P9-DFI-130

Islamic Political Identity in Turkey

M. HAKAN YAVUZ

OXFORD
UNIVERSITY PRESS

OXFORD
UNIVERSITY PRESS

Oxford University Press, Inc., publishes works that further
Oxford University's objective of excellence
in research, scholarship, and education.

Oxford   New York
Auckland   Cape Town   Dar es Salaam   Hong Kong   Karachi
Kuala Lumpur   Madrid   Melbourne   Mexico City   Nairobi
New Delhi   Shanghai   Taipei   Toronto

With offices in
Argentina   Austria   Brazil   Chile   Czech Republic   France   Greece
Guatemala   Hungary   Italy   Japan   Poland   Portugal   Singapore
South Korea   Switzerland   Thailand   Turkey   Ukraine   Vietnam

Copyright © 2003 by Oxford University Press, Inc.

First published in 2003 by Oxford University Press, Inc.
198 Madison Avenue, New York, New York 10016

www.oup.com

First issued as an Oxford University Press paperback, 2005
Oxford is a registered trademark of Oxford University Press, Inc.

All rights reserved. No part of this publication may be reproduced,
stored in a retrieval system, or transmitted, in any form or by any means,
electronic, mechanical, photocopying, recording, or otherwise,
without the prior permission of Oxford University Press.

Library of Congress Cataloging-in-Publication Data
Yavuz, M. Hakan.
Islamic political identity in Turkey / M. Hakan Yavuz.
p. cm. — (Religion and global politics)
Includes bibliographical references and index.
ISBN-13 978-0-19-518823-3 (pbk.)
ISBN 0-19-516085-1; 0-19-518823-3 (pbk.)
1. Islam and politics—Turkey.   2. Turkey—Politics and
government—1980–   I. Title.   II. Series.
BP173.7 .Y375 2003
320.5'5'09561—dc21   2002015380

9 8 7 6 5 4 3 2 1

Printed in the United States of America
on acid-free paper

Islamic Political Identity in Turkey

RELIGION AND GLOBAL POLITICS

Series Editor

John L. Esposito
University Professor and Director
Center for Muslim-Christian Understanding
Georgetown University

The Islamic Leviathan
State Power and Islam in Malaysia and Pakistan
Seyyed Vali Reza Nasr

Rachid Ghannouchi
A Democrat within Islamism
Azzam S. Tamimi

Balkan Idols
Religion and Nationalism in Yugoslav States
Vjekoslav Perica

Islamic Political Identity in Turkey
M. Hakan Yavuz

To

Kazim Yavuz (1938–1996)
Father, friend, and teacher

and

Aynur Yavuz
Mother and guiding light

I

Preface

Having grown up in a small town in Turkey's Black Sea region, I have been disturbed by the negative accounts of Islam and Islamic movements frequently encountered among the Turkish Republican elite and also in some Western intellectual forums because my understanding of Islam and its role in Turkish society has been very different. In rural and provincial Turkey, dominant religious organizations and ritual activity were shaped by the Nakşibendi Sufi order, although in my hometown of Bayburt they were shaped by the Nur movement. In Bayburt, the small shops around the main public square, known as Saat Kulesi Meydanı, hosted the reading circles of the devotees of the founder of the Nur movement, Said Nursi. One often would see the "red books" (kırmızı kitaplar) of Nursi in the hands of shop owners or state employees who came to chat in these shops. They were not only centers of trade but also places of ideas and discussion. People would open the books of Nursi and start to read, interpret, and debate. The debate eventually would move to totally different topics of discussion, but the idioms tended to be similar. I realized that this version of Islam and the eclectic teaching of Nursi often served for the townsmen as a philosophy of everyday life. My curiosity never died down, and I always wondered: Why Islam and this particular tradition? Could the Muslims of Turkey meaningfully discuss and engage in social, ethical, and political issues if they did not seem to share this common religious and cultural idiom? Could there be a social consensus outside Islam in modern Turkey? How did these fairly typical lower-middle-class provincial citizens reconcile their attachment to their religious traditions with their loyalty and devotion to the modern Turkish Republic and its political and military leaders, who often represented an ideological antithesis?

With these questions in mind, I commenced higher education at the Political Science Faculty of the University of Ankara. Here I encountered a very different intellectual setting and discourse. It was not a dialogue but rather a carefully structured program of indoctrination. This didactic education had very little connection with the often open and critical discussion found in Bayburt. It had its own elitist grammar, concepts, and modes of discourse that viewed the traditional Turkey of Anatolia as its greatest foe and danger. The Political Science Faculty was the hotbed of official Kemalist ideology, and the professors I met rarely had contact with the "other" Turkey, whether in the towns and villages or the teeming *gecekondus* (shantytowns) of Istanbul and Ankara. Yet they all claimed to know the "truth" of this "other Turkey" in their capacity as official stewards of what ostensibly was a meticulously planned program of "Westernization." We, the selected mandarins of this future order, were taught to think in terms of simplistic dichotomies: progress versus backwardness, elite versus masses, secularism versus Islam, nationalists versus subversives, and state versus civil society.

The "West" I encountered in my higher education in Milwaukee and Madison, Wisconsin, was starkly different from the one presented by my teachers in Ankara. Rather than rigid obedience, absolute truths, and stark dichotomies, I encountered a contentious and open society touchingly embodying many of the contradictory stances and concerns expressed by the citizens of Bayburt. The University of Wisconsin system provided me with a liberating and sustaining intellectual and emotional home, for which I always shall be grateful. While completing my dissertation in political science, I obtained an academic position at Ankara's new Bilkent University, which ostensibly was established on the model of Western and particularly American institutions of higher learning. Having published a few academic articles in the critical mode of thinking taught by my Wisconsin professors, I quickly was informed by Bilkent administrators that my nonorthodox views and criticism were unacceptable and if I continued to question official dogma I would not find a place in Turkish academe. Once again, America came to the rescue with a tenure track position at the Department of Political Science and Center for Middle Eastern Studies at the University of Utah. While traditionally Mormon and conservative Utah is quite distinct from liberal Wisconsin, I found both the state and university to share the same values of tolerance, critical thinking, and hospitality. For this I will always be indebted to my colleagues and the students and staff of the University of Utah.

It is especially vital to emphasize that categories like "the West" and "Islam" must be disaggregated to reveal the complexity, commonalities, and dynamic contradictions that each embodies. This book is the story of the "other Turkey" and an outcome of my 10-year fieldwork and interviews with the makers of contemporary Turkish Islam. I offer a dynamic map of actors, ideas, and actions that are shaped by a number of social, political, and economic factors. The dominant actors of the modern Turkish political landscape are the civilian and military bureaucracies, along with Islamic, Kurdish, and Alevi social and political movements. I identify Turgut Özal's neoliberalism of 1983 as the turning point in the reconfiguration of the political and intellectual landscape in Turkey. I argue that reinvigorated Turkish Islam(s) in the political and social spheres cannot be explained by the failure of Kemalism but rather is an outcome of new opportunity spaces—social and economic networks and vehicles for activism and the dissemination of meaning, identity, and cultural codes—in which the Kemalist project played an important albeit inadvertent role. This relationship has not been purely antagonistic but rather also contingent and transformative. The history of the last 80 years of the Republic shows that the Turkish authorities seldom have been consistent in counterpoising nationalism and Islam, secularism and religion. If any concept could capture this tendentious relationship it is that of contradiction.

While focusing on contemporary Turkish Islamic social and political movements, this study will also be useful in shedding light on the vexed issue of Islam, democratization, and politics in the broader Muslim world. Turkish Islamic social and political movements have sought to consolidate civil society by redrawing the boundaries between the state and society and attempting to form their own intellectual and moral charter, seeking not necessarily to replace the existing secularist state but rather to reconstitute everyday life. The Islamic movements of Turkey have created their own middle-class ethos and accommodations with modernity. Thus the contemporary debate in Turkey is not about restoring Islamic government or imposing Islamic law but about carving new spaces, constituting new identities, and diversifying voices in the public sphere with an idiom that would not be alien to most Western societies.

By utilizing new opportunity spaces, these Turkish Islamic movements are making new actors of intellectuals, businessmen, scholars, and artists and creating new sites of sociability. One of the major impacts of these opportunity spaces has been facilitating the emergence of private identities, commitments, and lifestyles in the public sphere. These new public spaces, along with new actors, have brought Islam to the forefront of public discussion. The second impact of these opportunity spaces is on the ultimately centrifugal trajectory of Islamic sociopolitical movements in democratic and pluralistic settings. As a result of new opportunity spaces, differentiation in terms of political practices, areas of specialization, and class dynamics has become quite apparent. Thus Muslim societies in general, and Turkish society in particular, and their various sociopolitical movements have allowed a "democratic space" to evince the same vital diversity and pluralism found in Western liberal democracies. New opportunity spaces have helped Turkish Muslims to acquire new skills to function in and shape modern practices and articulate their visions of the good life. For instance, new communication networks helped to create a new class of Muslim intellectuals, columnists, and news anchorpersons, quite distinct from the traditional ulema. Thus competing Islamic movements have less in common with each other than with various secular counterparts in Turkish society. This book further examines the state policy of using Islam to overcome the disintegration and tension created by neoliberal economic policies—and the way various social groups have utilized Islam to make identity claims and justify their entry into the political and economic spheres.

This book is the product of intellectual engagement over many years. In this long period I have incurred many debts. First I thank my friend and colleague Mujeeb R. Khan, whose amazing grasp of both Western and Islamic political thought and history has been deeply inspiring. I am also indebted for the input of friends, colleagues, and teachers, including Eric Hooglund, John L. Esposito, Saleha Abedin, İsmail Kara, Nilüfer Göle, Ümit Cizre, Becir Tanovic, Yasin Aktay, Paul Lubeck, Dale Eickelman, Alpaslan Açıkgenç, Charles Kuzman, İbrahim Kalın, Saleha Mahmood, Sükran Vahide, Mustafa Erdoğan, Ali Aslan, Faris Kaya, İsmail Engin, Edibe Sözen, Linda Butler, Etga Uğur, and, last but not least, my doctoral advisor, Crawford Young.

I

Contents

I

Abbreviations

AKP	Adalet ve Kalkınma Partisi (Justice and Development Party)
ANAP	Anavatan Partisi (Motherland Party)
AP	Adalet Partisi (Justice Party)
BP	Birlik Partisi (Unity Party)
BBP	Büyük Birlik Partisi (Great Unity Party)
CHP	Cumhuriyet Halk Partisi (Republican People's Party)
DEP	Demokrasi Partisi (Democracy Party)
DEHAP	Demokratik Halk Partisi (Democratic People's Party)
DİB	Diyanet İşleri Başkanlığı (Directorate of Religious Affairs)
DP	Demokrat Parti (Democrat Party)
DSP	Demokratik Sol Parti (Democratic Left Party)
DYP	Doğru Yol Partisi (True Path Party)
FP	Fazilet Partisi (Virtue Party)
HADEP	Halkın Demokrasi Partisi (People's Democracy Party)
HaP	Halkçı Parti (Populist Party)
HEP	Halkın Emek Partisi (People's Work Party)
MCP	Milliyetçi Calışma Partisi (Nationalist Work Party)
MDP	Milliyetçi Demokrasi Partisi (Nationalist Democracy Party)
MGH	Milli Görüş Hareketi (National Outlook Movement)
MHP	Milliyetçi Hareket Partisi (Nationalist Action Party)
MNP	Milli Nizam Partisi (National Order Party)
MSP	Milli Selamet Partisi (National Salvation Party)
MÜSİAD	Müstakil Sanayici ve İşadamları Derneği (Independent Industrialists' and Businessmen's Association)

PKK   Partiya Karkaren Kurdistan (Kurdistan Workers Party)
RG   *Resmi Gazete* (Official Gazette)
RNK   *Risale-i Nur Külliyatı* (The Epistles of Light) of Said Nursi
RP   Refah Partisi (Welfare Party)
SP   Saadet Partisi (Felicity Party)
SODEP   Sosyal Demokrasi Partisi (Social Democracy Party)
SHP   Sosyal Demokrat Halçi Parti (Social Democrat Populist Party)
T.B.M.M.   Türkiye Büyük Millet Meclisi (Turkish Grand National Assembly)
TİP   Türkiye İşçi Partisi (Turkish Workers Party)
TÜSİAD   Türk İşadamları ve Sanayiciler Derneği (Association of Turkish Industrialists and Businessmen)

Islamic Political Identity in Turkey

I

Introduction

On June 28, 1996, for the first time since the formation of the
Turkish Republic in 1923, Turkey's prime minister was a leader
whose avowed political philosophy and personal identity was based
on Islam. By winning 21.3 percent of the total vote, along with 158
seats in the 550-seat Parliament, the Welfare Party (RP: Refah
Partisi), after intensive maneuvering, was able to form a coalition
government with the True Path Party (DYP: Doğru Yol Partisi) of
Tansu Çiller. This coalition between the pro-Islamic prime minister
Necmettin Erbakan and the Europhile-secularist Çiller aptly reflected
the dualistic tensions inherent in contemporary Turkish identity and
held promise for the dawn of a new era in state-society interactions
in Turkey. However, this promising start at reconciling the deep
social fissures introduced by the radical secular reforms of Mustafa
Kemal and his followers was derailed abruptly by the military-
bureaucratic establishment's "soft coup" of February 28, 1997.[1] The
soft coup plunged the Turkish state into a renewed legitimacy crisis.
Not wanting to cede power to civil society, the Kemalist military-
bureaucratic establishment once again had launched a counterattack
against what it considered "enemies of the state," this time focusing
intensely on politically active Turkish Muslims rather than Alevis
and leftists.

This Kemalist (those who espouse Mustafa Kemal's ideas of
nationalism and secularism) effort to preserve authoritarianism,
however, confronts the law of diminishing returns. The Turkish
state faces the imperative of liberalizing its economy to meet global
demands—a process begun under Turgut Özal (1980–1993)—and
over the long term cannot avoid liberalizing its political system as
well. However, traditional Western and Turkish scholarship, overly

influenced by the Republican establishment, has presented the Kemalist state elite not as authoritarian but rather as an engine for "reform" and Westernization against a recalcitrant and "reactionary" traditional Islamic society.[2] Since the mid-1980s, writers such as Nilüfer Göle, İsmail Kara, Şerif Mardin, and Mete Tunçay have challenged this view, arguing that Islamic social movements are central agents for promoting a democratic and pluralistic society and that the Turkish example holds long-term promise for the rest of the Muslim world as well.

How can we account for the construction of Islamic political identity, and what does this modern construction of identity suggest for the legacy of Mustafa Kemal's radical secularizing reforms of the 1920s and 1930s, especially since the post-1982 era of burgeoning political and economic liberalism? We begin by addressing the question of why the Islamic identity movement assumed such significance in contemporary Turkey. I argue that Islamic idioms and practices constitute a set of social, moral, and political cognitive maps for the Muslim imagination. Three complex processes foster the modern construction of Islamic political identity in Turkey. After the foundation of the Republic in 1923, the secularizing, state-centric elite failed effectively to penetrate and transform traditional society, and was similarly unsuccessful in developing an alternative value system and associational life for the rural population of the country. This failure was underscored further when political and economic development inevitably raised previously muted social questions of identity, justice, and participation. Islamic social and political groups of diverse backgrounds and agendas were able to step into this vacuum and articulate viable alternative social and ethical paradigms. These paradigms differed from those provided by official Kemalism, which hitherto had failed to supply ideas and guidance convincingly for the newly urbanized poor and the emerging Anatolian middle class. Finally, the success of the Republican elite's policies of socioeconomic development and the subsequent shift to political and economic liberalization in the 1980s inevitably contributed to the political participation of hitherto excluded social groups. In this sense, Islamic movements in Turkey are not fueled by a deep-seated rage and frustration with the authoritarian policies of the secular elites, as is the case in Algeria and Egypt. The Turkish example of Islamically oriented political and social movements committed to playing within a legal framework of democratic and pluralistic parameters points to a potential model for less-developed Muslim countries confronting Islamically based demands for social and political change.

The construction of an Islamic political identity and the emergence of the renascent Turkish-Islamic ethos raises one of the paradoxes in the study of developing countries, namely, that of a people experiencing both the processes of rapid socioeconomic development and the reimagination of religion within new political and cultural spheres. Contrary to the expectations of earlier modernization theory, in the Turkish case secularization recast and inadvertently revitalized the very religious and cultural idioms and identities that it was supposed to have eliminated.[3] It may be noted that Turkey is not unique in experiencing this global paradox where modernity resides in tension between the forces of orthodoxy and heterodoxy, universalism and particularism.

Politically active Muslims in Turkey have evoked Islamic symbols and in-stitutions to express their notions of community, identity, self, and justice. More important, they have utilized Islam to construct their own version of moder-nity. By struggling to revitalize Ottoman-Islamic culture, Islamic social move-ments have brought with them something entirely new: the vernacularization of modernity and the internal secularization of Islam in terms of rationaliza-tion, nationalization, and the accommodation of faith to the overriding exigencies of reason and evidence. In the context of this study, I define "vernacularization of modernity" as the efforts of Islamic intellectuals and movements to redefine the discourses of modernity (nationalism, secularism, democracy, human rights, the liberal market, and personal autonomy) in their own Islamic terms. "Vernacu-larization" is a somewhat paradoxical process, in which the boundaries of the Islamic normative tradition are simultaneously preserved and radically altered. It both configures and assimilates certain aspects of modernity; however, it re-jects and contests them at the same time. This attempt combines religious val-ues with ideas supporting the emergence of an autonomous human agent. A key cultural aspect of modernity centers on the notion of autonomous human agency. Individual autonomy is protected by the rule of law and by the expan-sions of rights and freedoms. There is emancipation from the hegemony of tra-ditional political and cultural forms of authority. Accordingly, the autonomous Muslim individual is expected to take part in the formation of a new political and cultural order, especially through protest and participation in social move-ments and related political parties. The modern themes of equality, freedom and justice, and identity and solidarity have become the central building blocs of the new, emancipation-oriented Islamic movements. These movements oppose both the hegemony of the nation-state and the domination of the traditional code of Islamic morality, and seek instead to promote the defense of cultural and politi-cal rights of individuals and identity groups. In the 1980s, the weakening of the nation-state in Turkey created new opportunities for Islamic movements to construct their own autonomous social, political, and cultural spaces. Thus, the state-controlled, "top-down" westernization aims and the Islamic, "bottom-up" emancipation process have come into conflict over the type of society they seek to create, over the goals of modernity itself. One of the crucial impacts of the vernacularization of modernity is the internal secularization of Islam. By "in-ternal secularization" I mean the rationalization of religious practices and ex-clusion of magical elements and the acceptance of a universal conception of the sacred. Moreover, secular thinking has been incorporated into mainstream Is-lamic thought. "Internal secularization" is the process by which Muslims focus all their energy and activism increasingly on this world and decreasingly on a postulated otherworld. For instance, Islamic time is measured from the estab-lishment of the Ottoman state (and its successes) in 1299. Islamic movements, as actors of social change, imagine Islam in terms of modern concepts of democracy, nationalism, and secularism. One major feature of the Islamic move-ments is the Turkification of Islam. For instance, the Islamic movement treats Turkish history not as a period within Islamic history, but rather Islamic history is examined within Turkish history. Moreover, Turkey for the Islamic movement is not merely a part of Islamic history and landscape but rather is "the leading country" of the Muslim world.

Although scholars of Muslim politics have tended to focus on Islamic movements engaged in violent struggles against established regimes, as in Algeria, Egypt, and Saudi Arabia, Turkey has been experiencing a quiet Muslim reformation, a trend that for some time has been overshadowed by more dramatic events in other parts of the Middle East. Furthermore, the few analytical studies about the Islamic movements in Turkey have been simplistic, if not sensational. Thus, in recent years, some scholars, rather than focusing on the deeper social, intellectual, and political processes involved in the constitution of Islamic political identity have focused on the manifestations and rhetoric of Erbakan's National Outlook Movement (MGH: Milli Görüş Hareketi). Therefore, they have tended to confuse the causes and outcomes of the electoral victory of the RP with the broader and deeper processes of the vernacularization (Islamization) of modernity. In this study, the rise of the RP will be treated as an outcome of much broader social, economic, and cultural transformations that have been under way in Turkey since the 1960s. The intellectual origins of the Milli Görüş (the Nakşibendi Sufi order) will be examined separately. This study will demonstrate that Islamic political identity is Janus-faced: modern and progressive in one aspect, with yearnings for democracy and economic development; and in the other aspect, conservative with a potentially authoritarian agenda for establishing a religiously defined moral code for society.

The purpose of this study is to examine both the social and political processes and consequences of the formation of a new Islamic political identity in Turkey. Since identity is a "frame of reference" within which the social and political situations are recognizable, I examine the way this new Islamic frame of reference has been construed and articulated by various social groups, in particular by the Milli Görüş. The shift from the primordiality of traditional Islamic identity to the assertiveness of the new Islamic identity is made possible by social movements. It is very important to study Islamic identity because it provides the basis for individual and communal interests and a map of action to deal with political and social situations. Islam, as a stock of belief and knowledge, facilitates participation in social life, and serves as a source of solidarity and societal transformation.

Islam has had such popular appeal in part because of the effectiveness of Islamic leaders and networks in mobilizing large sections of the populace in pursuit of social justice and political representation. A social movement presupposes "a particular belief system, on which the goals, standards of behavior, and legitimacy (and, ultimately, the power) of the authorities spring."[4] A particular belief system is necessary but not sufficient for a social movement. In the case of Turkey, the coincidence of Islamic ideas and material interests mutually shape one another to provide the framework for postulating a more "just" society.

By Islamic political identity I mean the process of becoming conscious of the social and political effects of religiously molded frames of reference, and utilizing these frames as political means for fulfilling worldly agendas. This transformation entails the strategic and conscious utilization of shared conceptions of ethics, justice, community, and history to develop new methods for advancing tangible social and economic goals. Focusing on this transformation is vital in studying the formation of contemporary Islamic political identity in Turkey because political identity provides a cognitive bridge between interest and action, society and state, and tradition and modernity in much of the Islamic world. Such a process in terms of various Buddhist, Christian, Hindu, and Jewish social and political movements is also occurring around the globe.

While the politicization of Islamic identity is by no means unique to Turkey, the Turkish case is of particular importance for understanding this phenomenon. This is a result of Turkey's early experience with Kemalism as a generic (prototypical) ideology of modernization and nation-building that was imitated in the experiences of other developing Muslim countries such as Tunisia (Bourgubaism), Iran (Pahlavism), Egypt (Nasserism), and Indonesia (Pancasila). The Turkish experience, for Ira Lapidus, was "prototypical of these secularized Muslim societies" in that it succeeded in disestablishing Islam in public life.[5] As Benedict Anderson indicates in the case of Indonesia, "a tiny hyphen links two very different entities [nation-state] with distinct histories, constituents, and 'interest[s].'"[6] The Turkish secular reforms not only hyphenated state and society but defined the Republican state against traditional society. Before the link between "nation" and "state" could be established, the Republican elite had to dissolve the link with the Ottoman past. Since most Middle Eastern countries have experienced similar processes of nation-state-building, the Turkish case offers a rich laboratory for understanding modern sociopolitical formations in the Middle East and elsewhere in the Muslim world. In light of current trends in the Islamic world, an examination of the relatively peaceful evolution of the Islamic movement in Turkey and its tentative incorporation into centers of power presents a useful case study in theorizing the possibility of similar developments in other Muslim countries.[7] Encompassing the first elected Islamist prime minister in an officially secular state and his subsequent removal by the 1997 "soft military coup," the Turkish case presents a rich opportunity for discerning and theorizing about the relationship among Islam, nationalism, and ethnicity, and also the relationship between democracy and the Islamic tradition.

A constructivist theoretical approach in studying the formation of an Islamic political identity in Turkey will be the basis of my study. Contemporary Islamic movements in Turkey seek to reclaim the Muslim self, which is perceived as having been robbed of its authenticity and heritage. Moreover, Islamic movements produce, and are being produced by, new opportunity spaces for discussion where they can develop and experience novel lifestyles and identities. Turkish Muslims have used the newspaper, television screens, and journals to rearticulate and reimagine Islamic political identity. These opportunity spaces have come to signify differentiation—multiple articulations of the Muslim "self" and interests—and generally have promoted pluralism and the fragmentation of any efforts at imposing a hegemonic Islamic ideology. The growth of the modern media and the expansion of universal education, instead of weakening the role and influence of Islam, have led to its redefinition as a form of political and social consciousness very different from traditional understandings of religion and identity (see chapter 5). Print technology and the formation of opportunity spaces sundered the trinity of religion, authority, and knowledge. As a result of this breakdown, which can be traced to the early 1950s, a new prototype of ulema/intellectual emerged along with a set of network-communities to restructure this flow of information and devise strategies to cope with modern urban conditions of fragmentation and anomie.

An examination of the Turkish case contributes to a broader understanding of the politicization and transformation of Islamic movements worldwide. This study reaches three conclusions concerning contemporary Islamic movements in Turkey that I believe are also applicable to other Muslim countries: First, the terrain on which contemporary Islamic movements operate is not homogenous but rather is marked by various competing groups seeking to redefine the meaning of an Islamic identity. Second, the expansion of the secular nation-state apparatus for surveillance, control, and standardization coupled with the emergence of new socioeconomic and cultural classes catalyzes the politicization of Islamic groups. Third, this results in Muslims seeking to carve new niches in the public sphere free from hegemonic state ideology and control. The purpose of this endeavor is to find opportunity spaces in which to craft modern Islamic identities and knit a shared moral fabric upon which to create consensual social and political discourse.

The Framework of the Study

As the rhythms and patterns of governance in state and society change, so do the understandings and uses of identity. This study contends that the identity- and justice-seeking Islamic movements in Turkey since the early 1960s have been molded by two major, interrelated developments: the new liberal political opening conceded by the secularist state and the subsequent appropriation of these new opportunity spaces by Islamist groups and intellectuals. I demonstrate these developments by examining the constitution and evolution of several Turkish Islamic identity movements.

This study consists of 10 integrated chapters. The first three chapters analyze the theoretical framework and the political context of the Islamic movements by stressing the role of state policies. I weigh the relative merits of various theoretical approaches to the studies of Islamic movements and identities. I divide these theoretical approaches into three broad typologies: (1) essentialist; (2) contextualist; and (3) constructivist. I then indicate the advantages and disadvantages of the first two and explore the utilization of the last approach in my study of the formation of Islamic political identity in Turkey. I seek to introduce an empirically overlapping yet conceptually distinct theory of the formation of Islamic identity movements along both vertical and horizontal axes.

After setting forth the theoretical framework, I then present the historical background of state-society relations in Turkey to comprehend the construction of Islamic political identity and answer the question: What is the role of state tradition and policies in the formation of an Islamic movement? I argue that Mustafa Kemal (Atatürk) melded a diversity of loyalties and identities together to create one nation-state by imposing an official state ideology. In the process, he also eliminated public spaces where traditional Ottoman-Islamic networks invested societal norms and meanings. Many scholars assumed that the thoroughgoing and extremely coercive Kemalist program had succeeded in creating a new "secular" Turkish Republican reality. In hindsight, however, these policies eventually set the ground for societal groups to turn to Islam as a counterideology to the authoritarian hegemony of the state and its administrative elite. This analysis of Islamic movements will start with the state not because my approach is state-centric but because Turkish political culture is state-centric.[8] In other words, in the case of Turkey, the concept of "nation" is derived very much from the state. The concept of the state and its authority is more embedded in the imagination of the Turks than is the notion of the Republican nation. Since the Turkish nation was a project fostered by the state, such a study must start with an examination of the state's role in shaping modern Turkish society. Moreover, an examination of contemporary Islamic movements indicates the way these movements have shifted from a state-centric to a society-based focus.

By exploring the interactions between the state and society within the context of politics and the market in Turkey, I will argue that Islamic movements have developed four sets of strategies in relation to changing circumstances. These strategies gradually became four competing visions about the role of religion in Turkish society. These social strategies chronologically are: a spiritual ethical Islamic movement, which seeks to treat faith as a source of norms and mores for creating a common moral language by rearticulating communal identity (1925–1950); a cultural Islamic movement, which perceives Islam as a form of civilization and seeks to influence cultural and social identities in this respect (1950–1970); a political Islamic movement, which seeks to attain political power either to improve the economic position of a segment of society or transform itself through the institutions of the state (1970–present); and a socioeconomic Islamic movement, which stresses the role of the market, associations, and the public sphere as a way of transforming society (1983–present). It is my contention that political and socioeconomic concerns articulated in Islamic idioms are falling into the larger sphere of cultural Islam because of competition with other ethnic and parochial (hometown) loyalties. Thus Islamic political identity gradually is becoming more amorphous, more durable. In other words, there is no set index for reference to "being a Muslim"; rather the present amorphousness of Islamic identity has led to stronger and more resilient political identities in the face of state opposition.

In chapter 4, I address a more specific question: Why is Islam, rather than nationalism or localism, used to articulate issues of justice and identity? How does Islamic identity compete with and complement other loyalties? In this chapter, I examine the informal, personal, and fluid nature of Turkish society. I argue that Islamic political consciousness, as a form of "imagined community," continuously is shaped and articulated by the competing claims of religious, social, economic, and political forces.[9]

After the first four chapters set the context of the Islamic identity movements, chapter 5 examines how Muslim agents construct and internalize Islamic political identities. The current identity debate in Turkey also illustrates the way power is constructed socially through religious symbols and networks. This is reflected in controversies over education and the dress code.[10] The main forces in the formation and politicization of new Islamic frames of reference are the print and visual media, religious education, and the formation of a new religiously inspired intelligentsia and bourgeoisie. This chapter therefore consists of a detailed examination of the media, schools, and the new intellectual class. Study of the politicization of Islamic identity makes clear that schools and the media are critical in this process. Through the institutional means of the schools and the media, the construction, internalization, and diffusion of Islamic identity take place. The production of Islamist intellectuals and cultural entrepreneurs was hindered in the past by the lack of finance capital, which was readily available only to those who were part of the Kemalist, state-centered intellectual class. This economic hurdle was overcome only after 1980 by an Islamist capitalist class that fully emerged in the wake of Özal's policies of political and market liberalization. This new class of Muslim entrepreneurs was able to circumvent state controls by creating its own alternative schools, printing presses, newspapers, journals, and radio and television stations.

After two decades of struggle, an elaborate infrastructure of Islamic culture has established itself in contemporary Turkey. Ironically, the policy of economic liberalization in Turkey encouraged by the International Monetary Fund (IMF) did not favor those sections of society that were well disposed toward Kemalism as a result of their long dependence on the privileges of the Republic's statist economic policies. Muslim entrepreneurs who were not dependent on state subsidies and who were concentrated in foreign exchange–earning export industries, such as food processing and textiles, were particularly well placed to prosper in this period. This new counterelite, for the writer Erol Göka, is "protean, open to global discourses, and seeks to overcome the 'lack of fit' between Turkish society and the state."[11] This new Muslim business elite is represented, for example, in the new daily newspapers *Türkiye*, *Yeni Şafak*, and *Zaman* and the magazines *Aksiyon*, *Cuma*, *Girişim*, *İzlenim*, and *Yeni Zemin*.

As I shall demonstrate, publishing sets modernity apart from previous modes of production and consumption of knowledge. Printing has a major impact on societies in terms of raising the consciousness of space and time and the imagining of social and cultural ties.[12] Anthony Giddens argues that "the development of writing greatly extends the scope of distanciated interaction in space as well as in time."[13] Writing allowed people to study history and develop a "linear time consciousness."[14]

Chapter 6 focuses on Sufi orders for two reasons: They provided structure and became a catalyst for the survival of religious-political education and spiritual development of Muslim society in Turkey, as they did in the case of similarly fierce repression by antireligious forces in the Soviet Caucasus and Central Asia. Moreover, Sufi orders played a formative role in the foundation of the political forerunners of the National Outlook Movement (MGH: Milli Görüş

Hareketi) of Erbakan and they were also the intellectual fulcrums for the Nur movement. A Muslim Sufi order is an institutionalization of the set of roles played between master and disciple that varies in time and space and from one Sufi lodge to another lodge. Sufi groups, for example, seek to liberate the inner being (e.g., religious consciousness) from constraining social and political conditions. I examine the externalization of Islamic political identity and what I term the Turkish Muslim Reformation equivalent of the Protestant Reformation. In Turkey, the new idiom of religion conceptualizes the individual as being capable of shaping the self and freeing it from alienating structural conditions. Salvation is not about giving up or withdrawing to an inner world but rather about a struggle over recognition and space. Traditionally, the *ulema* (religious scholars of Islam)concerned themselves with the outward behavior of the Muslim community and its conformity with the body politic, while Sufism stressed the spiritual life of the believer and the inner dimensions of faith.[15] This chapter indicates how the web of religious networks has been transformed as a result of new social-economic conditions.

In particular, I demonstrate how the Nakşibendi Sufi order served as the matrix for the emergence in the 1970s of the four leading contemporary Turkish Islamic political and social movements: the neo-Nakşibendi Sufi order of *Süleymancı* and other orders; the new Islamist intellectuals; the Nurcu movement of Bediüzzaman Said Nursi, with its offshoot led by the charismatic Fethullah Gülen; and the MGH of Necmettin Erbakan. In order to understand the formation of Islamic political identity, one needs to look at its intellectual and epistemological roots. During the 1970s, the juncture of leftist ideology and far-right nationalism influenced social thought, but it was the writings of Nursi and Sufi groups that played the most vital embryonic role for the present generation of Muslim intellectuals and community leaders.

In chapter 7, I examine the social dynamics of Islamic discourses, that is, how and why Said Nursi (1876–1960), the writer of the volumes of exegesis on the Qur'an known as *The Epistles of Light* (*RNK: Risale-i Nur Külliyatı*), became a founder of the strongest and largest text-based Islamic movement in Turkey. The Nur (Light) movement, as it is known, seeks to move from an oral-based tradition to one of print culture.[16] One also must consider how the meanings of Nursi's writings are reproduced and read across the ethnic, social, and economic spectrum. The number of adherents of the Nur movement, known as Nurcular, varies between five and six million believers.[17] Thus, without a proper understanding of the Nur movement and its societal impact, one cannot grasp the peaceful and gradual mobilization of an Islamic identity movement in Turkey.

In this chapter on the Nur movement, I demonstrate that the understanding of political Islam in Turkey requires an awareness of the seminal role of Nurcu intellectuals and study circles as informal networks in articulating and disseminating Islamic idioms into society. The Nurcu textual reading circles, known as *dershanes*, function as a cradle for a new class of intellectual entrepreneurs possessing a different cultural capital vis-à-vis secular intellectuals. The number of these reading groups, which meet twice a week in different apartments and neighborhoods, is around 5,500. Since the entry requirements to

Nurcu circles are very loose, there is a constant movement of members from one circle to another. These reading groups are based on interpersonal trust and reciprocity. These informal networks are meant to be an instrument for building a religiously based Muslim society by raising spiritual consciousness and also less directly by wielding informal political power through unofficial ties to politicians. These dershanes are important elements of Turkish civil society, as they are outside the control of the state, self-supporting, voluntary, and informal in nature.

In chapter 8, I seek to examine how Fethullah Gülen, the most active and visible contemporary leader of the neo-Nur movement, with national television and newspaper franchises, reimagines the role of Islam within the nation-state system. In a way, Islamic movements and Islamic political identity are not "Islamic" in a solely religious sense but rather "national" in terms of seeking to use an Islamic ethos for fostering a regionally powerful Turkish state. Gülen has succeeded in creating a new language of politics by mixing nationalistic, religious, and global discourses together. Although Gülen has been highly critical of the RP,[18] his ideas and actions softened the opposition to Islamic political activity among powerful sections of Turkish society and helped to create a new outlook on the role of religion in contemporary Turkey. This, in turn, indirectly prepared the ground for the Islamic RP's rise to power with initially muted opposition from the military and the traditional state establishment.

Chapter 9 focuses on the MGH of Erbakan and examines the change in the discourse of this political Islamic movement. This chapter analyzes the rise of the RP into the government by examining its organization, leadership, ideology, and communication channels. Since I treat the RP as an outcome rather than a cause of the unfolding sociopolitical processes in modern Turkey, I argue that the RP in effect has integrated most of the prominent Islamic groups (even those that are bitter rivals) into the political process. Although the party has managed to expand its support base by addressing the questions of identity and justice, it has had limited success in shaping individual identities and loyalties on its own ideological terms.

Finally, in chapter 10, I examine the way the military-bureaucratic establishment used the national security concept to strike back at civil society. I examine the causes and implications of the military's soft coup of February 28, 1997. I argue that the ongoing rearguard action by the Turkish state's military-bureaucratic establishment to preserve its authoritarian privileges could not be sustained over the long term. By treating Kurdish and Islamic identities as threats to the existence of the state, the military prepared the ground for the nationalist takeover in the 1999 elections. However, the coup in the long run not only narrowed the legitimacy of the state but also forced traditional Sunni Turks and Kurds to regard the Copenhagen criteria and EU membership as the only hope for drastically reforming the authoritarian Turkish state and its ideology.

Although many scholars and journalists have treated recent political developments in Turkey as a march backward from the "highway of Westernization," such a view is as problematic as the teleological assumptions of the proponents of early modernization theory. Contrary to the expectations of secularization and national integration, Turkish society simultaneously is experiencing economic and political liberalization as well as Islamic and ethnic revivals. Neither the process of secularization nor Islamic revivalism is going to set the final mark on society because the process of Islamic identity formation resides neither in a specific textual locality nor in a particular person or party. Rather, it is to be found in a vibrant set of webs and networks that constantly are being negotiated and rearticulated by societal groups.

Turkey needs a new and more inclusive "social contract" that addresses the questions of identity, justice, and participation. I conclude that the Turkish case is of broad importance for scholars studying identity formation and religious-political movements worldwide. Similar movements and processes are the dominant social and political discourses in many developing countries. By uncovering the processes of the pluralization of Islamic groups and competing images of Islamic and national identity in Jordan, Malaysia, and Turkey on the one hand and the radicalization of Islamic political identity in Algeria and Egypt on the other, I argue that economic growth, along with a democratic political opening, is the essential path for countries to pursue if they are to avoid the pitfalls of political upheaval and societal polarization. Recent troubling recurrences of authoritarianism and retreat from reformist policies in Iran, Jordan, Malaysia, and Turkey does not invalidate the contention of this book that these Muslim countries will not be able to avoid democratizing and liberalizing their political systems in the medium to long term.

I

Islamic Social Movements

A comparison of different contemporary Islamic social movements shows that they are Janus-faced. That is, on the one hand they are modern and socially and politically "progressive" and express yearnings for democracy and economic development; on the other hand they are conservative and "authoritarian," calling for a strict moral-religious code in society.

Consequently, tension is an inherent characteristic of most Islamic social movements. Ironically, this tension between "progressive" and "authoritarian" aspects of religious movements is the source of religious innovation. Unfortunately, many scholars of Islam fail to see the complex nature of modern Islamic social movements and seek to explain them according to textual (essentialist) or economic reductionist (contextualist) readings of Islam. This book challenges such interpretations, arguing instead that, by embracing certain opportunity spaces within the public sphere, Islamic movements could become a motivating force for economic expansion, democratization, and the popular acceptance of many aspects of modernity.

I believe that a third approach, that of the constructivists, offers a sounder and more nuanced theoretical framework to analyze the formation of Islamic political identity in contemporary Islamic movements. Thus I use the constructivist approach to differentiate opportunity spaces from the political opportunity structure and then examine the way Muslims have utilized these spaces to make demands for political, social, and economic inclusion, in addition to justice. Specifically, by reexamining the interplay between the governmental policies of Turkey and societal resistance, I have been able to introduce a new typology of Islamic social movements based on the expansion and shrinking of opportunity spaces.

Approaches to the Study of Political Islam

There are three main theoretical currents in the study of religion and politics: essentialist, contextualist, and constructivist.[1] Interactions between these three approaches have been multifarious and by no means always conflictual. By setting up these categories, I am aware that I slight subtle distinctions and simplify profound analyses of particular cases. However, in order to organize the vast body of social science literature on this subject, it is useful to demarcate these three broad conceptual categories.

Essentialism: The "Text" and Political Developments

Essentialism seeks to reduce the diverse spectrum of human relations to a few "essential" causes and to identify certain defining traits and texts as keys to understanding a particular religious or cultural community.[2] This tendency, which can be seen in the textualism of Bernard Lewis, played a dominant role in the formation of modernization theory and the "cluster of absences" long noted by development specialists. Tradition and modernity were counterposed, and it was axiomatic for modernization theorists to view tradition as the main culprit standing in the way of "progress." The focus on the textual sources of Islamic revivalism in much of contemporary scholarship implies that Muslims do not reimagine and rearticulate what it means to be a Muslim in rapidly developing societies but only *act on* fixed Islamic principles. Lewis, for example, argues that Islam is a fixed and enduring tradition and cultural system.[3] Bassam Tibi's book *Islam and the Cultural Accommodation of Social Change* is another example of this tendency to fix a purported Islamic essence; Tibi argues that "Islam" is a set of fixed texts, doctrines, and practices by which a Muslim sense of self is determined.[4] Religious discourse, for Tibi, seemingly is produced in a vacuum, hermetically sealed from changing contexts and interpretations. In the end, he creates a model of a *homo Islamicus* who is ahistorical and similar to a fundamentalist caricature of "true" Islam. The essentialists attribute agency to Islam as an institution and as a set of fixed doctrines but negate the interactive agency of Muslims themselves. Tibi, for example, concludes that political Islam "provides no innovative prospects for the future but is solely a vision of the future as a restoration of the past. . . . Political Islam may therefore—with some restrictions—be interpreted as a backward-oriented utopia."[5] Lewis, like Tibi, has tended to assume that "Islam rather than any other element is the ultimate basis of identity, of loyalty, of authority."[6] Islamic identity is viewed as being a primordial, essentially political, all-encompassing, and determining force.[7] Similarly, Emmanuel Sivan claims that "Islamic revival—while activist and militant—is thus essentially defensive; a sort of holding operation against modernity."[8] Sivan sees the problem in the antimodern nature of Islam and concludes that Islamic groups are "all united by intense hatred of the 'evil of evils,' modernity. Modernity is inherently alien to Islam."[9]

Lewis, Tibi, and Sivan have exaggerated the impact of Islamic doctrine on the conduct of individuals and on the patterns of institutions in society as a whole. In addition to their problematic approach to the issue of agency, they tend to argue that there is a fixed political language and idiom in Islam that guides Muslim conduct in the public sphere. Thus essentialist scholars have treated diverse and competing Islamic movements as homogenous ideological movements that primarily are influenced by the Qur'an and the writings of certain individuals such as Abu'l al-Ala Mawdudi (1903–1979), Sayyid Qutb (1906–1964), Hasan al-Banna (1906–1949), and Muhammad Husayn Fadlallah (1935–).[10] This approach maintains that all contemporary Islamic social and political movements are motivated and guided by an Islamic worldview. One aim of this book is to show that the diversity of Muslim beliefs and practices is not compatible with an analysis that regards a monolithic, consistent, and unchanging "Islam" as the foundation of all social and political movements that call themselves Islamic.

Furthermore, by employing an ethnocentric and teleological definition of modernity, such scholars essentially are claiming that Muslim societies are inherently traditional and unable to modernize. In fact, some scholars of modernization have attributed the failure of democratization and capitalism in Muslim societies to a certain "cluster of absences, a missing middle class, the missing city, the absence of political rights."[11] Daniel P. Lerner, for example, argued that Islam was a traditional ideology, reacting to the processes of modernization, and that in the case of Turkey it forced the country to choose between "Mecca and mechanization."[12] Turkish scholars, no doubt influenced by the affinities of this approach with the Kemalist state ideology of Comtean positivism, have internalized Lerner's framework in their studies of political development in their own country.[13] They, as well as a number of Western scholars, have tended to treat the Islamic movement as a reactionary force fighting a vain rearguard action against the processes of Westernization and secularization.[14] These theories tend to explain human conduct in terms of simplistic dichotomies, modern and traditional, while ignoring the causal mechanisms that influence the evolution of Islamic movements, economic expansion, popular imagination, and social change.

Modernization theory dominated the social science research on Turkey, and explicit assumptions about old versus new, tradition versus modernity, religion versus secularism, the inexorable march toward Westernization, and sociopolitical reactions being religious fanaticism informed these studies. They presented the establishment of the Republican regime as the inevitable "emergence of modern Turkey" and depicted its founding Kemalist ideology as the fulfillment of destiny for the modernizing forces. This teleological, state-centric, and structuralist reading of the Turkish polity and society ignored the destruction of the Anatolian mosaic of Armenians, Assyrians, Greeks, Kurds, and other ethnic and religious groups. Tarık Z. Tunaya, Niyazi Berkes, and Bernard Lewis set the framework of Turkish studies in terms of "discovering" Turkish nationalism as a primordial identity that was awakened by Mustafa Kemal through his policies of progressive secularism that cleansed this identity of its Islamic-Ottoman layers. These writers all focused on the history of ideas and treated the state as a positive agent to put "modernity" into practice. Their understanding of the state as a progressive force informed their analyses of societal reactions, which they treated as "Muslim fanaticism." In addition, their works ignored the deep ethnic and religious cleavages in Turkish society and the state violence periodically employed to suppress identity claims. Only the new generation of scholars have offered a more nuanced reading of the state-society relations (Nilüfer Göle, Reşat Kasaba, Şerif Mardin, Robert Olson, and Martin van Bruinessen).[15] We need a more nuanced and theoretically sophisticated understanding of the processes by which religious and ethnic identities become politicized in response to economic and political problems in modern societies such as that of contemporary Turkey.

Contextualism

In opposition to these essentialist and reductionist approaches, a new genre of scholarship, known as contextualism, has emerged. This approach stresses contingencies in the study of Islamic social movements and rules out the irreversibility and teleology of modernization theory and the concomitant essentialization of Islam.[16] This approach has three different strands: The first strand, deprivation theory, presents Islamic movements as modern reactions against a corrupt state elite, overpopulation, and massive unemployment.[17] Özay Mehmet sees these factors as putting the Muslim world in an "intense crisis, [and as constituting] the catalysts that have triggered Islamic fundamentalist responses."[18] Mehmet argues that "Islamic resurgence in both Turkey and Malaysia appears as a response to uneven and badly managed secularist growth."[19] Those on the margins of society are more likely to be recruited into these religious-political movements, which express through religious idioms their goal of achieving social transformation. According to deprivation theory, Islamist entrepreneurs mobilize religious symbols and metaphors to gain access to economic goods, security for the individual, and a harmonious communal identity. Such movements utilize Islam as a populist ideology aimed at mobilizing society in the name of tradition and authenticity.[20] Diverse Islamic movements have had recourse to Islamic idioms in order to push back the authoritarian control of the state and create public spaces that they control. For example, Islamic groups in Egypt, Jordan, and Turkey have sought to carve new niches in education and health services, two of the most effective spheres through which to influence society. They also have sought to infiltrate the armed forces and the bureaucracy as the ultimate repositories of state power.

Clifford Geertz argues that in developing countries religion or tradition offers the "cognitive road map" or "ethos" that helps to bring diverse groups together for political action.[21] Even if we assume that Islamic movements are political protest movements, contextualist studies do not explain why it is Islam, and only certain interpretations of Islam, that the most powerful mass movements in many Muslim countries invoke. The contextualist approach adopts an instrumentalist reading of Islamic identity and idioms in a way that denies weight to

ideas and values and considers Islamic political identity primarily an epiphe-
nomenon of rapid social transformation.

The second strand of contextualism stresses organizational and leadership
qualities as well as the characteristics of the masses in the study of Islamic
movements and assumes that, despite overt appearances, they all have different causes and demands.[22] Some scholars who study Islamic movements argue
that religion is dynamic because it provides a set of mobilizing symbols, a formal structure to organize people, and a leadership network to deflect and ultimately to penetrate the state. Scholars who adopt this line of argument treat Islam
as the cement that binds together blocs of historically opposed forces to challenge authoritarian regimes. Nevertheless, this strand fails to explain why diverse competing groups tend to coalesce around Islamic symbols and idioms.
By focusing on institutions and leaders, this approach fails to explain how the
modern cognitive framework provided by Islam is formed and how it guides
the actions of individual believers. It also prevents general theorizing about
not only how various Islamic movements differ but also what they may have in
common.

The third group of contextualist writers emphasizes the dominant role that
is played by the twin processes of state-building and nation formation during
colonial rule.[23] Scholars of Middle East politics influenced by this school of
thought tend to stress the particular pattern of state formation as the reason for
the lack of democracy and the rise of authoritarian social movements. Some
scholars have tried to understand the Middle Eastern state as a republic based
on oppression rather than consent. Their studies view Islamic sociopolitical
movements as fragmented reactions to the "oppressive state." These studies do
not examine the state in relation to its "socioeconomic and sociocultural context"[24] but rather see the state itself as the cause of the lack of democracy and
civil society in the Middle East. For example, Simon Bromley argues that "the
relative absence of democracy in the Middle East has little to do with the region's
Islamic culture and much to do with its particular patterns of state formation."[25]
The "rentier state" model has become a leading conceptual tool to explain social movements in Arab countries.[26] According to this model, the state derives
income largely from oil, remittances, tourism, and external financial aid; and
citizens with little or no taxation do not demand political participation as long
as social services and food are subsidized. This approach, however, is overly
deterministic because it links oil wealth with authoritarian governments and
ignores sociocultural and historical contexts. For example, while the rentier state
model may help to explain political liberalization in Iran, Jordan, and Kuwait to
a certain extent, it does not explain why people invoke an Islamic identity rather
than national or class-based identities when the social welfare safety net of the
government no longer is deemed adequate.

This approach also overlooks other features of state and society, such as the
problem of well-off and upwardly mobile segments of society whose economic
and social success translates not into complacency but rather into increased
political frustration. Eric Davis criticizes the state-centric explanations of the
sociopolitical movements in the region and argues that "causal change emanat-

ing from the state was emphasized while societal constraints on state behavior were downplayed."[27]

The more nuanced and historically informed works of Lisa Anderson, Robert Bianchi, and Alan Richards and John Waterbury examine changes in the political landscape in terms of the internal and external economic and historical constraints in which state-society relations are embedded. Anderson, for example, treats the existence of authoritarian regimes in the Middle East as one of the imperatives of state- and nation-building.[28] Richards and Waterbury argue that it is the powerful autonomous corporate state and its interventionist tradition that shapes, even creates, socioeconomic classes through its policies. These classes, in turn, influence and determine the state's economic policies. Richards and Waterbury, like Anderson, assert that this autonomous state is the result of "the politics of decolonization and development."[29] They argue that

> the formulation of public policies shapes the allocation of resources within societies *and* the political consequences that flow therefrom.
> . . . As we shall show repeatedly, those authorities, the people who make up the governments and staff the upper echelons of the bureaucracies and public enterprises, frequently constitute an autonomous set of actors and interests in their own right.[30]

While the contextualist approach is a great improvement over the previous essentialism, it has ignored the dynamic changes that have occurred in numerous Islamic movements over time and the constitutive and framing role of popular Islamic culture. In order to understand the rise of a new Islamic political consciousness, we need a new framework that incorporates ideas and traditions within evolving social and political contexts.

Constructivism

Constructivism assumes that any society is a human construction and subject to multiple interpretations and influences. These constructions, such as Sufi orders, states, nations, and religions, condition and inform new modes of understanding. Thus Islamic political identity only can be properly understood through hermeneutical and mutually interactive causal techniques. This approach illustrates the unending tension between human understanding and multiple, yet conditioned, constructions of reality. It stresses human agency as the prime mover of history since individual subjectivity is formed reflexively by interactions between individuals. For constructivism, individual actions are neither caused by social structure nor the outcome of individual choices.[31] By focusing on the relationships between the individual and society (or between agency and structures), one may be able to understand how social structures (e.g., Islamic frames of reference that inform rules and practices) are constituted in the individual (internalizing the external through socialization). One also can understand how individuals build social structure through objectification of political and cultural consciousness (externalizing the internal). Using the constructivist approach, one can discern Islamic identity-based movements emerging along two diametrically opposed axes: state-centric (vertical and dogmatic) and societal-centric (horizontal and pragmatic). The expansion of public spaces plays a critical role in the formation and articulation of the competing Islamic identity movements. These identity movements entail a yearning quest for public ethics and justice in Muslim societies. In short, these movements are sites of articulating and bringing a different conception of the "good life" through negotiating with modernity.

The constructivist approach to Islamic political identity has three advantages over those just outlined. First, it does not confer agency to a reified Islam but rather to living Muslims whose actions are embedded in particular loyalties and networks. Second, it recognizes the power of ideas and everyday practices either to constrain or stimulate sociopolitical transformation. Third, it views (Islamic) social movements as not necessarily representing the disintegration of civil society but rather as contributing to its strengthening.[32]

Islamic Political Identity

Identities "are not things we think *about*, but things we think *with*. As such they have no existence beyond our politics, our social relations, and our histories."[33] The instrumental and strategic qualities of identities are expressed in the following definition by Crawford Young: identity "at bottom is a subjective self-concept or social role; it is often variable, overlapping and situational. . . . 'We' is defined in part by 'they'; the relevant other in a social setting is central in shaping role selection."[34] Using this definition of identity, I understand Islamic political identity as a frame of reference that unconsciously is internalized through socialization and becomes politicized and objectified in relation to desired ends and a changing social context. Islamic identity has two interwoven dimensions. One aspect governs an individual's religious devotion and adherence to ritual practices and offers a normative charter of roles and a conception of self and other. The second aspect of Islamic identity—one that often is neglected in scholarly works—presupposes a wide range of notions of justice and rule-governed conduct, ideas that facilitate the constitution of a community. In other words, Islamic frames of reference provide the cognitive basis for individual and collective interests and a map of action. The first aspect of Islamic identity becomes a sine qua non for the second aspect, but it is not sufficient for the construction of an Islamic *political* identity. Because of this connection between these two aspects of Islamic identity, Muslims are conditioned by religious tradition and existing sociopolitical contexts in the way they construct identity.

Islamic identity is politicized and stressed vis-à-vis other forms of national identities as a result of competition between different groups in society—such as intellectuals, Sufi orders, and political parties. These groups articulate and disseminate their political identities using modern forms of mass communication. Depending on the particular political and social context, Islamic groups and intellectuals may emphasize one layer of identity over others: religious, gender, status/class, ethnic, regional, tribal, territorial, or linguistic. These multiple layers of identity allow individuals to create and negotiate multiple and overlapping self-constructs and loyalties. Thus, among the questions that need to be examined are: When and under what conditions is Islamic religious identity transformed into something with a concrete communal aspect? Under what circumstances is the Islamic layer of identity emphasized over tribal or ethnic identities? Can the community adhere to both an Islamic and a national political identity simultaneously? I contend that Islamic political consciousness, as it develops in relation to other identities and within differing contexts such as that of a state-based nationalism in a secular state, must be understood as a contextual, relational, and situational phenomenon.

In this study, Islamic political identity is treated as a contingent and relational entity. By contingent I mean that Islamic political identity is dependent on the construction of difference vis-à-vis an "other" that helps to define identities in an ongoing process. By relational I mean that the social powers that help to construct difference are not closed systems but rather are constructed in oppositional moments. In other words, every identity, by definition, carries its "other" within it as a constituting element. The "significant other" is not only an oppositional "other" but also a constitutive part of identity. No identity has its own self-referential standpoint. In the case of Islamic political identity, one is confronted with internal "others" within competing Islamic movements as well as with the external "other" (i.e., the secular state or "the West").

In the construction of Islamic political identity, one needs to take the processes of modernity and imagination into account to understand the way Islamic movements become agents of identity formation. The experiment of modernity resulted in the formation of new opportunity spaces within which Muslims imagine Islamic identity and reconfigure new social relations. The demands of modernity and the human ability to imagine, interpret, and adjust to such contingencies are the main forces promoting the contemporary construction of Islamic political identity. The practical and theoretical bridge between modernity and imagination is built through the praxis of social movements. By modernity I do not mean a state-led transformation according to so-called universal principles that lead to the emergence of a "Westernized" society. Instead, I mean the ability of a society to transform itself in the face of modern conditions without futile attempts to shed completely its past culture and identity. One of the major implications of modernity is the autonomization of politics and other social spheres from all-encompassing ideologies, for example, religion or secularism. The attempts by Islamic groups to cope with the fragmentary nature of modernity have created contradictory positions and languages. These contradictions impel Islamic movements toward a more liberal and pluralistic self-understanding. These contradictions and ruptures within Islamic movements provide the breeding ground for the emergence of a modern civil society.

In recent years, the Nakşibendi orders and Nurcu movements in Turkey have struggled to free marginal voices from the dominance of the authoritarian state by using modern methods of mass communication. These movements should not be treated simply as reactionary opponents of modernity but as challenges to undemocratic aspects of modernism. Political developments in Turkey since the early 1990s demonstrate the naiveté of the conclusions presented by such leading proponents of the school of "modernization as Westernization" as Daniel Lerner and Bernard Lewis. Lerner, for example, confidently claimed that "the production of 'New Turks' can now be halted, in all probability, only by the countervailence of some stochastic factor of cataclysmic proportions—such as the atomic war."[35] In other words, Lerner and similar scholars had a very subjective, albeit unconscious, notion of modernity by which they meant "them" would become like "us." In contrast, I propose a more objective definition: modernity is a global condition in which individuals and groups are able to redefine social relations on the basis of social imagination. This imagination presupposes a rich repository of tradition, without which traditional societies would lose their inner cohesiveness and viability, the very precursors for modern development.

Imagination plays a critical role in the process of constructing Islamic political identity. Since Islam lies at the core of the symbolic structure of Turkish society and is the main source of shared moral understanding, Islam is the repository from which Muslim actors draw values, critiques, and judgments. Imagination, among Muslim agents, provides the healing power that opposes modern forces of fragmentation that threaten both the individual personality and society as a whole. Imagination acts to link individuals with society, spirit with matter, the present with the past, and the world with the mind. Imagination facilitates the withdrawal from the outer to the inner domain in which the self is formed. Imagination thus helps us to go beyond the limits of our experiences. For Said Nursi, imagination provided a dynamic bridge between the principles of reason and the empirical senses, thus allowing an understanding of the wholeness of the human and natural worlds.

Islamic Social Movements

In the construction of Islamic *political* identity out of primordial religious attachments, social movements form a critical bridge between the primordiality of Islam and the modern genesis of Islamic *political* identity. But what is a social movement? Sidney Tarrow has provided a comprehensive definition of social movement as a "collective challenge by people with common purposes and solidarity in sustained interaction with elites, opponents and authorities."[36] Alberto Melucci and Alain Touraine have taken this definition a step further with their new social movement theory.[37] This theory is based on a set of beliefs, symbols, and values with the goal of restructuring everyday life practices. New social movement literature, which links identity and ethics to the processes of cultural transformation, offers a useful conceptual avenue to follow in order to penetrate the construction of Islamic political identity in Turkey.[38] Islamic movements seek to reconstitute identities, institutional structures, ways of life, and the moral code of society through participating, influencing, or controlling cultural, educational and economic spheres. These movements are comprised of diverse, complex, and multisided Muslim agents with different goals and means by which they interact, shape, and guide political and social action. They supply a vernacular and flexible worldview with the means of mobilization and an oppositional platform for oppressed groups, from Kurds to farmers to workers. New social movements create new collective identities—that is, "a shared definition of the field of opportunities and constraints offered to collective action"—enabling participant actors to "calculate their cost and benefits of their actions" by using cognitive maps of identity.[39] The meaning of Islamic concepts such as just order (*adil düzen*) and virtues (*fazilet*) inheres in action. Thus, any study of Islamic social movements must bridge the gap between internal and external resources and utilize everyday life practices to understand the impact of Islamic movements.

By introducing the concept of opportunity spaces, I seek to overcome the dichotomy between individual versus collective, private versus public, and internal (piety) versus external (socioeconomic opportunity spaces) resources. Since social movements are "specialized in creating political space for newcomers, marginal populations, neglected programs, and unheard grievances,"[40] the study of opportunity spaces is essential in order to understand the causes and consequences of Islamic social movements. By opportunity space I mean a forum of social interaction that creates new possibilities for augmenting networks of shared meaning and associational life. Such arenas include civic and political forums and electronic and print media and cyberspace, as well as the market. Opportunity spaces are also not simply mobilizing structures, because they adhere through social interactions and expressive space rather than formal or informal organizational structures. The key opportunity space is the market, since economic prosperity allows one to become plugged in to broader cultural and political processes of social change. Opportunity spaces allow one to pick and choose in defining personal identity; to resist the policies of the state or the market; and to change the meaning of everyday life. Opportunity spaces undermine state-based or society-based attempts to generate a hegemonic ideology and mixed private and public spheres. These spaces free diverse voices and transform religiously shaped stocks of knowledge into a *project* and shared rules of cooperation and competition.

The concept of "opportunity spaces" is more useful than "opportunity structure" since it brings micro and macro forces together and identifies the interactions between external and internal resources to indicate direction of change. Moreover, since social movements "are 'acted out' in individual actions," opportunity spaces are central to the understanding of the transformation of everyday life.[41] In these spaces, not only are individual and collective actions blurred but also the boundary between the public and private is constantly redrawn. Islamic social movements represent the "coming out" of private Muslim identity in the public spaces. It is not only a struggle for recognition of identity but also a "going public" through private identities. In these public spaces, identities and lifestyles are performed, contested, and implemented. Thus the emergence of Muslim public sphere is very much about the history of the emergence of Islamic social movements. The Muslim public sphere does not only constitute but also emerges from these movements. These movements open up new spaces outside the control of the state and form a counterpublic sphere.[42] They transcend rigid class lines by framing the everyday issues of women, children, youth, and minorities in popular religious terms.

Economic growth fueled by the export-driven market has led to the dynamism and proliferation of opportunity spaces, as seen in the explosion of magazines, newspapers, television channels, the Internet, cultural foundations, and a private education system. These new opportunity spaces opened up new possibilities for Muslim actors to have their own distinct voice and institutional networks in public discussions. Thus Islamic movements, like civil rights and labor movements, involve participation in a rational game to carve out space and seek recognition vis-à-vis the state. Islamic groups strategically use new economic and political opportunities to create counterhegemonic spaces and discourses that are autonomous in relation to the secular state. These opportunity spaces have helped to form a new sociopolitical consciousness, and this, in turn, has become a source for social change in Turkish society. It should be stressed, however, that the immediate and primary goal of Islamic movements such as those of the Nurcus and the Nakşibendis has not been control of the state. Rather they seek the reconstitution of everyday life by transforming personal identity and consciousness by means of societal microinteractions that take place through contact with Sufi orders, the media, printed texts, and local communities. The construction of an Islamic political identity is the story of the transformation of macrostructures through microinteractions. Islamic movements transform these issues into a contest with the state over control of social and cultural spaces. But Islamic social movements are less about the resurgence of religion and mostly about "communal/empowerment," the introduction of a new moral language and the reconstitution of a "repertoire of action" that is very much dependent on opportunity spaces.[43] New opportunity spaces and the dominant discourse of privatization of social life have helped people to live as they wish outside the fixed patterns of the state. This privatization and pluralism of fashion, journalism, new tastes, architecture, and music have allowed multiple Islamic forms to become public. At the same time, these spaces have empowered economically and culturally excluded groups vis-à-vis the state, allowing excluded communities a means by which to bring their ethnic, religious, regional, and linguistic differences to the forefront and to attempt to shape the policies of the state. Those who have benefited from the access to foreign capital and markets have formed thousands of associations and foundations that attempt to recast "Islamic" discourse completely in valorizing civil society, pluralism, technology, capitalist consumerism, and the market.

Turkey's new Islamic intellectuals are not rooted in state positions but rather are advisors to major private companies or are well-paid essayists in newspapers and journals. The formation of this new class represents a shift from the Sufi lodge (tekke) to the printed text, or from oral culture to print culture. As a result of these changes, one encounters democratization of religious knowledge and a shift of authority from traditional ulema to new urban intellectuals. These young and very popular Islamist intellectuals are engaged in serious debates among themselves, as well as with "secular" members of the intelligentsia. This development inevitably has meant the fragmentation of what the "ideal Islamic society" entails. Despite the new pluralism of ideas, there is a consensus that a liberal political and economic order, including a marketplace of ideas as well as one of goods and services, is essential if most Muslims are to be secure and enjoy tolerance and the opportunity to participate. In the writings of these new intellectuals, the questions of justice and identity have been the two dominant terms of discourses.[44]

Islamic social movements, because of the blurring boundary between public and private space, concentrate on personal aspects of human life. They seek to use Islam to punctuate, monitor, and control arenas of daily life: what Muslims eat, read, wear, and enjoy, and how they behave. Islam is both a "resource" that can be manipulated and fashioned to pursue personal goals and interests and a "disciplining complex" that constitutes identity and interest. By focusing on Islam as a "resource" and constitutive block of personality and social capital, one can examine how material concerns constrain and shape the way people construct different Islamic movements such as Islam of the market and Islam of the welfare state. In the case of Turkey, the supporters of Islamic movements are the economically and culturally excluded sectors of society, as well as, very significantly, a new dynamic and confident Anatolian bourgeoisie. These groups are

> clearly people with modernist orientation who are experiencing a rising status in society, and [are] not yet fully incorporated into an elite group. . . . The religious symbolism associated with political Islam provides the unifying bond that helps to engineer a cross-class alliance, bringing together individuals with markedly different social status in society.[45]

The boundary between what is considered Islamic and what is non-Islamic is not fixed by Islam but rather by Muslims themselves. That is, Muslims are not passive receptacles of Islamic tradition, nor is their behavior determined by Islamic precepts. Islamic political identity is formed as a result of constructing new inner and outer boundaries through modern consumer goods, dress styles, manners, educational networks, demeanor, and diets; raising political consciousness by framing issues through the political language of Islam; and diffusing these identity markers in everyday life strategies. Purposive agents, such as Muslim intellectuals, traditionally have produced a body of principles, norms, and practices that constantly are being redefined as "Islamic" in relation to the Qur'an and the sayings of the Prophet Muhammad (hadith). These historic practices and principles are not prisons for Muslims but provide, instead, evaluative resources for them to use in shaping their cognitive worldview and value system. When traditional local frames of reference prove inadequate in modern conditions, Muslims, and in particular Muslim intellectuals, invoke the process of reimagination to redefine a new cognitive map, reading new meanings into traditional concepts and institutions. For example, the prominent Turkish Islamist intellectual Ali Bulaç has articulated a new social contract stressing human rights and pluralism by drawing on the charter of Medina as laid down by the Prophet Muhammad.

This reimagination creates a perpetual controversy between the customary meanings and practices associated with Islamic identity and the modern issues with which contemporary intellectuals must contend. This conflict is well illustrated by my model of the vertical and horizontal axes along which debates of Islamic authenticity and identity are argued (see table 1.1). The emergence of new opportunity spaces on the horizontal axis preserves and at the same time undermines traditional Islamic doctrines. It rearticulates them, allowing them to respond to changing social circumstances. However, this process also raises the issue of whether there are any limits on or guidelines for the reinterpretation of tradition and whether this opening up of discursive spaces to a wide range of interpretations is not undermining the long-term stability of tradition and its very survival. Such fears lead to attempts to reimpose some scriptural control and oversight by recognized traditional religious authorities on the vertical axis of this paradigm.

Islamic movements, as actors of social change, shift their goals and tactics as a result of two intertwined processes. First are the new structural conditions that either shrink or expand opportunity spaces, which in turn shape the goals and strategies of Islamic movement as "withdrawal," "confrontation," or "participation" in politics and the market. Second are the abilities of intellectuals or communal leaders to use opportunity spaces to frame everyday issues in terms of the shared cultural idiom of their community. Frames and the process of framing, which are shaped by the discursive practices of Qur'anic and prophetic tradition, face the uncertainties of editing, interpolation, and contamination by subsequent events and ideological currents. These two conditions address the question of *why* Muslims mobilize and *how* they do it. These movements reasonably could be referred to as "identity movements" because they carry certain meanings, lifestyles, and identities that challenge state-centric identities.[46] By bringing the concept of imagination to the forefront, I seek to stress the social construction of identities and resources by societal groups. In the case of Turkey, an Islamic ethos together with religious networks (mosques, Sufi orders, the textual reading circles) "supply" a powerful notion of justice and identity to express the "demand" of contemporary Turkish society for something that can overcome its ideological vacuity.[47]

Horizontal and Vertical Islamic Political Movements and Identities

Two distinct and opposing understandings of identity movements have developed in Turkey. This differentiation is based on each group's goals and strategies to produce change. Their goals range from state-oriented to societal-oriented changes, and their strategies range from legal to illegal. Although some social movements can be placed along a continuum, the classification suggested here offers four generic typologies of Islamic movements. At one end is a state-oriented and elite-based vanguard movement that is more ideological and stat-

TABLE 1.1. A Typology of Islamic Social Movements

Goal	Repertoire of action (strategies and means)	
	Legitimate	Illegitimate
Vertical		
State-oriented; elite vanguard; social change from above	*Reformist*: Participation in the hope of controlling the state or shaping policies through forming their own Islamic party or in alliance with other parties	*Revolutionary*: Rejects the system and uses violence and intimidation
	Target: education, legal system, social welfare *Outcome*: accommodation	*Target*: the state *Outcome*: confrontation
Horizontal		
Society-oriented; associational; identity- oriented; social change from below	*Societal (everyday life-based movements)* Groups using the media and communications networks to develop discursive spaces for the construction of Islamic identity; seeking to use the market to create heaven on earth; viewing Islam as a cultural capital; use of associational networks to empower community	*Spiritual/Inward*: Withdraws from political life to promote self-purification and self-consciousness
	Target: media, economy, (private) *Education Outcome*: integration	*Target*: religious consciousness *Outcome*: withdrawal

ist, while at the other is a society-centric, gradual, and reformative pragmatic movement. This classification is diagramed in table 1.1.

State-Oriented Islamic Movements

State-oriented vertical Islamic movements tend to be authoritarian and elitist in terms of decision-making and believe that the ills of society are best corrected by the control of the state through its enforcement of a uniform and homogenizing religious ideology. These movements are more likely to form when the state is oppressive or is in the process of opening new opportunity spaces. State-centric Islamic identity evolved in Turkey as society was encouraged to proceed along a "civilizing" project to create a homogeneous nation-state. The Republican state broke down traditional ties and culture with the intention of forging a homogeneous and obedient nation-state. Some individuals and groups, however, refused to submit to this new state-sponsored secular-rationalistic faith. Ernest Gellner has compared the secular ideologues to a type of rationalist ulema, who, instead of promoting Western-style tolerance and pluralism in Turkey, undermine it.[48] This nationalist project of constructing a new society has had a great "model-setting" impact on current Islamic movements. Thus many current identity-centered Islamic movements in Turkey have a powerful nationalist dimension and state-centric orientation.

Those who seek state-imposed change from above stand on the vertical level of the model of socioreligious movements. Such movements consist of people who perceive both religion and nationalism as belonging within the framework of the nation-state. They seek total transformation of society by means of the state. The degree of change sought is cataclysmic. The goal of replacing the state or, at the very least, providing a substitute for it means that this becomes the locus for the production of popular identity. The goal of forging a standardized modern religious identity requires a leader to determine the definitive dogma and practices. Thus dialogue is problematic for state-oriented Islamic movements and may cause erosion of their memberships.

Another defining feature of state-oriented Islamic identity is that this identity, in seeking to accommodate itself to a hostile environment, has attempted to assimilate the external world into its own religious dogma. This identity is characterized by textual uniformity and a desire for homogeneity. It perceives diversity and differences generated by market forces, emerging discursive spaces, and technology as threats to its faith in unity. At the same time, however, state-oriented Islamic movements depend on populist democracy to mobilize followers toward the goal of capturing the state.

How do we account for this paradoxical increase in rigidity, which is occurring among some Islamic groups even as the new public spaces occupied by electronic media publications and associations create many more options for adaptation and differentiated interpretations of Islamic identity and ideology? The explanation for this development lies in the search for an absolute foundation to prevent pluralistic readings of Islamic practices and identity (see chapter 4). Economic and political liberalization allows these movements the freedom to advance their agenda while at the same time promoting pluralism and the fragmentation of social control, which Islamist movements find very disturbing. These movements therefore are engaged in a search for an absolutist reading of Islamic practices and identity that will leave no room for pluralistic readings.

We can divide the state-oriented Islamic movements into two subcategories on the basis of their strategies for accessing power and shaping society. *Revolutionary* Islamic movements reject the legitimacy of the prevailing political system and use violence as their means of accessing power, usually because all other avenues are blocked by the establishment.[49] Some Islamic groups treat violence as a means to create opportunity spaces; other movements seek a complete overthrow of the current sociopolitical system. The purpose of their violence is to establish an Islamic state and apply Islamic law. *Reformist* Islamic movements, in contrast, participate in the political processes (as political opportunity space) currently available to them in the hope of gaining control of the state or shaping state policy; such movements take the form of Islamic political parties or alliances with other parties. In keeping with their ideological and social priorities, their main focus is on matters within the spheres of education, law, and the welfare program. For example, Necmettin Erbakan, leader of the MGH, envisioned a world order based on the current international structure but transformed so as to satisfy Islamist worldviews.[50] However, when a state-centric reformist movement seizes new opportunity spaces to penetrate the state, the same movement can be penetrated by the state and forced to moderate its positions.[51]

Society-Oriented Islamic Movements

Society-oriented Islamic movements seek to transform society from within by utilizing new opportunity spaces in the market and media to change individual habits and social relations. In terms of strategies and means, there are two distinct subhorizontal movements. First are the *inward-oriented contemplative movements*, which seek to withdraw into their own private realm in order to disengage, or exit, from what are viewed as illegitimate sociopolitical systems. These movements focus on individuals as the object of change by cultivating the inner self as the inner space in order to construct a reinvigorated Islamic consciousness along very traditional lines. Muslim activists seek to raise social consciousness by deeply involving religious rituals of praying, fasting, reading the Qur'an, and giving alms to the poor and needy. Through the repertoire of pious activism, they achieve personal transformation and contruct a shared moral discourse to critique power relations. For instance, the Nur faith movement and Sufi orders believe that if individuals are redeemed, a larger societal transformation will become possible. Thus personal redemption is seen as the key to societal change. This inner and microlevel mobilization has attracted those who are looking for self-enriching and satisfying emotional experiences, some of which are produced during collective rituals and meetings. This highly individualistic approach to social change was advocated by the late Said Nursi. The Nur movement and the Sufi groups in general aim to control negative emotions such as anger, shame, and outrage through inner mobilization. In contemporary Turkey, the Nakşibendi Sufi order has been the major institutional expression of this inner mobilization.

In contrast, the second category, *everyday life–based movements*, are concerned with influencing society and individuals, and they use both modern and traditional communication networks to develop new arguments for the construction of newly imagined identities and worldviews. These groups consider the market the space in which spiritual goals and material prosperity can best be achieved; and they view prosperity as demonstrating God's grace to his believers. Since societal movements target the media, economy, and information industry, they favor active participation in all facets of life. As rural communities migrate to cities, they seek to revive old communal ties as a way of sheltering themselves from the anomie of modern lower-class urban life. They construct networks along the lines of hometown solidarity and neighborhood religious associations. It is within these horizontal religious-communal spaces and networks that the socialization of a newly urbanized individual takes place. Turkey's development of a capitalist market economy, institutionalized rules of law, and increased acceptance of liberal values—and its membership within European organizations—have created new opportunity spaces for the understanding of the "self" within a broader community. Everyday life–based movements indicate that Islamic identity is about defining and living "the good life." One's political engagement is informed by one's moral commitment. Religious faith, or religiously informed moral character, propels one into action. Islamic practices and ideas are utilized to legitimize alternative practices and lifestyles. Questions like these— What is the good life and how does one realize it?—are very much at the center of the contemporary religious revival. One of the structural outcomes of new opportunity spaces is the emergence of new Muslim actors and more conscious and assertive Islamic social movements as agents of social change.

The Cycle of Islamic Movements and the Shifting Opportunity Spaces

Kemalism is the term used for the top-down, state-imposed political and cultural reforms of Mustafa Kemal Atatürk (1881–1938) to create a secular society and state in Turkey. Since the 1920s, the goal of the Kemalists (those who espouse Atatürk's ideas) has been to Westernize every aspect of social, cultural, and political life to create a secular, national, and republican state with a Western identity. Despite this state-led secularization policy, Islam has continued to offer a set of rules for regulating and constituting everyday life. Given the ongoing struggle between a militantly antireligious state elite and ideology and the majority of society, for many Turkish Muslims, Islam continues to serve as a repertoire and a site of counterstatist discourse and an organizational framework for social mobilization to deal with the stresses of development.

Between 1922 and the 1950s, the Kemalist reforms aimed to create state-monitored public spaces to secularize and nationalize society. The opportunity spaces were limited, and the repertoire of action varied from rebellion to full withdrawal to create inner spaces safe from the penetration of state power. This differentiation was based on each group's access to opportunity spaces, and their goals and strategies to further expand these spaces to produce social change (see table 1.2). The centralization and interference of the state politicized religion to an unprecedented degree. Rigid state policies led many people to perceive Islam increasingly as the language of opposition. Thus the large Sunni periphery embraced Islam as a way of challenging the policies of the center. This "oppositional Muslimness" of the periphery tried to develop a new language to counter Kemalism on the one hand and struggled against folk Islam by stressing the textual basis (the Qur'an and *hadith*) of Islam on the other. Secularism ceased to denote just the separation of state and religion in Turkey but instead became a virtual creed and designation for the ruling elite. Thus the debate between Islam and secularism is a debate about the boundary of state and society, the public and private. It is also a debate over the codes of everyday life.

TABLE 1.2. The evolution of Islamic movements in Republican Turkey

	Repertoire of action (strategies and means)	
Goal	Legitimate	Illegitimate
Vertical		
State-centric; elite vanguard; from above	*Reformist*: Nakşibendi and Nurcu political support to Democrat Party (1950–1960) and alliance with the Justice Party (1960–1970) and the formation of the first Islamic political party (1970–1980) and the Welfare/Virtue Party (1983–2001) in the hope of controlling the state.	*Revolutionary*: The Nakşibendi rebellions of 1925 and 1930
	Targets: education, legal system, social welfare	*Target*: the state
	Outcome: accommodation	*Outcome*: confrontation and defeat
Horizontal		
Society-centric; associational identity; oriented from below	*Societal (everyday life–based movements)*: As a result of new opportunity spaces in economy, politics, and the cultural domain, Nakşibendi and Nurcu groups are using the media and communications networks to develop discursive spaces for the construction of Islamic identities; the utilization of the market to create heaven on earth (MÜSİAD); views Islam as cultural capital; use of associational networks to empower community (Mazlum-der).	*Spiritual/Inward* Nakşibendi and Nurcu withdrawal from political life to promote self-purification and self-consciousness (1930-1950)
	Targets: Media, Economy, (Private) Education	*Target*: increasing moral and religious consciousness
	Outcome: Integration	*Outcome*: withdrawal

Greater insight can be gained if we stress continuities and ruptures by situating this inductive typology of Islamic movements within a historical context. Islamic movements have been evolving in different stages and each stage is shaped according to the boundaries of each new opportunity space as a result of political openings, liberalization of economy, increasing autonomy of business classes, and expansion of discursive spaces of radio, television, and print media. As a result of these opportunity spaces, the Islamic movement shifted from armed reaction (1923–1937) to the inward-oriented contemplative movement (1937–1950) to state-centric participatory movement (1950–present) to more everyday life–based movement (1983–present). However, within the overall Islamic movement of Turkey, revolutionary, spiritual, participatory, and societal movements coexist together, even though one tendency becomes more dominant in some stages. The chronological classification in table 1.2 should not be read as a linear "progress" of Islamic movements but rather as the growing pluralism of Islamic movements within new opportunity spaces.

The first reaction to the state's secularizing policies took the form of numerous uncoordinated revolts during the 1920s and 1930s. These revolts failed to overcome sociocultural cleavages in society, and the state brutally crushed them. For instance, the Nakşibendi orders stressed confrontation and even rebellion, when there was no possibility of a political opening. These orders not only stirred up inner mobilization with their religious doctrine but also offered themselves as the social movement of the excluded and marginalized Muslim population. The orders mobilized communal resources by offering a religious code of ethics based on sacrifice, leadership, and a network to disseminate the insurgent consciousness.

After the violent reaction from the state, religious leaders such as Said Nursi, the founder of the faith-based Nur movement, and Süleyman Hilmi Tunahan (1888–1959) developed a new repertoire of action by forming new networks based on inward-oriented faith. The writings of Nursi created the most powerful faith movement, one that stressed spiritual withdrawal and patience. Islamic practices and idioms offered Muslims a means for spiritual development and a stock of knowledge for their maturation as individuals and in the building of their personalities. The Nurcus and Nakşibendis used Islam as a repository to intellectualize everyday life and to keep the state at bay. Moreover, Sufi-led internal mobilization provided a map of community action. During this period, Turkish Islamic groups decided to move inward to cultivate Islamic consciousness at the personal level. Because of the oppressive policies of the state and limited financial resources, the groups had very limited access to printing and dissemination of religious literature. This, in turn, forced the Islamic groups to become inward-looking, closed circles, with the activist Islamic movement base limited mainly to the small, urban middle class. These groups lacked financial means and resources and were dependent on the state; moreover, the state-controlled media presented any form of antigovernment protest as being "reactionary."

Only with the advent of the multiparty system in 1950 did some Islamic groups begin to create covert and overt alliances with the center-right Democrat Party (DP: Demokrat Parti) of Adnan Menderes, who ruled Turkey between 1950 and 1960.[52] The first decision of the DP was the reinstitutionalization of *ezan* (call for prayer) in Arabic. It also stopped the persecution of Nursi. This new political opening facilitated the dissemination of his message of raising religious consciousness. Groups that met to read Nursi's works constituted a "reading public" or "textual-community." These textual communities evolved into a major social movement, the Nur movement, with powerful economic, cultural, and political capital. The Nur movement represents a shift from oral to print Islam. This process of allowing Nursi's students to participate in politics and to distribute his writings was the turning point for the open emergence of Islamic social movements in the Republican period. After the closure of the DP by the military coup in 1960, the Nur and Nakşibendi communities supported the Justice Party (AP: Adalet Partisi) of Süleyman Demirel in the 1960s and 1970s.

With the 1961 constitution, which extended civil liberties, Islamic groups started to create their own nongovernmental organizations and engage in sociocultural activities. The first Islamist party, the National Order Party (MNP: Milli Nizam Partisi) of Necmettin Erbakan, was established in 1970 and was the predecessor of the National Salvation Party (MSP: Milli Selamet Partisi, 1972–1980), the Welfare Party (RP: Refah Partisi, 1983–1998), the Virtue Party (FP: Fazilet Partisi, 1997–2001), and the Felicity Party (SP: Saadet Partisi, 2001–present). Before 1970, Islamic groups either worked with conservative factions of the Justice Party or remained underground.[53]

In addition to benefiting from the political openings created by a multiparty political system, the Islamic movement also profited from Turkey's involvement in the Cold War as a partisan of one of the two rival superpowers. In particular, as the Kemalist elite increasingly came to view the communist movement in Turkey as a security threat, it also saw the Islamic movement as an antidote to the perceived ills created by the Left. Thus the deepening of electoral democracy and "the repression of democratic leftist forces" helped to create political opportunities for Islamic movements.[54]

Although the 1980 military coup disrupted existing power arrangements, it also created opportunities for new actors who desired to restructure power relations and the distribution of resources. Even more so than during the 1960s and 1970s, the military perceived leftist forces as a threat and thus encouraged the mobilization of Turkey's historically excluded groups such as the Nakşibendi and the Nurcus during the 1983 elections. The latter groups activated their indigenous religious networks between 1983 and 1990 to offer welfare services, communal solidarity, and mobility to newly educated social groups and businesses. Turgut Özal's legal openings in terms of expanding the freedom of association, speech, and assembly and removing the state monopoly over broadcasting further facilitated the communication and dissemination of local and global idioms. As a result of these factors, Islamic movements constructed activist "consciousness" to shape the sociopolitical landscape of Turkey.

Conclusion

The typology of Islamic movements hereby developed and the conditions under which they vary suggest an empirically rooted and theoretically nuanced thesis about the evolving role of Islam in Turkey. The Turkish case proves that the predictions of the modernization school failed to materialize because of each Muslim's ability to reimagine his or her faith in a flexible and subtle fashion. This approach stresses the adaptability of religious tradition and its ability to reproduce itself within new spaces and forms of communication. This should not be seen as retraditionalization but rather as a creation of new forms "in the process of trying to adapt the old."[55] This study offers a better explanation of Islam as a living reality, not a body of rigid and closed "social-structural principles which constantly constrain the Muslims to behave in particular ways."[56] Rather, it is a repository of practices that present a vision of justice and the good life. In order to understand the meaning and the role of Islam, one needs to focus on "the individual Muslim actors, knowledgeable human agents who are possessors and strategic utilizers of local Islamic knowledge"[57] and the macrohistorical forces that either expand or shrink opportunity spaces.

Islamic political movements articulate complex social and economic issues and concerns. Mosques, Sufi orders, and small religious circles constitute an institutional network that relies on its repository of Islamic symbols for framing social and political issues to disseminate its ideas and articulate a new set of blueprints for the reconstruction of state and society, individual faith, and community. I have introduced four distinct typologies of Islamic movements and have identified three conditions under which Islamic movements are transformed from revolutionary to societal movements: changing state policies, movements' cooperation and alliances with business classes, and the expansion of discursive spaces. In the following chapters, I will examine the ideological and institutional power of the state and its goal of creating a homogenous nation-state. After examining state policies and their role in the construction of Islamic movements, I examine the economic landscape, along with urbanization as a site and a bundle of practices that create opportunity spaces for Muslims to imagine activist Islamic identities. Finally, I deal with the emergence of Islamic intellectuals, new communication networks, and the educational system as a habitat for the articulation of Islamic political identity.

2

The Enduring
Ottoman Legacy

In order to understand the origin and evolution of contemporary
Turkish Islamic movements and their relationship with the Kemalist
Republic, it is necessary to understand the formative impact of the
Ottoman state tradition. This continuity of the state tradition
continued through the Kemalist period, as the Republican regime
consciously aggregated political and economic power in order to
create a rationalized homogenous nation-state. Societal groups,
however, reacted strongly against the Republican elite's policies of
forced homogenization and the displacement of Ottoman-Islamic
institutions and traditions. This overt hostility was repressed during
the early years of the Republic but surfaced after a multiparty
political system tentatively was instituted in 1945–1946. In the case
of Turkey, democratization and liberalization have brought Islamic
and Ottoman traditions and idioms closer to the center of politics.
The relationship between democratization and Islamic movements is
not causal but rather constitutive. A diffuse Islamic political and
cultural identity served as a focal point around which popular
discontent with the authoritarian policies of the ruling Republican
People's Party (CHP: Cumhuriyet Halk Partisi) rallied.

The issue examined in this chapter is why an Islamic identity—
rather than one focused on nationality, ethnicity, or class—developed
as the primary outlet through which the population chose to vent its
frustrations with the Kemalist Republican elite. It should be noted
that an Islamic-oriented identity, although existing prior to the
foundation of the Republican state's radical homogenizing reforms,
lay dormant in Turkey for some time. Once "awakened," it had to be
reimagined or rearticulated to meet drastically changed circumstances. Moreover, because this reaction and rearticulation took

place within the confines of state-society interactions, the process of reimagining Islamic identity utilized the instruments of the state to redefine the society. Thus the primary aim of modern Islamic movements in Turkey is either to carve new spaces in society or to penetrate the state and reshape it according to their own counteridentities and perceptions of the Seljuk and Ottoman past.

Identities are very much constructed as a result of dynamic interactions between agents of the state and society. To trace the historical and social lineages of identity discourse, one needs to understand the evolution of these interactions. Print media, education, communications, and the commercialization of social relations were key factors in the expansion and consolidation of the state in the early Republican era. This, in turn, politicized societal groups by forcing them to construct an alternative Islamic political identity to counter the pressure of the state-led "civilizing" policies. The factors that were instrumental for the expansion of the state, paradoxically and simultaneously, also allowed societal groups to penetrate the state. Since 1980, Turkey has experienced the gradual Islamization of society, the market, and the state, coinciding with the construction of a new official Turkish-Islamic state ideology. The official policy of promoting a "Turkish-Islamic synthesis" was meant to co-opt socially powerful Islamic movements, whose emergence prior to the 1980 military take-over was evident, and to use them against what in hindsight was a much-exaggerated leftist "threat." The Republican state was transformed and in the process transformed those Islamic groups that sought to penetrate its previously off-limits political sphere. The Islamic groups, in the process of gaining access to the state, have transformed themselves from what once were purely social groups into a complex amalgamation of sociopolitical networks. These interconnections between Islamists and the state are dynamic and evolutionary. A closer examination of the formation of Islamic political identity and its externalization at the state level offers a useful prism for examining the inner dynamics of state-society interaction in contemporary Turkey.

The Sources of the Ottoman State

Throughout Ottoman history (1299–1922), religion served as a mediating cultural and political bridge between the state and society. The dominant Sunni Muslims of the empire shared a frame of reference based on the Qur'an and the traditions of the Prophet, which were used to define notions of virtue and justice in society. The most critical period of Ottoman state transformation took place in the nineteenth century. The seeds of the modern Republic were sown in this period, when Islamism was mobilized as a form of nationalism, with the aim of constructing a "Muslim nation" out of diverse ethnic groups. The Ottoman imprint on state and society created a peculiar conception of the state in modern Turkey. The Ottoman political system was notable for its attempt to create independent sources of legitimacy outside the strict framework of religion. The autonomous state structure became a battleground for the formulation and implementation of modernizing reforms during the Tanzimat era

(1839–1876). Two of the main legacies of the Ottoman state were its "patrimonial" and "transcendental" characteristics. By "patrimonial" I mean a political administration in which the ruler was the main source of legitimacy. The Ottoman ruler (the sultan) sought to maintain his control not through mediatory associations or groups such as the nobility but rather through his "patrimonial bureaucracy." The state remained above all local identities, and the ruler's bureaucrats had ostensibly but one loyalty: to the Ottoman sultan. By "transcendental" I mean that the state maintained itself above particular interests by adjudicating particularities on the basis of its role as a universal center. The state sought to promote itself as being above the rivalries and particular interests of its subject populations.[1] The state acted from above, according to its own transcendent logic, referred to in Ottoman by the phrase *hikmet-i hükümet*. *Hikmet* means wisdom in Turkish, and *hükümet* stands for government or state, hence: the wisdom of the state. Hikmet-i hükümet is similar to the notion of *raison d'état*, or actions according to the requirements of the state. In the Ottoman Empire, the requirements of state gained primacy over the requirements of religion.

Another legacy of the Ottoman state was that its formative development as a frontier society and ideology paradoxically helped to promote a "liberal" Islam and a highly differentiated state with an ambiguous, yet constructive, boundary between the temporal and the spiritual. This state felt a continual need to assert its authority over diverse and centrifugal elements of its far-flung empire. Bernard Lewis argues that "the Turks first encountered Islam on the frontiers—and their faith has from then till now retained some of the peculiar quality of frontier Islam."[2] One of the main characteristics of frontier Islam is that it is cosmopolitan in character and usually dominated by wandering ascetics and Sufi mystics. Frontier societies tend to be fluid, institutionally fragmented, and multiple in their loyalties and shared understandings—laws, norms, customs, and overlapping roles. As the Ottoman state was institutionalized, its center was gradually dominated by orthodox Islam, whereas the periphery maintained its segmentary Sufi and eclectic character.

The Ottoman state lacked corporate associations, and neither the landowners nor the merchant guilds could challenge it effectively because there was no landed aristocracy or recognized mediatory institutions between the sultan and his common subjects. The Ottoman state did not allow the existence of crosscutting identities or corporate institutions to challenge its hegemony. Indeed, society was segmented in Ottoman times in terms of religious, ethnic, regional, and neighborhood loyalties. At the local level, personal relations were structured by religious norms. These characteristics of the Ottoman state, although varying and evolving across time, were nowhere more pronounced than in certain key institutions associated with the Sublime Porte. These included the famous institution of the *devşirme*, or child levy, whereby the state raised a family of elite military and bureaucratic leaders whose only attachment in theory was to the state and the objective fulfillment of its purpose.[3] The state established its own bureaucratic schools and trained the devşirme-recruited children to perpetuate the norms and rule of the state. The military component (Janissary corps) played the key role in the expansion of the empire, making it an essential element in the survival of the state. A military career was one of the most prestigious professions in the state, and the Janissary tradition of being a force unto itself, above society and even above the direct control of the state's bureaucratic apparatus, was a tradition that continued into the Republican period.

A second important institution was the *millet* system, the organization and incorporation of the population in terms of confessional ties for administrative purposes.[4] With the *millet* system, the state developed a quasilegal framework for controlling different religious communities by recognizing a large degree of autonomy in their intracommunal affairs.[5] Each religious group, known as a *millet*, was organized as a corporate communal legal entity under its own religious leadership. This system helped to institutionalize a "tolerable" minority status for different religious groups.[6] However, it also placed rigid restrictions on individual freedoms within each millet. This system not only allowed the state to control communities through religious institutions but also allowed religious hierarchies to control internal dissent and combat heterodoxy.

A third institutional source of state autonomy was the guild system. This system, which was engineered by the state, provided some degree of government control over economic activity and prevented the emergence of an independent merchant class. The guilds functioned as an administrative link between the state and the merchant class.[7] The existence of the millet system and guilds demonstrates that power was structured vertically from the ruler to the ruled and that there was a dearth of horizontally integrating institutions. The communities of Ottoman society managed to live together by living apart. One of the main reasons for this peaceful coexistence was the lack of horizontal integration and limited interactions between diverse communities. When communal boundaries were sundered in order to create a citizen state, there was little left to mediate personal relations with the state. Thus Ottoman citizens in the nineteenth century "stood in a *direct* rather than a mediated relationship to supreme authority."[8]

Islam was not only the source of social cohesion and an important organizing set of norms for the horizontal ties of diverse Muslim communities but also a reference for the rulers in their relations to the ruled. Religious scholars of Islam (ulema) served a vital role as an informal bridge between state and society. As the guardians of the "high Islamic tradition," they both legitimized the status of the sultan and his state and ensured that Islamic injunctions of justice and obligation toward the sultan's subjects were upheld as much as possible, mitigating any tendencies toward unbridled despotism. Ruling classes "included those to whom the sultan delegated religious or executive power through an imperial diploma, namely, officers of the court and the army, civil servants, and ulema."[9] The ulema were integrated into the state system along with other administrative elements, and the primary task of this bureaucracy was "the preservation of the integrity of the state and the promotion of Islam."[10] In short, the state, even though it derived its popular legitimacy from Islam, strictly organized and controlled religious institutions and scholars (ulema). There was no tension between the state and an independent "church" similar to that which existed for centuries in Europe, ultimately leading to the gradual separation of church and state and the secularization of European societies.

The affairs of the Ottoman state were carried out according to the sovereign's laws, known as *kanun*, which were seen as separate from Islamic law (*sharia*). Since Ottoman social life was regulated as much by the sultan's laws as by Islamic legal injunctions, some historians have hesitated to describe the Ottoman Empire as an "Islamic state," that is, one in which Islamic law prevailed. For example, Halil İnalcık, a leading Ottoman historian, argues that "a kanun, in principle, had to conform to the Islamic law and had to deal with a case which was not covered by the *Shari'a*."[11] These laws, known in Turkish as *kanunnames*, governed the affairs of the state and the public domain. The Ottoman state can be seen as, first and foremost, a legal association. As a result of the kanun, an independent and secular legal system developed, complementing the sharia and its vision of a virtuous and just society. In effect, the Ottoman state attempted to use religious law and "high tradition" to control and homogenize Muslim society and to combat separatist tendencies exhibited at its frontier zones; the latter often were associated with heterodox Islamic movements. The state built mosques in most villages to combat heterodoxy and promote loyalty to the orthodox Islamic faith and to its protector and sovereign, the Ottoman state.[12] As the state expanded, cultural diversity came to be seen as a potential threat, and thus religion was used to destroy alternative sources of solidarity.[13]

The administrative trinity of the devşirme, the millet system, and the guilds began to break down as a result of the diffusion of new European ideas of secularism, nationalism, endless wars, and the penetration of Western capitalism. The multifaceted crisis of the state, which no longer could be ignored by the beginning of the nineteenth century, led to concerted efforts at revitalization through administrative reforms.

Shifting from a Dynastic State to an *Ummet* (National) State

Turkish scholars raised during the Kemalist era tend to ignore the emergence of a proto-Islamic nation-state in the nineteenth century and instead eulogize the nation-building enterprise of the Republican state.[14] But the Ottoman Empire, in the brief interlude between the Tanzimat Edict (1839) and the disastrous Russo-Ottoman war of 1877–1878, witnessed a brief period of far reaching liberalization that had profound cultural and social effects.[15] The Tanzimat reforms sought to expand the influence of the state by means of new administrative tools—a parliament, new engineering schools, and the reorganization of administrative units into "departments." A policy of "Ottomanism" was implemented; this was designed to minimize cultural, ethnic, and religious differences within the diverse empire by giving strong legal protection to all groups along with a feeling of Ottoman citizenship. During this period (1839–1876) commerce flourished, a new merchant class emerged, and expanding trade fueled the development of bourgeois taste and individualism.[16] The individual in this modern idiom was ready to emerge in something akin to the European enlightenment. This individualism was expressed in the literary and artistic renaissance of the time.[17] Print-based dialogue appeared in various journals. These journals played homage to the individual, a protean character, and attempted to modify and change people to meet the needs of the time. This policy of Ottomanism failed, however, because of the rise of nationalism in the Balkans and the state's failure to respond to external challenges. Nonetheless, these reforms and their impact promoted the secularization of Turkish society and introduced new ideas of citizenship, equality, and constitutionalism.

The reformists had one goal, to preserve the existence and authority of the state. Thus most reforms were implemented with the aim of consolidating the state's social base. These policies did not have the original liberal intention of limiting the power of the state or creating public spaces for the expression of individual freedom. Nevertheless, a new environment was created in which ideas of citizenship and scientific reasoning evolved. The nineteenth-century Ottoman elite sought to consolidate state power primarily by modernizing the army, a process that transformed the army into a trend-setter and an agent for ordering the society in accordance with the needs of the state. In addition to the modernization of the army, the second instrument for consolidating state power was the introduction of science and technology for economic development. Science, for Ottoman bureaucratic intellectuals, became the progressive force to order and regulate society and alter the modes of thinking. The "carriers" of this positivist worldview exploited the reform campaign to consolidate their power vis-à-vis the religious scholars by framing all opposition as "religious fanaticism."

Whereas the state bureaucratic class saw European-inspired reform policies as an effective means of coping with the empire's problems, the ulema viewed the reforms as weakening the state. Their argument gained ground as a series of reforms failed to stem the decline of the empire or placate its cynical European critics. The ulema began to argue that the Ottoman state should accept European scientific and technological expertise but not its social and political institutions and ideologies. This group argued that Islam was the cement of Ottoman society and that it should become the state ideology as well. With the reign of Sultan Abdülhamid II (r. 1876–1908), this latter argument started to have a greater impact on the Ottoman government.

During the reign of Abdülhamid II, a new group of reformers, known as Young Turks, presented themselves as progressive on the grounds that they had scientific education and were guided by science and reason rather than by religion. The major characteristics of the Young Turks, who were trained in secular military schools, were an unquestioned faith in positivism as a guide to politics and society, a determination to create a modern society to consolidate the power of the state, and a belief in elite rule. Because of these three characteristics, the Young Turks were neither liberal nor democratic, although they stressed the significance of the parliamentary system and constitutionalism as a way of coping with ethnic challenges in the Balkans. Their first and foremost goal was to protect and consolidate the power of the Ottoman state. Even their attempts to create "Ottoman citizenship" were aimed at expanding the social basis of the state. Thus, for the Young Turks, the parents of the Republican elite, identity was constituted by the two contradictory trends of radicalism (by stressing science and rationality) and conservatism (by seeking to consolidate state power). Even though they presented themselves as "revolutionary" leaders determined to change society, they also used the state to consolidate their own power beginning in 1908.

Transformation of the Ottoman State

During the long reign of Sultan Abdülhamid II, the Ottoman state began to promote Islamic nationalism. Profound changes within and outside the Ottoman state facilitated the promotion of this Islamic political consciousness. The cycle of wars and reforms revitalized religious identities, and nineteenth-century Ottoman nationalist discourse was framed in terms of Islamic identity. The Ottoman political elite utilized Islamic concepts to promote the idea of territory as the new foundation for statehood and to disseminate the view that the fatherland comprised the space that was necessary for the survival of this Islamic community. By the end of the nineteenth century, the Ottoman elite had begun to use fragments of Ottoman-Islamic political thinking to articulate new concepts such as homeland (*vatan*),[18] nation (millet), and public opinion (*kamuoyu*).[19]

Bureaucratically led reform policies, such as the Tanzimat, sought to shift the center of loyalty from the sultan to a more broadly based understanding of legal citizenship and to promote the concept of "Ottoman" nationhood. Realizing the difficulty of creating a nation through strictly legalistic means, the state bureaucrats stressed the necessity of a common cultural axis in forming a nation. Islam was presented as a vital part of the cultural glue that would hold the population together. The state invoked an Islamic identity to blend various Muslim ethnic groups into a "Muslim nation" after the 1878 war. This constituted a major revolution in the Ottoman state tradition. The source of legitimacy began to shift from the Ottoman dynasty toward the caliphate and the Muslim community; a new center of loyalty began to develop, along with more concrete concepts of homeland. This feeling, in turn, gave impetus to the rise of the notion of citizenship in the Ottoman state. The existence of the state was rationalized by the need to ensure the survival of the nation.

As the state began to fragment as a result of Balkan national movements grounded in the nationalisms of their respective churches, a massive influx of Balkan and Caucasian Muslim refugees into Anatolia took place. The Russian and Balkan states' atrocities these Muslims described served as a catalyst for a new Islamic political and national consciousness following the 1878 Treaty of Berlin, which reduced Ottoman territory by two-fifths and resulted in the loss of one-half of its subjects, including one-fifth of its Muslim population.[20] The migrations from territories ceded to European powers under the Treaty of Berlin transformed the multireligious empire into a Muslim country. After the treaty left Muslims as the clear majority in the Ottoman state, its promotion as the spiritual home of Muslims proved to be easier. Over four million Muslims migrated from the Crimea, the Caucasus, and the Balkans to settle in Anatolia and eastern Thrace. This influx required the Ottoman state to provide some concept that would unite these newcomers, many of whom were non-Turks (Albanians, Bosnians, Circassians, Chechens, etc.) and spoke different languages. The migrants, who had been expelled or forced to leave because of their religion, found in Islam the source of their common bond with the people of Anatolia. The sultan sought to strengthen this common bond and to replace the various group loyalties and identities with loyalty to and identification with an Islamic state apparatus—namely, the institution of the caliphate.[21]

Only British-Russian rivalry kept the Ottoman Empire from being dismembered totally in 1878. The sultan recognized that he needed to forge strong political unity within the remaining empire if he were to preserve it. In the aftermath of the Treaty of Berlin and following the administrative occupation of Egypt by the British in 1882, Sultan Abdülhamid II sought to integrate the remaining Anatolian, Arab, and Balkan regions of his state through a series of new administrative, economic, and cultural programs.[22] In particular, he tried to create among his Muslim subjects a political consciousness and sense of unity based on the twin pillars of state (*devlet*) and religion (*din*). However, in practice, religion was subordinate and acted primarily as a shield for the preservation of the state. Abdülhamid II pursued his efforts to create a form of Islamic nationalism through numerous avenues; these included the centralization of authority, building schools, an emphasis on the role of Arabic culture in the empire, the creation of new communication and transportation channels such as the Hijaz railroad and telegraph lines, the provision of financial support to select Arabic and Turkish newspapers, the retention of leaders of Sufi orders as advisors, and investment in the protection and reconstruction of Mecca and Medina. During this period the state's profound social and political transformation was also manifested in the public debate over national identity, centered on three possible sources of identity for citizens: Ottomanism, Islamism, and Turkism.[23]

Sultan Abdülhamid II also took steps to form connections with the widespread networks of Sufi orders and emphasized the pilgrimage to Mecca and Medina, as well as the caliph's role as organizer of this important Muslim activity.[24] He invited the şeyhs of the prominent Sufi orders to Istanbul and established a close relationship with the leaders of the Şazeli and Rufai orders, who became his advisors. He resumed use of the title "caliph" to show Muslims around the world that he served as guarantor of the Holy Places in Mecca, Medina, and Jerusalem.[25]

Since Abdülhamid II's conception of an Ottoman political community required the subordination of local identities and loyalties to an Islamic identity, he created a new ideology (Islamism) and state organization. He reactivated and further politicized traditional societal networks to form a national communal identity. The main instrument he used to foster a common identity and feeling of loyalty to the state was the school system.[26] During his rule, 10,000 new semi-religious elementary (*sıbyan*) schools opened, while the numbers of *ibtidai* (more secular elementary) schools increased from 200 to 4,000, *rüştiye* (mid-level high schools) from 250 to 600, *idadi* (middle schools) from 5 to 104, and teachers' colleges from 4 to 32. The founders of the modern Republic in fact were educated in these very schools. Abdülhamid II also brought the German General Colmar von der Goltz to train new military cadets. During a twelve-year period (1883–1895), von der Goltz formed a new cadre of army officers in accord with the Prussian model, and this cadre would play a major role in the formation of the secular nation-state beginning in 1923.[27]

New personnel hired from these Hamidian schools in order to expand state positions placed the mark of Islamic culture on their offices. In other words, in the process of transforming society, the state itself was transformed by societal forces. Sufi orders were able to penetrate different levels of the state. This reciprocal transformation of the state and society, which was an outcome of the mutual redefinition of state and society, created a new state-identity, and this identity in turn shaped the "national interest" of the state.

One may argue that the seeds of the Kemalist nationalist project ironically were planted during the Hamidian period. The nationalist struggles of 1919–1922 were fought in Anatolia at the popular level as a war in defense of the faith. In fact, the Islamic layer of identity was heightened and used by Mustafa Kemal Atatürk to mobilize the population against the occupying powers that sought to implement the Sevres Treaty of 1920, which divided much of what is now Turkey among European powers, and carved an independent Armenia and Kurdistan in eastern Anatolia. The Turks were left only with Ankara and a swath of land around central Anatolia. This humiliating treaty raised Islamic political conciousness against the occupying European powers by bringing the external other (the West) into actual contact with a defeated and now technically subordinated Muslim population. The ulema played a key role in this mobilization; in the first Turkish parliament, 20 percent of the deputies were ulema.[28] The founding charters of the Turkish Republic and the decisions of the Erzurum and Sivas conferences constantly refer to those "Muslims who form one nation" or "all Islamic elements of the population." These charters hardly mention the "Turkish nation" as a separate entity and always include "Kurd" alongside "Turk."[29] In other words, it was not a "Turkish" war of liberation, as claimed in the official historiography, but rather a war of "Muslim elements" to free the caliphate from the occupation. During the opening speech of the Grand National Assembly (Büyük Millet Meclisi) in April 1920, Atatürk said: "It should not be assumed that there is only one kind of nation from the communities of Islam inside these borders. Within these borders, there are Turks. There are the Çerkes; as well as other Muslim communities."[30]

During the war years, Atatürk defined the nation in Islamic terms and argued that "the nation that we are trying to protect similarly not only consists of one community. It is composed of different Muslim communities."[31] Under the leadership of Atatürk, the Muslims of Anatolia defeated foreign armies. The 1923 Lausanne Treaty recognized Turkey's new borders and scrapped Sevres.[32] Although Sevres is not remembered by many Europeans, Turks turned it into a major trauma and a living document to understand European policies toward Turkey. This preserved "chosen trauma" is a powerful tool that has been used to delegitimize European criticism of Turkey's human rights record.

The Kemalist Cultural Revolution (1922–1950)

In order to understand contemporary Turkish Islamic movements, one needs to comprehend the essentially antagonistic and intersubjective role played by a still largely Muslim Anatolian civil society and a Kemalist state establishment whose *raison d'être* is to combat it. Since its inception the Kemalist military-bureaucratic establishment has viewed large sections of its own society, rather than foreign countries, as its main threat. Kemalism, like other ideologies generally, serves as a means for the acquisition and maintenance of its own power. To comprehend the political and ideological crisis confronting the Turkish state, one must explicate Kemalism in terms of its conception of politics and community, which is informed by its secular-nationalist worldview. There is an inherent contradiction between Kemalism and democracy, since the former defines politics as a means to realize an elite-defined and administered common good: a docile, homogeneous, and secular nation-state.

Kemalism, in the manner of other radical revolutionary movements, defined itself in obsessive antagonism to the *ancien regime*, in this case the Ottoman-Muslim state and society. Kemalist "secularism" was meant to represent "progress" and "civilization" against alleged Islamic "backwardness" and "Oriental barbarism."[33] For this reason, Kemalist ideology has been obsessed with "the security of secularism," which is manifested as fierce hostility to public manifestation of Islam. Resistance to or even mild questioning of secular objectives has been viewed as tantamount to high treason against the state, and such challenges always have been regarded as security issues to be dealt with outside the normal political processes. For the sake of the security of secularism, the Kemalist system sought to create its own secularism-friendly Islam, known as enlightened Islam, or *çağdaş İslam*. In order to protect its founding ideology, the Kemalist elite opportunistically employed Islam for the realization of a modern and secular Turkey.

There are several political consequences of the Kemalist worldview. First, it prevents open and participatory public debate over the formation of a social contract by insisting on its own predetermined ideal society: a secularized and Westernized homogenous nation-state. Second, it does not tolerate the articulation of different identities or lifestyles in the public domain since they undermine the Kemalist vision of an ideal society. Third, it treats "politics" as a management issue to realize predetermined Kemalist ends. Finally, it limits political participation to those who subscribe to Kemalist goals and seek to promote them; those who are not fully committed to Kemalist ideals are depicted as backward, irrational, or divisive and are excluded from the public sphere. The overall effect, then, is to delegitimize dissent and opposition in public space. Politics, therefore, is an "administration" in accordance with predefined principles. The military's main task is to supervise and monitor the public sphere and punish those who do not act in accord with Kemalist principles. Even the Turkish Parliament is not free to determine legislation but rather is an institution that passes laws that accord with the views of the main guardian of Kemalism, the National Security Council (NSC).

The latter body comprises the military-bureaucratic elite and considers genuine participatory politics as a threat to national unity and the territorial integrity of Turkey. Thus, whenever the NSC perceives politics to be moving beyond the constraints of Kemalism, it intervenes.

The Politics of Identity in the Early Republican Era

To understand the meaning and role of the secular Turkish identity that the new Republican regime introduced in 1923, one must be aware of how the state elite used institutional means to shift the basis of popular identification from an imperial/Islamic identity to a Western-influenced nation-state identity. The main task of the new Republic was to consolidate the *Turkish* state and its new establishment by homogenizing the plethora of ethnoreligious groups centered in Anatolia. In the process of forging the "hyphen" between nation and state, Atatürk and his allies stressed a largely linguistically determined sense of "nationhood." Yet there was a pronounced sense of contradiction inherent to this Kemalist project. In order to become a Turk, it was necessary first to be a Muslim and second to learn a standardized form of Turkish. This transformation was easy for many Balkan immigrants, since the terms "Turk" and "Muslim" often were used synonymously in the regions from which they had come. However, the situation was different in Anatolia, where tribal, sectarian, and ethnic loyalties competed for allegiance among a diverse population.

After 1925, the multiple identities that had existed during the Ottoman period "officially" coalesced into a secular Turkish nationalism. The historians of the Kemalist period and the official Turkish Historical and Language Society redefined identity in terms of ethnicity and language. They used the army, schools, media, and the arts to make a clean break from Islam and the Ottoman legacy. Major public buildings such as the Turkish Grand National Assembly in Ankara were built by the Republican regime intentionally to express not any Ottoman heritage but rather an elite-manufactured "Hittite" foundation for the new Turkish identity. Despite these great efforts, however, two versions of nationalism have continued to compete in Turkey: secular linguistic nationalism and religious-communal nationalism. Even for the secular intellectuals, there always has been an ironic ambivalence surrounding the Islamic component of Turkish identity. For example, one "author" of secular Turkish nationalism, Ali Haydar, viewed Islam as a sine qua non for being a Turk; a non-Muslim, even one whose mother language was Turkish, could not be a real Turk.[34] He categorically said: "It is impossible to make non-Muslims sincere Turkish citizens. But at least we can make them respect the Turks."[35] Haydar's ideas were not exceptional and indicate that, at a fundamental level, Turkish identity, even during the most doctrinaire Republican period, could not elude religion as an important component of its supposedly secular, national identity. One could be a non-Turkish Pomak from Greece, a Bosnian from Sanjak, or a Torbesh from Macedonia and become a Turkish citizen, but a Gagauz-Turk of the Orthodox Christian faith from Moldova could not.[36] Ironically, despite its fierce hostility to religion, Kemalist secular nationalism never was able to disengage itself or its putative nation from its Islamic heritage.[37]

Strategies for Creating "The Turk"

Since 1926, the state has created and disseminated its version of a Turkish state–based national identity through its educational system and the media. This state-based nationalism not only has excluded Islamic institutions from political and social life but also has controlled the dissemination of Islamic knowledge by strictly monitoring and controlling Islamic teaching through the Directorate of Religious Affairs. The purpose of the state-run educational system was to build a modern nation-state and a homogeneous citizenry. The image of a tutelary state was enhanced as a result of Turkish nationalism and the positivism of the Kemalist period. Modernist intellectuals viewed the sciences as the key to liberating Turkish society from the shackles of tradition, history, and superstition. Atatürk claimed that his agenda was shaped by the laws of nature rather than the laws of God. He stressed the authority of science over that of religion and tried to form a new society centered around rational-positivism and nationalism. The Republican state also played an emancipatory role with regard to the rights of women by offering them a better education than had been available to them in the traditional school system. The emancipation of women regularly was presented as an example of the civilizing role of this new elite. This "state feminism," however, subordinated gender identity, as all else, to the exigencies and whims of the Republican authorities.

The elite tried to engineer a modern society by making full use of the mechanisms of the state, without, however, a genuine commitment to pluralism and critical thinking. The ideological basis of this political engineering was the tradition of French positivism. The positivist elite came to view the state as an end in itself and society as simultaneously a threat and a means to enhance the state and its new elite. Because identity is constructed in relation to an "other," identity formation is always in a state of flux. Constructing a new internal and external "other" for political purposes was at the center of Turkish-Republican identity formation. For example, the Turkish elite identified Islamic tradition and the masses as the other, and the internal otherness of Islam was also extended to the external otherness of the Arabs. Indeed, the new Kemalist regime deliberately tried to ignore Muslim countries in its foreign relations.

This attempt to disengage the Turkish state from an Islamic worldview considerably widened the gap between the elite (the center) and the masses (periphery).[38] After a few years of consolidation, Kemal and his associates were ready to launch a fierce attack on traditional society and indeed on everything and everyone that might pose a real or potential challenge to their authority. The republican policies included, among others: abolishing the caliphate and establishing the Directorate of Religious Affairs in 1924;[39] closing the traditional religious seminaries (*medrese*) in favor of a unified educational system in 1924, and banning Sufi orders in 1925; prohibiting the *fez* and the veil in 1925; adopting European criminal, civil, and commercial codes in 1926; replacing Arabic script with Latin in 1928; removing Islam as the state religion in 1928; recognizing full political rights of women in 1934; introducing secularism as a constitutional principle in 1937; and prohibiting the establishment of a society or party based on religion or sect in 1938. These radical measures did not result from any popular pressure from below. Rather they amounted to a revolution-from-above imposed by a military-bureaucratic elite whose aim was not simply reform but the creation of a completely new state and society in full accordance with its own vision.

The popular perception of the military as a sacred institution facilitated the implementations of these reforms without much opposition from the people. The contradictory sources of the legitimacy of the Turkish military have been very much ignored by scholars of Turkey. The military derives its legitimacy from its mission of modernizing the society (Europeanization) and creating a secular nation-state. The masses see the military as a sacred institution protecting the sacred values of the Turks: the state and religion. There is not much distrust and fear between the populace and the military. One reason the military was able to implement its modernizing policies has to do with its "imagined" sacred roots among ordinary Turks. The military remains a very popular and trusted organization, even among those who don't seem to share its radical secularist agenda. The goal of the military is the *preservation of the state*. Since Turks usually see the state as the necessary condition for the survival of Islam, they always justify any act for the preservation of the state as a sacred duty. For instance, every member of the Turkish army is called *"mehmetcik"* (Turkified version of Muhammad, or the soldier of Muhammad). Thus, the armed forces are regarded as the *Peygamber Ocağı* (the Heart of the Prophet). Every soldier who is killed in the line of duty, therefore, is also regarded as *sehid* (martyr), and those involved in military conflict are called *gazi* (a fighter for Islam and homeland). During the establishment of the conscript army in the late nineteenth century, Islamic concepts were utilized to make military service acceptable, a sacred duty.

Mustafa Kemal was not opposed to religion per se, but he wanted to construct a progressive Islam that would be in the service of nation-building and the economic development of Turkey. In line with this thinking, a Directorate of Religious Affairs (DİB: Diyanet İşleri Başkanlığı), under the office of the prime minister, was established. The goal of the DİB is to "administer the Islamic affairs of faith, rituals, moral principles, and to enlighten the society about religion and govern the places of worship."[40] Thus the task of the DİB has not been to educate "good Muslims" or raise Muslim "consciousness." Instead its objective is to create "good citizens" with civic responsibility toward the state.[41] Indeed, the DİB exists to promote love of homeland, the sacredness of the military and civil service, respect for law and order, and hard work for the development of Turkey.[42] In other words, it has the arm of the state to educate and socialize new "Turks" according to the needs of the Republic. The establishment of the DİB also was expected to nationalize Islam. Turkish secularization therefore has not recognized the autonomy of religion but rather has tried to control it strictly and has used religion for its own nationalizing and secularizing goals. The state integrated the religious institutions and functionaries into the government structure to create a Turkish version of enlightened Islam. Since diverse versions of Islam (e.g., Sufi orders) were the source of pluralism in the public sphere, the state decision to create a homogenous and nationalized public sphere required their elimination in favor of a national religious structure. In 1928, the government established a committee to reform religious life in accordance with the precepts of reason and science. The committee, under the leadership of the prominent historian Mehmet Fuad Köprülü and educator İsmail Hakkı (Baltacıoğlu), declared that "religious life, like moral and economic life, must be reformed along scientific lines, that it may be in harmony with other institutions."[43] It recommended that people not take their shoes off in the mosque, the language of worship be Turkish, and the prayer times be adjusted to the needs of the work day; it even called for the introduction of church-style pews and music instead of Qur'anic recitation.[44] The fundamental goal of this report was the Turkification and the subordination of Islam.[45] Although its recommendations were not implemented because of the fear of hostile public reaction, it facilitated some changes, such as introducing the first call to prayer (ezan) in Turkish on January 22, 1928, in Istanbul. After the 1930 Menemen incident, the state gave up its attempts to create a national (Turkish) and enlightened Islam and adopted a militant secularist policy to eliminate the public manifestation of Islam.

Education: The Medium of Social Engineering

National universal education was also central to the Republican campaign of forging a new national identity and creating a hegemonic culture.[46] Atatürk's main goal was to create a disciplined and obedient Turkish nation according to his ideological worldview. The Law of Unification of Education (Tevhid-i Tedrisat) created a national educational system with the aim of fostering a secular and patriotic collective consciousness. The Republican regime aspired to invent a new nation whose standardized subjects would be guided by a secular and positivist ethos hostile to all manifestations of tradition. It was commonly believed that the high level of illiteracy demonstrated in the first national census of 1927 (89.4 percent of the Turkish population) was the result of education being primarily the responsibility of the private sphere. This contributed to the government's desire to see education become the exclusive responsibility of the state. The high level of illiteracy also encouraged Atatürk to push for the adoption of the Latin alphabet, which was better suited for Turkish phonetics. However, adopting the Latin script also represented a marked break with the Islamic-Arabic past.[47] The famous feminist writer of the period and associate of Atatürk during the War of Liberation, Halide Edip (Adıvar), criticized this policy:

> The continuity of Turkish culture has been abruptly broken. The
> younger people will read and write, but will not be at home with any
> culture half a century old. Without a past, without a [collective]

memory of the accumulated beauty in the national consciousness, there will be a certain crudeness, a lowering of aesthetic standards.[48]

This abrupt rupture with the past did not trouble Atatürk; on the contrary, he viewed the influence of the religion of the Arabs as the main factor contributing to the perceived backwardness of his society and thus adopted a set of reforms to promote the "disestablishment" of Islam. Atatürk argued that "our national morality should be cleansed and supported with modern principles and free thought."[49] Science and rationalism were to be the true liberators and moral guides in the construction of this new Turkish society. The Kemalist understanding of rational-positivism was imposed on every aspect of society within reach of the state. Once the Ottoman-Islamic past had been discarded, the Republican elite had an opportunity to fill this lacuna by fabricating a new history and language tailored to its vision of the "new Turk." Atatürk himself encouraged historians to create pseudohistorical theories such as "the Turkish History Thesis" and the "Sun-Language Theory" in the first half of the 1930s.[50] In the Third Language Convention, which met in the historical Dolmabahçe Palace (Istanbul) on September 24, 1934, it was generally accepted that the Sun Language Theory proved that all other languages and civilizations sprang from Turkish.[51] In keeping with the Kemalist insistence that Turks were "really Europeans," a number of papers at this convention insisted that the Turkish language belonged to the Indo-European language family.[52]

In analyzing efforts to create a pseudoscientific national theory, Eric Hobsbawm argued that historical writings play a key role in the "invention of traditions" by contributing "to the creation, dismantling and restructuring of images of the past which belong not only to the world of specialist investigation but to the public sphere of man as a political being."[53] Such texts, over time, become more "real" than the "reality" of unwritten memory, according to Hobsbawm:

> The element of invention is particularly clear here, since the history
> which became part of the fund of knowledge or the ideology of the
> nation-state or movement is not what has actually been preserved
> in popular memory, but what has been selected, written, pictured,
> popularized and institutionalized by those whose functions it is to
> do so.[54]

In the case of Turkey, state-sponsored historical theories stressed the pre-Islamic roots of the Turks and were meant to forge a politically correct continuity between the Republican present and an imagined pre-Islamic past. Although this attempt to exclude Islam and Ottoman history from modern Turkish nationalism was criticized by some intellectuals, Atatürk suppressed their dissent. Dissident historians, such as Rıza Nur, the first minister of education, and Hamdullah Suphi, Rıza Nur's successor, continued to be discredited until 1950, when the introduction of the multiparty system made it possible for them to demand a redefinition of Turkish nationalism that incorporated Islam and Ottoman history as legitimate and even essential aspects of modern Turkish national identity. In the twentieth century, therefore, Turkish nationalism has vacillated between two poles with regard to the place of religion in Turkish national identity and culture. The first trend sought a closer synthesis between Islam and nationalism, arguing for a reinterpretation of Islam to cope with modern challenges. The second trend sought to divorce religion from nationalism and create a secularist ethnolinguistic nationalism.

Although Atatürk's "civilizing" project utilized the educational system to transmit a new sense of identity and a new value system, this purpose was in conflict with the deeply internalized Islamic value system found within the family and the traditional neighborhoods. In other words, the Kemalist system could not be totally successful in breaking down traditional patterns of the production and transmission of knowledge. In the Turkish context, therefore, two different cultural patterns existed side by side in competition with one another. Furthermore, in attempting to create a nation out of diverse ethnic groups who were unified and also at times divided by their own conceptions of identity and the past, Atatürk's secular policies also—and ironically—breathed life into religious institutions of the periphery. As the state moved to penetrate every aspect of social life to mold a nation, it helped to turn peripheral groupings, such as Sufi orders and the Kurdish tribal groups, into centers of resistance and alternative sources of meaning. In short, the exclusion of citizens from political decisions and the attempts to impose a new identity on them forced them to turn to home-based identities to reinforce personal, tribal, neighborhood (*mahalle*), and regional loyalties. The dynamism of Turkish society thus resided in these areas that were outside the control of the state. The Kemalist reforms, contrary to the commonly held view, did not unify society but rather helped to politicize nascent identities such as Kurdish ethnicity and Sunni/Alevi Islam. As a result of nation-building and militant secularization, society came to be divided along the now familiar cleavages of Turkish versus Kurdish and state versus society. In contrast, the caliphate, abolished in 1924, had represented an Islamicly sanctioned union of multiethnic groups and had recognized ethnic diversity without assigning it any political role. In other words, the caliphate was the symbol of a multiethnic polity and authority; it symbolized the unity of Muslims as a faith-based community and allowed space for diverse loyalties and local autonomy for the periphery.

With the processes of de-Islamization and centralization of political power, peripheral groups expressed their opposition in terms of Islamic symbols. When an initial experiment in multiparty politics was tried in 1924, it lasted only seven months (November–June 1925) because the state aborted this tentative opening in response to antiestablishment demonstrations. However, the stage already was set for the outbreak of widespread (Kurdish) ethnoreligious rebellions against the secular reforms of the state.[55] Although the impetus and demands of Sheik Said's revolt were largely religious, the organizing group, known as the *Azadi*, aimed to create an independent Kurdish state. However, tribal rivalry and religious divisions prevented full Kurdish participation. Although the Turkish army captured Sheik Said (1865–1925) and hanged him in Diyarbakır, his rebellion, the first ethnoreligious uprising, made the Turkish Republic very suspicious of any form of Kurdish and Islamic (Nakşibendi) activities.

In response to this major rural religious popular revolt, in which the Nakşibendi Sufi order provided an organizational framework, the liberal government of Fethi Bey (Okyar) was forced to resign, and the new government of İsmet İnönü introduced a draconian legal system that closed all Sufi orders and removed other potential obstacles to its secularizing revolution. The decision to ban all Sufi orders had two consequences. By removing the traditional Sufi network system, the ban, in the short run, prevented the potential utilization of Sufism by nationalist Kurdish intellectuals. In the long run, by removing Sufi loyalties and leadership, which had made it relatively easy to blur ethnic lines by stressing Islamic brotherhood between Turks and Kurds, the ban consolidated Kurdish ethnic identity and politicized Kurdish national consciousness. In October 1927 a group of Kurdish tribal leaders and intellectuals formed the Kurdish National League (*Hoyboun*) under the leadership of İhsan Nuri Paşa of Bitlis, a successful Ottoman general. This group organized the revolt of Ağrı (Ararat) Mountain in 1930–1931. The Turkish army had difficulty putting the rebellion down in its early stages because the rebels received better arms from outside, but eventually prevailed, and İhsan Paşa took refuge in Iran. In order to establish law and order in the region, the 1934 Resettlement Law organized a selective deportation and exiled some Kurdish tribal chiefs to western Turkey.[56] Meanwhile Atatürk again decided to expand the political base of the state and ordered his close friend Fethi Okyar to establish the Free Republican Party (Serbest Cumhuriyet Fırkası) in August 1930.[57] This experiment at controlled two-party politics lasted only three months because the population of rural and small-town areas immediately utilized the party as a means of expressing their discontent with Kemalist policies, especially those of radical secularization.[58] Atatürk grew apprehensive about these protests and ended the experiment on November 17, 1930. On December 22, 1930, six weeks after this short-lived and limited experiment in political openness to the masses, the Menemen rebellion took place.[59] In this incident, a group of militant Muslims rebelled under the leadership of the Nakşibendi sheik Derviş Mehmet in the city of Menemen and killed a military officer, Mustafa Fehmi (Kubilay). The events of 1925 and 1930 awakened Ankara to the fact that its new national ideology had not really taken root. Atatürk subsequently made a three-month visit to the countryside and came to the conclusion that his "reforms" had not penetrated the periphery.[60]

The failure to penetrate the periphery was demonstrated again in 1937–1938, when Kemalist policies triggered a new revolt in and around the mountainous areas of Dersim, inhabited mostly by the Alevi Kurds, known as Zazas. After suppressing the rebellion, during which several key military posts were attacked and hundreds of soldiers were killed, the Turkish state destroyed Dersim and created a new town, Tunceli, in its place.[61] These rebellions against the young and inexperienced Republic created a cumulative image of the people of the rural Anatolia as socially tribal, religiously fanatical, economically backward, and most important, a threat to the national integrity of the Republic of Turkey. For example, in the way the state framed the Kurdish resistance it sought to legitimize its own claims and justify its domination. In other words, the Kemalist state discourse on the Kurdish issue evolved as a result of these rebellions, with the state becoming more sensitive about its policies of creating a secular Turkish nation. Thus one needs to take these rebellions into account to explain the securitization of Kurdish and Islamic identity claims by the state. After the rebellions, politicized Sunni-Islam evolved as a surrogate Kurdish identity in southeastern Anatolia.

Vernacular of Political Opposition

The Sheik Said and Menemen rebellions helped to redefine the concept of politics in Turkish society. After 1930, the state elite considered participatory political activity to be a dangerous and potentially regime-threatening phenomenon, whereas society as a whole viewed politics as the arena of the ruling elite and sought an apolitical and cultural venue for challenging radical Kemalist secularism. The excluded groups developed a new vernacular in which to express their notions of a political reality that would enable them to protect their personal conceptualizations of morality and definitions of "the good life" and undermine the state policies of "civilizing" society.

These rebellions heightened the fears of the Republican elite concerning an ethnoreligious counterreaction. Their initial response was to attempt to sever Islam from nationalism completely, that is, to Turkify society without religion through the institutions of the state. The Republican elite developed three strategies in order to penetrate the periphery with its reforms: to create a reformist elite to carry the reform message to small towns; to establish People's Houses, which were supposed to provide the bridge between the masses and the Republican elite; and to raise the social and economic standards of rural areas by establishing Village Institutes (Köy Enstitüleri).[62] However, the Republican purges of traditional institutions and networks undermined the state's ability to carry its reforms to the periphery. In other words, by destroying traditional networks, the secularist Republic destroyed its own means of penetrating and reshaping the traditional periphery. By closing the Association of Turkish Hearths (Türk Ocakları) and opening the People's Houses (Halkevleri), the Republicans alienated large segments of society.[63] The former institution, founded in 1912, had played an embryonic role in the formation of Turkish nationalism. Its understanding of nationalism recognized the constitutive role of Islam as an inseparable part of national culture and identity. This was, of course, in contradiction to "Atatürk's" notion of a pre-Islamic Turkish nationalism confined to Anatolia and completely loyal and subservient to himself. The Hearths were closed in 1932, and People's Houses were opened in 14 provinces to introduce the new vision of Kemalist society to the periphery. The People's Houses sought to disseminate secularism and nationalism by creating connections between the rural and urban populations.[64]

The Kemalist state justified its coercive secularism by presenting Islam as the main reason for the economic underdevelopment and social malaise that confronted Turkish society in the 1920s and 1930s. The reforms of the Republic maintained the dominance of the state elite until 1950, treating society as an arena to be mapped, controlled, and civilized without any say of its own. As the state's hostility to religion became clear, societal groups that did not share in the political and economic benefits reaped by the new elite saw Islam as an ideology they could use to challenge the Kemalist state. Islam thus became a political tool in the hands of marginalized segments, which made up the bulk of Turkish society.

By seeking to suppress virtually all manifestations of Islam in what was a deeply religious society, the Kemalist elite actually promoted the politicization of a furtive Islamic identity and ensured a struggle between the secular and Muslim groups' control of the state. The secular elite considered any attempt by marginalized societal groups to seek representation within the state center as an example of an "Islamic revival."[65]

The Republican goal of comprehensive secularization of all aspects of social and political life naturally generated intense hostility and resistance that could not be overcome by sheer force. The Kemalist elite did not take into account that Islam was embedded in various layers of Turkish social life and was more conducive to mass mobilization than either a constructed "ethnic" nationalism or socialism. Its power in this respect stems from its flexible network system, norms, and symbolic value. With respect to the mobilization of Turkish society, the abstract concept of "humanism" as expounded by secular discourse was no match for the concreteness and familiarity of Islamic idioms and symbols. Indeed, Islamic cosmology conveyed a clear vision of the phenomenal world for the true believer, and this enabled him to sustain the imaginary and emotional life of the archetypical Muslim, the Prophet Muhammad. Through imagination, Muslims constantly reexamine their present condition in terms of Islamic ideals, and, in the process Islam is freed from the danger of becoming a sterile and fossilized tradition.[66] By imagination I mean the ability to invest familiar symbols with new meanings, or even to create new symbols based on an image of what the current situation requires. Through imagination, Islam is freed from the reductionism of literal texts (Qur'an and hadith) and turned into a living text that is embodied in the practices of Muslims. Therefore, in almost every century one witnesses the phenomenon of Islamic movements and a period of radical imagination by prominent Islamic thinkers. By radical imagination I mean the rethinking of images and concepts of self and society. The existence of an imaginary horizon "acts as a schema which organizes categories and marks out the frame of the imaginable."[67] This, in turn, helps in creating interpretations and explanations of a more holistic understanding of social relations. This is so because the imagination is but a layer of thought on thought, where existing constructs either are superseded or sublimated to a new level.

Islamic consciousness remained at the foundation of communal identity among large segments of society, occasionally transcending national consciousness but never viewed as alien to it. Islam, unlike a nationalism based strictly on language and ethnicity, offered a more durable political community and language for communication. It had a familiar set of transcendent symbols for interpreting the world that the Muslims in the periphery could readily use to voice their discontent and opposition.

The Inward Migration of Turkish Islam

In the period between 1923 and 1950, two forms of oppositional movements took place in response to the cultural revolution that Turkish society was forced to undergo. These movements were led by Nakşibendi and Nurcu religious groups. The Nurcus led a spiritual or inward-looking Islamic movement whose goals were self-purification and self-consciousness. This inward-oriented movement sought ways to free itself from state control, which was perceived as illegitimate, and viewed self-transformation and individual piety as the basis for societal and eventual state control. The Nakşibendi orders, unlike the inward-looking Nur movement, pursued a more revolutionary and confrontational strategy by leading several conspicuous antisecular disturbances. The main goal of the Nakşibendi order was to make tangible inroads into centers of state authority. Both movements, however, stressed the constitutive role of Islam as a shared language and practice for a community to have a meaningful life.

By removing Islam from the public domain, the Kemalist revolutionaries were seeking to cut off the populace from their own shared language of imagination. This policy succeeded in large urban centers but failed to transform the majority of the populace in rural areas of Turkey. The new political discourse was rigid and did not have the flexibility and symbolic nature of Islam, which offered ever-changing meanings in a given context. During the years of Kemalist repression, three social institutions (family, neighborhood, and religious groups) became the only habitat for the preservation and reproduction of traditional values and identities. With the removal of the caliphate and other symbolic structures of the Ottoman state, society experienced the loss of authority and power, since politics became a matter of nation-building and was largely confined to a small authoritarian circle in Ankara. With this loss of public space and vernacular political language, devout Muslims focused on the home as the new stronghold for maintaining Muslim morality and identity within an antireligious state. The household became the center of a sacred arena where the outer door represented the boundary between private belief and the unstable bifurcated personality that Muslims were forced to adopt in the open. Outside, the Muslim was a fictitious public citizen in the Kemalist secular-positivist order, but within his sacred zone he could be true to an earlier identity. The door not only distinguished the inside from the outside but also exemplified the divide between the earlier moral normative ground of Ottoman-Islam and what many viewed as the moral vacuum of Kemalist positivism. İsmet Özel, an ex-Marxist convert and the most prominent Islamist intellectual, argued that it was Atatürk's reforms that, ironically, Islamicized Turkey by forcing people to internalize and value their religious identity and not simply take it for granted as in the past. The suppression of the outward manifestations of Islam encouraged in many Turks a deeper inner contemplation of their faith.

The metaphors of the household and the neighborhood, however, should not be limited to their literal meanings but instead should be understood as inclusive. Indeed, residential quarters, whether a household, a quarter of a town, or a village, became a bounded cultural whole where the local mosque played an important role. Historically, the Ottoman quarter, known as a *mahalle*, "consisted of a religious community grouped around its mosques (or church or synagogue) and headed by its religious chief."[68] The quarter, as a religious-administrative unit, also ran its own educational and public facilities during the Ottoman Empire. During the Republican period, the mahalle maintained its autonomy as a place in which an established code of ethics must be preserved. Everyday life required a set of norms and strategies to deal with new situations. In the Turkish quarter, there was a strong sense of communal identity and solidarity, but this had been eroded as modernization led to the massive dislocation of populations and as economic development and urbanization shook the code of ethics in the neighborhood.

The main institution in the construction of Islamic political identity in this environment has been the textual and *tekke*-based Islamic groups of the Nakşibendi (see chapter 6) and the Nurcus (see chapter 7). Confronted with political oppression and coercive control of their conduct, the Nurcu groups and the Sufis encouraged the process of withdrawal and the creation of an inner world of faith. Moreover, Sufism was also a reaction to the legalist-formalism of state-centric Islam. Sufism became, as a result, more powerful in those regions where a strong state tradition existed. This is so because as the level of state penetration increases in relation to society, Sufism, which relies on inner withdrawal, can generate and maintain greater faith in the face of coercion.[69]

In addition to the Sufi orders, textually based communities that evolved from them, such as the Nurcus, also helped to internalize and externalize Islamic political identity by redefining the function of the state. Said Nursi called on believers to shield their inner self from the oppressive "reforms" of the Republic. Mehmet Kırkıncı, a prominent Nurcu leader of Erzurum, has referred to this process as an internal *hijra* or migration of Muslims.[70] He argues that "the sun of Islam set down in 1925 and dawned in 1950 with the writings of Said, which enlighten the darkness of Kemalism with its light [nur]."[71] When Kırkıncı was questioned concerning his definition of *hijra* in 2000, he said: "I mean the believer's mental movement away from unbelief. The Muslims moved to an inner world to examine themselves and develop a better understanding and arguments to overcome the forces of darkness, so that God's existence was of apodictic certainty."[72] It was not a withdrawal from sociopolitical life but a strategic retreat and renewal.

The internal dynamics of Turkish Islamism were shaped during this period of withdrawal, from 1925 to 1950. The intellectual origins of modern Turkish Islamic social movements matured in this period. The secularization policies of the state did not succeed fully because they focused on the public sphere and were not able to touch the grassroots level of informal societal networks.

Conclusion

Secularism, the official discourse of the Republic, failed to establish real connections with much of the population, and it left a void in the inner life of many segments of society. Islam as a spiritual and communal force was well positioned to address some of the more alienating consequences of modernity and the Republican state- and nation-building project. The Republican discourse of modernity and development ironically has been hijacked and transformed by the religious and cultural forces that the Kemalist authorities saw as the main obstacles to progress and to their own hold on power.

3

The Tempering of the Kemalist Revolution

The Emergence of Multiparty Politics

The 1950s represent an ambiguous period for the Turkish Republic; the state gradually came to view religion as a possible antidote for coping with embryonic leftist/communist movements. During the period 1950–1980, as a result of the circumscribed emergence of participatory politics, the reinfiltration of Islam into public life became quite apparent. This was most striking in the case of the DP, which quickly trounced Mustafa Kemal's own Republican CHP in the pivotal election of May 1950. The political opening in terms of a multiparty system in 1950 was a catalyst for Islamic groups to participate in the system. The 1961 constitution enabled associational life and created new autonomous institutions to curtail party politics. Islamic groups very much invested in party politics, whereas the leftist movement focused on the associational life. The 1971 coup tried to curtail this associational life and opened the way for conservative nationalist-Islamic groups to become politically active. When diverse groups started to penetrate the state and redefine it, the military intervened again to insulate the state from the society.

The period following the 1980 military coup was, ironically, another turning point, as the "praetorian guard"—that is, the secular nationalistic Turkish armed forces—sought unsuccessfully to utilize a nationalized version of Islam as a "unifying" glue for a deeply polarized Turkish society.

In this chapter I argue that the advent of limited democratization and political opportunity spaces during the 1950s enabled some social groups to express their pent-up discontent in Islamic idioms. Then I examine the ways social groups managed to force the state to incorporate some manifestations of Islam into its nationalist ideology, ultimately leading to what in the 1980s was termed a "Turkish-Islamic synthesis." I also shall examine the competing visions within the DP over national identity and religion. Many in the DP leadership remained committed to "Westernizing" reforms, even as popular society demanded a reduction in state hostility toward their traditional beliefs. This contradiction and ambiguity was never resolved within the party.

Overview, 1950–1980

As a result of external and domestic pressures, the ruling CHP decided in early 1946 to permit a multiparty system, and the DP was established on January 7.[1] The DP became the only institutionalized force allowed to express opposition to the ruling party, which still was seen as the embodiment of the state. New industrialists who were critical of statism, landowners who opposed the 1945 Land Reform Bill, intellectuals who wanted greater freedom of speech, small merchants who resented the patronage of the state enjoyed by leading merchants, Sufi leaders who had been persecuted, and most villages voted for the DP, which consciously depicted itself as the voice of the peripheral and marginalized masses of society and depicted the CHP as the party of the oppressive bureaucrats. In the July 1947 elections, the DP won 62 of 465 seats in the National Assembly. This election played a critical role in transforming the meaning of politics in the minds of many Anatolian Turks. For the first time since the establishment of the Republic, they felt that they had a political say in government. One may ask why the population mobilized around a cluster of Islamic idioms concerning justice, dignity, and community instead of secular nationalism. The most critical reason was that the Republican elite justified its authoritarian ways and defined itself as "progressive" in the face of "Islamic backwardness." This secular approach politicized Islam and helped to turn it into an inspiration for the disenchanted periphery. As the elite became more involved in corruption and oppression, those who felt disenfranchised viewed Islam as a medium for expressing demands of justice, identity, and representation.

To maintain its hold on power, the CHP in its 1947 Seventh Congress took several steps to placate public opinion by proposing the "normalization" of religious affairs. These steps included the introduction of voluntary courses on religion in the primary school curriculum and the establishment of a limited number of preacher (*imam*) training centers, known as İmam Hatip schools, to train religious functionaries. The CHP even allowed a limited number of Muslims to make the pilgrimage to Mecca in 1948.

These measures proved ineffective in terms of rallying popular support for the ruling party. In the election of May 14, 1950, an overwhelming majority of the electorate voted for the DP, which gained 408 seats in Parliament and promised greater freedom for religious practices and greater respect for Islam. This DP victory represented a victory of the periphery over the center, since "the common denominator of the DP supporters was their opposition to the center of officialdom."[2] The DP articulated the power and voices of associations of proto-civil society. These included provincial business associations, extended families (aşiret), and Nurcu and Nakşibendi groups. These associations wanted a say in political life and state policies. With the DP victory, the social bases of Turkish politics began to change, and for the first time a large segment of popular society had a voice at the center. Although the CHP, the army, and the civil bureaucracy sharply criticized the DP's close ties with the ostracized informal religious networks,[3] the structural transformation (urbanization, political participation, and education) since the 1920s had empowered the marginalized sectors of Turkish society and facilitated their return to politics, the marketplace, and education. The return of religious activism and religiously framed movement was not a fearsome "return of the repressed" but rather an attempt to vernacularize modernity.

The DP relied on these local informal networks, and this, in turn, reproduced and consolidated authoritative, hierarchical patron-client relations—that is, people exchanged their votes in return for expected favors.[4] The DP was supported by the rural population that had suffered under the World War II tax system, while the urban bourgeoisie had prospered from its ties to the Republican elite. During the 1950s these people became conscious of the power of their votes, and this awareness helped them to internalize democracy as a way of redefining state-society relations. Thus a sense of citizenship began to evolve around the DP, with the concomitant feeling that the state could, for the first time, be made responsive to the needs of the people.[5] By establishing new linkages between the center and the periphery and bringing the views and aspirations of the periphery closer to the center, the DP presented politics for the first time as having deliberative aspects rather than being simply an administrative means to implement an elite-defined civilizational project. The Kemalist elite, which saw only state-guided reforms as modern, did not know how to respond to the emerging social groups, since a goal of Kemalism was to create a classless society. The DP thus differentiated itself from the CHP by recognizing the newly emerging bourgeoisie, rather than the state, as the agent of modernity.

On the basis of actual DP policies toward Islam, one must conclude that the party's leadership was still quite ambiguous on the subject of allowing open expression, despite claims of both their supporters and their critics in the CHP. The DP policies were conditioned by the secular state structure and the leadership of the DP, which was dominated by secular politicians. The original DP leadership included Celal Bayar, Adnan Menderes, Fuat Köprülü, Fatin Rüştü Zorlu, and Refik Koraltan. On the whole, they remained prosecular and fully supported the Kemalist programs. For instance, Celal Bayar told a cheering crowd in 1947: "We will not let sharia live on."[6] Therefore, it was not the DP leadership but rather the DP's popular grassroots supporters who forced the DP to pursue a more confrontational policy toward militant secular injunctions. Thus DP policies for the normalization of the status of religion vacillated. One main reason for this vacillation was the critical opposition of the CHP, which charged the DP with "undermining secularism." For example, on June 16, 1950, after Parliament passed a DP resolution to nullify article 526 of the Criminal Code, which penalized the call to prayer in Arabic with a jail sentence of three to six months and a fine of one to three thousand Turkish liras, the DP rushed to pass a new rigid law to protect the stature and reputation of Mustafa Kemal.

Actually, there was a rising tide of anti-Atatürk sentiment and actions in the country after 1950. In response, the DP passed the Law to Penalize Anti-Atatürk Criminal Conduct on July 25, 1951. This law was aimed at the Tijani Sufi order's attacks on Atatürk's officially omnipresent busts and statues as hated symbols of persecution and representatives of a pagan ideology.[7] The law made it illegal to deface images of Atatürk or to insult his memory, and the leader of the Tijani order, Kemal Pilavoğlu, was sentenced to fifteen years for his actions against Atatürk memorabilia.[8] The DP also used its parliamentary power to enact a law closing the Peoples' Houses on August 8, 1951.[9]

While trying to protect the Kemalist legacy, the DP also created conditions favorable for the publication of Said Nursi's long-banned *Epistles of Light* after the Higher Criminal Court of Afyon decided on May 25, 1956, that "there is no criminal and threatening element" in the writings of Said Nursi.[10] While the opposition CHP criticized the DP for violating the principle of secularism and politicizing religion, ambiguity continued to be reflected in the DP's contradictory responses to the desires of the periphery and the center. In 1959, for example, the minister of home affairs used police force to prevent the burial of the most prominent Nakşibendi sheik of the period, Süleyman Hilmi Tunahan, in the garden of Istanbul's Fatih Mosque.[11] In addition, the government did not allow Said Nursi to enter Ankara, although following his death on March 23, 1960, some high-ranking local DP politicians participated in his funeral in Urfa. These ambiguous policies toward religious issues force me to conclude that the argument about the DP pursuing a pro-Islamic policy, especially after its setback in the 1957 election, are inaccurate.[12]

The co-optation of Islamic groups varied according to time and the issue concerned. During this period, the DP government carefully co-opted certain Islamic groups, for example, the Nurcus and Nakşibendis, into the political system to expand its electoral base. This co-optation helped the DP to consolidate its position within society as a network of politics and the state under the DP gradually realized the significance of Islam and tried to "normalize" its policies toward Islamic institutions and informal networks. The DP's liberal policies toward Islam prevented the radicalization of religious groups and expanded the social basis of the state by integrating religious groups into the system. However, under the Cold War conditions, the Turkish state, alongside American strategy, gradually utilized Islamic movements as a front against communism and the Left in Turkey. During this period, Islamic movements blended with anti-Russian Turkish nationalism to protect the status quo. In the 1950s and 1960s, Islamic movements acquired nationalistic, anticommunist, and conservative features. Thus Islamic movements fully integrated into the center-right of the Turkish political spectrum. The main goal of the Islamic movement became fighting against leftist forces.

The 1960 Military Coup and Its Political Consequences

Despite what on balance must be seen as a very limited conciliatory attitude of the part of the DP toward Islamic groups, the policies permitting greater religious activities in public space convinced the Turkish military that the Republic and its Kemalist program was in danger. Consequently, the military carried out a coup against the DP government on May 27, 1960. The military sought to purify not only the state but also its own ranks by purging two thousand officers, along with 147 university professors. The military coup derailed Turkey's gradual evolution into a full-fledged liberal democracy. The political system, in effect, failed to cope with the massive increase of popular political participation and the political mobilization of an Islamic identity it had engendered.

The 1960 military coup created a set of political institutions that were intended to preserve the ideological purity of the state from perceived leftist and Islamic threats.[13] The 1961 constitution embodied two competing principles. First, it tried to depoliticize society by increasing the power of bureaucrats so that they could balance that of elected officials and thus reduce socioeconomic issues to "technical" problems that could be solved by rational planning. Second, it ironically deepened associationalism, which reduced the monopoly on political life enjoyed by political parties.

The new constitution presented a reinvigorated (and left-leaning) Kemalist ideology as being the main source for public policy. Article 4 redefined sovereignty and argued that sovereignty is exercised through "Parliament and *autho- rized* agencies as prescribed by the principles laid down in the Constitution." It established the Constitutional Court, with the power of judicial review over the decisions of Parliament and the cabinet. Most significantly, Article 111 established the National Security Council—consisting of the chiefs of the land, air, navy, and gendarmerie forces, as well as the chief of staff, and the secretary of the Council, who is also a three-star general—to "inform the cabinet of its relevant opinions by the way of assisting in the taking of national security decisions and providing coordination."[14] (A 1971 amendment replaced the terms "by the way of assisting" and "is to inform" with "is to advise.") The constitution also recognized the autonomy of the Turkish military by removing the chief of Staff from the supervision of the civilian Ministry of Defense. The 1961 constitution added a second chamber to the legislative body, the Senate, which was created from a mix of permanent members from among the coup leaders to counterbalance popular representation. Moreover, the state-run Directorate of Turkish Radio and Television Board (TRT) and universities theoretically were made autonomous from peripheral political pressures but not from those of the state.

The coup bitterly divided Turkish society, as it led to the purging of pro-DP local leaders, including some Kurdish tribal chiefs and 485 Kurdish politicians. However, the junta's most disturbing act was the hanging of the popular prime minister Adnan Menderes and his two top ministers. The coup leaders in the military reimposed a strict implementation of Kemalist secular dogma in public life. The tomb of the charismatic founder of the Nurcu religious movement,

Said Nursi, who had passed away in 1960 after a long internal exile, was des-
ecrated, and his corpse was disposed of in an unknown place in a vain attempt
to exorcise the devotion of many of his pious followers. In the face of rising
popular discontent in August 1961, the military junta, known as the National
Unity Committee, assured the people that the call to prayer would remain in
Arabic, that TRT would maintain its broadcasts of Qur'anic recitations, and the
state would allow the normal functioning of mosques.[15]

One sees a constant ambiguity and tension at this time in the policy of the
Republican state toward Islam. The source of this inherent tension was Kemalist
political philosophy on the one hand and modern participatory politics on the
other. By recognizing the significance of Islam in everyday life, the military coup
leaders started to treat religion not only as a force to be crushed but also as an
ideology to be co-opted for its own ends. The coup reestablished the old Kemalist
distinction between "reactionary" and "enlightened" Islam and employed a
number of policies to train and educate enlightened religious leaders. General
Cemal Gürses, the leader of the coup, said in Erzurum:

> Those who blame religion for our backwardness are wrong. No, the
> cause of our backwardness is not religion but those who have
> misrepresented our religion to us. Islam is the most sacred, most
> constructive, most dynamic and powerful religion in the world.[16]

The economic and social changes that had transformed Turkey by 1960
forced the Kemalist old guard to give up its dream of creating a "classless society" and redefining Kemalism as the national security ideology of the state. Its
main goal became the protection of the state and its purity against societal pen-
etrations. Thus, in response to new emerging social and political actors,
Kemalism became a more conservative ideology to protect the state against assertive class, religious, and ethnic identities. However, a group of leftist intellectuals, gathered around the socialist weekly *Yön*, tried to redefine Kemalism
as an antiimperialist and "nationalist liberation" ideology.[17] They stressed the
statist aspects of Kemalism and sought to consolidate state power against the
newly emerging bourgeoisie. In short, the 1960 coup marked the fragmentation of Kemalism into a security doctrine of the state and a protoleftist ideology.
This fragmentation, in turn, further alienated the large conservative sector of
the Turkish population from Kemalist ideology.

The 1961 constitution ultimately created a freer environment for associational life, although such an outcome was neither the intent of nor foreseen by
its framers. Their goal was to check parliamentary majoritarianism by creating
new autonomous institutions outside the control of the elected deputies and give
more rights to ordinary citizens. This new-found freedom allowed diverse groups
to penetrate the state indirectly. In the 1950s and 1960s, the patron-client relationships that were established to court the popular vote reactivated religious,
ethnic, and kinship-based networks. Following new elections in 1964, 46.6
percent of the electorate voted for the new AP because it adopted a pro-Menderes
and -DP position and implicitly criticized the coup supporters in the CHP, which
received only 38.4 percent of the total vote.[18] However, the military induced the

AP to form a coalition under the leadership of İsmet İnönü, then head of the CHP. Nevertheless, the AP proved to be more popular than the CHP, primarily because it was based on the same informal networks as the DP and increasingly challenged the role of nonelected state agencies in the exercise of sovereignty.[19] The AP dominated the Turkish political scene between 1963 and 1970 and helped to achieve the integration of the rural and provincial populations into urban life with its policies of building bridges between society and the state, including the mutual interpenetration of state and society mediated by political parties, associations, and interest groups.[20] Moreover, the AP developed a more nuanced approach to secularism by arguing that the state "must be secular" but not the individuals. In a way, it offered a way of blending personal religious piety with political secularism and the market economy. Süleyman Demirel, the head of the AP, defined Islam as a respectful form of personal piety and treated it as an antidote to the leftist movements. He developed close ties with the Nur movement to enhance his pious credentials against those of the MGH of Erbakan.

Despite the return of civilian government, the system designed by the military leaders could not address the political and economic problems of society. Leftist views even became increasingly more dominant in autonomous state institutions such as the universities. When the AP government failed to cope with the problems of ethnopolitical polarization, the military forced all parties to form a national unity government from 1971 to 1973. The military purged itself of possible left-leaning officers and declared martial law to deal with leftist associations and intellectuals. The coup leaders asked the Constitutional Court to close the MNP and the pro-Marxist Turkish Workers Party (TİP: Türkiye İşçi Partisi).

The victories of the CHP in the 1973 and 1977 elections did not give it a majority in Parliament. From 1973 to 1980, therefore, Turkey had unstable coalition governments that failed to address the growing structural problems of the country. In the 1970s, political divisions were mostly based on ideological divisions between the Left and Right. These ideological divisions, however, relied on the cultural cleavages they helped to politicize. Societal polarization inevitably was reflected in electoral politics. The formerly statist CHP after 1971 defected to the left and became an advocate for ethnic (Kurdish) and religious (Alevi) minorities. Indeed, as Arnold Leder aptly puts it, "conflicting solidarity groups may dictate party affiliation."[21] This transformation helped the CHP to contain Kurdish and Alevi identities within the universal framework of socialist solidarity. In a way, left-wing ideology became a container for ethnoreligious (Kurdish-Alevi) identities.

The Emergence of the Alevi Communal Identity

The Alevi community, whose membership is defined by descent and which was previously known as Kızılbaş and Bektaşi, represents approximately 15 to 20 percent (approximately 10–12 million of 64 million) of Turkey's population.[22] The community is divided along ethnic (Turkish, 8–9 million; Kurdish, 2–3 million; and Zaza Alevi-Dersimli, 1 million), regional, and class lines.[23] Kızılbaş identity was an outcome of the tension between sedentary and nomadic lifestyles of Turkic tribes, the rivalry between the Ottoman and Safavid empires, and the presence of heretical ideas in Anatolia. The nomadic Turks sought to preserve their way of life and freedom against sedentary Ottoman polity, which sought to control the population through Sunni Islam. After the establishment of the Safavid state in the sixteenth century, nomadic heterodox Anatolian tribes cooperated with the Safavids. Those who adapted a sedentary life and settled in cities with their Sufi lodges were called Bektaşi, and those who remained seminomadic and resisted the state's control came to be known as Alevi.

The Ottoman state historically had viewed the Alevi community as a potential fifth column for Shi'a Iran and accordingly treated Alevis as blasphemers and heretics.[24] The Alevis suffered a number of massacres at the hands of the central government, and they were forced to live in small isolated communities in the mountainous areas of Turkey. Within these rural and marginalized communities, Alevis formed their own syncretic religious-social worldview. The Alevi worldview tends to be about resistance and escape from the power of the state and a way of building alternative communal life in the mountains of Anatolia. Almost all Alevi teaching and ceremonies stress communal autonomy and cohesion of the group vis-à-vis the state. Since the Sunni ulema and the state regarded the Alevis as heretics, the Alevis could not build their own educational structures, and their sacred traditions were transmitted orally. Teaching and preservation of religious knowledge took place by means of stories and anecdotes. Communal actions are informed by lived habit. These oral narratives allowed a plurality of beliefs and ideas to coexist, and it also kept the doors open for outside ideas and beliefs to color Alevi narrative stories. In order to avoid the Ottoman bureaucracy, the Alevis developed their own communal justice system to solve disputes in their secret religious gatherings, known as *cem* or *ayin-i cem*. In these religious communal gatherings, they discuss and resolve disputes, reserving the imposition of *düşkünlük* (excommunication) for those who have committed grievous transgression against Alevi norms.[25]

This collective yet isolated psychology of solidarity played a key role in maintaining the inner boundaries of the community, especially through dissimulation as a way of overcoming Sunni prejudices. The cohesion of Alevi collective identity historically has been determined by external threats rather than a fully articulated shared code of theology or conduct. This communal experience of oppression at the hands of the Ottoman state inclined the Alevi community to become a main supporter of the Kemalist reforms, if not of the War of Independence itself. Alevis welcomed the disestablishment of Sunni Islam—which had long excluded them—in public life and the creation of a secular polity; initially, many Alevi notables actually presented themselves as ardent supporters of the Kemalist project of radical secularization and a homogeneous ethnolinguistic nationalism.[26]

Multiparty electoral systems tend to mobilize latent ethnocultural and sectarian solidarities because politicians often appeal to the politics of regional, ethnic, and sectarian difference. This was the case in Turkey after 1946. Many in the Alevi community, for example, tended to support the DP in the historic 1950 national elections because they, like much of the rest of the country, had become dissatisfied with the authoritarian and inefficient leadership of İsmet İnönü (r. 1938–1950) and the worsening economic conditions with which he seemed unable to come to terms. However, this early enthusiasm quickly faded when Alevis realized that the DP was interested in increasing its popularity by appealing to the Sunni majority and easing up on the Kemalist policy of antireligious oppression. Many Alevis withdrew their support from the DP in the 1957 election and became staunch supporters of the CHP.

In the mid-1950s and 1960s, massive Alevi migration to major cities in Turkey and Germany caused social disorganization by destroying the closed rural communal structure and forcing the newcomers in the cities to reconfigure a new set of networks on the basis of common origin, known as *hemşerilik*.[27] The Alevis formed hometown and Alevi saint–based associations and solidarities to meet urban challenges and restructure intensified interactions with the Sunni majority. Migration brought new opportunity spaces in the media, education, politics, and the market. With the legal opportunities of the 1961 constitution, the Alevis started to form their own separate hometown-associational networks in which identities and histories were re-created. For instance, the Ankara Hacı Bektaşi Veli Tourism Association, which was formed in 1965 and included Mustafa Timisi and Seyfi Oktay, became a center of Alevi university student activism. In 1966, a group of Alevi political entrepreneurs took the next logical step and formed their own recognizably "confessional" Alevi party, the Unity Party (BP: Birlik Partisi).[28] Growing Alevi assertion led to the first major sectarian conflict of the Republican period in Elbistan during a festival of folk musicians on June 12, 1967. The Alevi poet Doğan Hızlan told the crowd that "there are 10 million Alevis but no single Alevi senator. Our rights are denied, we are forced into exile throughout the country, we are deprived of a share in the economy."[29] In reaction to this proclamation and to the widespread popular perception of Alevis as enthusiastic supporters of the Kemalists' anti-Islamic campaign, a group of radical Sunni youths attacked the assembled Alevis, and Elbistan became a battleground between the two communities. This incident contributed to the politicization of Alevi identity; in the 1969 national elections, the BP received 2.8 percent of the vote and won 8 seats in Parliament.

During the rapid urbanization, expansion of universal education, and the sharp ideological polarization of the 1960s and 1970s, many Alevis adopted a nonconformist strategy of seeking greater access to wealth and power by supporting revolutionary leftist ideologies. This was complemented by their continued support for the CHP as the main bulwark against the resurgence of Sunni Islam. A close examination of the 1973 and 1977 elections reveals the politicization of ethnoreligious identities and faultlines within the framework of left-versus-right polarization.

Alevism, therefore, continued to be used oppositionally to the dominant Sunni majority and functioned as a local cultural habitat for the construction and dissemination of a politicized Alevi identity closely tied to leftist movements. Alevi poems and hymns were redefined and propagated as crucial components of the broader Left, with Alevi and socialist demands complementing one another and blending together. The Alevi community evoked socialism to address issues of social justice and equality, whereas the socialist movement used grassroots Alevi networks and symbols to enhance its broader movement. Newly urbanized Alevi youth in squatter towns had little interest in Alevism as a religion but reimagined it as a cultural source for socialist values and communal solidarity. The Marxist TİP and later the CHP sought to expand on this Alevi base and also to integrate left-oriented Kurdish movements. Thus the relationship between party affiliation and sectarian identity increasingly became articulated in terms of Marxist-Leninist ideology, and "the radical left, construing the Alevi rebellions of the past as protocommunist movements, considered the Alevis natural allies."[30] This vernacularization of communist ideology frightened the Turkish military establishment, which still saw Turkey as a bulwark of the anticommunist West in the Cold War contest with the Marxist Soviet Union. Thus many right-wing Turkish nationalists came to perceive Alevis, not as strong supporters of Kemalist laicism but as potential tools of Moscow.

During the 1970s, some scholars argued that Alevi identity had been assimilated by mainstream secular Turkish nationalism and was on the wane.[31] The 1977 and 1978 communal massacres against Alevis in five major cities (Tokat, Çankırı, Çorum, Sivas, and Kahramanmaraş), however, challenged this view and further demonstrated the connection between party affiliation and ethnoreligious identity. The communal-sectarian conflicts between the Alevis and Sunnis of Kahramanmaraş in December 1978 forced the government to impose martial law in 11 provinces. This communal conflict ended with 106 deaths (mostly Alevis), 176 injured, 210 homes destroyed, and 70 stores ruined. The sectarian conflict soon merged into a political one, as the Alevis tended to support a variety of militant leftist groups and their opponents sided with rightist nationalist militants who were Sunni Turks. Another serious incident took place on July 4, 1980, when a group of right-wing Sunni Turks attacked Alevi neighborhoods in the town of Çorum, killing 26 people and destroying 36 homes and 12 stores. This background of severe violence and class polarization along sectarian cleavages paved the way for the 1980 military coup.

By the late 1970s, society was polarized by intense ethnic, sectarian, and ideological conflict. Some Islamic groups exploited the apparent weaknesses of the state in this period to voice their long-pent-up demands. For example, the followers of the Nakşibendi sheik Süleyman Hilmi Tunahan organized a big public rally in istanbul under the leadership of Kemal Kaçar on May 21, 1979. But the immediate event that triggered the 1980 coup was a political meeting of Erbakan's MSP on September 6, 1980, in Konya, a central Anatolian town long associated with the renowned Celaleddin Rumi and Sunni Islam. In this meeting, a large group of Turkish and Kurdish-Islamists refused to pay homage to the Turkish national anthem and chanted slogans supporting the restoration of an Islamic government in Turkey.[32] The military perceived this behavior as an open challenge and decided to end the cycle of left-right and Alevi-Sunni violence by direct intervention in Turkish domestic politics.

The State as a Cultural Ecumene

The 1980 coup was carried out by a group of military officers who sought to overcome the country's political and social divisions and to implement an IMF-led structural adjustment program to curb the hyperinflation that was contributing significantly to the political turmoil. The military administration led by General Kenan Evren viewed leftist groups as the greatest threat to its authority in this period and sought to diminish their influence by promoting a "Turkish-Islamic synthesis." This policy garnered considerable support and, more important, paved the way for the near-revolutionary liberalizing reforms of Turgut Özal. A close examination of the magazine *Diyanet Dergisi*, a monthly periodical published by the Directorate of Religious Affairs, and the new *İslam Ansiklopedisi* (Encyclopedia of Islam) of the Religious Affairs Foundation indicates the degree to which this official state ideology had taken root.

Instead of showing the traditional military hostility toward Islam, the coup leaders took several steps to utilize religion. They opened new Qur'anic courses; made religious instruction compulsory in public schools; and employed new preachers. Moreover, in the 1982 constitution, the military restricted the activities of labor unions and voluntary associations, abolished the autonomous status of the universities and state-run television and radio, and banned all political parties. The NSC took over the legislative functions of Parliament and appointed a mixed civilian-military cabinet lead by the retired admiral Bülent Ulusu. Having purged those officers who were reluctant to intervene directly in civilian affairs, the military was united within its own ranks on the need for drastic intervention in politics.[33] The NSC sought to restructure the country through its edicts and the 1982 constitution, which created a strong presidential role. As a result of the September 12 military coup, 650,000 people were arrested; 1,683,000 cases were prepared; and 517 people were sentenced to death, although only 49 of the sentences were carried out. In addition, 30,000 people were fired from their jobs for holding objectionable political views, 14,000 had their Turkish citizenship revoked, and 667 associations and foundations were banned.[34]

The 1980 Military Coup and the Turkish-Islamic Synthesis

Three factors shaped the military's policies of culture and identity. These factors, in order of importance, were the perception of threat (leftist movement), the personal Islam of Evren, and the availability of resources. Because many Kurdish and Alevi activist groups were allied closely with Marxist organizations and movements, the military coup leaders felt compelled to use Islamic institutions and symbols as a legitimizing counterweight. By encouraging the fusing of Sunni Islamic ideas with national goals, the military government planned to foster a co-opted and less political Islam to confront a much-exaggerated "leftist threat." Military leaders believed that this officially determined "Turkish-Islamic Synthesis" potentially could diffuse the growing conflict between Sunnis and Alevis on the one hand and Kurdish nationalists and the Turkish State on the other. They established a new Department of Propagation (*İrşad Dairesi*) within the DİB in 1981 to fight against Kurdish nationalism in southeast Anatolia. Since then, the department regularly has organized conferences and lectures in the region to inform people about the dangers of the Kurdistan Workers' Party (PKK: Partiya Karkaren Kurdistan) and its Marxist-nationalist ideology.[35] The military government apparently preferred to exploit religious sentiment and traditional allegiances rather than encourage pluralism and participatory democracy to achieve political stability and national unity. According to Arif Soytürk, the deputy head of the the DİB, since 1980

> our national and religious feelings are interwoven, the DİB seeks to consolidate and cultivate national and religious consciousness at the same time. Our task is not confined to religion only but it also includes preservation of Turkish nationalism. The Turk in Germany needs to know the history of the War of Independence along with Islam.[36]

The DİB has tried to expand its power and legitimacy within the state by becoming the bastion of Turkish nationalism. It defined itself as the institution that was to "protect and preserve Turkish national identity" and protect the new generation against "communist and atheistic" ideologies. As the DİB used nationalism to consolidate and expand its position within the state, the military used religion to expand its legitimacy within society and enhance Turkish nationalism. This alliance between nationalism and Islam is what differentiated the 1980 coup from previous military interventions. General Kenan Evren even established a close relationship with Mehmet Kırkıncı, a prominent nationalist Nurcu leader in Erzurum.[37]

Evren's Islam

General Evren, a son of an imam and the leader of the coup, set the policies of the military government. He employed Islam to promote his secular ideas and policies as well as to expand the social base of the military government. Evren believed that there is an enlightened Islam that is open to change and secularism. He used religious arguments for raising national consciousness, social responsibility, and health concerns, promoting birth control and social cohesion of the Turkish society to overcome its ethnic and ideological divisions. He underlined the rational nature of Islam to promote modernity and stressed religion's role as a unifying agent or social cement. His goal was to free Islam from backward interpretations and political influences. For Evren, Islam "is the most rational religion, and it has high regard for knowledge and science."[38] His speeches and policies demonstrated the compatibility of Islam and Kemalism.

During the coup, in order to demonstrate the compatibility of Islam and Kemalism, the military redefined Kemalism and published a three-volume work, *Atatürkçülük* (Ataturkism).[39] These volumes constitute a major new interpretation of and contribution to the understanding of Kemalism. These books rediscover a new pious Mustafa Kemal who realized the necessity of enlightened Islam and implemented modernizing reforms to free Islam from reactionary forces. These books have three messages: religion is necessary for the social cohesiveness of the nation; Kemalism and Islam are compatible; and secularism is necessary for the development of "true Islam," that is, enlightened Islam and Kemal's reforms aimed for the development of "a rational and logical religion."[40]

Evren had a much better understanding of the role of religion as the cement of society, the source of morality, and an intellectual force to arm ordinary Muslims against the communist threat.[41] The rhetoric and policies of the 1980 coup treated Islam as an element in the service of the nation and nationalism rather than as an autonomous force to compete with either secularism or nationalism. The idea that Islam is the most important cement of the Turkish nation and nationalism was not new.[42] Those nationalist-conservative intellectuals who stressed the ethnoreligious aspect of Turkish nationalism had a major opportunity to put their ideas into practice. Islam, for them, inspired as well as brought a sense of personal and communal identity to Turks. It is in this nationalist context that the issue of the sacred as the source of duty-oriented moral responsibility to homeland, state, and nation has been addressed collectively.

The military courts decided that "the Basic Law of Education encourages the teaching of love of God and the Prophet as a way of cultivating moral values in students, and these would lead to the love of fatherland, state, and family."[43] Thus the military-dominated court did not see all religious instruction in high schools as an antisecular act. The military sought to cement national unity by using Islam as its shared social bond. Its Turkish-Islamic Synthesis was constructed by a group of conservative scholars who were members of the Intellectuals' Hearth Association, an organization founded in 1970 supposedly to protect the Turkish soul from foreign cultures.[44] This new ideology sought to create public consent for the consolidation of state power. The Intellectuals' Hearth Association was sympathetic to the Islamic dimension of modern Turkish identity and enjoyed good relations with the state-civil apparatus. The military leadership viewed this group of intellectuals as ideal for constructing this new ideology because the sterility of Kemalist positivism as an ideology of state legitimization had become obvious by 1980. The Intellectuals' Hearth Association attempted to create a new ideology out of Ottoman, Islamic, and Turkish popular culture in order to justify the hegemony of the ruling elite. They reinterpreted the state as being integral to the nation and society, and their repertoire of Ottoman-Islamic myths and symbols was selectively deployed, for the first time in the Republican era, to make the past seem relevant to the present. One can see the codeterminacy of Islam and Turkish nationalism in this statement by Mustafa Erkal, the leading member of the Hearth:

Islam is a religion that seeks unity without negating differences
above all diversity. How can you bring the Turks together or unify

with other groups by ignoring their customs and tradition and mother tongue, national history, literature, music, Turkish-Islamic architecture, *mevlid*, the Ottoman military march (*Mehter Marşı*), their cleanness and respectfulness? The difference between a Protestant Russian and a Protestant German, between Catholic Italian and Catholic Spaniard is a fact of life; our differences with other Muslim nations are just the same kind of national differences.[45]

This ideology was aimed at overriding particularistic interests by stressing the danger of anarchy and social divisions to the family, nation, and state. The ideology and solutions of the Intellectuals' Hearth Association—Islam and nationalism—helped to shape the 1982 constitution, as two Hearth members were also key members of the Constitutional Preparation Committee.

The military coup leaders thus used religion, among other means, to secure acceptance of their authority. For example, they turned the DİB into a constitutional institution. Article 136 of the 1982 constitution sets the goal of the DİB as "promoting and consolidating national solidarity and unity."[46] In addition, article 24 required the state to carry out religious and ethical education within the context of "national solidarity and unity," stipulating that the state is the only institution to carry out religious education and making religious education and ethics courses compulsory in elementary and high schools. In the preparation of article 24 in the Consultative Assembly, the framers of the constitution justified compulsory religious teaching as a means of offering a "standardized knowledge on Islam" and "a source of national culture, which is the primary task of the state."[47] The constitution expressed the views of the coup leaders, who considered religious education at the time to be an essential "glue" for national unity. Nonetheless, the constitutional framers argued that the role of teaching "proper" Islamic beliefs was the sole business of the state-run educational system, not a task of private institutions or schools. Thus, while the coup leadership eased up on the intense antireligious hostility of the early Kemalist period, they also sought to confine and control all Islamic thought and associational life to suit their narrow power goals.

Whereas the Intellectuals' Hearth Association utilized Islam to override other interests and identities, the official DİB simultaneously employed Turkish nationalism to open up more spaces for religious practice. Working in tandem, these two organizations were effective to a large degree in persuading much of the public and state officials to internalize the new Turkish-Islamic synthesis. This new hegemonic ideology, however, neglected the multicultural character of Turkish society and the particularity of Kurdish ethnic and Alevi sectarian identities. Moreover, antinationalist Islamist writers criticized the Turkish-Islamic synthesis as a new pro-American ideology that aimed cynically to manipulate Islamic sentiments to undermine the universality of Islam and the unity of Muslim solidarity by stressing Turkish ethnicity.[48] The left-wing and agnostic Kemalists were also critical of the thesis because it toned down the secular aspect of Turkish nationalism and undermined the authenticity of religion-resistant Kemalist secularism.[49]

In their efforts to engineer a new form of depoliticized Turkish-Islamic culture, the coup leaders published the National Culture Report.[50] Prepared with the help of the Intellectuals' Hearth Association, the report based its Turkish-Islamic synthesis on the pillars of family, the mosque, and the military,[51] three institutional pillars that were to produce a disciplined and unified society.[52] The historic Islamic *umma* (community of believers) seems to have set the model for a new sense of community that hypothetically could consolidate social unity and solidarity and thereby eliminate the conflicts of opposing ideologies.[53] In effect, the 1980 coup leaders emphasized for the first time at the official level the religious component of the nation and state as being important and worthy of respect. In order to solve this legitimacy problem, state officials did not hesitate to adapt the model of the umma in their new articulation of state ideology. The coup leaders, in fact, pursued pro-Islamic domestic and international policies. For example, the coup leaders allowed Mehmet Zahid Kotku, a Nakşibendi sheik, to be buried in the garden of the Süleymaniye Mosque in Istanbul and shied away from closing the religious seminaries and dormitories of the Süleymancı order.[54]

Even though the military coup leaders conceded space for Islam in the definition of state ideology and national identity, they still stressed the central role of the state in Turkish politics. This is apparent in the 1982 constitution, which makes the nonelected NSC the ultimate source of authority. According to the description of the NSC's duties in article 118 of the 1982 constitution,

> the NSC shall submit to the Cabinet its views on taking decisions
> and ensuring necessary coordination with regard to the formulation,
> establishment and implementation of the national security policy of
> the state. The cabinet shall give priority consideration to the deci-
> sions of the NSC concerning the measures that it deems necessary
> for the preservation of the existence and independence of the state,
> the integrity and indivisibility of the country and the peace and
> security of society.

The NSC law further sets out the basic duties of the NSC as (1) formulating the necessary measures that will preserve the constitutional order, guarantee national unity and integrity, and guide the Turkish nation toward national targets in accordance with Kemalist principles and reforms by uniting the nation around national ideals and values, and (2) formulating officially prescribed NSC views to be held and followed by the government in times of emergency rule, martial law, mobilization, or war. Under the 1982 constitution, the military has full autonomy in determining its recruitment and promotion rules, its budget, and how it defines and implements the national security policy. This military role varies from direct to covert guardianship by preserving political will and the capacity to take direct political action. In the 1982 constitution and in postcoup practices, the Turkish military regards itself as the guardian of the state and identifies its interests as the interests of the state. The military conflates its own autonomy with state autonomy. In other words, state autonomy, for the military, means the insulation of the military from social forces and the freedom to define the existential threats to the state and maintain the parameters of the Kemalist system above and around the governments. In Turkey, the military rather than the people or their elected representatives is the ultimate sovereign in the defining of security threats. This conflation of the state with military autonomy and interests has effectively militarized the state and turned the state into a security agent. The military's understanding of Kemalism as a "modernization" project to create a secular and national society supposedly justifies its autonomy. As the protector and executioner of modernization projects, the military defines secularism and nationalism as the two pillars of the Kemalist modernization project. It views any challenge to secularism and nationalism with suspicion and frames them as "antimodern" reactionism and "divisive."[55] Institutionally, Turkish military officers are well educated and have a corporate identity and sense of mission to be "guardians of Kemalism." They are recruited mostly from the lower and middle classes, and as cadets in the military high school from age 13, they are indoctrinated in the Kemalist dogma of a secular (that is, a nonreligious), national (Turkish), and Western-looking Turkey. This corporate military identity, which includes professionalism, guardianship, and distaste of civilian politicians, has an inherent impetus to "guard and guide" the society and prevent the formation of independent power centers outside the control of the state.[56]

In addition to the NSC, the new constitution granted authority to the president to make appointments to the Higher Education Council (YÖK: Yüksek Öğretim Kurumu), dissolve the Parliament, appoint justices to the Constitutional Court and the Military Court of Appeals, and appoint all members of the Supreme Council of Judges.[57] The constitution also prohibited any connection among trade unions, professional associations, interest groups, and political parties. Furthermore, since much of the pre-1980 ideological violence had been centered around university campuses, the coup leaders created the YÖK with the goal of purging left-leaning professors and centralizing the curriculum and administration of the universities. The YÖK also had the power to hire and fire faculty, determine curriculum and research agendas, and set the dress code for faculty and students.[58]

The 1982 constitution demonstrates that the Turkish military, despite its surface-level reforms, was not interested in shedding its real power as the sovereign guarantor of the state and Kemalist ideology in favor of a true civilian democratic government. In response to the totalitarian vision of the state—its intervention in every aspect of social life—as formulated in the 1982 constitution, social groups reacted with liberal agendas, demanding free spaces and no state control of the economy and education. This liberal reaction unleashed a new debate about the legitimate boundaries between the state and society and between the individual and society. This new post-1980 political and economic setting eventually facilitated the activities of Islamic groups and Sufi orders.

The military wanted to have a regulated and gradual transition to electoral politics. They therefore barred over seven hundred ex-politicians from politics for a period of five to ten years. The NSC empowered itself to screen new political parties and candidates and legalized only 3 of 17 parties that applied for participation in the 1983 general elections. The military fully supported the pro-military Nationalist Democracy Party (MDP: Milliyetçi Demokrasi Partisi), led by the retired general Turgut Sunalp, and tolerated a "loyal social democrat" Populist Party (HaP: Halkçı Parti) headed by a retired high-ranking pro-coup bureaucrat, Necdet Calp. The military openly criticized the third party, the Motherland Party (ANAP: Anavatan Partisi) of Turgut Özal, the evening before the election. This election-eve meddling badly backfired, and Özal's connection with informal associations and traditional authority networks contributed significantly to his party's electoral victory.

The Opening of New Opportunity Spaces

In the first elections after the 1980 military coup, Özal's ANAP came to power with 45.2 percent of the total vote and gained 211 seats in the four-hundred-seat Parliament. Özal served as prime minister between 1983 and 1989 and then as president from 1989 until his death in office in 1993. One of the most far-reaching legacies of the Özal years was the official legitimization of radically new perspectives on the role of Islam and the Ottoman heritage in contemporary Turkish society. He used the Sufi orders, kinship ties, and mosque associations to build dynamic bridges with society, resulting in the adaptation of these traditional networks to a modern urban environment. Özal also pursued a policy of Islamicizing the educational system. His minister of education, Vehbi Dinçerler, a known Nakşibendi disciple, prepared a new curriculum focusing on rewriting the presentation of national history and culture. In the new curriculum, the term "national" (*milli*) was often used in a religious sense.[59] The inner core of Özal's administration included leading members of the defunct pro-Islamic MSP and prominent disciples of Nakşibendi. Özal himself came from a religious Nakşibendi family.

Özal's economic liberalism, antibureaucratism, and pro-Islamic attitude made him very popular. He was the first prime minister of the Republic era to make a pilgrimage to Mecca and to be open about his religious practices.[60] The ANAP encouraged religious expression and increased state support for religious institutions. One of the signs of the increasing Islamicization of the governing elite was the introduction and institutionalization of *iftar* ("break the fast") dinners during Ramadan. These dinners, in the fashion of the national prayer breakfast in Washington, became a spectacle for the purpose of acknowledging and bestowing prestige on a pious elite in tune with popular sentiment at the center of government.

Özal also initiated a fresh set of policies on the Kurdish question, allowing greater cultural freedom for the Kurds, who prior to this period had not been recognized as a distinct ethnic group. In addition, Özal always supported Turkey's full integration into the European Union (EU), treating potential membership as a way to undermine the authoritarian position of the powerful Kemalist state–centric institutions, public sector industries, and those who profited from their patronage. In line with application for EU membership, Özal in 1987 accepted the right of individual Turkish citizens to petition the European Commission on Human Rights. Since then Kurdish-speaking citizens of Turkey have used this forum to challenge the state's oppressive conduct. In 1988, Özal also signed the European Convention on the Prevention of Torture and the United Nations instruments on the same issue. In 1990, after Özal had become president, the Turkish government recognized the compulsory jurisdiction of the European Court of Human Rights. In the same year, Özal led the government in ratifying the Ninth Additional Protocol to the European Convention on Human Rights, which grants the right of individual petition to the European Court of Justice. In the same month, the government ratified the revised version of the European Social Code and the Paris Charter. The ratification of these international conventions was important because according to article 90 of the 1982 constitution the provisions of international instruments to which Turkey is a party become integral parts of national law.

During Özal's presidency, the government also repealed (April 1991) the draconian Law No. 2932, which had banned the use of the Kurdish language in public and private places.[61] The military coup leaders had imposed that law in October 1983 in response to growing manifestations of Kurdish ethnonationalism.[62] This law, however, failed to suppress efforts to create political and social space for Kurds within Turkey. In fact, the law may have pushed the PKK to take up armed struggle against the government in 1984, nearly one year after its enactment. But most Kurdish politicians continued to press their demands within legal parties. In 1989, when Kurdish members of the left-wing Social Democrat Populist Party (SHP: Sosyal Demokrat Halkçı Parti) participated in a Kurdish congress held in Paris, the resultant controversy led to their expulsion from the SHP and then to the formation of the first pro-Kurdish party, the People's Labor Party (HEP: Halkın Emek Partisi), in June 1990. During the 1991 general election, the HEP had formed an alliance with the SHP and won 22 seats in Parliament. This election alliance was a result of the Turkish electoral law that stipulated that each political party had to organize and contest elections in every province and surpass a 10 percent national threshold in order to gain a seat in Parliament—conditions the HEP was not able to meet as an independent party. This alliance broke up when some newly elected Kurdish deputies swore allegiance to the Turkish constitution in Kurdish during an official ceremony and also wore the colors of the PKK flag (green, yellow, and red). This event and the refusal of Kurdish deputies to condemn PKK terrorism led to the breakup of the coalition. The HEP was banned soon afterward by the Constitutional Court for "promoting ethnic separatism." On October 19, 1992, former members of the HEP established the new Freedom and Democracy Party (ÖZDEP: Özgürlük ve Demokrasi Partisi); within three months the public prosecutor began procedures to close this new party because it called for a federalist solution to the Kurdish problem, and it was formally banned by the Constitutional Court on July 14, 1993.[63] Before this formal closure could come about, Kurdish deputies maneuvered to register yet another party, the Democracy Party (DEP: Demokrasi Partisi). The legal pressures radicalized the DEP leadership, and Hatip Dicle, the deputy from Diyarbakır, who was known as being openly sympathic to the PKK, became the trendsetter in the party. In February 1994 PKK activists killed five young military cadets in Tuzla railroad station, near Istanbul. Dicle defended the attack as "legitimite target" and also argued that the "PKK is not a terrorist but rather a political organization."[64] Before the local election campaign of March 27, 1994, the DEP became one of the main targets of Tansu Çiller's DYP. Çiller managed to have the immunity of eight DEP deputies removed on March 2, and six DEP deputies were arrested; four of them (Leyla Zana, Hatip Dicle, Orhan Doğan, and Selim Saddak) were condemned to 15 years in prison, and six DEP deputies fled the country. The Constitutional Court banned the party in June 1994. The DEP parliamentarians who managed to flee the country established the Kurdish parliament in exile. In May 1994 Murat Bozlak, a prominent Kurdish lawyer, established the People's Democracy Party (HADEP: Halkın Demokrasi Partisi) and took part in the 1995 and 1999 elections. Although its members are constantly harassed, persecuted, and even killed, the Kurds used new political and social opportunities to carve a political space for themselves in terms of HEP, DEP, HADEP, and DEHAP.

In addition to Islamic and Kurdish movements, the construction of an autonomous Alevi identity began to emerge in the mid-1980s as a result of the fall of socialism, which had been the surrogate identity for the Alevis, and the rise of the political Islamic movement and of the assertive Kurdish nationalism that forced many Kurdish Alevis to switch to their "religious/Alevi" identity.[65] Moreover, in the aftermath of the 1980 coup, many leftists (mostly Alevis) either were arrested or fled the country to Europe, primarily Germany.

The 1990s witnessed the revival of Alevi identity in terms of establishing new media outlets, associations, festivals, and conferences. Alevi publications, along with festivals, became the main institutions for political and religious mobilization. Within the same sociopolitical site, different versions of Alevism competed for control of these symbols. For example, when prominent left-wing Alevi intellectuals gathered in Sivas (a fault-line province for sectarian conflict) to commemorate teachings of the Alevi saint Pir Sultan Abdal, a major conflict took place on July 2, 1993. The gathering also included the late Aziz Nesin, one of Turkey's leading writers, who had published segments of *The Satanic Verses* of Salman Rushdie and had openly declared himself an atheist. A mob mobilized by a group of pro-RP activists attacked the Madımak Hotel where the meeting was taking place, and a subsequent fire killed many of the intellectuals present. This incident was filmed by the city police force, and the police video was leaked to private television channels and was played on television stations for almost a week. The film showed that the police force clearly sided with the mob and did not use force to disperse it. The airing of this film became an occasion for diverse Alevi groups to imagine themselves as a unified community that shares the same treatment from the state and Sunni majority. The conduct of the police force, the government, and Parliament in dealing with this assault against Alevi intellectuals was a turning point for the Alevi community. The community perceived that the state was not "theirs"—a view that has heightened their feelings of insecurity vis-à-vis the state and Sunni majority and catalyzed their mobilization and organization.

After the 1993 Sivas incident, Alevis became more assertive and increasingly have stressed that they are a separate ethnoreligious group vis-à-vis the state. Television and radio popularize this feeling and now provide a new network to mobilize the Alevi community as was never before possible. For example, when a group of unknown gunmen opened fire on Alevi teahouses, killing two and wounding three people in the Gazi neighborhood of Istanbul on March 12, 1995, the volatile and tenuous relationship between the state and the Alevi community was ruptured. The police were slow to react, and a rumor spread around the neighborhood that the local police station also might have been involved in the attack. This rumor, combined with a previous event in which an Alevi detainee had been killed at the same police station, galvanized the Alevi community, which mobilized in opposition to the state. As was reported on radio and television channels, Alevis from all over Istanbul poured into the neighborhood. As the television cameras and journalists moved to the area to cover the story, the demonstrators further hardened their rhetoric and actions. They subsequently encircled the police station and demanded justice. When a group of armed demonstrators started to fire at the police, the police reacted. The clash ended with 22 deaths, mostly Alevis. Alevism then became a symbol of the denial of justice and rights by the state. The 1990s was a period of "coming out" for a potential Alevi identity, as is evident in journals, conferences, and associations. The Sivas and Gazi incidents, along with the rising Sunni-Islamic movement, became a catalyst for the articulation of Alevi political identity. Between the years 1993–2002, the Alevis also managed to express their political demands as a religious group and make effective use of opportunity spaces. With the help of the new Alevi bourgeoisie, Alevi intellectuals utilized new opportunity spaces in the media, market, and education to articulate an autonomous Alevi identity. The transformation in the Alevi community and the (re)forming of an autonomous Alevi identity took place through associational life, that is, the establishment of village or town-based cultural associations. These associations consolidated themselves and entered into the public sphere by establishing their own magazines or radio stations. The Alevi intellectuals utilized these associations and their magazines as opportunity spaces to reconstruct an Alevi identity that is print-based and in tune with the global discourses of human rights. The attempts at becoming a print-based theology led to contradictory reinterpretations of the oral Alevi tradition as a "secular belief system outside Islam," "real Islam," "Turkish Islam," "Kurdish Islam," or "a way of life."[66] The politics of Alevi identity have been produced and consolidated in these associations. They are not only centers of gathering and discussion but also socializing places where skills in public relations and politics are acquired. They prepare for the conversion of a heavily rural population to an urban mode of life through training and establishing connections. At the same time, the weakening position of the main Alevi religious functionary, known as the *dede*, also promoted communal fragmentation, and the Alevi community was further divided into ethnic Turkish and Kurdish groups. Kurdish nationalism, for instance, facilitated the formation of a separate Zaza ethnolinguistic identity. As a result of opportunity spaces, traditional group boundaries have been undermined, and new identity groups are emerging. For instance, despite their unique language, the Zazas—speakers of an Iranian language—never regarded themselves as a separate ethnic group. Religious identity shaped their public identity and alignment. However, the last two decades have witnessed the construction of an Alevi Zaza consciousness and the creation of a separate Zaza ethnolinguistic identity.

Conclusion

The political developments in Turkey during the 1980s and early 1990s demonstrate that the state is contested not only as a set of institutions determining policies but also, and more important, as a source of societal legitimacy and identity. İsmail Kara, a leading scholar of political Islam, has argued that the state stresses the public role of Islam to ensure social harmony and to serve as an ultimate source of legitimization just as it did in Ottoman times.[67] However, Kara's stress on the state by itself does not explain the situation fully, because one needs to take social transformation and pressures into account to understand the marked policy changes pursued by the Turkish state in this period.

Since 1980, Turkish Muslims have begun to feel that the worst period of Kemalist oppression has passed and that their state could and should represent their Ottoman-Islamic culture and identity. Democratization nationalizes political institutions by carrying collective identities into the public sphere. Due to increased democratization, the gap between state and society has been reduced, and this process, in turn, has catalyzed other groups to resist the further penetration of Sunni Islam into the state. The assertion of Alevi identity, for example, is a response to the tentative alliance between the state and Sunni Islam.

Drastic changes also occurred during the 1980s in the composition of the state elite. Although some scholars claim a certain continuity of the state-centric culture because of the power of the post-1980s bureaucracy, I would argue that there has been a major break with past Turkish political practice as a result of several factors. For example, the state elite is not as homogenous as it used to be. There is no single path to socioeconomic development as defined in the old ideology of "Westernization." Universal education and the expanding economy brought new recruits into state institutions who had a greater empathy for Islamic sentiments. Finally, with the end of the Cold War, the security situation of Turkey has been normalized. All of these factors have made possible the emergence of a new "organic elite"—that is, an elite that identifies with society and is attuned for electoral reasons to public concerns.

4

The Political Economy
of Islamic Discourse

Contemporary Turkish society is experiencing simultaneously the
processes of economic growth and political liberalization on the one
hand and the development of an assertive Islamic political movement on the other. This chapter seeks to address this seeming
paradox by demonstrating how several decades of economic expansion and political liberalization have provided the grounds for the
construction of a modern Islamic political identity. One must ask
whether these processes are causal or constitutive. What is the
impact of economic transformation on local, national, and Islamic
identity? How do these identities, in turn, shape economic interests
and policies?

The current Islamic identity movement is not a revival of old
religious loyalties but is rather a modern creation, constructed in
relation to neoliberal economic politics. This form of Islamic identity
is detached from its traditional rural context and is rooted instead in
the urban market. Economic liberalization, the expansion of education, and urbanization have offered new opportunity spaces for
contesting notions of identity. These new spaces, where identities
can be formed and contested as a result of new economic and
political forces, were formed not only for identity purposes but also
to cultivate business and social connections within the new market
economy. As the state's inadequacy in the social, economic, educational, and health care spheres became apparent, Islamic groups
increasingly moved into these spheres with financial means, organizational experience, and dedicated workers. The primordial quality of
religious communal bonds and a coherent sense of mission concerning the future revitalization of the Turkish state and society help
explain why Islamic groups have been so active.

The political economy of Turkey has witnessed far-reaching changes since the official import substitution policies of the 1960s and 1970s. The new export-oriented economic policy of the 1980s led to liberalization, economic development, and the emergence of an Islamic communal discourse. Sufi orders and Islamic groups were the vehicles for the formation of an associational life through the financial resources they derived from the capitalist market. In Turkey, which is far from being a rentier state that derives its legitimacy by distributing goods in exchange for political consent, the power of the state, following the liberalization that occurred during the Özal era (1983–1993), has been gradually circumscribed by social and economic groups.[1] The emergence of the middle classes has influenced religious attitudes and practices and the framing of social issues. Islamic doctrine and practices increasingly are becoming rationalized as a result of the combination of religious discipline, ethical solidarity, and entrepreneurial dynamism that has occurred under the leadership of the successful small and medium enterprises known as "Anatolian tigers."

By examining the socioeconomic context of the Islamic revival and the assertion of a political identity, one can demonstrate how this process has been facilitated by the new discursive spaces that have been created as a result of urbanization, capitalist development, and the revolution in mass media and publishing. The mass migration of the rural population to urban centers has led to socioeconomic pressures, promoting the embrace of Islam as an instrument for attaining social equality and justice.

Urbanization and Migration

Turkey's economic growth has taken place against a backdrop of severe socioeconomic imbalances among regions and social groups.[2] High income disparities between the towns and the countryside led to rural-to-urban migration, which in turn politicized and sharpened regional and ethnic differences in society.[3] During the reformist era (1920–1950), the population was hardly integrated in terms of social ethos and ideological outlook. Secular Kemalist ideology held sway in the major cities, with its own symbols and institutions, whereas traditional forms of Islam maintained their dominance in the large rural areas of Anatolia. The role of religion and the boundary between state and society were transformed in part by the dislocation of the populace between 1950 and 1970, when over 18 percent of the population moved away from the provinces in which they were born. The direction of migration, virtually without exception, has been from rural areas to urban centers.[4] According to a report of the State Statistic Institute, 60 out of every 100 people living in Istanbul in 1980 originally came from another part of the country. In Ankara, 40 percent of the 1980 population was born outside the provincial borders.[5]

Rural-to-urban migration has been a source of both dynamism and tension. As a result of migration, people have changed not only their locale but also their worldviews. What they bring with them to the cities is the residue of their Islamically shaped moral understanding and a sense of community. Official state statistics bear out this great demographic transformation: in 1950, only 25 percent of the population lived in cities; by 1993, this figure had increased to 59 percent.[6] But it is important to appreciate that the scale of this migration has also had an impact on the villages. In fact, Turkey has been experiencing "two-directional urbanization . . . the village has been reached by urban Turkey after vast improvements in road networks . . . and telephone installation. And correspondingly, the city has also been reached by rural Turkey."[7]

The average annual urban growth rate has been about 7 percent since 1950. A closer examination of the population movement indicates regional patterns. For example, while people from the Black Sea region tended to move to Istanbul because of the ease of transportation by sea, the people of central Anatolia have tended to move to Ankara. The latter migration has had political implications in terms of the transformation of Kemalist ideology from that of secular/positivism to a Turkish-Islamic synthesis. Before the 1950s, the bureaucracy was dominated by the cadres made up of people from the ex-Ottoman bureaucracy who were mostly immigrants from the Balkans. The heartland of Anatolia, in contrast, was ethnically Turkish, mostly Sunni Muslim, and had remained more conservative vis-à-vis other regions; it thus has been a strong support base for religious and nationalist parties.[8] Following migration to Ankara in the 1960s and 1970s because of geographic proximity, central Anatolian Turks came to be overrepresented in the national bureaucracy. The political consequences were evident by the 1990s. For example, the pro-Islamic RP and the Nationalist Action Party (MHP: Milliyetçi Hareket Partisi) received their greatest support from the central Anatolian provinces in the 1995 national election.

One of the main causes of massive rural emigration has been the state-sponsored policy favoring the mechanization of agriculture and import substitution in the industrial sector, which came at the expense of traditional agriculture. This policy led to increasing poverty in the countryside, encouraging mass migrations to the cities in the 1960s and 1970s. These newcomers were not integrated into the formal economy but instead came to form an informal sector at the margins of the economy. They needed low-cost housing, but when the state failed to make the necessary provisions for this, the low-income migrants built squatter housing, or *gecekondu* ("condos" built overnight), on illegally occupied state land without construction permits. By 1975, one quarter of the urban population lived in such squatter housing, and these areas became important centers for political parties seeking to mobilize support.

Within these squatter towns, Islam became a means of communication and alliance formation. Islamic rituals and teachings are reinterpreted under these new urban conditions to provide the cognitive means to understand the social and political world of a new and unsettling urban life. In this context, Muslims use Islam as a medium for communicating standards of meaningful conduct and a repository of traditions that can regulate everyday life. Islam therefore constitutes a community by offering a set of symbols and norms that connect events and social interactions. Islamic political movements have flourished in the squatter towns, which in the 1970s were breeding grounds for left-wing movements. Squatter towns, it must be emphasized, are not exactly equivalent to the slums one confronts in places in Latin America or South Asia. While squatter towns originally did not have electricity or sewage services, this underclass participated in local politics, managed to gain very basic social services, and linked the gecekondus to the city. The inhabitants of the gecekondus are not alienated and isolated from urban life in the manner of many impoverished rural migrants to Sao Paulo or Calcutta; rather they tend to be upwardly mobile, energetic, and initiative oriented. They seek integration rather than isolation. Moreover, they generate a sense of cultural dynamism that allows them to succeed in their reinterpretation of rural traditions and adaptation to urban life.

In the beginning, Turkish government officials did not have a clear vision or plan regarding urban development. However, the governments gradually accommodated themselves to these new patterns of urbanization, and electoral politics became a tool for bringing public services to these areas and mobilizing them politically. Governments have been forced to legalize these public land appropriations, either by selling the occupied lands at nominal rates to their new tenants or giving them away for free. Such policies, in fact, have encouraged the further occupation of lands and the establishment of new squatter neighborhoods. As a result, over 70 percent of the population of Ankara live in squatter housing; this figure is 55 percent in Istanbul, Izmir, and Adana and 40 percent in the case of Erzurum and Samsun.[9] In 1985, 30 percent of the total urban population lived in the gecekondus of the squatter towns.[10] Since 1983, conflicts such as that between the Turkish army and Kurdish insurgents have resulted in further massive population movements from southeastern Anatolian villages to the large urban centers of western Anatolia.[11] The anomie of modern urban life raised a whole set of issues concerning social ethics, justice, aesthetics, and the broader search for meaning and identity in the context of rapid socioeconomic development. It was exactly these pressing issues that Kemalist ideology never addressed adequately because of the vacuum it had created by forcefully displacing traditional Islamic norms and ethics.

In squatter towns, new migrants become laborers without the support of trade unions to protect their interests and provide a sense of security and solidarity. This has forced the newcomers to rely on networks centered around older, rural-based solidarity associations (hemşerilik) and religiously oriented welfare associations.[12] The hemşerilik ("hometowners") is an informal group that forms to assist members in social, political, and economic fields. It does not mobilize nationalism but rather fosters pre-nationalistic loyalties (to the rural, hometown, and religious solidarity networks) that emerge as dominant markers of identity and loyalty in the urban market economy. Newcomers "gravitate toward networks based on places of origin, ethnicity, or religious beliefs partly to maintain their ties with their villages but more importantly as a means of integration into the city. "[13] These pre-nationalist networks have been modernized and reinvested to meet the needs of urban society—housing, jobs, education, and a degree of security against the corrupt bureaucratic system. The existence of "crime-free slums . . . demonstrates how formidable is the fabric of which Turkish Muslim culture is made."[14]

The leading residents (notables) of the cities in the early Republican period were primarily people who closely identified with Atatürk's policies and saw themselves as far removed from the traditional values of the small towns and countryside. The large cities at this time tended to be bastions of Kemalism. Thus newcomers, including the provincial elite who were not without financial means, traditionally found themselves ostracized from the center of city life and were forced to form their own neighborhood associations on the fringes of urban society. In many ways, rural migrants were changed by the dominant secular urban culture they encountered, but they also managed to mark this urban space with their own rural-Islamic identity.

One of the major implications of this pattern of urbanization has been the growing dominance of the social practices of the provincial town. This social adaptation to urban life is constituted by the confluence of imitation and innovation. In the process of mass migration from villages to cities, the first groups to leave the village were notables and other economically well-off groups. Reflecting traditional Islamic culture, with its close-knit families, the patterns of migration reveal that families migrate as a whole rather than as individuals. Therefore, family and village kinship networks tended to reconstitute themselves within their own quarters (*mahalle*) in large urban centers. Squatter housing further promoted the development of communal ties because people needed help to build squatter houses and to protect them from the state bureaucracy. These family-based migration patterns created a new ring of conservative clusters around the cities, and this in turn reinforced the conservativism of urban centers. Neighborhoods (*mahalle*) evolved around hometown loyalties and an Islamic code of ethics. The local mosque often became the center for integrating and assisting newcomers. Thus both the material and psychological needs of the new migrants were met at the neighborhood level. Between 1973 and 1999, the number of mosques sharply increased from 45,152 to 75,000 and punctuated Turkey's urban landscape.[15] Before people build schools, roads, and a sewage system, they come together to build a mosque in the new neighborhood. The mosque-building, which includes the establishment of a religious association, collection of money, and voluntary work, helps newcomers to get to know each other through their shared language of Islam and to create a web of interactions that can be used in other spheres of social life. Building mosque, for many pious Sunni Turks, means creating a moral frame of reference and a sacred reference center of the new community.

The successful ability of rural migrants to shape their environment is seen in their adaptation of cultural forms. Not only were new solidarities in urban centers formed on the basis of rural origins but also these squatter towns became the centers of new subcultures. These geocultural spaces included both rural and urban culture, practices, decorative arts, and music. Nothing signified Islam and a shared Ottoman past more than the rise of a new form of music known as *Arabesk*; it rekindled the animosity of the Kemalist elite. The migrants gradually reintroduced into major urban centers this "traditional" culture and music that the Republican custodians thought had been purged forever. In the minds of many Anatolian migrants, their choice of music, dress, and literature was an act of conscious resistance and rebellion against the attempts by the state to inscribe an official and radically different high culture. *Arabesk* songs genuinely attempted to reflect the pain and hardship of modernization, as experienced by vast yet marginalized sectors of Turkey's nascent capitalist economy. These songs articulated the feeling newcomers had that they were "strangers" within their own country; their lyrics emphasize themes of poverty, social mobility, and alienation. Another common theme in this music is the presentation of the city as both a locus of opportunity and a place of corruption and dissolution.

Arabesk music was officially banned on public broadcasting stations until the early 1990s because it evoked a different set of cultural norms than what the Kemalist state sought to promote.[16] The Republican regime attempted to use music via the radio as a tool for creating uniform sensibilities and tastes. The state-owned radio regularly broadcast European classical music in order to encourage Turks to accept the Kemalist agenda of realizing a European identity.[17] However, the Turkish urban poor either turned their radios off or turned their dials to Egyptian popular music broadcasts, which were a closer reflection of their authentic tastes. With the Islamization of urban life, a new form of popular music evolved, stressing the heritage of Ottoman classical music. Although the second generation of Arabesk singers has its origins in village culture, they constructed a hybrid music that bridges rural and urban culture in Turkey.[18] They conceive of the city no longer as a source of fear and isolation but rather as a space that can be shaped and improved. This generation, unlike the previous one, demonstrates a confidence that results from growing up in the squatter towns. They have had greater opportunity to be trained in Ottoman classical music, and their close ties with the Turkish diaspora in Europe allow them to keep up with changing fashions.

As a result of the expansion of urbanization and education and the development of print and video media, first- and second-generation urban intellectuals adapted local and oral Islamic traditions and idioms into new discourses on urban life.[19] Islam constituted a language for new urban dwellers, a cement for bringing diverse groups together, and a social security network that the government was unable to rival. The children of the first wave of migrants seized the educational opportunities of the 1970s and began to hold public offices in the early 1980s. Some of them have come to form a new and important group of vernacular Islamic intellectuals and musicians. Their image of Islam is different from that of their fathers; it is rearticulated to meet the challenges of modern urban life and the overtly Europeanizing program of the Republican old guard.

The Treacherous Path to a Market Economy: Economic Development in the 1980s

The young Turkish Republic intended to pursue a liberal economic policy; however, the depression in the global market prevented this from happening, and Turkey instead pursued a statist policy designed to protect its own economy.[20] However, economic étatism soon became enshrined because it overlapped with the statist-political culture and the interests of the Republican elite. The state pursued industrialization and capital formation with the aim of creating not a national bourgeoisie per se, as many historians have alleged, but one that would be loyal to and indeed part of the new Republican elite.[21] The Turkish bourgeoisie, unlike that of Europe, was a product of state-led economic policies and most of the time supported high customs tariffs to protect itself against foreign competition. This state bourgeoisie failed to develop its own cultural code and organic ties with the larger society and culture. It functioned as the agent of the state and tried to imitate European cultural practices without seeking any synthesis with local tradition. It thus effectively has functioned as a pampered ward and an agent of the state establishment.

The State Economic Enterprises (SEE) became a source of "rapid employment expansion, motivated by the political concerns of generating support for the government in power."[22] The Republic thus successfully created its own bourgeoisie, but because of its dependence on the state, this new class could not emerge as an independent force in politics and society. The liberal economic policies of Adnan Menderes's government in the 1950s broke from this early Republican tradition and promoted the interests of commercial farmers and the industrial bourgeoisie. The bourgeoisie, however, continued to be state dependent. Turkey made good use of import-substitution strategies in the 1960s and thus "enjoyed a vigorous economic recovery together with high growth rates in GNP ... 6.4 percent (1963–1967), 6.7 percent (1968–1972), and 7.2 percent (1973–1977)."[23] The 1973 oil crisis and the division of political parties and state institutions along rigid ideological lines led to the fragmentation of the state and the breakdown of the economy in 1977. The government was forced to implement harsh IMF structural adjustment programs. The government devalued the Turkish lira twice—by 23 percent in March 1978 and 44 percent in June 1979. These measures did not help because Turkey needed an even more ruthless structural adjustment policy that the weak government was not willing or able to implement. The inflation rate rose to 120 percent, and unemployment was 15 percent in 1980. Per capita GDP fell by more than 2.6 percent a year in 1979 and 1980, while manufacturing output declined by 5.2 percent in the same period.[24]

This economic crisis greatly contributed to the social unrest that impelled the Turkish military to intervene in 1980. The military coup created the authoritarian political climate that was needed for implementation of the structural adjustment program, which moved from import-substitution to a growth-led export strategy.[25] This strategy reduced state intervention, alleviated payment difficulties, liberalized domestic pricing, and rationalized the public sector. The coup also made other adjustments possible: prices were freed, agricultural and other state subsidies were removed, and trade unions were banned. Özal, who became prime minister in 1983, closely cooperated with the IMF and the World Bank in assuring that these reforms were implemented fully. Turkey received nine structural adjustment loans during the 1980s.[26] In the short term, the structural adjustment program yielded positive results. Turkey reduced inflation from 104 percent to 28 percent in 1982, and achieved its first positive growth rates as exports took off.[27] However, privatization was implemented in the 1980s program only to a limited extent because of opposition from the bureaucracy, large industrialists, and statist politicians.[28]

Nevertheless, Turkey at last had opened its economy to the outside world, bringing in large-scale foreign investment, new technology, and management skills. These in turn led to a sevenfold expansion in exports between 1979 and 1981. Özal's economic policy encouraged foreign trade generally, not just exports, because he removed a number of trade barriers and introduced export credits. This expansion of the economy, however, did not have the same effect on all segments of society; there were distinct inequalities in the distribution of goods and finance capital. In 1980, public sector wages were 25 percent higher than those of private sector workers. But by 1987 private sector wages were 30 percent higher than in the public sector; in 1995 this figure rose to 56 percent.[29] Large industrialists had difficulty orienting their production toward the export market, and this situation led to a major campaign to oppose export-led economic restructuring. Özal, in turn, assisted ambitious small and medium-sized producers in overcoming opposition from the large Association of Turkish Industrialists and Businessmen (TÜSİAD) bloc. The Istanbul-based, pro-state bourgeoisie was forced to stand on its own feet beginning with the 1980 economic decisions. It is hardly suprising, then, that this group, rather than promoting democratization and empowerment of the people, became an obstacle to the aspirations of a more national and democratic Anatolian bourgeoisie.

As a result of 1980s economic policies, two distinct bourgeoisies, often in conflict, have emerged in Turkey. Not only do they compete over market share but, more important, they compete over the ideological and cultural orientation of the country. The new Anatolian bourgeoisie is less dependent on the state and more embedded in Turko-Islamic culture and demands a smaller government, larger political space, and freedom for civil society. Therefore, the conflict in Turkey is not only between the haves and have-nots but also between these two bourgeoisies.[30]

Small and medium-sized enterprise development was the primary goal of Özal's economic policies. Called the "Anatolian tigers," such enterprises played an important role in the "globalization" of some major Anatolian cities.[31] Özal tried to overcome the problem of an oligarchic capitalism, characterized by the dominance of giant conglomerates and a handful of wealthy tycoons who enjoy special privileges and a cozy relationship with the state.[32] The "Anatolian tigers" prefer the institutionalization of market competition over the oligarchic capitalism of TÜSİAD.[33] In the enterprises of these Anatolian tigers, management is less rigid, and contact between workers and management has become more personalized. Social trust, solidarity, and loyalty are at the center of the regional economic development successes. The shared culture produced by communal ties, Sufi networks, and village connections ease conflict and facilitate economic activity.

Lucrative trade and large remittances by Turkish guest workers in neighboring Muslim countries following the oil boom of the 1970s served to reestablish economic and cultural ties with these countries that the Republican elite long had tried to downplay. Those who were involved in trade relations with oil-rich Muslim countries used some of their profits to promote Islamic activities—such as opening private schools or supporting publications of new journals and books. Cultural interaction and the restoration of historic connections—rather than a deliberate program of Islamicization funded by Gulf Arabs—contributed to a significant reconsideration of past ties with West Asian neighbors. This oil money was distributed to new Islamic groups through well-funded financial circles.[34] In fact, one of the first policy decrees of the Özal government, on December 16, 1983, provided legal grounds for charitable donations to be used for religious purposes in Turkey. Nurcu groups helped to form the Faisal Finance Company in August 1984. Korkut Özal, the prime minister's brother and a prominent Nakşibendi follower, and Eymen Topbaş, the brother of Nakşibendi sheik Musa Topbaş, founded Al-Baraka Türk. The Özal government introduced tax reform laws that exempted these financial institutions, which operated according to Islamic principles forbidding interest payments.[35]

In the late 1980s and early 1990s, Özal's antibureaucratic and free market policies were supported by small-scale provincial business owners and the petite bourgeoisie of the large cities. This petite bourgeoisie consists of peddlers, dealers, small constructors, restaurant owners, small industrialists, textile factory owners, and food processors. This sector does not want state intervention in the economy; it is therefore the main supporter of economic liberalization. This sector finds in Islamic symbols and ethics useful weapons for fomenting public opinion against state regulation of the economy and against the big industrialists who enjoy state patronage. The Islamic voices within this informal sector believe that society would prosper if the state would stop intervening on behalf of big business. Islamic associations (MÜSİAD and HÜRSİAD) also offer small business owners a critical network where they can meet to voice shared concerns and frustrations and also to engage in business transactions.

In this period, as noted, a new class of bourgeoisie emerged that has been closely identified with Islamically inclined segments of the urban populace. However, the Islamic capitalists who benefited from the liberal policies of the 1980s represent only one privileged section of the broader Islamic movement in Turkey. In the long term, the structural adjustment policies of the Özal government did not solve Turkey's chronic inflation (which has continued to hover at over 70 percent), high interest rates, or mounting external debt (which had reached US$70 billion by 2000). The program to privatize fully inefficient public sector industries has not been realized because the ruling parties utilize state enterprises as a source for allocating patronage to their supporters. During the 1990s, the earlier success of the structural adjustment program soured, and the benefits of economic liberalization failed to "trickle down" to the squatter towns, where the urban poor are beset by high inflation and bereft of welfare assistance. The squatter town environment has become a breeding ground for radical ethnic and religious ideologies.[36] It is thus clear that macroeconomic policies have diverse impacts on the goals and strategies of Islamic political movements. As a result of the economic expansion, class cleavages have begun to emerge as a source of internal division within the Islamic groups and to shape their competing political alliances. Indeed, those who have not benefited from economic liberalization are embittered toward those who have. This has become a major source of tension in the interpretation of political Islam in relation to issues of social justice, equity, and economic redistribution. Those who have benefited, such as the Nakşibendi and Nurcu groups, supported parties of the center-right (ANAP and DYP) that favor economically liberal policies and stress a cultural and ethical Islam, as opposed to a more overtly political Islam. These right-of-center parties have become much more socially conservative as their constituents have come to hold Islam as the guiding ethic of social life. On the other hand, those who felt the negative brunt of the 1980s economic policies tended to support the RP of Erbakan because that party allowed for social mobility through Islam and stressed a platform of social justice and economic redistribution led by the state.

The power of Islamic factions within particular political parties has dissipated because each group seeks a different economic reality. These ideological rifts over the correct economic policies led the RP to draw back from its earlier enthusiasm for state intervention in the economy. The Turkish state, caught at the intersection between a fluid international economy and a restless domestic society, has had to restructure itself to respond to these pressures. It has had to find a balance between economic growth and decentralization; foreign investment and national industry; Islamism and secularism; local interest and national interest; rural and urban needs; security and freedom. Moreover, in order to be competitive in the global market, Turkey has had to achieve domestic stability. This in turn requires a large degree of political decentralization, recognition of the political rights of the Kurds and the cultural rights of Alevis, and tolerance of broad-based democratic institutions so that a culturally diverse nation can cooperate in meeting the challenge of globalization.

Political Islam and Competing Loyalties: Sufi Brotherhoods and Hometown Solidarities

In the "get rich quick" environment of the 1980s, "profit" often became an end in itself. Even love of God was quantified by the amount of money one gave to charity. This atmosphere created for many a sense of fraying in the moral fabric of society. This perceived moral crisis led some to argue that society must work to emphasize ethical and moral values. Individuals joined religious associations and Sufi orders both to sanction capitalist profits and to alleviate their moral unease over social inequality by placing stress on charity and social justice. In other words, liberalization and industrialization have helped foster the emergence of a form of the Protestant ethic along with Islamic communalism, that is, a common political and economic ethos that may be expressed and contained within religious affiliations. This communalism has allowed provincial capitals to enhance their economic and social bases and gradually to compete with the established centers of finance and industry.

The 1990s have been marked by the continued migration of the Anatolian bourgeoisie toward the economic and political centers of power. Since the 1980 economic restructuring, Islamic movements have not sought to control the state directly but rather have focused on "community-related goals without sharing their state-oriented ideologies."[37] On moving to new neighborhoods, persons need a new value system to preserve their families and to create a new moral language to regulate their relations with their environment. The village-based values were not sufficient to regulate the complex relations that exist in big metropolitan cities. The rhythms of Islamic movements in Turkey thus are not geared toward the consolidation of individual autonomy but rather toward the maintenance of communal ties and solidarity.[38] Since Islam constituted a shared code of conduct for Turkish society, Islam has become the ideology of these newcomers, who have sought a place and voice in the political domain and economic sphere against a center that identified itself with laicism. In this process, the Sufi orders have functioned as informal networks for raising capital and promoting the business interests of fellow members. In other words, the economic growth of the mid-1980s transformed Islamic organizational networks into mechanisms for achieving upward mobility. For instance, according to the pro-Kemalist daily *Cumhuriyet*, the West Working Group of the Military determined that there are more than 4,000 pro-Islamic corporations in Turkey; about 203 out of 385 major corporations are owned by interests aligned with Fethullah Gülen.[39]

In addition to the Islamic identity nurtured in Sufi neighborhood networks, another form of identity, generated in hometown solidarity (*hemşeri*) associations, also emerged. *Hemşeri* networks are the most natural and pervasive magnets of loyalty for those who are new arrivals in the lower class neighborhoods ringing large cities. The hometown identity remains a central sentimental bond among a group of people who share a common geographical origin, mainly rural, and a common status, for the most part, of beginning life anew on the lower rungs of the urban capitalist economy. Hometown networks of solidarity involve mutual expectations and obligations on the part of their members. In other words, the phenomenon of hometown affinity is consolidated, stressed, and matured as an identity instead of fading away in the big-city environment.[40] The neighborhoods in the 1980s became distinct units of shared provincial, religious, and ethnic loyalties.

The mobilization of Islamic identity in these new urban centers assumed a guise that reflects the more loosely structured and interpretive aspect of what I earlier defined as a society-centric Islamic movement, as opposed to what I called the doctrinal and rigidly defined state-centric Islamic movement. Neighborhood associations and Sufi orders contribute to the development of a flexible and adaptive Islamic identity and a discourse that is able to respond to the complex stresses and changes of modern urban life. At this horizontal level, the expansion of education and technological innovation lead to an awareness of the power of agency and individualism.

The Sociopolitical Implications of the Market
as a "Public Space" in the 1990s

During the free market transition of the 1980s and 1990s, the market spaces provided a material base on which diverse and competing visions of Islam were produced. These competing visions have crystallized into three general forms. Political Islam seeks to attain political power and transform society through the institutions of the state. Cultural Islam perceives religion as a form of civilization and seeks to influence cultural and social identities in this regard. Ethical Islam seeks to treat the faith as a source of norms and mores that creates a common moral language by rearticulating experiences. It is my contention that political and ethical Islam fall within the larger sphere of cultural Islam.

Turkey's "market space" has had four major impacts on the formation of Islamic identity. First, the associational life that takes place in the market leads to the establishment of thousands of new foundations and associations in which group consciousness is expressed in terms of the market rather than the individual. Second, technological advances have helped to disseminate diverse voices and thus facilitate the fracture of an authoritative Islam. Third, entrepreneurship, characterized by market efficiency and rationality, has created a protoindividuality that is marked and conditioned by Islam. And fourth, patterns of consumption are used to objectify Islam and create boundaries.

The Emergence of an Islamic Bourgeoisie: The Case of the MÜSİAD

The marketplace has been instrumental in creating an associational life that is outside the purview of the state. The goal of these civil society–based associations (as opposed to state-formed and operated associations) has been to weaken the state's bureaucratic power and open new spaces for the politics of identity. Identity formation in Turkey in fact has been driven by these associational societies. Turkish civil society has "thickened" considerably as a consequence of the 1980 economic liberalization and the 1989–1991 collapse of the Cold War, which removed the "communist" security threat that antiassociational state officials had been able to exploit in the past. In short, economic resources formed the basis of a richer and thicker associational life in Turkey, and these associations, in turn, became the habitat for the construction and articulation of an Islamic consciousness in accordance with market needs. For instance, between 1980 and 1995 a total 39,369 new associations were established, compared with only 24,272 in the entire period from 1926 to 1980. As of 1995, there were 63,641 associations and foundations in Turkey (table 4.1).[41] During the Özal period, Turkey experienced a major expansion of associations and foundations.

Özal, the man most associated with the liberalization of the Turkish economy, helped to transform the market into a space for identity formation. He strengthened associational societies by establishing coalitions between various emerging Islamic groups, intellectuals, provincial medium-scale businesses, and new

TABLE 4. 1. The Growth of Associational Life in Turkey (number of associations per year)

Goals	1980	1983	1984	1985	1986	1987	1988	1989	1992	1995
Social	5,348	5,870	6,215	7,695	8,822	9,776	11,730	12,218	12,896	19,515
Cultural	9,116	9,629	9,955	11,115	12,594	13,805	15,335	15,740	16,430	19,401
Religious	6,038	6,514	6,917	7,722	8,830	9,789	10,242	10,582	11,817	14,743
Athletics	3,343	3,792	4,168	4,710	5,366	5,849	6,206	6,373	7,185	8,936
Higher education, student associations	1	—	2	8	40	50	64	69	79	80
Public-good association	320	324	325	340	355	370	371	371	384	426
International branches	106	—	108	128	—	198	202	221	354	540

Anatolian industrialists. The expansion of associational life along economic and cultural lines has become a source of social stability in Turkey. Associational life has consolidated political stability by creating organic ties between the state and society. One of the main institutional developments in the modern Islamic revival has been the establishment in May 1990 of the Independent Industrialists' and Busninessmen's Association (MÜSİAD: Müstakil Sanayici ve İşadamları Derneği). It has branches throughout Turkey, with its headquarters in Istanbul. Its membership was 1,718 in 1995 but had increased to 2,897 by 1997; nearly half (1,318) of these companies were founded after 1983, with 580 being established between 1990 and 1995. Only 27 of the 2,897 companies were founded before 1950.

The MÜSİAD was organized in 41 major cities to oppose the state's continued favoritism toward a handful of business conglomerates, which are represented by a rival group, the Association of Turkish Indusrialists and Businessmen (TÜSİAD: Türk İşadamları ve Sanayiciler Derneği). To counter the uncompetitive environment created by state support of the TÜSİAD and big business in general, the MÜSİAD has advocated full liberalization and privatization of the Turkish economy. The MÜSİAD is not anti-capitalist but opposes "crony capitalism," that is, the close connections between political power centers and a limited number of oligopolist companies, political ties that make the Istanbul-based bourgeoisie "both state-protected and monopolistic" vis-à-vis the free market–oriented, Anatolian-based national bourgeoisie.[42]

The MÜSİAD's literature enthusiastically promotes the virtues of free market capitalism. The MÜSİAD has produced an Islamic economic manifesto that is derived from its booklet, Homo Islamicus.[43] The association extols the life of the Prophet Muhammed as an ideal guide for conducting one's own life. By invoking the example of the Prophet as a merchant, the MÜSİAD seeks to justify a free market system and to oppose the state's intrusive role in the economy. For example, the Konya-based Kombassan Corporation funded a MÜSİAD conference that helped to shape the Anatolian tigers' economic agenda in support of "free markets."[44] The MÜSİAD also opposes heavy taxes, the distributive role of the state, and trade unions (which it regards as un-Islamic). The MÜSİAD's economic model is likely to politicize ethnic, religious, and rural solidarity networks to provide economic security to those left outside the market. In effect, Islam is used as *social capital* to promote cooperation and solidarity on behalf of economic interests.[45]

To become a member of the MÜSİAD, a firm needs to have attained a reputation in business circles and society in general for honesty and probity. The association includes some of Turkey's fastest growing firms. One of its most important features is its development of an Islamic network of businesses. Regular Friday meetings are held to which the MÜSİAD typically invites a prominent Islamic writer or journalist to discuss social, economic, and political issues from an Islamic perspective. In addition, the association prepares research reports about Turkey's economic situation and organizes visits to foreign, generally Muslim, countries to study their economic potential.

The MÜSİAD's economic interests overlap with provincial/ideological ties to create a more effective and rooted associational life. For instance, the majority of MÜSİAD members in Konya are also members of diverse cultural associations.[46] The MÜSİAD derives its strength from the opportunities of the 1980 economic restructuring and its ability to use sociocultural networks for economic advancement. Religious networks help to create social synergy—the willingness of believers to act from their cultural ideas. MÜSİAD members thus are members of overlapping networks. Informal characteristics of these networks, which are based on interpersonal trust and are derived from Islamic identity, help to promote work ethics and new channels of communication for collaborating and sharing business information. Since one of the constituting norms of Turkish society is to "render one's service for the state and nation" (*devlete ve millete hizmet etmek*), self-promotion and self-interested activities are not necessarily welcomed. Self-serving business activity for the sake of becoming rich is questioned in traditional Turkish society. Thus, in order to become a respected businessman, one has to justify economic activity in terms of serving the "state and nation." Therefore, the conservative Muslim bourgeoisie try to meet societal expectations by stressing religious norms in their interaction with society at large. In other words, they present a religious identity to society and a nationalist identity to the state. As a result of new economic spaces, a new Anatolian business identity is developing. This new bourgeoisie has three major characteristics: they are religiously and socially conservative, economically liberal, and oriented toward private initiative; able to generate initial capital through family and religious networks and thus more prone to accumulate wealth; and very critical of state intervention in the economy. This causes them to support free market conditions, in contrast to the state, which supports the big secularist business oligarchs. The new Muslim economic actors also are shaping a new social and cultural landscape in Turkey through Islamic literature, television stations, newspapers, and an Islamic conception of leisure. Hence, as Islamic practices and norms become more public, they are transformed to meet modern expectations and conditions. Thus one can see the transformation of an "Islamic way of living and thinking" in Turkey.

Reconstruction of the Prophet's Merchant Ethics

The MÜSİAD represents the complex intersection of religion and economics among the new Anatolian bourgeoisie. This process could only have been consolidated with the help of Özal's economic liberalization. This policy also promoted the construction of an Islamic "Protestant ethic" by stressing puritanical, this-worldly values that seemed to anticipate rewards for a virtuous life in the hereafter as well. This new bourgeoisie, organized around either Nurcu or Nakşibendi groups, criticized "superstitious" beliefs, stressed a surprisingly rational understanding of faith, and defined Islam (in MÜSİAD publications) as the religion of progress.

The dynamic interaction between contemporary Islamic movements and market forces, however, indicates that Turkish modernization is not necessarily a carbon copy of Westernization. Whereas in the West, the embourgeoisement of religion led to the process of disenchantment, the Turkish case indicates that disenchantment and reenchantment can coexist.[47] For example, in the case of the MÜSİAD, religion has become intertwined with the market economy. This phenomenon illustrates the different form modernity is taking in Turkey. Civil society–based modernization from below, unlike the state-led modernization from above, has created a hybrid that combines local practices and networks with global and universal discourses of human rights. The utilization of religious practices and idioms to justify the market economy has become the major source for the inner secularization of Islam.

The main obstacle to the inner secularization of Islam, however, is state control over Islam. The existence of a "market" of religious ideas is a requirement for achieving a pluralistic democracy. Muslim merchants in the MÜSİAD compete to offer an economic basis for the sustenance of a moral community. They tend to see Islam as a pool of ideas and strategies that can be employed to justify social acts in the market environment. Thus religious enthusiasm, along with earning profits, are the main motivating forces behind the expanding Turkish market. The Nakşibendi and Nurcu communities emphasize the merchant ethics of the Prophet Muhammad and try to fuse these with the values of modern capitalism. For example, Mehmet Zahit Kotku, a leading Nakşibendi leader, argues that the search for profit in the service of the Muslim umma is on an equal level, in terms of religious practice, with praying and fasting.[48] The Islamic identity of the new bourgeoisie, which is rooted in the market and shaped by Islamic ethics, not only differentiates MÜSİAD members from the members of the TÜSİAD but also provides a powerful link between them and the members of larger segments of society who are their consumers.

Turkey had attempted to create a perceptible balance between state, community, and market forces through "Çankaya corporatism" (a state-guided attempt at corporatist control of society, named after the Çankaya district of Ankara, where the presidential palace is located), but this effort was very much weakened by the 1980 military coup. The Özal government, in contrast with the leaders of the military coup, recognized that private associations did not represent an obstacle to the state but rather an opportunity to expand legitimacy and to create dynamism within society. This dynamism came as a result of the expansion of Turkey's domestic and external markets. This process resulted in "Mecidiyeköy pluralism" (named for a business district of Istanbul where major corporations are located, including the headquarters of the MÜSİAD) replacing Çankaya corporatism. Mecidiyeköy pluralism genuinely promoted associational life and tenuously integrated the Islamic movements into the economy through the filters of the expanding market.

In addition to the MÜSİAD, several other associations and many charitable foundations were established. These charitable associations usually have a religious-social dimension that plays a key role by offering educational services, running printing houses, operating television and radio stations, and staffing health clinics. Thus a vibrant market freed from dependence on state subsidies and these associations have jointly carved out a larger space for voluntary activism and the externalization of Islamic identity. With independent access to market resources, these associations have gained greater autonomy. This economic independence has led to cultural independence, which has allowed these groups to offer diverse and original interpretations of Islam to the public.

The emergence of an independent Islamic bourgeoisie has threatened the Kemalist establishment. Since the 1980s, there has been an enormous accumulation of capital in major Anatolian towns.[49] This capital is invested in both local and world markets.[50] In contrast, the "Istanbul bourgeoisie" of the TÜSİAD has been reluctant to enter into open trade with the EU. Since 1995, TÜSİAD has been lobbying the state to introduce new customs policies to protect its members from the competitive global market and, most important, from the MÜSİAD entrepreneurs of Anatolia. The increasing tensions between the Istanbul and Anatolian bourgeoisie were a major factor in the political problems of the coalition government led by Erbakan's RP. For example, when Erbakan tried unsuccessfully to undermine the dominance of the Istanbul bourgeoisie by removing protectionism, certain tax exemptions, and incentives that had overall negative effects on the economy, the media controlled by the "Istanbul bourgeoisie" enthusiastically encouraged the military to overthrow his elected government. The TÜSİAD remained silent when the military issued a list of over one hundred "Islamic" corporations, including some of Turkey's leading exporters, that were to be put under surveillance and denied access to state sector contracts.[51] The Istanbul bourgeoisie similarly did not protest when the Constitutional Court shut down the RP or subsequently when the prosecutor demanded the closure of the MÜSİAD (April 1998), accusing its president of "inciting hatred" in his speeches.[52]

Entrepreneurship and Protoindividuality

The political culture of the 1980s was characterized by two contradictory processes: the struggle for recognition and the search for a new consensus. These two processes forced social groups to develop a shared code of conduct through political means. In other words, the separation of the economic domain from the dominance of the state has been the major source for the emergence of a protoindividual (see next paragraph) in Turkey. As a result of this economic confidence, Turkish society redefined politics as "deliberation" and used it to reorganize the state-society boundary. These economic processes helped to unpack the imagined homogenous "people" of Turkey, such as Kurds, Islamists, liberals, women, and Turks.

Turkey has experienced the growth of an entrepreneurial spirit that has had an important impact on Islamic identity. Risk taking, the emergence of group individuality, and joint venturism are features of this entrepreneurial spirit. Willingness to take risks is significant because it involves liberation from blind submission to a higher order. The spirit of risk taking brings to the Turkish identity debate an approximation (protoindividualism) of the idiomatic character of individualism as understood in the West. This is so because, as noted by Max Weber, the character of an entrepreneur virtually requires an elective affinity to risk taking. Because of the correspondence between these "leaps of faith" (that are necessary to both religion and risk taking) the synergy between the two is at the same time psychologically and socially satisfying.

Sufi groups and other solidarity associations have stabilized the uncertainty inherent in market situations by developing ethical and normative ties of membership that enable Muslim entrepreneurs to embrace the all-important virtue of trust in their business relations. These relations, in turn, further consolidate the religious groups and their role in society. This process promotes trade connections among the followers of religious groups and creates a set of business codes and ethics. Trust and the promise of future interactions in turn play a key role in the formation of prosperous trade networks. Those who are strangers in the market (such as the state bourgeoisie) are also strangers in a deeper cultural sense.

Joint ventures are the method by which two distinct groups or individuals become partners to achieve a desired end that is made more efficient or more profitable through their cooperation. In other words, without one of the parties, the desired end cannot be accomplished with a viable profit margin. Joint ventures can occur within the same group category (Sufi and Sufi) or with outsiders. Intragroup collaboration is guided by the defining characteristics of the group. However, what of intergroup ventures? In the United States, the possibility of corporations or individuals of diverse backgrounds joining together in a high-risk venture is not something remarkable, as a strong legal framework that protects the parties from risk and breach of contract has developed. In Turkey, such intergroup ventures can only rely on Islam in its horizontal character as providing a guiding framework and basis of trust for maintaining the venture's integrity and that of its partners. Market relations thus also demonstrate the need for ethical practices and bonds of trust that religion is well suited to provide.

Patterns of Consumption

A closer examination of Islamic groups indicates visible class demarcations. These lines are manifested through patterns of consumption. The followers of the İskenderpaşa Sufi order, for example, regularly meet to discuss social and religious issues in five-star hotels. They even have their own shopping malls and have developed haute bourgeoisie tastes. New members of the İskenderpaşa order are encouraged to internalize new sets of norms and roles. Through re-defining consumer patterns, these Islamists seek to differentiate themselves first from other Islamic groups and then from the Kemalist/secularist section of society. The İskenderpaşa order seeks a foretaste of heaven by validating a ma-terial paradise on earth. The asceticism of the Nakşibendis and Nurcus, coupled with their positive views of capitalist profit, have played a key role in the accu-mulation of capital and the economic development of Turkey. God is reinvented for the needs of the capitalist market. However, this stress on capitalist virtues inevitably undermines asceticism in the long run, as Weber demonstrates with respect to the Protestant ethic.

Consumption patterns in modern Turkey reify and articulate differences in identities. Muslim journals and television stations, through their ad campaigns, clearly demarcate the boundaries of consumption and class interests. Consump-tion patterns thus signify who Islamists are and to which social group they be-long. Consumption is not limited to the purchase of goods but also encompasses such activities as enrolling children in the private high schools run by the neo-Nurcu followers of Fethullah Gülen, watching the TGRT and Samanyolu televi-sion channels (both Islamic), and listening to the BURÇ and AKRA (both Islamic) radio stations. The Islamic movements have their own music companies, cafes, restaurants, and publishing houses. Thus a feature of modern Turkish Islamic identity formation is that vertical Islamic movements are bending under the stress of class distinctions and thus find themselves on a plain with horizontal Islam. Indeed, God has come down to earth, and Muslims are preoccupied with building his kingdom here.

The five-star Caprice Hotel is an example of how "Islamic holidays" have been invented in accordance with modern consumerism. It represents a mix-ture of Islam and capitalism. The luxury hotel is a site where modernity inter-mingles with Islam and molds the conduct and expectations of Muslims in accordance with the capitalist system. In order to capture the business of in-creasingly prosperous Muslims, this "Islamicized" hotel neither sells nor serves alcohol and maintains gender-segregated swimming pools. Its customs are those of the traditionally inclined Anatolian bourgeoisie, who support full economic liberalization against the "statist" Istanbul-based oligarchs. While more conser-vative Muslims have criticized the presentation of the Caprice Hotel as an "Is-lamic vacation site" and contend that it is evidence of the total dominance of neoliberal values over Islamic ones,[53] one may argue that this hotel represents the internal secularization of Islam, that is, making Islam into a commodity for the sake of market competition. This is not an act of "Islamic radicalism" but rather a reconstitution of Islam within modern conditions.

As Islamic groups move to differentiate themselves from others in terms of patterns of consumption, they do not enhance individualization but rather repersonalize social interactions. In contrast with the late Ottoman Empire, where the introduction of Western fashion and consumer products encouraged a growing sense of individualism, the present phenomenon of consumerism acts to cement communal solidarity and identity. Particular dress codes, restaurants, cafes, and home furnishings indicate group tastes and consumer patterns, and Islamists have adopted consumption patterns that can easily be distinguished in schools and on the streets. This creates a highly visible group culture. In this respect, the various forms of dress worn by Muslim women have become the distinct means to differentiate Islamist women both from one another and from secular women.

The Political Discourse of the Headscarf

Following the 1997 soft coup, the Kemalist military forcefully pushed for a ban on the wearing of headscarves in public institutions. This policy led to continuing large-scale protests and acts of defiance, with many police officers and midlevel state officials sabotaging the edicts of the military. The issue came to a head with the expulsion of the FP deputy Merve Kavakçı from Parliament and the stripping of her citizenship, as demanded by the generals. The great controversy this issue aroused in Turkish society demonstrated that individual rights and Islamic traditions continue to provide sources of fierce contestation that the state cannot control. The insertion of Islamic identities into controlled and predefined secular spheres will continue to generate debate over the state-society and public-private boundaries in Turkey. Far from "liberating" women from above, as claimed by the Kemalists, a generation of religious women once again is being disenfranchised and denied the right to an education and the ability to serve in political life by an allegedly "reforming" state.

In examining the symbolism of devout "modern" women who wear headscarves, it becomes clear that these Muslim women are using their bodies to inscribe on themselves a particular religious identity.[54] The decision to wear a form of headscarf represents women's attempts to negotiate and balance their own new roles as working women and mothers by resorting to the shelter of traditional symbols.[55] By "stepping backward," women in fact make a "leap" ahead to modernity.[56] Modern Islamic attire allows Muslim women to carve out new spaces for themselves between the private and public spheres. Cihan Aktaş, a leading Islamic woman writer, argues that by covering their hair Muslim women challenge the policies of the modernizing state and even some traditional norms of society that seek to keep women inside the household.[57] Scarves become an exit from the traditional restrictions on women in the public sphere and allow them to take part in modern society. Women increasingly are making public demands and organizing themselves with their own resources.

In a group discussion of a number of pro-Islamic women students at Bilkent University in Ankara, I realized that covering one's head, for these women, is an essential part of their identity and moral position in society.[58] It is also a way for them to gain access to political and social positions within religious society. They are critical of "state-feminism" for negating their womanhood for the sake of the adoption of a Western identity. They argue that this Western identity is

alien to their history and is associated with negative values, such as sexual pro-
miscuity and bodily exhibitionism, that they find personally offensive. The
Kemalist version of Turkish secularism constructed a binary opposition between
Muslim women as rural, traditional, and uneducated versus modern women as
educated, secular, and urban. This version regularly has refused to incorporate
a Muslim presence in its conception of modern Turkish identity. The Kemalist
elite fears that recognition of an Islamic presence in the public sphere would
mean the surrender of their privileged presentation of the secular as the universal and modern.

The presence of educated Muslims in the universities and in the market,
particularly the emergence of a new bourgeoisie in the public sphere, has undermined the Kemalist efforts to project Islam as opposed to modernity. However, one should not think that headscarves and uniform Islamic attire have
covered up ethnic and class boundaries. On the contrary, they create a new set
of criteria for the determination of status distinctions. Within the Islamic
women's movement, everyday markers of family and provincial backgrounds
have not disappeared; they simply are suspended for the time being. Lila Abu-
Lughod has indicated that in the case of Egypt "the new veil works to produce a
false sense of egalitarianism that distracts from the significant and ongoing
problems of class inequality."[59] Moreover, some Islamic feminists have begun
to question "Islamic male identity" vis-à-vis the politicized female identity and
dress code.[60]

Conclusion

As a result of economic liberalization, the state now exercises even less control
over society than before 1983. New groups and movements have arisen to contest the boundary between state and society. The exact constitution of this boundary has been the subject of a significant ongoing social debate in modern Turkey.
The increasing role of Islam in Turkey does not represent a "return to religion"
but another level of self-understanding: the repersonalization of relations with
a "new" articulation of community and identity. This understanding embodies
certain contradictions in that it promotes community and individualism at the
same time. Economic and social development has led to rapid urbanization and
the creation of vast squatter settlements that surround the major cities of the
country. For this new underclass of rural migrants, religious identity in the earlier forms of Sufi orders and rural-based hometown associations have been rep-
licated in their new urban neighborhoods, providing an invaluable source of
social support and psychic comfort in the face of the dislocation and alienation
of modern life at the urban margins.

Farther up on the socioeconomic scale, the capitalist market has integrated
the newly wealthy Muslim entrepreneurial class of traditional Anatolian background and is recasting their religious affiliations and beliefs. For this business
class, Islam becomes an ethic that complements such commercial virtues as
thrift, investment, and trust. This new Muslim business elite finds itself at odds

with the state bureaucracy and the large industrialists who benefit from the Kemalist state's patronage. The championing by this Muslim entrepreneurial class of free market enterprise also puts it at odds with the Islamic underclass made up of recent migrants to the city. The role of Islam as a source of identity and political and social mobilization embodies a number of contradictions that encourage both individualism and a lively reinterpretation of the faith with increased collective group solidarity. Thus market forces and economic development have played a major role in recasting state and society relations and the political role of Islam in contemporary Turkey.

5

The Role of Literacy
and the Media in the
Islamic Movement

We are always changing and becoming. . . . But this is to state
another basic condition of making sense of ourselves, that we grasp
our life in a narrative. . . . In order to have a sense of who we are, we
have to have a notion of how we have become, and of where we are
going.

Charles Taylor, *Sources of the Self*

The momentous transformation of primordial religious identity into
a modern political identity in Turkey has been carried out via a
revolution in mass printing and education and the creation of a new
genre of Muslim intellectuals.[1] This transformation, which promises
paradoxically a renaissance of Turkish Islamic thought and culture
and its internal secularization and pluralization, is the most profound phenomenon on the horizon, transcending any particular
individual or movement. The locus for this, as well as much else, in
terms of Turkish Islamic sociopolitical movements, has been the
Nakşibendi order. It served as the conduit of change and allowed
the transformation of orally based *tekkes* (Sufi lodges) into textual
communities, a change made possible by the revolution in media
technology and mediated by a new autonomous class of Muslim
intellectuals. This process, in turn, has endowed the current generation of Turkish Muslims with a sense of agency, encouraging them
to participate in politics so that they may better shape the society
they live in.

    Although the media/technological revolution is tied to sociocul-
tural transformations that compelled Sufi lodges to adapt modern
means of communication, these developments did not eliminate the
traditional Sufi lodges entirely; these traditional networks continue

to coexist with modern means of communication. In constituting the community and constructing an Islamic identity, the Nakşibendi shifted their formative ground from the tekke to printed texts, and this has proven to be more effective in promoting the internalization of their identity.[2] Even such traditional Sufi orders as the Nakşibendi of İskenderpaşa and Erenköy, both located in Istanbul, publish periodicals to propagate their messages and influence. Esad Coşan, the sheik of the İskenderpaşa community—the most prominent Nakşibendi order in Turkey—justified his printing and publications activities thus:

> Why am I involved in a magazine? Because this is the most crucial service! In my mosque, when I deliver a sermon, I have about two or three thousand people there. This is not enough! It is not sufficient. The press is important. . . . We cannot divorce ourselves from daily activities and events. Why do we have a weekly magazine? To get involved in current debate and activities.[3]

Coşan considered the essential work of the press to be "a form of *jihad*,"[4] or a struggle to raise the political consciousness of Muslims in order to create a harmonious and powerful Turkey.

New Islamic circles, such as the Nurcus and the İskenderpaşa Nakşibendi order, are more socially dynamic than the traditional Sufi orders and are formed around magazines and radio stations rather than a tekke. The demonstrated effectiveness of this medium resulted in major Nakşibendi orders adopting the media as a necessary means for ensuring their survivability and as a way of consolidating modern Sufi identity. Coşan directs his followers to support the media activities of the order, justifying his call in the following way.

> Almost everything is organized and shaped by the press and publication. The most important weapon is the press. . . . It is the most potent force; and an effective medium to get people conscious. You must conquer the press either by working for it or you should own it.[5]

After the 1980 military coup, a powerful mainstream Islamic media was created, and it has played a key role in producing and disseminating new doctrines and critiques of state and society. In addition to print media, the religious groups also are involved in sophisticated and effective broadcasting. By 1994, there were 525 privately owned radio and television stations in Turkey; out of this total number, Islamic groups owned 19 television stations and 45 radio stations.[6] Nakşibendi and Nurcu radio stations (AKRA, BURÇ, and Moral FM) have been among the most popular ones in Istanbul. Islamic radio stations also play an important role in the construction and articulation of a collective Islamic consciousness. The magazines and radios link followers by developing a common cognitive matrix for interpreting events. Printing and mass education lead to novel ways of understanding the Qur'an and the self. The new Islamic political identity is formed within the matrix of communications and education revolutions. Technological innovations in communication and the spread of education have had several important social consequences. (1) They have created a more skeptical and relativistic understanding of the absolute and have popularized the perpetual epistemological question: How do we know that God exists? (2) They have undermined the authority of the traditional ulema and facilitated the emergence of new urban Islamic intellectuals who operate under the guise of popular media pundits. (3) They have led to the disintegration of large Islamic communities in favor of emerging smaller publication-based groups. These developments have had unexpected long-term social consequences. For instance, the processes of producing and disseminating knowledge, once firmly based in tradition, have been exhaustively secularized. In addition, the discursive fragmentation that results from the spread and economization of print technology has increased opportunities for marginal voices to contest a totalistic and uniform interpretation of Islam and also challenged the state's secular dogmas. This in turn has facilitated the evolution of the Turkish-Islamic synthesis.

Print as the Habitat for Identity Construction

Some scholars have examined the social and political impact of printing on Muslim societies. However, they have not examined the role of literacy and printing from the perspective of articulating and objectifying difference and promoting what Robert Hefner aptly calls "civic pluralism."[7] I argue that print culture frees creative forces by offering opportunity spaces for groups and individuals to challenge prevailing practices and to establish new roles and relationships. In the case of Turkey, the government expanded its power over education and printing to create a new secular and national public culture.[8] The regulation of universal education and print were two of the "most powerful and effective tools of the program of secular reforms."[9] Since the 1970s, the Islamic groups have been using the same tools to challenge the hegemonic state ideology and "reinvent local and oral Islam in Turkish urban life."[10] The spread of education and mass communication prepared the ground for the transformation of political Islam. The Islamic component of identity in the Turkish Republic has taken on a new saliency. Islamic and ethnic groups (Alevis, Albanians, Caucasians, Bosnians, and Kurds) increasingly have made use of the media to dissolve centralized hegemonic voices emanating from both the state and society. Literacy and printing opportunities bring diverse Muslim groups together as part of an overarching Islamic identity and discourse that, paradoxically, also promotes further internal differentiation and pluralism among Islamic groups. The current vibrancy of Islamic political identity and activism would be neither very appealing nor widespread in the absence of modern print and communications technology. The written word and the press have allowed for the emergence of a new Islamic intelligentsia capable of challenging the authority of the ulema and of traditional Sufi groups.

Modern communications are not based on face-to-face dialogue or confined to a sacred zone (mosques or Sufi lodge) but are carried out by a variety of means, from newspapers and radios to television and other visual symbolic images that condense time and space. Condensing time and space brings the other into the home, the office, the shopping malls. And while the other can now be said to be physically very near, psychologically it remains remote, thus sharpening political consciousness. This sharpened political consciousness distinguishes between the Muslim "self" and the perceived other. Confronted with this new sociopolitical environment, the newly defined Muslim identity struggles to exist and adapt to modern conditions. Moreover, by creating common images, the print media help to mold images and values and shape Muslim actions. The configuration of print, intellectuals, and education has several social impacts on Muslim societies, including the shift of epistemology and authority and the pluralization of Islamic voices.

Muslims, like other religious peoples, move between their particular and universal worldviews, between a sense of loyalty and skepticism toward tradition and faith. Brinkley Messick illustrates this tension: "a central problem in Muslim thought concerns the difficult transition from the unity and authenticity of the text of God to the multiplicity and inherently disputed quality of the texts of men."[11] In other words, "divinely constituted truth and humanly constituted versions of that truth" have been at the heart of Islamic hermeneutics for centuries.[12] As the printed text has become generally accessible to the rank and file of Muslims through universal education and cheaper technology, the debate over interpretation, authority, and authenticity has sharpened. The distance between divine injunction and human interpretation renders a critical space to free Islam from ossified tradition. The opening up of discursive spaces makes loyalty to a single "center of truth inconceivable."[13]

Popular Islamic education takes place not inside the mosque, with the ulema serving as educators, but rather in printed pages and on television screens, with urban intellectuals serving as the main conduits of interpretation and authority. With the help of the media and publishing outlets, contemporary Islamic groups, rather than the Kemalist elite, shape norms of everyday life and define mainstream culture. In a way, mainstream Turkish culture simultaneously has been "communalized" and personalized by these Islamic groups.[14] This communalization of mainstream culture has a democratizing impact on the production of Islamic knowledge by freeing Islam from the control of the state-centric ulema. The production of Islamic knowledge is democratized and diversified through competing interpretations. Dissemination of new interpretations through printed-works promotes the formation of new groups, for example, the Nurcus (see chapter 7). Interaction and print-based discourses can increase both solidarity and contestation and gradually create new boundary formations.

Muslim media channels also politicize Islamic consciousness by developing connections between social events and Islamic principles. This offers an alternative source for constructing new meanings. For example, a "born again" Nakşibendi said:

> My sense of self has altered as a result of reading Islamic magazines about the genocide of Bosnians in which I found a similar voice of a painful man. You don't feel alone anymore. You become a part of a larger collectivity. This gives me a sense of security and consolidates

my dignity. I subscribed to the magazine so as to discipline my thought. It provides an alternative perspective to understand the events.[15]

One no longer needs to go to a mosque to develop one's spiritual and communal dimension. New Islamic urban intellectuals construct their own version of Islam and transmit it to the masses with new concepts and genres of literature. These literary public spaces are sites in which diverse role models are explored, and are used as a vehicle through which new Islamic consciousness and practices are carried to the margins of Turkish society.[16] For instance, the literature of Islamic novels has played a key role in the articulation and diffusion of shared frames of reference. Rasim Özdenören, a leading contemporary writer, defines "Islamic literature" as "literature, regardless of its topic, expressing the Islamic consciousness of the author who approaches his subject with Islamic spectacles."[17] Through these novels the writers have sought to address the inner dimension of the spiritual self. The most influential novel is Hekimoğlu İsmail's *Minyeli Abdullah*. The power of this novel lies in its rich folkloric symbolism and ability to speak to the reader's sense of alienation and uncertainty in the modern world. A central theme of these novels is usually the fight against injustice and corruption, which is justified by appeals to religious morality.

Epistemology and Authority

Print culture, along with universal education, has helped to undermine the vertical relationship between the master and the disciple in the construction and dissemination of knowledge, replacing it with horizontally diffused and objectified Islamic knowledge.[18] Moreover, within this modern educational system students learn to validate knowledge with proof and to become skeptical about received wisdom. In the Muslim context, this created a crisis among the ulema, who were not prepared to offer an explanation for doctrinal faith.

Furthermore, the confusion that results from this rapid circulation of ideas undermines "old forms of solidarity and creates exclusion, [and consequently] an immense need for identity is being expressed through the revival of religion, of charismatic father-figures, and 'populist' politicians who promise tangible identifications and warm organic relations."[19] This "revival of religion," however, is not a return to traditional practices and charismatic father figures but rather a construction of new practices and the objectification of previous Islamic ones. The expansion of print Islam may be seen as a continuous struggle to eliminate folk/mystical Islam in favor of a more rational, textual urban Islam. Jack Goody argues that

> the fact [is] that writing establishes a different kind of relationship between the word and its referent, a relationship that is more general and more abstract, and less closely connected with particularities of person, place and time, than obtain in oral communication.[20]

Print plays a rationalizing role both in the production and transmission of knowledge and also in thinking.

Traditional education in Muslim societies was face-to-face and informal and stressed the transmission of knowledge from master to student.[21] Even written commentaries were mediated through the master to his students. One of the impacts of print technology on Islam in modern Turkey has been the increasing accessibility of Islamic knowledge and the theoretical debates that have surrounded it. In the case of the Nur movement, one witnesses a deep vernacularization of religious debates as urban Islamic intellectuals have displaced the traditional ulema. Journals and books are not only repositories of ideas but also discursive opportunity spaces for the definition of Islamic issues and the offering of interpretative solutions to social problems. Print plays a functional role in storing, transmitting, and generating thought. Moreover, journals set the coordinates of identity groups in Turkey.

The printed word, combined with a free political environment and private economic resources, has impacted societal formation in two crucial ways. First, easy access to knowledge and the dissemination of ideas fractures the structures of authority and creates a more widespread understanding of the common idiom of politics. The printed word opened new possibilities for acquiring knowledge and transmitting it. This in turn created a new form of political and moral discourse. The printed word, unlike oral communication, has a sense of permanence and timelessness about it. Muslim intellectuals can preserve ideas and knowledge and disseminate them across political boundaries and through authoritarian information blockades with the means of modern communication.

Print has challenged both the authority of the traditional ulema and modern postcolonial Muslim social and political elites. It has provided a means and space for the emergence of a new urban intellectual who in the guise of a journalist is able to reach a vast audience across the social and ideological spectrum. In a way, printing and literacy have made the written word a source of authority, usurping what was the traditional domain of the ulema. A university degree became a requirement for intellectual recognition. The authority to produce knowledge, so important in modern states, has shifted in Turkey from the ulema-based imitative/oral tradition to an urban intellectual/print-based one.

Thus printing promotes the necessary ground for the formation of individuality. This perception of originality and independence allowed Islamic intellectuals to create a discursive space outside the hegemony of both the state and the traditional hierarchy of Islam. Turkish Islamic intellectuals are situated outside the religious establishment, and they have marked a new beginning in this secular context by establishing a more open and critical discourse with respect to the interpretation of the Qur'an. Their goal has not been to establish an Islamic political regime but to raise Islamic cultural and political consciousness. However, this activity of constructing an Islamic cultural and social consciousness leads to a new and more complex image of Islam that increasingly is taking on a political and civilizational dimension.

Print and mass media communications technology have also induced Islamic intellectuals to expound new forms of discursive knowledge that are more abstract, reflective, and universal in content. In other words, the production of knowledge is freed from its traditional oral-based accounts of proper Islamic practice and doctrine dating to the time of the Prophet. Therefore, newspapers, magazines, television stations, and radios are a means to transmit not only decontextualized Islamic viewpoints but also discursive spaces for critical thinking and dialogue. To manipulate Islamic meanings of social and political practices in a communication-based modern society, one needs an "elaborate code" of Islam, that is, a code in which "the message is contained in the code and not in the context."[22] The current articulation and dissemination of Islamic commentary is context-free in terms of the traditional narrative. The understanding of these context-free Islamic commentaries becomes feasible as a result of mass education. The new sacred places of reviving Islamic consciousness are Islamic literary circles and magazines. The role and impact of new urban Islamic intellectuals thus is tied closely to print and universal mass education.

Civic Pluralism, Difference, and Modernity

The debate over Islam's role in society in the earlier years of the Republic was pushed to the margins, and it gradually became an issue to mull over for those who were excluded from the center. During the 1990s, these marginal voices moved to the center and have become an integral part of the national debate over identity through the mass circulation of Islamic magazines. In the 1970s and 1980s, however, these magazines remained marginal vis-à-vis the dominant secular and nationalistic public culture. As statist ideology fractured, these marginal voices gradually moved to the center.

These discursive spaces have three main characteristics. First, they remain fragmented over the basic issues of society, and these amorphous spaces bring writers and readers together in public, without bracketing their identities and suppressing their particular voices, to create issue-based consensus and common ground. Second, these spaces are zones of struggle, resistance, and radical imagination. There always has been a struggle in Islamic journals to express their respective differences from each other. Third, the plurality of the Islamic media and journals mirrors the diverse social structures of Islamic groups.

The diversity of periodicals allows one to conclude that three broad trends exist in the Islamic publishing arena. These trends are: (1) socially oriented Islam, which embraces the Sufi orders and their publications (*İslam, Altınoluk, İlim ve Sanat, Kadın ve Aile, Semerkant*) and the Nurcu publications (*Sur, Yeni Ümit, Köprü, Karakalem, Nubihar, Yeni Dergi, Sızıntı, Zafer*); (2) intellectually oriented Islamic publications, which incorporate Western-influenced Islamic intellectuals (*Tezkire*,[23] *Dergah, Değişim Yarın, Yeni Zemin*,[24] *İzlenim*,[25] *Bilgi ve Hikmet, Sözleşme, Bilgive Düşünce*); (3) politically oriented Islamic publications that were connected to Islamic political parties and to other smaller factions within larger conservative parties (*Cuma, Nehir, Yörünge, Yeni Şafak* [AKP], *Milli Gazete*); and (4) radical Islamist publications that advocate struggle outside the legal means (*Haksöz, İktibas, Tevhid*). The radical Islamic journals and writers defend violent resistance to the secular system in Turkey. These journals become spaces of dissemination of radical ideas and places of recruitment of revolutionary and romantic believers in the establishment of an Islamic state to engineer an Islamic society by force. Politics, for the radical Islamists of Turkey, is about finding and fighting against the enemies of Islam. Their journals are sites of Islamic fascist ideas and thick anti-Semitism. The competition among these publications is important in terms of articulating differences in the framing of diverse social and political issues through the symbolic language of Islam. In airing differences through the media, one sees the competing versions of society and politics within the Islamic movement. Therefore, mass communication plays an emancipatory role in terms of bringing marginal voices into the public sphere. Yet the differences among Islamic groups increasingly have been articulated in the media. This has led some Islamicly oriented people to read only the books of a specific publishing house. Certain publishers try to avoid being associated with a particular interpretation and aim to create, through diverse Islamic publications, a reading public that identifies with general Islamic consciousness rather than specific sects.

These journals have challenged the state's understanding and presentation of Islam and Islamic institutions as instruments for fostering national unity. For example, *Yeni Zemin* was very critical of the state's attempts to use Islam as a common bond to neutralize Kurdish grievances. In effect, Islamic publications provided spaces that promoted the evolution of a more pluralist understanding of Islam. Print-Islam, then, facilitated a decentering of hegemonic Islamic voices and prevented any group from dominating the presentation of Islam as a monolithic civilization and religion. Therefore, the proliferation of Islamic journals, magazines, and radio and television stations opened new spaces of imagination, and helped to foster new discourses.

In order to understand the organic ties between the media and Sufi orders on the one hand and modern intellectuals and the media on the other, one needs to grasp the pluralizing implications of modernity. Modernity has led to differentiation and individualism more than it has led to homogenization largely because of the dissolving effects of mass communication and a "consumer culture that celebrates diversity, so that fashion and taste in religion become one more 'good' to be consumed."[26] This dissemination and incorporation of diverse and, in some cases, historically separate cultures creates a debate over authenticity and paradoxically generates movements against extreme syncretization. In modern Turkey, the syncretization of Islamic political identity means the fusion of liberalism, nationalism, democracy, and religious beliefs all together. This syncretization assists the integration of the marginal voices at the periphery into the national discourse. Indeed, the peripheral idiom of the Nurcu movement in the 1950s had become the central voice of the Islamic identity debate in the 1990s as a result the syncretizing ability of a series of magazines, newspapers, and radio stations to bring contradictory forces of religion, democracy, and the market together.

The Commodification of Islamic Knowledge

In a free market economy, knowledge becomes a commodity produced for exchange. Muslims, too, are consumers of Islamic ideas. Treating Islamic knowledge as a commodity demystifies religious knowledge, and it becomes another commodity that competes with other forms of circulating knowledge. Commodifying religious knowledge has a profound social and political impact on society. Its value becomes evaluated in relation to other forms of knowledge and beliefs. Since 1983, Turkish Muslim groups have dominated the publishing market in terms of the number of books printed. The expansion of education and the emergence of a new group of intellectuals has led to a flowering of the Islamic printing industry. Publishing houses that gained prominence and enjoyed a leading position in the publishing market as a whole include *Pınar, İnsan, Yöneliş , Beyan, Dergah, Nehir, Ağaç, Vadi,* and *İz.* Although there has been no major increase in overall book publication since 1985, most of the new books being printed are about either Islamic religious issues or Islamic history. Since the 1990s, these publishing houses have focused on Islamic modernity, a critique of orientalism, and new alternative methodologies of the humanities and social sciences.

The publishing houses earned enough money to reinvest funds in the business of writing and translation. The wealth generated by this activity provided the financial basis for the emergence of an autonomous class of Muslim intellectuals who thus were able to write on Islamic and social issues outside of state or non-Islamic corporate control. One can consider the latest Islamic intellectuals "Islamic entrepreneurs" who articulate the nature and role of Islamic identity in relation to certain political and economic goals. For example, Ali Bulaç, Sezai Karakoç, and Abdurrahman Dilipak have managed to earn their livelihood solely from their publishing royalties, an independent source of income that fosters a degree of intellectual freedom.

Islamic intellectuals have responded to this new opportunity by developing arguments for freedom of speech, press, and conscience and the right of association because of the desire to gain such freedoms for themselves. Political events have forced Islamic groups to take positions on issues, and this has led either to the building of an issue-based coalition or to further fragmentation. The Gulf War sharpened the differences within the Islamic media, reflecting the lack of consensus on the merits of the conflict in the wider Islamic world, but the war in Bosnia unified them and promoted a broader Islamic solidarity and political consciousness. For example, during the Gulf crisis, the Islamic media and intellectuals were divided into two groups, so the understanding of the Gulf War was constructed within the configuration of domestic politics, social pressures, and historical experiences. The debate demonstrated that Islamic intellectuals and groups referring to the same texts and faith can reach radically different conclusions concerning a particular issue. Although appeals to an "Islamic understanding and doctrines" are significant, class, ideological, personal, and hermeneutical factors often lead to divergent conclusions not only among Islamic groups but also within each one.

The commercialization of Islamic knowledge through the media leads to competition and a search for new compelling and competitive voices. This competition facilitates the rationalization of Islamic arguments. The major consequence of this commodification of Islamic knowledge has been the diversification and secularization of Islamic knowledge. The new Islamic media is connected to the emergence of a new Islamic-oriented bourgeoisie.

Vanguard of the Islamic Movement: Evolution of an Islamic Intellectual Class

Since political and religious knowledge is embedded in interactive social relations, its production and control is the key to the intellectuals' self-understanding. Because Islamic writings present many contradictory views on basic social and political issues, one may raise the vital question of whether there is an Islamic discourse. Such contradictory positions often are reflected by the same thinkers at various stages of their thinking and reveal that "Islamic thought" can encompass a broad range of conflicting views and ideologies. I argue that what makes a thinker or school of thought "Islamic" is simply the self-awareness of a thinker as such and his or her claim to refer to some Islamic body of doctrine or text in formulating at least a part of his or her thought.

The Islamic intellectuals of the second generation who reconstructed Islam as an integral component of Turkish identity (1950–1970s) and those who treated it as an identity and a cognitive map (1970–1990s) share several characteristics. First, they were not trained formally in the manner of the ulema in the traditional Islamic sciences (with the notable exception of Ali Bulaç). Second, they all were shaped by modern urban issues and educated in modern universities where Kemalism dominated. Third, they do not write strictly about religion or religious issues but rather address contemporary political issues through Islamic concepts; their writings Islamicize political issues; and they either speak about Islamic "civilization" or "Islamic political consciousness" but seldom about ritual and doctrine. Fourth, they are critical of the traditional ulema and feel that they lack the critical intellectual skills to tackle contemporary social and economic problems.

The term "modern Islamic intellectual" is commonly used in Turkish to indicate those who are "modern" in dealing with contemporary issues. They are "Islamic" because they seek to examine contemporary issues from an Islamic viewpoint; and they are "intellectuals" because, like secular intellectuals, they also are inspired by the critical thought of the West and Islam to critique the established political and social order. Islamic intellectuals act like cultural entrepreneurs in the construction and externalization of an Islamic political consciousness in Turkish society. One of the major sources of current Islamic political movements is the empowering impact of technology, market forces, and increasing higher education. The self-conscious attempt at becoming "contemporary" has created a new intellectual profile within Islamic movements. This genre of intellectuals reimagines Islam either within the context of modernity or in relation to modernity to offer a broad political language of Islam. This positioning within or in relation to modernity has conditioned Islamic understanding of Islam. As an end product, these intellectuals have managed to mold the content of Islam with contemporary social and political issues rather than strictly traditional understandings of religious norms. They have managed to hijack the spiritual aspect of religion and turn Islam into a rationally interconnected system that can only be experienced if Islamic identity is diffused throughout society. Islam, for them, is not only a religion with a rich spiritual depository but also an ideological partner for a modern Turkish identity.

The modern Islamic intellectual tends to believe that by transforming the mind or the consciousness of the populace one can transform society. This is in contrast to the understanding of the Ottoman Tanzimat-era intellectuals, who sought to transform society by reforming the administrative system.[27] To carry out these reforms, the tacit acceptance of public opinion was essential. Islamic intellectuals also see this public opinion as being vital for the public production of Islamic idioms and symbols. However, their version of Islam is colored by the Ottoman/Turkish historical legacy.

The difference between Islamic and secular intellectuals is also manifested in their readership. The main difference between Islamic and secular readers is that the former behave as agents of a faith, whereas the latter behave as a reader with reservations. Moreover, among the Islamic readers, the author's position on contemporary issues is more important than his or her ideas. Islamic intellectuals are expected to participate in religious rituals and support actions that are motivated by the Islamic faith. This has led some writers even to rationalize the actions of a Sunni mob that burned 11 prominent Alevi intellectuals in a fire in the city of Sivas in central Anatolia in July 1993.[28]

The First-Generation Islamic Intellectuals

As part of the secular campaign of the Republic in the 1920s and 1930s, virtually all manifestations of organized Islamic activity were banned and forced underground. This policy, in turn, caused Muslim households to become surreptitious bastions for preserving the faith. It was in this period that the Nakş ibendi orders organized their underground networks, which eventually would become a fulcrum for the formation of a new Islamic intellectual class. Their primary task was not the political revival of Islam but rather the preservation of Muslim practices within the household. These networks were successful in "preserving" Islamic knowledge but intellectually unable to develop a new Islamically shaped cognitive map to conceptualize the issues of identity and ethics in everyday life. Only with the emergence of a new genre of intellectuals, who modified Islamic concepts in accordance with the modern quest for identity and ethics among the youth, did Islamic knowledge and practices move from the private to the public sphere. Despite the updating and the utilization of the new opportunity spaces in media, one quickly perceives an enduring pattern of traditional Muslim attitudes and frames in the writings of this generation of Islamic intellectuals because their personalities were shaped by the Nakşibendi orders. In some respects, then, Nakşibendi orders became a "womb" for the formation of a new intellectual class in Turkey.[29] Since the Turkish community was organized by means of religious rituals, and everyday life was interpreted in the light of Islamic concepts, this genre of intellectuals did not confront major problems in communicating their Islamic ideas through the medium of poetry and novels. In fact, this group of poets and novelists became popular among ordinary people because they were intellectually connected with Turkish-Islamic tradition and history. In addition, this group of poets and novelist tried to maintain collective memory as a necessary base for identity and to create a moral language for everyday life by maintaining close ties with the Nakşibendi order.

The Islamic intellectuals, by using poetry, plays, and novels, managed to transcend the narrow ideologization of Islam. Thus, with the print culture as an opportunity space, these Muslim intellectuals managed to cultivate human emotions of love, fear, struggle, and hope. These books and poems offered an alternative site for the imagination of a more humane society. Political oppression forced Islamic thinkers to stress the inner spiritual aspects of the faith, the importance of individual moral consciousness, and a transformation that would reform society from the bottom up. For years, however, Islamic thought was confined to the pages of literary and cultural periodicals. Only in the 1950s did various Muslim intellectual groups seek to organize around magazines and newspapers, which became centers for examining domestic and international events from an Islamic perspective. These efforts represented the first step toward developing an Islamic perspective in the media since the anti-Islamic policies of the Kemalist regime in the 1930s. Such journals played a key role in the preservation and articulation of Islamic identity with an intellectual dimension. With the help of these new opportunity spaces, Islamic intellectuals tried to demonstrate that Islam was not the religion of the "backward periphery" incapable of revitalization, as the Kemalists claimed, but rather a dynamic force and source for inspiration.

The main thesis of these literary magazines was that Islam has its own "civilization"; for Muslims and for Turkey to prosper, they must be rooted in a sense of authenticity. Necip Fazıl (1904–1983),[30] Nurettin Topçu (1909–1975),[31] and Sezai Karakoç (1932–)[32] may be considered the three pillars of this civilizational intellectual movement. They all take the historical Ottoman period as a conceptual reference for examining social and political issues. Thus they did not treat Islam strictly as a religion but rather as a civilization with its own identity and code of ethics. By civilization they meant that the principles, ideals, and precepts of Islam are abridgements of a lived experience with their histories and particular geography. For example, they reinvented the Ottoman past as being the essence of Islamic civilization, according to their definition. This historical consciousness induced the first generation of Islamic intellectuals to embrace statist views, because Ottoman history was written as the story of the state rather than of the society. This new Muslim intellectual elite created a new language that merged Islamic esoteric traditions of inner dimensionality with the outward modern idiom of individuality. In other words, their conceptions of society and self have at the same time modern and traditional imprints. This new phenomenon of a Turkish urban Islamic intelligentsia evoking communal idioms with a decidedly modern twist to address social, political, and cultural concerns of Turkish society demonstrates the likely course to be taken by modern Islamic revivalist thinkers in general around the globe.

One of the major implications of this historicization (Ottomanization) of Islam has been the nationalization of Islam and the emergence of Turkish Islam as the basis for right-wing groups that sought to revive the suppressed collective memory of the Ottoman-Islamic past and fill the existing ethical void in society. They reimagined their own tradition by adopting and modifying some Kemalist terms and concepts to modern discourses of nationalism. Therefore, the first generation Turkish Muslim intellectuals consciously promoted an Islamic discourse that incorporated and domesticated the Turkish nationalism of the Republican intelligentsia into its own project of synthesizing the Ottoman-Islamic past with the modern Turkish present. These intellectuals did not create a separate and autonomous communal religious identity but rather reproduced an ethnoreligious Turkish Islamic identity.

Nurettin Topçu, the founder of *Hareket Dergisi* (1939–1974), who was heavily influenced by the French philosopher Maurice Blondel and by the Nakşibendi sheik Abdülaziz Bekkine, sought to construct Turkish-Islamic nationalism.[33] Because it utilized new opportunity spaces in media and the expanding educational system in Turkey, Topçu's magazine became the center of a new Islamic and Anatolian Turkish identity movement. Topçu defended the Nakşibendi conception of the self and community by utilizing the ideas of French philosophers such as Blondel and Henri Bergson. Topçu's understanding of religion informed his ideas of self, community, and nationalism.[34] Religion, for Topçu, is a faith in God that is formed within the inner self, a psychological experience and realization of God within oneself. This faith is manifested and articulated in human conduct as ethics. Thus, religious ideas and experience form ethics, and this ethics, in turn, informs social order in community. He treats Islam as a religion of inner self and criticizes its politicization by religious groups or utilization by the state. However, Topçu supports the role of religious scholars in the formation of public policy and believes that religion must stay outside and above state policy. His main concern is the inner mobilization of the Anatolian population through "building their core center as spirituality" to overcome alienation created by the Kemalist form of top-down modernization. In short, Islam, for Topçu, is first a source of ethics, this ethics is the source of identity, and this identity forms its own authentic civilization: social institutions and practices.

Topçu offered the first comprehensive critique of positivism and the dominant form of structuralist/functionalist explanations that denied any role for human agency in the constitution of society and social events. Topçu, unlike

Necip Fazıl, was not a populist but rather a well-grounded Islamic intellectual who sought to identify inner religious experience as a way of developing personality. The goal was to invite all the faithful to form themselves by cultivating the inner self so as to overcome the fragmentation of modern society. Topçu's main concern is human dignity and its preservation against manmade ideologies and systems. Because of his concern for human dignity, he stressed the constitutive role of ethics in forming an Islamic identity. Identity, for Topçu, is a concrete manifestation of religiously informed ethics. Thus, due to his stress on ethics and human dignity, Topçu's conception of nationalism is contained within an Islamic conception of community.[35] He always rejected ethnic- or race-based nationalism and defended the more inclusive religious-cultural nationalism in Turkey. In his writings, he introduced two forms of nationalisms: Gökalp-led ethnic-linguistic versus religious-cultural nationalisms. The first form of ethnic nationalism, for Topçu, was introduced by an elite group of Masons from the Balkans and was based on positivist social engineering, that is, the disestablishment of the Ottoman ethos of community, and the revival of utopic Central Asian roots. The second form of religious-cultural nationalism (solidarity) was rooted in the Turkish experience in Anatolia and articulated itself with the Ottoman state. In a way, Islamic solidarity is the fundamental constitutive essence of this Anatolian-Turkish nationalism and is embedded in the everyday life of Anatolia. Thus Topçu's conception of Turkish nationalism is an outcome of Anatolian Turkish-Islamic synthesis. Moreover, Topçu, unlike Gökalp, does not see civilization as separate from culture. He treats civilization as the technical and institutional achievements of a society that is formed by its own culture. He rejects the Kemalist project of Westernization, believing that it creates a "split society and personality" by failing to offer a relevant code of ethics.

The journals *Ağaç* (1936) and *Büyük Doğu* (1943), which were edited by Necip Fazıl, played a primary role in the politization of Islamic identity.[36] In the 1940s and 1950s, he was the first Turkish Muslim intellectual to frame Islam as a holistic and totalist ideology, known as *Büyük Doğu* (Great Orient). The process of ideologization of Islam was carried out in "opposition" to the Kemalist project of Westernization. With his books, Necip Fazıl elucidated the search for a deeper self and an Islamic cognitive map of meaning and action for himself and his society.[37] He dealt with the lack of shared primordial language and emotions that led to the deep existential pain of his generation. This emptiness stems from the lack of a moral and symbolic repertoire to organize and regulate everyday life. Necip Fazıl's nationalism was informed by his Islamism and sought to create shared ethnoreligious symbols, heroes, and emotions.

The third major Islamic intellectual of this period, who has been largely overlooked in scholarly studies, is Sezai Karakoç, the founder of the Resurrection (*Diriliş*) movement in Turkey. He was part of the inner circle of Necip Fazıl and a regular contributor to *Büyük Doğu*. He argued that the source of modern angst afflicting many individuals was the spiritual and civilizational crisis that had destroyed the bridge between individuals and their inner spiritual and cultural consciousness connected to the Ottoman-Islamic past and their contemporary outer manifestations of "self" as citizens of a modernizing secular republic. In an attempt at mediating a solution to this crisis of modernity, Karakoç was involved in widespread printing activity to disseminate his ideas. He aimed at the resurrection of a new consciousness (*diriliş nesli*) to revive and rearticulate the memory of Ottoman civilization and identity. He focused on the inner resurrection of the self as the necessary condition for the resurrection of the Muslim community and this in turn he hoped would lead to the resurrection of the whole of humanity. He proposed the concept of "Resurrection" as an alternative model of change to revolution and evolution by identifying the inner self as the engine of social change. Thus this change strives toward unity from within and moving outward from a center that Muslims themselves achieved. This resurrected self, for Karakoç, must achieve a systematic unity of life and society by elevating and taming rather than developing or growing. The magazine *Diriliş* emphasized that Islam as a faith and civilization was well suited, after being appropriately reinterpreted, for addressing many of the ills of modernity.[38]

Literary magazines provided a discursive space to express an aesthetic understanding of Turkish Islam. More important, however, the authors camouflaged their messages in literary form to avoid charges by the state that the authors were subversives. Periodicals such as *Sebilürreşad*,[39] *Büyük Doğu*, *Serdengeçti*,[40] *İslam*,[41] and *Hareket*[42] provided an intellectual womb for the development of the latest generation of Muslim intellectuals, who manifest the bicultural and dual characteristics of Turkish society. In the literary magazine *Mavera* of Bahri Zengin, Rasim Özdenören, Ersin Gürdoğan, and Erdem Beyazıt, a company of novelists and poets, Islamic identity and knowledge became a matter of open debate.[43] They stress the role of poetry and literature in the construction of Islamic role models.

Islamic Skeptics: Postmodern Islamic Intellectuals (1970s–Present)

The current generation of Islamic intellectuals, such as Ali Bulaç (1951–), Rasim Özdenören (1940–), and İsmet Özel (1944–), rejects the glorification of the historic past (the Ottomans), criticizes the Kemalist project of "civilization," and seeks to offer a new vision for the future Muslim society.[44] This generation's main characteristic is its rebellious attitude toward science, technology, civilization, and democracy. I have labeled this group of thinkers "postmodern Islamic intellectuals" because they have been questioning the epistemological origins and political consequences of modernity and seek to deconstruct Kemalist narratives and place them within their own all-encompassing totalistic Islamic narrative in the name of promoting "difference." They define themselves by defining the "other" as being Kemalist or modernist. Thus their identity is very much an oppositional identity, and their project is a rational reconstruction of the sacred. They construct an Islam that can serve as a vital source which nourishes new lifestyles and modes of thought to create a systemic ideology to resist the expanding impact of modernity.

The post-1980 generation has adapted a critical approach to the "civilizational project" and its conservative and nationalistic position in the political domain. It has stressed the Qur'an and *sunna* (recorded sayings and acts of Muhammad) vis-à-vis the historicization of Islam within the framework of the Ottoman Empire. By returning to the text (Qur'an and *sunna*), it sought to free Islam from the constraints of tradition and history. This latest generation of Islamic writers emphasized the limitation of human reasoning for attaining complete knowledge; therefore, revelation in the form of the Qur'an is the ultimate source of knowledge, and the conduct, sayings, and practices of the Prophet Muhammad are the guiding structures of Muslim life. These intellectuals have utilized postmodernist skepticism against the Kemalist positivist tradition to deconstruct the Kemalist faith in science and reason. This radical position makes them postmodernists who wish to blunt the Enlightenment's claim of the triumph of rationality by seeking a self-reflexive and renewed appreciation of tradition.

These Islamic intellectuals mostly originate from lower-middle-class backgrounds, and their writings have clustered around the themes of identity and justice. It is because of these themes that these authors have managed to carve a powerful and effective intellectual space for themselves. Moreover, these writers do not seek a state-centered solution to societal problems but rather treat each Muslim believer as a potential agent for positive change and self-liberation.[45] Özel, for example, defines the Islamic movement as the movement of those who are "conscious of their Muslim identity."[46] The contemporary Islamic movement for these intellectuals is located "in-between the state and society."[47]

Because of their provincial small town and village experiences, intellectuals like Bulaç, Özdenören, and Özel knew that an oral and local form of Islam dominated the worldview of the countryside. Even though the architects of the Kemalist cultural transformation tried hard to penetrate this periphery, local and oral traditional culture maintained its hegemonic position in the traditional structure of Turkish neighborhoods and households. Nevertheless, the Kemalist reforms greatly influenced the intellectual development of the Islamic intellectuals. According to Bulaç, "the educational reforms made skepticism a corner stone of our own thinking and this skepticism helps to form a better faith. The reforms forced us to make a choice between secular national identity and Islamic identity."[48]

By stressing the Qur'an and the sunna, these intellectuals seek to transcend tradition. In other words, these postmodern Islamic writers realized that Muslims cannot fully address the challenge of modernity by insisting on traditional institutions and interpretations. By "going-back to pristine Islam," they sought to overcome the problematique of tradition. This attempt at moving back to the origins of the faith was not an obstacle to modernity but rather a way of building new understandings about Islam that would help dissolve the accretion of centuries of tradition. By "going-back to Islam" they actually retrieve a new "revealed" understanding that is quite novel. Within this genre of skeptics the most radical is Özel, who has had no formal training in Islamic sciences and is an ex-Marxist convert to Islamism. Less skeptical and not willing to break completely with tradition is Özdenören, who has been more influential in the Anatolian heartland than either Özel or Bulaç. Özel differs from other Islamic writers by stressing the constitutive role of Islam in the construction of self-identity. He stresses every-day life and the "system" in which everyday life flows. His problem is not with the Republican ethos, or the "West," but rather with the way the world system, that is, the forces of modernity, produces itself in terms of colonizing thinking and everyday life. Islamic identity, for Özel, is the only site of resistance to the colonization of everyday life by the totalizing consequences of modernity.[49] He invites Muslims to ignore modernity by not defining Islam in opposition or in relation to it. In fact, Islamic movements that seek to create an Islamic state be-come extensions of the world system. Religion, particularly Islam, is the only space for remaining outside this system. While Özel is successful in problematizing and questioning modernity and its impact on society, one can say that he fails to link Islamic consciousness with political and social action. In fact, he does not advo-cate resistance to the state at all. On the contrary, Özel treats the state as the ulti-mate institutional retainer of "the nation" and seeks to preserve it from societal subversion. Consequently, he views cultural pluralism as a potentially imperial-ist project trying to undermine Turkish sovereignty.

Ali Bulaç, in contrast, sees the state as a national institution that should reflect societal cleavages and be subordinated to the principles of social coexist-ence. He argues that much of contemporary Islamic political ideology and no-tions of the Islamic state are constructed through the lenses of nationalism and the nation-state. His own project, which is derived from the Prophet Muham-mad's Constitution of Medina, is to construct a contemporary civil society based on his concept of multilegal communities.[50] According to Bulaç,

> there are 10 million Alevis in this society and democracy is not a
> solution for them. You need to allow these people to utilize their
> legal rights within a framework. The solution is not democracy
> within the nation-state but rather legal pluralism within the state.[51]

His writings have been quite influential. For example, Bahri Zengin, then deputy chairman of the RP, sought to place democracy within this Islamic framework by introducing into the election platform of the RP in 1995 Bulaç's concept of multilegal communities, which dates back to the Ottoman millet system, where each community was allowed to be ruled according to its own norms and laws. The Turkish Constitutional Court regarded the concept of "multilegal commu-nities" as an indication of the RP's anti-secularism and banned the party.

A closer examination of the writings of Özel and Bulaç indicates that their concepts of an Islamic society and polity are not conditioned by a reactive re-turn to tradition but rather by the unfolding impact of modernity and capitalist development in Turkish society.[52] In fact, the intellectual issues and debates within Islamic thought are to a large degree derivatives from European intellec-tual thought. Islamization of society and politics, therefore, tends to be a vernacu-larization of prevailing controversies surrounding issues of the nation-state, civil society, and modernity. These postmodern-influenced Islamic intellectuals are involved in a dual task: modernizing Islamic discourses on politics, civil soci-ety, gender, and technology; and Islamicizing sociocultural discourses in Tur-key. For example, Bulaç argues that

One cannot understand Islamic movements by examining
sociopolitical factors. They shape but they hardly determine these
movements. Those who study the Islamic movement in Turkey have
two rigid categories in their mind: modern versus Islam. You will find
this in the writings of Binnaz Toprak and others. I am also shaped by
these categories but I differentiate Islam from tradition. Let me give
you one example. They argue that it was Atatürk who gave the right to
women to elect and be elected to positions of power since Islam was
against it. In fact, during the Abbasid and Umayyad periods, women
were excluded from the public sphere and the Ottoman state maintained this. However, if you examine the period of the Prophet and the
four caliphs, you will see that women engaged in war and were
involved in political activities. We cannot argue that Islam is modernized by recognizing the place of women in the public sphere. We need
to think of Islam and tradition on the one hand, modernity and Islam
on the other. Tradition cannot be considered as synonymous with
Islam nor can simple notions of progress and modernity.[53]

Modern Islamic intellectuals present a profound paradox: they want to be
contemporary and up-to-date in terms of their references and theoretical tools,
but they also want to overcome this sense of contemporaneousness by positing
a "retrieved" tradition to challenge modernity. Identity, for this new group of
skeptical Muslim intellectuals, is a mode of imagination that is externalized in
life patterns. They argue that these patterns of interactions are the externalization
of an Islamic consciousness. The source of this imagined Islamic consciousness, for the postmodern Islamic writers, should be the Qur'an and sunna. For
example, Rasim Özdenören defines Islamic culture

as a way of everyday life and thinking. By 'a way of everyday life,' I
mean the external world, a world where objects have shape, and our
patterns of behaviors. By 'a mode of thinking', I mean Islamic
consciousness . . . Outside is expression of our inner world and
Islamic consciousness.[54]

Özdenören treats Islamic consciousness as a frame for evaluating sociopolitical issues in Turkish society. As far as the issue of technology is concerned,
Özdenören is critical of the ideological implications of technology, which he
feels subjects the inner soul of the individual to an instrumental and consum-
erist ethos. Özdenören argues that "the goal of Islamic intellectuals is to define
the meaning of the good life in accordance with Islam. What is a good moral
life and how should we as Muslims realize that morally justifiable life?"[55] This
genre of Islamic intellectuals has worked to adopt local and oral Islamic traditions to urban/print culture and sought to arm a new generation of Turkish
Muslims with new Islamic critical terminology to evaluate present conditions
and policies.

Islamic thinkers in Turkey are particularly distinguished from the Kemalists
by their profound sense of connection to Islamic norms and the residual collec-

tive memory. In the case of Republican Turkey, one of the primary goals of the Kemalist intelligentsia was to foster a radical sense of forgetting in order to embark on a radically new future. This lack of a sense of collective memory prevents individuals from understanding the constructiveness of social relations and organizations. The loss of memory deprives people of the historical consciousness necessary for the organizing of alternative practices or institutions. Thus collective memory and identity became one of the primary grounds for resistance for those thinkers who reject the radical Kemalist attempt to write a new script for Turkish society. This resistance should not be seen as a radical rejection of modernity but rather a recontextualization of modern relations in light of a consciousness of the past.

Building an Islamic Education System

Appreciating the role of education in the construction of Islamic consciousness, the Nakşibendi orders and the Nur groups also are involved in educational activities such as establishing new high schools and *Kuran Kursları* (Qur'anic schools for children). The struggle between state and society therefore is focused largely on achieving influence in the educational sphere, which naturally is seen as central to shaping the future of the country. Kemalists perceive the spread of religious schools as a threat to their secular educational objectives. Consequently, on February 28, 1997, the NSC demanded that the Ministry of Education undertake reforms aimed at curbing private schools that are funded by religious associations and closing the public İmam Hatip middle schools and Qur'anic seminaries. The purpose was to curtail the growth of Islamic schools, which the NSC claimed were breeding grounds for Islamic "fundamentalism" and thus threatened the country's stability. In reaction to these demands, large mass rallies were organized in the name of "freedom of education" and "privatization of the educational sector."[56] When the Erbakan government hesitated to implement these directives, it was forced out by the military's orchestrated soft coup.

After the mid-1920s, the Republican state, by controlling education through the 1924 Law of Unification of Education, aimed to appropriate ideas, symbols, texts, and norms to fashion a new citizen committed to Kemalist principles.[57] Through this means, the state sought to condition the individual's thought patterns by encouraging students to think in terms of specific secular-nationalistic frames. These particular patterns of thought were promoted in order to create a unified nation. The Kemalist state had come into being without a corresponding "nation" and society suitable to the new Republican elite's vision of its destiny. Therefore, the state bureaucrats, who were also the functional intellectuals of the period, employed the instruments of education to mold a new secularist Turkey.[58] Universal state-sponsored education, however, did not result in the formation of a uniform secular Turkish citizenry but rather facilitated the emergence of competing Kurdish, Alevi, and Sunni Islamic political identities. These groups manifested their resistance either in Islamic symbols, such as the dress code, or by attacking Kemalist icons. The educational sphere, therefore, became a site for the struggle over the soul of society between secularist Turkish nationalists and popular Ottoman Islamism. This major change took place in the 1980s and 1990s, when high rates of literacy and mass printing converged with the emergence of a middle-class. A new "reading public" formed with an ability to buy and sponsor new forms of literary journals.

With the opening of private, religiously oriented high schools, the state lost control over the production of a state-centric secular identity.[59] These religious schools offer their students a very different interpretation of Islam, Ottoman history, and the Republic than do the secular state schools. The Özal era witnessed a rapid expansion of Islamic groups in the educational sector. By the 1996–1997 academic year, a total of 120 out of 376 private high schools (32 percent) belonged to Islamic foundations and associations, and they enrolled about three hundred thousand students.[60] The Kemalist elite was alarmed by the growth of these schools (as well as by the growth of public İmam Hatip schools, discussed hereafter) and reacted via the military-dominated NSC, as noted earlier.

İmam Hatip Schools and the Privatization of Education

One of the major sources of cultural transformation in Turkey in recent years took place as a result of the evolution of the state's İmam Hatip schools from religious seminaries into full-fledged high schools providing to graduates an opportunity to study at any university. By incorporating both a religious curriculum and a modern secular one emphasizing the sciences and humanities, these have served as a vital bridge between traditional Anatolian society and the emergence of a confident and dynamic modern Islamic-oriented intellectual and business class. These schools made explicit previously unstated cultural assumptions and used them to frame a Turkish Islamic identity. Although these schools never were allowed to become sites for critical thinking and appreciation of divergent sub-Islamic cultures, they still constituted an alternative space to the official state-defined secular education program.

The development of İmam Hatip seminaries into schools and the proliferation of public religious education in general remained a very sensitive and politically symbolic issue.[61] The debate over these schools also exposed the intensity of the culture wars in Turkey. The Law of Unification of Education had brought all educational institutions under the control of the Ministry of Education, closed all *medreses* (traditional theological seminaries), and created a strictly limited number of İmam Hatip schools for the education of carefully controlled and indoctrinated religious preachers who were expected to endorse any policy put forth by the Republican establishment. In addition the Faculty of Divinity (İlahiyat Fakültesi) within Istanbul University was established with the same intentions under Article 4 of the Law of Unification of Education.[62] On the basis of this Law, the Ministry of Education opened twenty-nine İmam Hatip schools (four-year middle level schools) and a Faculty of Divinity in 1924. The İmam Hatip schools filled the gap in religious functionaries that had resulted when the *medreses* were closed down. The İmam Hatip schools were treated as vocational schools meant to produce a limited number of imams whose training and education would be controlled strictly by the state.[63] However, the İmam Hatip schools and the Faculty of Divinity were closed down in 1930 and 1933 respectively, as the Kemalists intensified their onslaught on religion and like their erstwhile Bolshevik allies to the north sought to have it displaced completely from Turkish society over a relatively short time.[64] The Republic in striving for a de-Islamized society sought not only to close down all public religious institutions but also sought to ban furtive private religious education as well. Even an innocuous book by a loyal state bureaucrat, A. Hamdi Akseki, then the deputy director of the Directorate of Religious Affairs, concerning the life of the Prophet Muhammad was banned by the governor of Ankara in 1946.[65]

After a 15-year campaign to disestablish religion, the legalization of limited religious education was considered in 1948, a decade after Mustafa Kemal had passed away. There was a lively debate in the Seventh Convention of the CHP on December 2, 1947, over the issues of secularism and religion, since the CHP had decided to transit into a multiparty system. This new political opening, as an expansion of the opportunity spaces played a key role in the relaxation of religious education and religious discourse. Hamdullah Suphi Tanrıöver, a member of Parliament from Istanbul and ex-minister of education, argued that

> one day after a debate in Parliament, six serving staff of Parliament came to me and said "there is only one imam who serves six villages. We have to keep the bodies of the deceased waiting for days before the imam can come to bury them. If you do not send us more imams, the bodies of our dead will decompose in the open like those of animals."[66]

After sharp debate, and because of upcoming multiparty elections, the CHP decided to open 10 İmam Hatip vocational programs to train preachers and religious functionaries under the authority of the Ministry of Education. The state reinstituted courses on religion in public schools and opened a new Faculty of Divinity within Ankara University in 1949.[67] In order to meet the need for more imams, the new government of Adnan Menderes turned the 10-month vocational project of training into a seven-year school and opened a series of schools in 1951 in Konya, Kayseri, Ankara, Isparta, Maraş, İstanbul, and Adana.[68] Tevfik İleri, then the minister of education, two years later opened eight more İmam Hatip Schools in Antalya, Çorum, Elazığ, Erzurum, İzmir, Tokat, Trabzon, and Yozgat and also opened the high school level of these schools. The number of İmam Hatip schools jumped from seven in 1951 to nineteen in 1961. The number of students increased from 876 in 1951 to 3,374 in the 1961–1962 academic year (see table 5.1). During the DP period, the publication of books and magazines on religious issues flourished.[69] The Ministry of Education created a special Department of Religious Education in 1959 to carry out its functions of public religious education.[70] In 1959, the Institute of Higher Islamic Studies was opened within Istanbul University, and a similar institute was opened in Konya in 1962.

The policies of the Republican establishment with regard to religion and education vacillated dramatically, depending on the exigencies of the moment. Religious education had been justified on the basis of consolidating the nation against perceived leftists threats and creating a well-ordered and stable society.[71] By 1971, however, the military coup authorities decided to close the first four-year period of middle (junior) school (known as Orta Okul) of the İmam Hatip schools and only kept the last three-year period open. They also restricted the

TABLE 5.1. Number of Imam Hatip schools, students, and teachers, 1951–2002

| Year | Number of Imam Hatip schools | | Number of students | | Number of teachers |
	Middle	High	Middle	High	Middle/high
1951-52	7	7	876	889	27
1960-61	19	17	3374	1,171	246
1965-66	30	19	11,832	1,646	366
1970-71	72	40	40,776	6,648	1,548
1971-72	72	42	36,303	8,886	1,535
1972-73	72	71	16,443	19,935	1,564
1973-74	58	71	10,522	23,960	1,612
1974-75	101	73	24,091	24,809	2,152
1975-76	171	72	51,829	25,809	2,933
1976-77	248	72	86,053	25,688	3,852
1977-78	334	103	108,309	26,177	4,922
1978-79	335	335	114,273	148,690	4,448
1979-80	339	339	130,072	178,013	5,500
1980-81	374	333	138,798	62,206	7,768
1981-82	374	336	147,071	69,793	9,212
1982-83	374	341	147,140	72,791	10,537
1983-84	374	341	144,798	76,193	11,113
1984-85	375	341	145,816	83,157	11,334
1985-86	376	341	150,465	87,560	11,439
1986-87	376	341	160,197	89,666	11,824
1987-88	376	342	170,066	87,972	12,261
1988-89	383	350	180,399	87,079	12,010
1989-90	383	366	190,176	92,585	12,995
1990-91	385	380	209,915	100,300	12,809
1991-92	406	390	229,570	117,706	13,581
1992-93	416	391	258,405	137,490	15,022
1993-94	443	392	283,971	160,720	16,344
1994-95	446	394	301,862	171,439	16,903
1995-96	497	434	306,684	188,896	18,330
1996-97	601	601	310,504	192,727	18,809
1997-98	604	604	218,631	178,046	18,702
1999-00	—	610	219,890	134,224	15,922
2001-02	—	558	—	71,583	8,482

Source: The Ministry of Education (2002); Ahmet Koç, "Türkiye'de Din Eğitimi ye Öğretimi Üzerine Bir Değerlendirme," Din Eğitimi Araştırmaları 7 (2000): 317-18; http://www.meb.gov.tr/Stats/Apk2002/64.htm

choices available for further university education for İmam Hatip graduates, thus rendering the option much less attractive. The Ministry of Education wanted most students to go to the state secular schools in their most critical period of socialization. One of the effects of this new regulation was the relative drop in the enrollment of students.

The first civilian government of Bülent Ecevit and Necmettin Erbakan, after the 1971 military intervention, reversed the 1971 decision, and İmam Hatip schools were expanded to middle and high schools. After five years of primary education, students could go to a three-year İmam Hatip Middle School and a four-year İmam Hatip High School. They became integrated into the regular school system. Finally, with the Basic Law on National Education (1739) of June 24, 1973, İmam Hatip Schools were designated as *lise* (lycees) and granted the same accreditation as the other state schools. Article 32 of the Basic Law on National Education changed the name İmam Hatip school to İmam Hatip Lise and stressed the dual functions of these schools:

> The İmam Hatip high schools were established by the Ministry of National Education, within the secondary educational system, to train religious functionaires who perform religious services such as being *imams, hatips*, and teaching staff of Qur'anic courses. These institutions implement a preparatory program for vocational training as well for higher education.[72]

This law broadened the curriculum and influence of the İmam Hatip high schools. For instance, in addition to the basic courses in religious training, students were required to take the regular mandatory courses in state secular high schools. At the middle school level of İmam Hatips, the vocational religious training courses constituted 20 percent of the curriculum, and the rest of the 80 percent covered academic courses.[73] In the religious vocational training curriculum, the courses covered exegesis, prophetic tradition, theology, jurisprudence, and the life of the Prophet Muhammad. At the İmam Hatip high school level, vocational courses varied from 31 percent in the ninth and tenth grade to 42 percent in the eleventh grade and 44 percent in the twelfth grade. Although this curriculum sought to bring religious and nonreligious courses together to train an "enlightened" religious cadre, it often was not as successful as the state would have liked. At one level these schools tended to be dominated by conservative teachers and usually stressed memorization over creative thinking. For their Kemalist critics, these schools also came to be seen as a Trojan horse, being the main source of religious conservatism in Turkey. Twenty-nine İmam Hatip schools were opened during the period of the 1974–1975 coalition government of Bülent Ecevit and Necmettin Erbakan.[74]

In the politicization of the İmam Hatip system, Islamic associations played a key role. These associations carried out a sustained campaign between 1973 to 1997 to build new İmam Hatip schools by collecting money and labor from ordinary people. Within unfolding Islamic activism, a new submovement was formed with the goal of building, maintaining, and improving the İmam Hatip education system. Growing political and economic capabilities of civil society in the 1970s and 1980s empowered Islamic groups to act on their resources and the need of the people to create new education system. The İmam Hatip movement was not directed at the state or modernity. Rather, its goal was to introduce the "way of education" in which knowledge and mores are reconfigured to sustain Islamic forms of conduct. This struggle for identity and ethics through carving a new education system explains the power of the İmam Hatip movement. This movement created an affinity between religious values and networks and the well-being of the society; and it mobilized economic and other resources for building new Imam Hatip schools. Many Turks were ready to contribute to this education movement because they wanted their children to have a set of cultural, ethical, and cognitive models for the constitution of everyday practices. If the goal was to create a new identity, along with a code of ethics, education was the main tool to realize it. However, the elite and many secularist Turks perceived the İmam Hatip education system as a challenge to the shared secularist Turkish identity of the nation and a source of cultural division.

A large segment of the population that is opposed to the state's highly centralized and overtly ideological educational system has perceived İmam Hatip high schools as a means of challenging, and even redefining, the state-centric *laic* (secular) identity the authorities sought to impose on their children.[75] Many traditional families see the İmam Hatip high schools, where Islamic principles are taught in tandem with a mainstream science- and literature-based curriculum, as the ideal balance between modernity and tradition. Even though limited, public religious education was legalized only in response to grassroots demands and pressures, the secular establishment hoped to control and regulate these schools, as well as to exploit them for electoral gains and the balancing of left and right blocs in society. Only the religiously oriented MSP of Necmettin Erbakan was committed ideologically to these schools from the beginning and viewed them as providing the most effective avenue for the redefinition of national identity.[76] Contrary to the original intention of the Republican elite, however, the İmam Hatip high schools developed from being strictly vocational schools for training preachers into an alternative educational system in which pupils attended both religious and secular courses while redefining an identity at odds with the official, state-imposed one. Students of the İmam Hatip high schools usually come from conservative Sunni families, and the schools are seen as important for preserving the conservative values of the youth. The research carried out at these schools indicates that they breed conservatism, even though the students of these schools read on the average more than their secular high school counterparts.[77] Indeed, these schools played a critical role in the Islamicization of society and the state. The İmam Hatip schools, for Necmettin Erbakan, represent the "fifth reason for the growth of the Welfare Party."[78] Moreover, Beşir Ayvazoğlu, a conservative writer, argues that in the formation of the new class of Islamic intellectuals "the first and the only source was the İmam Hatip schools."[79] An RP booklet claims that

when the Milli Görüş [MGH] was the partner of the coalition government between 1974 and 1978, it took the following steps: (1)

within this four-year period we opened 450 new İmam Hatip
schools; (2) 10 Institutes of Higher Islamic Studies; [and] (3) 3,000
Qur'an vocational projects. Over half a million youth have studied in
these schools. Within the last 15 years many youths have graduated
from these schools. The graduates of İmam Hatip high schools
number over 1,300,000. We have trained a new and moral generation.[80]

Bahattin Akşit, a professor at Middle East Technical University who has carried
out survey research on the İmam Hatip high school students, notes that "the
students' education reinforces their religious sentiments and opposition to
Kemalist secularism."[81]

The opening of İmam Hatip schools has been one of the main demands of
Muslim groups in Turkey and has been one of the main concessions granted
by center-right parties in return for electoral support. These schools have played
a critical role in the Islamicization of society and the state. Consequently, the
secular authorities have adopted a very ambivalent attitude toward them. Kenan
Evren, the 1980 coup leader and president of Turkey between 1983 and 1989,
labeled the İmam Hatip schools sources of "fanaticism" and blamed the coalition governments prior to his coup for allowing their expansion.[82] However, it
was during his leadership that the state promoted a Turkish-Islamic synthesis
and presented Atatürk as a "religious leader" who had engaged in a jihad to
protect his nation. Although no new İmam Hatip high schools were opened
during the coup period (1980–1983), none were disbanded or curtailed either.

Between 1983 and 1997, the number of İmam Hatip schools grew by 59
percent, from 374 middle and high schools to 604, but their student enrollment
actually increased from 220,991 total middle and high school students to
511,502. The discrepancy is due the fact that parents and school associations, with
the help of administrators, opened new annexes to existing İmam Hatip schools,
which then expanded their enrollments. Pious foundations and a newly emerging Muslim bourgeoisie not only supported established schools financially but
also provided money for new construction.

Ministry of Education data for 1991 show that 66 percent of all public İmam
Hatip schools had been constructed almost entirely with funds from private
social and cultural associations. Another 19 percent of these schools had been
built by joint state and private cooperation; only 9.65 percent had been built
largely with state funds.[83] Over time, the ratio of İmam Hatip students as a
percentage of all secondary school students increased from 2.6 percent in 1965
to 8 percent in 1985 and 10 percent in 1997.

The İmam Hatip schools became the main source of tension between 1990
and 1997 with the rise of the RP.[84] Many Kemalists believed that these schools
bred Islamism in society.[85] After the military forced Erbakan out of office in 1997,
the NSC demanded the immediate introduction of compulsory eight-year secular education to stop the growth of religious schools. The first official decision
of the government of Mesut Yılmaz was to implement the new education law
"suggested" by the NSC. By expanding compulsory education from five to eight

years, the new law prevented the acceptance of new students to İmam Hatip middle schools and also curtailed the opportunity of İmam Hatip graduates to attend a regular university program. This draconian law also closed down all private Qur'anic School courses.[86] These sweeping decrees faced stiff opposition from conservative Turkish Muslims who openly denounced the laws and engaged in nationwide mass demonstrations and letterwriting campaigns to prevent their implementation. The conservative wing of Yılmaz's own ANAP also reacted very negatively to the decree, and some members of Parliament resigned.

In an apt illustration of how distant the Kemalist vision of "progress" and "Westernization" remains from that prevailing in the liberal-democratic West, the new minister of education, Hikmet Uluğbay of the DSP (Demokratik Sol Parti), presented the law as "an important step toward attaining the modern society Atatürk wanted."[87] Bülent Ecevit, then the deputy prime minister, told a group of journalists that "the first condition of national unity is unified education."[88] Indeed, the Kemalist establishment saw the main issue as not the improvement of the woefully inadequate public education sector but rather the indoctrination of future generations. Neither side has been able to reach a compromise on an education system that would be open and tolerant. As a result of the closure of the middle school level of İmam Hatip schools and other military-imposed restrictions, only 2,000 students applied to these schools in 1997, compared with 35,000 in 1995.[89] The number of students decreased from 396,677 in 1998 to 71,583 in 2002.[90]

Public Religious Education

No one shaped religious education in Republican Turkey as much as Ahmet H. Akseki (1887–1951), who was the major developer of Atatürk's "enlightened Islam" project. He maintained a balance between the needs of the state and its reformist project and the needs of the Anatolian population. Akseki was commissioned to write new books on the religious instructions and teachings in the new (Latin) alphabet because the old books were all in the Arabic alphabet. On the request of General Fevzi Çakmak, then the chief of staff, Akseki wrote a textbook on religious instructions for soldiers in 1925.[91] In these books, Akseki argues that the military values of sacrifice, unity, self-discipline, and considering the interests of the Turkish nation before those of the individual were the core aspects of Islamic morality. Citizens, for Akseki, are more likely to obey the laws, and believe in them, if these laws are backed and sanctioned by a religious ethics as well. Islamic belief system helps foster and sustain the political community, with the promise—and threat—of divine sanction, in a way that a mere compact between ordinary individuals cannot. Religion, for Akseki, is a necessary underpinning to the republican political system, but it should not take a direct role in politics—destructive of both religion and politics. He argues that enlightened religious virtues could help to bring a "modern" citizenry into existence in Turkey. These are well-written and compelling books that synthesize nationalism and Islam and recognize the autonomy of revelation and reason. He constructed and disseminated enlightened and Turkified Islam through the means of the state and defended the state's right to provide religious education. After the Menemen incident, the state's policies changed, and so did the content of Akseki's new books. A closer examination of his life and writings reveals his personal and professional commitment to educate the populace about an enlightened Islam in which revelation and reason are two autonomous domains.[92] His books became the canon of the textbooks on "religion and ethics" in the public schools. The goal of religious education, for Akseki, was to bring "enlightened" Islam into the religious sphere and put it in service to Turkish nationalism and modernity.

In addition to these vocational schools, the Ministry of Education offers courses on religion and ethics in all public and private schools. In 1949 the Ministry started to allow voluntary courses on religion in the fourth and fifth years of primary education, although limited to one lecture a week. In 1953, religion became a mandatory course in the ninth and tenth year of high school education.[93] In 1956, the Ministry allowed sixth- and seventh-year students to take courses once a week on religious education.[94] Following the 1980 military coup and as part of their Turkish-Islamic Synthesis, the generals made a course on religious culture and ethics mandatory. Article 24 of the revised 1982 constitution reads:

> Education and instruction in religion and ethics shall be conducted
> under the supervision and control of the state. Instruction in religious
> culture and moral education shall be compulsory in the curricula of
> primary and secondary schools. Other religious education and
> instruction shall be subject to the individual's own desire, and in the
> case of minors, at the request of their legal representatives.

All Turkish students from grade 4 through secondary and high school, whether public or private, are required to take a course entitled "Religious Culture and Ethical Knowledge." The course is conducted once a week with a textbook approved by the Ministry of Education. Although in theory the course is expected to preserve the line between teaching about religion in general and teaching Islam in particular, in practice it becomes an opportunity to teach the Islamic faith. An examination of four textbooks that are widely used in these mandatory courses reveals that the chapters stress five themes: (1) the major world religions; (2) the history of Islam and the life of Prophet Muhammad; (3) the ways to perform Islamic rituals; (4) the role of religion in Turkish history; and (5) Islamic ethics and good manners. These textbooks fail to take into account Muslim sectarian differences and are written from a Sunni perspective. The section on the role of Islam in Turkish history seeks to fuse Turkish nationalism with Islam. The Turks are presented as the defenders of Islam, and the love of fatherland is equated with the love of faith.

Conclusion

The impact of print in shaping identity and ideology in Muslim societies depends on the level of literacy, the saliency of the arguments put forth by charismatic figures and intellectuals, and the commodification of books and knowledge. The impact of these discursive spaces is therefore uneven in different sectors of society. However, print-based discursive spaces have been at the core of Islamic political activism and have resulted in the invention of a new Islamic self-understanding in Turkey. Even the traditional Sufi orders could not divorce themselves from the impact of print and therefore have entered the publishing market with their own journals and magazines after a period of hesitancy.

The revolution in print and modern technologies of mass communication has had profound consequences for the revitalization of Islamic discourse in contemporary Turkish society. The opening up of discursive spaces has been instrumental in promoting a new dynamic Islamic consciousness that is implicated in virtually all discussions of state, society, and culture in contemporary Turkey. The popularization of Islamic discourse as reflected in the veritable explosion in the publication of newspapers, magazines, and journals paradoxically has undermined any efforts at establishing a single hegemonic Islamic discourse. The market in print and the mass media can be viewed as forces for emancipation and pluralization as various Islamic and non-Islamic ideologies and viewpoints must contend with one another continuously in the hyper-competitive marketplace of ideas.

By raising new questions and challenging dominant perspectives, the media has allowed the *differences* among Islamic groups to become public knowledge. To put it differently, as a result of the media, differences are freed both within the Islamic worldview and also between competing nonreligious worldviews. Moreover, small and idiosyncratic differences concerning the reading and interpretation of Islamic doctrine and history easily can constitute a separate magazine-based intellectual circle. This phenomenon leads to constant transmutations and splits within Islamic groups. The text-centric Nurcu movement, unlike the Sufi groups, has been divided into more than 12 such subgroups. Each interpretation of the standard Nurcu text, the *Risale-i Nur*, offers a ground to compare variances in reading and understanding.

The text-centered Islamic groups are more prone to the processes of swift dissemination and quick fragmentation because what Said Nursi wrote and what the reader understands are not the same. The war of interpretations over the soul of Nursi's writings illustrates that no single voice can speak authoritatively about Nursi's works. Certainly differences of age, gender, class, political context, and educational level play a role in the fragmentation of an authoritative consensus in the movement, but this awareness of the lack of consensus at a popular level only becomes public with the spread of mass communication.

As the Nurcu and Nakşibendi groups venture to arrange the boundaries of interpretive communities through their periodicals, they become further fragmented. In a liberal political and economic context, the Islamic groups are more likely to experience fragmentation than in an authoritarian system. As Turkey tentatively moved toward becoming a full democracy with freedom of speech and other civic rights before the 1997 coup, Islamic periodicals multiplied and diversified in their competition with one another as well as with the secular establishment.

The commodification of Islamic knowledge through print has had a revolutionary impact on traditional religious authority in Turkey and the production and dissemination of Islamic knowledge. Beginning in the 1980s, one witnesses a shift in religious authority from the traditional religious class of the state-centered ulema and the provincial leaders of Sufi orders. Replacing them is a new urban-based and university-educated class of Islamic intellectuals who use their wide access to the print and the electronic media effectively to propagate their learned theories and critiques. In contemporary Turkey, those religious groups and leaders who enthusiastically have adapted to the revolution in print and mass communications are the ones whose power and social stature have grown most rapidly. These leaders include the charismatic and highly influential Fethullah Gülen of the neo-Nurcu movement and Esad Coşan of the Nakşibendi order. Thus the opening up of discursive spaces through the media is having a profound impact on debates over identity and state and society relations while also simultaneously transforming traditional Islamic doctrines and institutions.

6

The Matrix of Turkish Islamic Movements

The Nakşibendi Sufi Order

The Nakşibendi order in its many different manifestations has been a part of Turkish history, culture, economics, politics, and individual identity for several centuries. Like other Sufi orders, this order has undergone an internal transformation and revival in recent decades, despite state-imposed secularization and repression. Not surprisingly, this revival has corresponded with the Turkish state's gradual liberalization and integration into the global market. Nakşibendi religious, social, and cultural networks have become suffused with political and economic associations. In response to repression, most of these orders gradually transformed themselves from strictly religious associations into competing informal educational and cultural associations with religious underpinnings. They gathered support from sections of traditional society that regarded the Kemalist variant of secularization as too radical and destructive with respect to Turkish history and traditions. The Nakşibendi orders provided a structure and functioned as a catalyst for maintaining the religious-moral education and spiritual development of Muslim society in Turkey.

In recent decades, the Nakşibendi order has become mobilized on an internal level because of increasingly worldly concerns. To a certain extent, the order has become secularized, and its religious views, in turn, have been modified by more profane interests. A close examination of the Nakşibendi orders, and specifically the Khalidiya lodge, can provide insights into Turkish Islamism for three reasons. First, the Nakşibendis are by far the most politically active of the tarikats and indeed represent a model for virtually all subsequent major contemporary Islamic sociopolitical movements in Turkey. Second, the order is also the most useful avenue for understanding the social interactions between politics and religion in the country. Finally, the Nakşibendi orders played a formative role in the evolution of Islamic identity in Turkey by developing three patterns of interaction with the state: confrontation, withdrawal, and engagement.

The Nakşibendi orders operate as a repository of virtually all cultural and religious traditions that have existed in Turkey; they bridge the gap between the Ottoman period and the current Islamic sociopolitical revival. They constitute a dense socioreligious network in which the exchange of ideas and the transmission of social norms take place. Moreover, by cutting across ethnic, regional, and linguistic lines, Nakşibendi orders have played an integrative role. Finally, the Turkish Muslim understanding of Islam is very much filtered through Sufi concepts and institutions. For example, both the National Outlook Movement and the powerful Nurcu movement were nurtured by and emerged from the Nakşibendi orders.[1]

Nakşibendi Tradition

The Nakşibendi order belongs to the Sufi tradition of Islam. This tradition focuses on disciplining the appetite (*nefs*) by educating the believer about the nature and function of the different faculties of the soul, from the sensual to the spiritual.[2] The struggle to control the nefs is carried out in the realm of the heart (*kalp*). Sufis are distinguished from other Muslims by, among other things, their interpretation of the Qur'an. In order to find the "true" meaning of the book, Sufis "read the [Qur'an] with the 'eyes of the heart,' not with the eyes of one's head."[3] With the phrase "eyes of the heart" Sufis refer to the need to grasp the inner nature and meaning of the text. Sufis seek to create a balance between the inner and outer dimensions of the believer. The esoteric life usually is regulated by Sufi teachings, while the exoteric (external) life is represented by the ritual obligations of prayer and acting in accordance with Islamic norms.[4]

Sufism is a discipline that aims to teach one how to live without confining oneself to the materialistic dimension of life. It argues that there is one true experience in existence and it is the encounter with the sacred, the numinous, that is beyond human reasoning and is grounded in an instinctual understanding that immediately calls a believer's attention to his or her finiteness in the face of God. This sacred presence penetrates the deepest psyche of the believer and in addition provides a conceptual map of meaning. This complex map is marked by a cluster of concepts such as *sabır* (patience), *tevekkül* (imagination), *fedekarlık* (sacrifice), and *edep ve haya* (ethics and morals).[5] While morality tends to organize relations between individuals, religion defines the relationship between the individual and God. Sufism organizes mental dispositions with respect to both human virtue and ritual activity. It seeks to instill higher moral values (*ihsan*) through the disciplining of the passions.[6] Sufism can be viewed as a constant search for new inner discoveries and a struggle for human perfection. The sacred or numinous is not rational, it is more a "feeling tone" in which a person facing the mystery and overwhelming nature of God is both awed and speechless, yet imbued with a sense of a commitment to struggle against one-dimensional life-worldliness.

Strangely, in the modern period, Sufism proved to be a dominant spiritual vehicle in urban areas of Turkey. This is contrary to the traditional image of the Sufi ascetic life. It has attached itself to the cities because it offers individuals a comprehensive source of normative principles by which to deal with the conditions of modern urban life. However, Sufism should not be mistaken for true numinous experience; instead it is an abridgement that allows the individual to chart new discoveries both within the "self" (moral) and outside the "self" (material), thus transcending the one-dimensionality of material existence.

Genesis and Organizational Structure

Although Nakşibendi spiritual genealogy started with Abu-Bakr al-Siddiq, the Nakşibendi order's eponymous founder was Bahaeddin Nakşibend of Turkistan (b. 1490). Its intellectual maturation took place under Ahmad Sirhindi of India (1563–1625), whose main goals were the elimination of corrupt innovation (bid'at)[7] and the revitalization of the Muslim community. There were several stages in the crystallization of Nakşibendi teachings.[8] The most significant period was that of Sirhindi, known as Imam Rabbani, who did not draw a rigid demarcation between the temporal and material world of the present and that of the hereafter. Sirhindi set an important example through his own personal involvement in society and politics.[9] His reformist writings redefined the Nakşibendi tradition; he thus became known as the Renewer (Mujaddid) of the tradition.[10] Sirhindi was deeply influenced by a descendent of the Central Asian Nakşibendi Khwaja Nasraddin Ubaydullah Ahrar (d. 1490).[11] By putting into practice the axiom of seclusion in the midst of society (khalvat dar anjuman), one of the eight Nakşibendi principles, Ahrar became both a sheik and a politician.[12] This axiom requires "being inwardly focused on God whilst outwardly taking an active part in the life of the community."[13] The genius of the Nakşibendi orders has been their ability to mobilize internal religiosity, a kind of psychological resource for activism that promotes self-esteem and renewal. Nakşibendis, therefore, incorporated their strong sense of faith and community into strategies of social activism and resistance against "alien" rule. Sajida Alvi argues that those who followed this Renewal tradition were at the forefront of the modernist Islamic movements in the nineteenth century as well as of modern Islamism in the late twentieth century.[14]

A combination of charismatic leadership and worsening social conditions led to a major transformation of the order in the nineteenth century. Sheik Mavlana Khalid al-Baghdadi (1776–1827) reinterpreted the doctrinal content of the order to respond to external challenges. Al-Baghdadi studied under the mujaddid sheik Abdullah Dihlavi of India and was appointed by the latter as his successor (caliph) in the Ottoman territories. Sheik Khalid's revitalizing influence forged the separation of the Nakşibendi-Khalidi autonomous suborder from the Nakşibendi-Mujaddidi order.[15] Sheik Khalid, like Sirhindi, argued that the

Muslim community as a whole was following a path of decadence, and as a cure, he called for the restoration of the sunna and sharia.[16] He was very much worried by the effects of syncretic innovation and the social disintegration of the Ottoman-Muslim community. He believed that the Muslim community was on the wrong path and tried to emphasize the significance of the Sunna for social life. He maintained that "if the umma had gone astray, it was because of its rulers." Thus, following Sirhindi, he seems to have thought that "the foremost duty of Nakşibendi-Mujaddidi sheiks is to seek to influence rulers and bring them to follow sharia rules."[17] One of the major reasons that the Khalidi branch managed to penetrate the Ottoman state was the religiously orthodox and politically activist doctrine of the order. Both the state and the Nakşibendis were critical of heterodoxy in society. The ulema of Istanbul favored the order, too, in their fight against the heterodox Bektaşis.[18]

Sheik Khalid, whose goal was the revitalization of the Muslim community qua Islam, trained hundreds of disciples to carry his ideas throughout Central Asia, Southeast Asia, the Caucasus, the Balkans, and the Crimea.[19] Both Sirhindi and Khalid stressed an imaginative "imitation" of the Prophet's life and sought to identify the universally applicable intentions of the Prophet in order to learn how to cope with prevailing problems. The durability and significance of the Nakşibendi-Khalidi order rests in its organizational structure and theoretical teaching. Sheik Khalid based his community on three complementary pillars: *rabıta* (spiritual bond), *zikr* (invocation to God), and the sheik. After expressing regret for wrongdoing, the disciple must proceed to strive for purification through *zikr*, a method of internal training and self-construction through which a new consciousness is formed and is expressed in good deeds.[20] In the Nakşibendi tradition, a believer discovers a universal and substantial self-consciousness that is objictied both in the personality of the Sufi leaders and in certain behavioral practices.

The contemporary Nakşibendi orders of Turkey are all diverse branches of the Khalidi-Nakşibendis.[21] In the nineteenth century, the Kadiri order was the dominant order in which the position of sheik became hereditary. The Nakşibendi order offered an alternative, that is, a nonhereditary order, to those who did not have the required hereditary lineage for religious mobility. In a way, the Nakşibendis, by issuing hundreds of *ijazas* (religious decrees recognizing the right of the named person to exercise independent reasoning) to those whose fathers were not sheiks, democratized and popularized Sufi orders. However, in due time Nakşibendi orders also adopted heredity as a basis for selecting new sheiks.

Sheik Khalid's main goal was to "promote the moral and spiritual rebirth of the Muslim community gathered around the Ottoman caliphate, in order to strengthen its cohesion against external attack," and he pursued a careful and deliberate policy to penetrate the state by recruiting ulema and some high-ranking bureaucrats.[22] However, since Sultan Mahmud II (r. 1808–1839) was always suspicious of charismatic popular leaders and alternative loyalties within the state, he banned the Khalidi-Nakşibendi order in Istanbul and exiled its sheiks.[23] Under Sultan Abdülmecid (r. 1839–1861), the Khalidi-Nakşibendi's expulsion and persecution ceased, and some Nakşibendi disciples were appointed to positions of authority. During the reigns of Abdülmecid, Abdülaziz (r. 1861–1876), and Abdülhamid II (r. 1876–1909), the Nakşibendi order expanded its influence and became one of the most important forces of mediation between ruler and ruled. Albert Hourani argues that

> throughout the nineteenth century most educated Muslims who took
> their religion seriously interpreted it within the framework created
> by the great [Nakşibendi] masters of spiritual life, and many still
> adhered to one or other of the brotherhoods founded by them.[24]

The factors that facilitated the expansion of the Khalidi-Nakşibendi orders included worsening economic conditions that were due to "the expansion of European imperialism and the political and intellectual responses this provoked"[25] and improved conditions of transportation and communication. The Nakşibendis increasingly treated the state as a necessary instrument not only for the realization of Islamic ideals but also for the very survival of the Muslim community, which was under severe pressure at this time from European powers. According to the Khalidi tradition, implementation of Islamic law at the state and societal level is the sine qua non for a just society. The state-centrism of the Nakşibendi was promoted by Sheik Khalid. He asked his followers to pray for the survival of "the exalted Ottoman state, upon which depends the victorious existence of Islam," and invited all Muslims to be active against the Christian and Shi'a expansionism.[26]

In the nineteenth century, important societal actors, including both bureaucrat-intellectuals and notables, were exploring ways to revitalize Muslim society in order to meet internal and external challenges. They sought to carry out the mission of societal transformation through traditional institutions such as the Nakşibendi orders. The orders focused on the life of the Prophet Muhammad for guidance. Muhammad was a highly successful social engineer who transformed an ignorance (jahiliyya)–based society into a new rule-based civil (medeni) society. The Nakşibendi orders examined the Prophet Muhammad's conduct and political leadership with a view to revitalizing their own contemporary society. The need for direct engagement with politics and social life was stressed by Sheik Khalid and was passed on to his successor, Ahmet Gümüşhanevi.[27]

The transformation of the Ottoman state in the second half of the nineteenth century took place as a result of the penetration of Western capitalism along with the introduction of the railroad, education, and a heightened attention to public opinion. This capitalist penetration made small business groups, artisans, and farmers vulnerable to external pressures. In order to protect their interests, these groups reacted to structural changes by resorting to Islamic symbols and rhetoric that, in turn, politicized Islamic identity. The European political and social "other" was brought into the cities and towns through the commercialization of agriculture and the penetration of capitalism; the position of the middle class thereby was undermined severely by Western imperialist penetration. The middle class expressed its reaction to European penetration by seeking to redefine society in terms of Islamic concepts. For those concerned with the economic and political weakness of the Muslims, the Nakşibendi orders provided leadership and an organizational vehicle through which political independence and the economic revival of the Muslim community might be achieved. The Nakşibendi order managed to confront the penetration into Turkish society of capitalism and modern ideas by establishing its own competing network system. The Nakşibendis protested vehemently against the Westernizing policies of the Tanzimat Reform.[28] They even instigated the Kuleli Incident of 1859, an antireform protest that demanded the full restoration of Islamic law.[29] The social basis of Nakşibendi activism was located among the merchants, literati, bureaucrats, and urban notables.

At the same time, the Nakşibendi order itself underwent certain internal and external changes. It played a key role in the laying down of a new political and social terrain for Turkish society by promoting the new idiom of constitutionalism and human rights. In contrast to many of those engaged in the theoretical debates that surrounded these new idioms in Ottoman society, the Nakşibendi order, by interpreting these new idioms through the prism of the sharia and the sunna, was able to appeal for activism at the grassroots level. Gümüşhanevi's direct involvement in the 1878 War in the Caucasus against the Russians, as well as in hadith study, was an important indicator of the formation of this new socially and politically activist Islam. The human story of the Prophet Muhammad helped to make abstract precepts more concrete and created a shared moral understanding among Muslims. In particular, it should be noted that the Nakşibendi order was more influential in cities than in rural areas. Although grassroots in origin, the Khalidi branch of the Nakşibendi order had elitist qualities, as most adherents were educated people, merchants, bureaucrats, and notables.

The 1878 Russo-Ottoman war was a catalyst in the transformation of the order's strategies. The Nakşibendi order quickly adopted modern notions such as love of the homeland and defense of the nation.[30] For example, Gümüshanevi rallied his disciples to volunteer in the 1878 war to protect the homeland, religion (din), and the state (devlet).[31] The disastrous Ottoman defeat and loss of large territories forced the order to engage in a far-reaching social, cultural, and political critique. One of the results of the war was a mass exodus of Ottoman Muslims from the Balkans and the Caucasus and the destruction of historic Muslim villages and towns, which caused communal trauma for many Muslims remaining in Ottoman territory. This confrontation forced the order to treat Islam as an identity of resistance and restructuring. During the mass exodus from the Caucasus, the Nakşibendi evolved into an institution that was able to unify ethnically diverse Muslims and help them to establish a sense of community. Thus the Nakşibendi of the nineteenth century became an effective force for the preservation of Islam and for mass mobilization against the penetration of foreign capital that undermined the socioeconomic viability of much of traditional Ottoman society. As a protest movement based on religious solidarity, the order became an instrument for articulating the interests of urbanized small business groups and farmers. In the last decades of the Ottoman Empire, the Nakşibendi order emerged as the largest and most influential independent Islamic group. By 1920, on the eve of the Kemalist revolution, there were 305 Sufi lodges in Istanbul, 65 of which were Nakşibendi.[32] This was more than any other order.[33]

The Nakşibendis' modern revival is a search for an "authentic" identity as well as a struggle for control of resources. Whereas nineteenth-century revivalism focused on political transformation, modern Islamic movements seek social and economic power that sometimes can be used to shape the policies of the state. During the War of Liberation, the Nakşibendis played a critical role in the mobilization of the populace. The Özbek Tekkesi in Üsküdar, for instance, provided shelter for high-ranking Turkish officials escaping the occupying Allied Forces. İsmet İnönü, Mustafa Kemal's deputy, stayed in this lodge, and it offered logistical support to many other nationalist figures.[34] Some other prominent Nakşibendi leaders took an active part in the War of Liberation. For example, Hasan Feyzi Efendi of Erzincan led the mobilization against occupation troops in Erzincan and Bayburt.[35] The history of the Nakşibendi order includes several breaks and renewals that have occurred during major sociopolitical upheavals. This ability to adjust to new situations along with an inherent intellectual flexibility has been able to neutralize the hostile propaganda of opponents who seek to identify the movement as "fundamentalist" or an enemy of modernity. In spite of Western efforts to use the captive sultan-caliph to neutralize nationalist opposition to foreign occupation, the Nakşibendi orders fully supported the Turkish War of Liberation. Turks and Kurds fought side by side in the war, and Muslims from as far afield as India provided their assistance in the name of a defensive jihad. This facet of the Liberation War later was elided completely by Kemalist historians who sought to erase the memory of the religious basis of Turkish resistance in this formative period of the Republic.[36] The Kemalist establishment always has been particularly fearful of the Nakşibendi movement, because the Nakşibendis were able to demonstrate their continuing ability to arouse mass resistance across ethnic and tribal lines in their protests against the radical antireligious programs of the Republican elite from 1925 through 1930.

Kemalist Persecution: Silent Transformation of the Order, 1930–1960s

One of the most significant consequences of the birth of the Turkish Republic under Mustafa Kemal was a sustained campaign against traditional Islamic institutions, Sufi orders being one of the chief targets. Under Legal Code 677, the Republic closed Sufi lodges on November 30, 1925, later replacing them with the Halkevleri, or People's Houses, which promoted radical secularization and obedience to the new state elite. Despite official purges of religious figures and institutions, the Nakşibendi order managed to lead or incite many rebellions against the radical reforms. According to Reşat Halli, between 1924 and 1938 18 such rebellions against the draconian policies of the state took place, and most were led by the Nakşibendi orders.[37]

The most important of these rebellions were the Sheik Said rebellion (1925) and the Menemen rebellion (1930). These incidents, in particular the Menemen rebellion, have been presented in the official historiography of the Republic as a clash between "the forces of darkness and those of the Enlightenment."[38] In the Menemem incident of December 23, 1930, a group of local Nakşibendis were involved in disturbances that, according to revisionist Muslim historians, actually were orchestrated by the state authorities as a pretext to murder the most prominent Nakşibendi sheik, Mehmet Esad (1847–1931).[39]

Facing severe persecution from the Kemalist state, the Sufi orders, which depended heavily on the Sufi lodge structure, began to wither. The program of persecution, arrest, and execution of members of the Nakşibendi community was pursued ruthlessly as authorities labeled them "a snake we have been unable to crush."[40] In spite of these purges, the Nakşibendi-Khalidi order was not affected by the elimination of all lodges to as great an extent as were other Sufi orders that relied more heavily on the figure of the sheik and his lodge. Sheik Khalid's particular interpretation of zikr and rabıta did not require any outward, institutionalized religious rituals. At the level of popular religion, many people replaced outward manifestations of faith with inner expressions as spirituality was restructured within the confines of the neighborhood and the family. Moreover, Nakşibendi orders adopted themselves to the new realities of the Republic by taking civil service jobs at the Directorate of Religious Affairs to "cover" their activities and utilize the state-owned mosques as new centers of Sufi activism. Thus these orders took refuge in the mosques and "covered" themselves as the "mosque community." The mosque in Turkey thus may be seen as a "lodge" building, since the mosques were the only spaces where formal and informal religious structures simultaneously coexisted. The Khalidi Nakşibendi order thus emerged as the Sufi order best suited to provide a matrix for the revival of organized Islamic sociopolitical movements in the thawing period of the 1950s. The order managed to survive in the Kemalist period because the state secularism regarded individuals as positivist abstract entities, without much concern for the ethical and spiritual dimensions of human life. The Nakşibendi order thus was strengthened and its purpose reinvigorated as it was able to meet certain vital, personal needs of many segments of the population who felt alienated and underrepresented by official Kemalist ideology and policies.

The Nakşibendi tradition became the intellectual and historical groundwork for a new urban Islamic intellectual discourse. Since intellectual activity not licensed by the state took place in private groups and networks, the Sufi orders were well positioned to become spaces for free thought and reflection for the religious segments of Turkish society. Religious intellectuals emerged in this period, such as Abdülaziz Bekkine (1895–1952), the spiritual leader of the Hareket movement of Nurettin Topçu, and Abdülhakim Arvasi (d. 1943), who played a critical leadership role in the print-based *Büyük Doğu* (Greater Orient) intellectual circle. In Istanbul, five main Nakşibendi branches emerged: the economically wealthiest and most influential one was the İskenderpaşa, led by Nureddin Coşan; the currently most powerful branch is the Erenköy Cemaati; the more conservative and neo-Nakşibendi are the Süleymancıs; and two more rural and conservative orders are the İsmail Ağa Cemaati, led by Mahmut Ustaosmanoğlu, and the Menzil Cemaati of Adıyaman.[41]

Mehmet Zahit Kotku and the Gümüşhanevi-Nakşibendi Order

The charismatic Mehmet Zahid Kotku (1897–1980) became the leader of the Gümüşhanevi Nakşibendi order after the death of Abdülaziz Bekkine in 1952.[42] In addition to its role as the incubator of the postwar generation of prominent Islamist intellectuals, the Nakşibendi order under the leadership of Kotku also played a crucial role in the formation of the pro-Islamic MNP and the MSP of Necmettin Erbakan. Perhaps Kotku's most significant contribution was as the spiritual advisor of Turgut Özal, in which position he strongly supported Özal's liberalizing, market-oriented economic policies. Kotku also mobilized his disciples Erbakan, Fehim Adak, Korkut Özal, Hasan Aksay, and Lütfü Doğan to form the Republic's first explicitly Islamic political party (the MNP), with the aim of healing the sharp rupture between traditional Turkish society and the Kemalist establishment. Kotku remained the spiritual guide of the MNP, and its successor the MSP, while he was alive.[43] During the years of the MSP, Kotku favored an incremental approach; he "warned against premature attempts to establish an Islamic state in Turkey and stated a preference for the moral and cultural reorientation of Turkish society as the pressing goal."[44] According to his biographer, Halit İlhan, Kotku "was in favor of technology and did not hesitate to make use of any machine. He always encouraged people to establish firms and corporations, and he stressed the significance of economic independence. His life was immersed in politics."[45]

It is important to examine Kotku's role as a Sufi sheik in the transformation of the Nakşibendi order and its development as the model for the matrix of the majority of contemporary Turkish Muslim sociopolitical movements. While Kotku was in the Ottoman army in Istanbul, during the empire's fragmentation, he became involved in discussing possible solutions with other prominent followers of the Nakşibendi order.[46] At the age of 21, he established a spiritual tie (*intisap*) to the Dagistani sheik Ömer Ziyauddin.[47] He worked as an official imam in different mosques and became the leader of the order in 1952. Many Sufi orders in modern Turkey, including different Nakşibendi orders, have claimed Kotku as the *Qutb*, the "pole" or "spiritual axis," of their movements since the 1960s and 1970s. One of the main reasons that Kotku emerged as the most significant Sufi leader after 1952 had to do with the people who surrounded him: Turgut and Korkut Özal, Cevat Ayhan, Temel Karamollaoğlu, Teoman Rıza Güneri, Hilmi Güler, Nazif Gürdoğan, Recep Tayyib Erdoğan, and many other public personalities who would become leading figures in Turkey's social and political life, including ministers (Korkut Özal, Lütfü Doğan, Fehim Adak), a prime minister and president (Turgut Özal), and another prime minister (Erbakan).

Kotku transformed the structure of the mosque-based community into a semipolitical movement. The mosque, in this case the İskenderpaşa Camii, was no longer a place for elders to sit and pray. It became a center for shaping young people, and many of his students, as noted, came to occupy critical positions in the higher echelons of the bureaucracy.[48] However, Kotku did not see politics as the only avenue available for shaping Turkey in accordance with his ideals.

Rather, he stressed economic progress and industrialization as the best ways to develop society and ease the iron grip of Kemalist authoritarianism.[49] Kotku's agenda modified the old Sufi saying "Bir lokma, bir hırka" (all a person needs is a morsel of food and a cloak to cover oneself) by adding to the list "one Mazda." By "one Mazda," Kotku meant that Muslims should control technology so they could control their own destiny; once Turkish Muslims had joined the ranks of the middle class and obtained the power that would accompany this rise in class, they could reshape their state and society from within.[50] Kotku stressed both religious (uhrevi) and worldly liberation (felah). His disciples were encouraged to become involved in trade as opposed to seeking jobs in the civil service, since success in trade, for Kotku, freed individuals from dependence on state authorities and created an economically and culturally powerful Turkey. In furtherance of this goal, he emphasized the centrality of education and individual development for his followers. Kotku was a man of deep intelligence with a clear understanding of the constraints of society. He treated the lack of ethics and self-discipline among individuals in Turkish society as the main impediment to the full realization of freedom and an Islamic ethos.

Kotku wrote 30 books, most of which have appeared in third or fourth editions.[51] An in-depth examination of these works reveals that Kotku's goal was to help Muslims find their inner selves by cultivating a progressive Islamic consciousness that would address the issues and needs of each Muslim's own period. Kotku's *Sermons to the Faithful (Mü'minlere Vaazlar)* seek to consolidate Muslim faith through moral allegories from the period of the Prophet Muhammad. In the corpus of his writings, a struggle emerges over the question of how to close the gap between daily human exigencies and practices and traditional Islamic morality.[52] In Kotku's appraisal, the high Islamic tradition is flexible and enlightened enough to address contemporary needs.

Islam, for Kotku, is a repository of moral arguments that are expressed in the shared language of a community and can be used to mold an unformed future. One might sum up the writings of Kotku in the following way: a harmonious community cannot exist without a shared ethical and spiritual language (mores); communal justice and tranquility only can be realized by the internalization of such mores; Sufism had a crucial role to play in this inner transformation. Kotku's focal point was disciplining the appetite/soul and constructing a cognitive map within each believer that could be followed to form a well-ordered society. After Kotku's death, Esad Coşan (1938–2001), his son-in-law and the new leader of the order, reinvented the Gümüşhanevi order as a model for political associations and economic corporations. In this process, the image of God was redefined; Coşan's emphasis on the market implied that Muslims should view the liberating and rationalizing "hidden hand" of market forces as a reflection of divine wisdom. After the 1997 coup, Coşan left Turkey; he died in Australia on February 4, 2001, and his son Muharrem Nureddin Coşan became the leader of the order.

The İskenderpaşa promoted the circulation of ideas and the development of new intellectuals in society by publishing them in its magazines and broadcasting them on its radio stations and, by doing so, marketed its own intellectuals and representatives. Coşan calls on his disciples to study foreign languages, use computers, establish connections with the outside world, and visit foreign countries. Coşan views engaging in trade and commerce as a way of shaping society and the collective consciousness. He argues that one must take foreign trade seriously because "one road to success is success in trade."[53] In his later writings, trade and economic enterprises are emphasized more than politics. Indeed, some of his speeches and articles were very similar to the speeches of presidents of corporations informing shareholders about the economic condition of a company. Worship of God, for a follower of Coşan, can be realized in the marketplace. Coşan says:

> Trade is real and permanent in an individual's life. Other activities are utopian, hypothetical, and imaginary; whereas trade is the most realistic. As far as I am concerned, those who do not have trade experience do not turn out to be good humans. The most pragmatic and realistic people are businessmen and merchants. If a business-man is also a Muslim, he is the most in tune with his religious station in life.[54]

In other words, Qur'anic verses were turned into slogans as a project in economic competition. The market conditions of the 1980s led to the process of recreating a new, abstract, highly centralized and economically conscious Islam, which was embraced by the modem urban population.

The İskenderpaşa offers both a case study of a society-oriented Islamic movement and a model of horizontal Islamic identity building. Specifically, I argue that İskenderpaşa's engagement within socioeconomic segments of society that are not overtly religious in nature—such as the mass media, education, business—while continuing nonetheless to emphasize the primary religious purpose of promoting individual piety constitutes an important model for Islam's future and peaceful co-existence with Western culture. In relating to the modern Turkish state and politics, the order emphasizes a gradualist, accommodationist program and concentrates its efforts on civil society. In the expanding private economy, the Nakşibendi order of İskenderpaşa has changed from a state-oriented Islamic movement to a society-oriented one.

The case of İskenderpaşa illustrates that Islamic social movements are not always a reaction to social change or massive deprivation, an effort by the poor to undermine modernism, but rather can be an attempt to capitalize on new opportunity spaces, an effort by the middle class to benefit from modernism; by opening private high schools, hospitals, radio stations, local television stations, commercial companies, printing houses, and summer camps and forming a reliable network among Nakşibendi businessmen, the order satisfies many needs of its followers. It also provides jobs in its own companies. Modem Islamic social movements in Turkey, therefore, respond to local as well as global aspects of social change. Strategies chosen depend on the political context. For example, there is a close link between the degree of autonomy permitted by the state and the cohesiveness of the order. If the political context is oppressive, ties between followers are intensified and solidarity produces consensus. When a

democratic environment flourishes, however, followers are inclined to emphasize other loyalties: to club, union, or business association. Therefore, as Turkey has been increasingly democratizing, the İskenderpaşa has developed new
means of communication such as periodicals and radio stations to keep its followers informed of current events. It has also opened new professional associations in medicine and law. All these activities compete with other loyalties by
transforming Nakşibendi loyalty into a framework or a ground for accommodating professional loyalties. In this case, solidarity among the followers of the
İskenderpaşa order is built through creating a consensus on social and political
issues. However, the order's remarkable adaptive powers and pragmatism may
led to its decline, not so much because of state suppression or rivalry from other
orders, but because of its smooth adaptation to capitalism and politics, both of
which undermined the spiritual and cultural aspects of the İskenderpaşa order.
The order may come to be characterized as a vacuous commercial enterprise
rather than as a Sufi fraternity.

The Erenköy Cemaati

In 2003, the most influential post-Republican Sufi order is that established by
Mehmet Esad Efendi, who eventually settled in the Istanbul neighborhood of
Erenköy.[55] Esad Efendi was born in Erbil, Iraq, and trained by Nakşibendi schol-
ars. His first book, Kenzü'l –İrfan (Treasury of wisdom), attempted to create a
system of morality by utilizing the reported sayings of the Prophet Muhammad.[56]
In addition to his religious writings, Esad Efendi was also a well-known poet who
used Persian and Turkish in his verses.[57] Because of his support of the Young
Turks against Abdülhamid II, he was forced to leave Istanbul and settle in Erbil.
There he collected his exchanges with his followers and other scholars and published these as Mektubat (The letters).[58] Some of these letters reflect the sociopolitical conditions of northern Iraq in the early 1900s. After the Young Turk
revolution in 1908, he returned to Istanbul and became the sheik of the Selimiye
lodge in Üsküdar.[59] He also played a significant role in the War of Liberation but
later became one of the leading critics of Mustafa Kemal's program of secular social
engineering. Even though there was no direct link between the Menemem incident of 1930 and Esad Efendi, state officials took this opportunity to arrest him
and his eldest son, M. Ali Efendi.[60] The son, whom Kemalists feared would become his father's charismatic successor, was hanged; Esad Efendi himself died
in prison on March 4, 1931. His followers believed he was poisoned.[61]

After Esad Efendi's death, Mahmut Sami Ramazanoğlu (1892–1984), an
accountant by profession, became leader of the community.[62] In the discussion
circle where he met with his followers in the Zihnipaşa mosque in Erenköy, he
stressed the importance of Islamic ethics as a "horizon within which Muslims
are expected to determine what is good and bad and what is just and unjust."
Islam, for Ramazanoğlu, was not "only an identity to determine one's location
but rather a lens through which Muslims must critically evaluate the world."[63]
Ramazanoğlu succeeded in training and influencing a sizeable number of pro-

fessors, journalists, intellectuals, and businessmen.[64] In 1984, Musa Topbaş, a rich businessman and lawyer, became the leader of the order; he continued in this role until his death in 1999, and was succeeded by his son, Osman Nuri Topbaş.[65] With new economic opportunities in the 1990s, the Erenköy order distanced itself from politics and increasingly became a civil society–oriented Islamic movement, with its own publishing houses, charity foundations, and educational networks.

Süleymancıs

The Nakşibendi sheik Süleyman Hilmi Tunahan (1888–1959), a conservative member of the ulema who cared more about "safeguarding" Islam than updating it, was the spiritual leader and founder of the second-largest Islamic movement in Turkey, with four million members.[66] The Süleymancıs, the followers of Tunahan, have developed a sectlike identity around the cult of Tunahan and a set of norms to protect its members from the contaminating ideas of secularism, political Islamism, Shi'a and Wahhabi interpretations of Islam, and consumer culture. The main goal of this movement is to "train" preachers to control and discipline Muslims in accordance with the "Sunni-Hanefi-Ottoman" version of Islam.[67] No one did more for religious training in Turkey during the Kemalist period than Tunahan. He endured constant police harassment for his religious activities but constantly reacted to the social, cultural, and political transformation of Turkey.

Tunahan was an émigré from Bulgaria and was a leading religious scholar of his period. He led a grassroots movement calling for a return to the textual sources of Islam. In spite of official harassment, he never wavered from his religious mission in tutoring students to recite the Qur'an. He converted his house into a Qur'an seminary and asked his followers to do the same. His desire to reform the method of teaching the Qur'an stemmed from his perception of the decline of Islamic thought, which had intensified following the implementation of the centralized and secular education system in accordance with the Law of Unification of Education of 1924 that closed all religious schools. Indeed, the expansion of state authority and mass culture raised fears of eroded religious and social boundaries, giving rise to new conservative religious movements. These movements developed contradictory agendas: the conservation of religious tradition and the establishment of new traditions based on communitarian principles.

The Turkish state constantly watched the activities of these movements and pursued a policy of "fear and favor." For instance, Tunahan was arrested three times, in 1939, 1944, and 1957. He spent three days in prison in connection with the first and eight days in connection with the second arrest, which ended without any charges being proven. The third arrest was his worst experience. In 1957 he was arrested during an incident in the historic Ulu Cami Mosque in Bursa, where a man declared himself the Mehdi (similar to the Christian messiah) and called for the overthrow of the government. Tunahan was charged with masterminding this event and spent several months in jail, where he was tortured by the police despite being 69 years old at the time. On September 16, 1959, a few months after his release from jail, he died. His son-in-law, Kemal Kacar (1917–2000), succeeded him as the organizational (not religious) leader of the movement. Kacar, an outspoken critic of Erbakan's political Islam, was elected to Parliament from Kütahya (1965–1973) and Istanbul (1977–1980) as AP deputy and played a significant role in expanding Qur'anic seminaries. The Süleymancı community differs somewhat from traditional Nakşibendi orders, although its followers insist that they are Nakşibendi. In their regular meeting, the followers read the classics of Nakşibendi thought, such as the *Mektubat* of Rabbani.

The Opportunity Spaces and the Süleymancıs

The economic and political opportunity spaces shaped the evolution of the Süleymancı movement. During the rigid period of secularization, Tunahan utilized the inner-self and private spheres to conserve and maintain Islamic ideas and practices. During the multiparty system, the state accommodated religious identity claims and allowed the establishment of Qur'an seminaries in 1949. This legal and political opening helped to shift the strategy of the Süleymancıs from "withdrawal" (1924–1949) to "engagement" (1949–1957), including even a degree of cooptation. As a result of the 1949 decision to open Qur'an seminaries and hire more preachers for the state mosques, Tunahan trained and employed preachers for the Directorate of Religious Affairs (DİB). The seminaries offered major employment opportunities to thousands of rural youth in the religious civil service. The movement also institutionalized itself as the Association of the Qur'an Seminaries and established a symbiotic relationship with the state. The Süleymancı preachers had to accommodate themselves to the national-secular philosophy of the state by incorporating nationalism and some Republicanism into religious identity and adopting a religious position that was pro-state, nationalist, anticommunist, and antipolitical Islam. This crossfertilization of nationalism and religion became the major characteristic of the Süleymancıs in the 1950s and 1960s. The Süleymancı preachers dominated the different levels of the DİB until the new 1965 Directorate of Religious Affairs Law, which allowed only the graduates of İmam Hatip and Divinity schools to be employed at the DİB. This sowed the seeds of an ongoing row between the Süleymancıs and the DİB. In order to present themselves as "acceptable" to the state, the Sülemancıs never hesitated to accuse the graduates of İmam Hatip schools of being "political Islamists and sympathizers of Arab radicalism." Indeed, Erbakan's campaign to establish more İmam Hatip schools enhanced their claims about the politicization of the DİB.

Despite the Süleymancı arguments, the 1971 military coup decided to "nationalize" the private Qur'an seminaries, which had to give up some of their buildings to the DİB. Thus, since the 1965 Law and the 1971 coup, the Süleymancıs have focused on the market and started to build a distinct "Turkish-

Islamic" community among Turkish workers in Germany. Moreover, new economic opportunities in Turkey and the financial resources of the Turkish workers helped the Süleymancıs to carve a new space for themselves in terms of meeting the housing and scholarship needs of the growing numbers of university students. In this respect, their aim was to protect the new generation against leftist-atheism and radical political Islam. In the 1970s, they started to organize among the Turkish workers in Europe, whose religious affairs were ignored totally by the DİB. The 1980 coup further enhanced the Süleymancı networks, as the state regarded the Turkish-Islamic synthesis as a new national identity. As of 2003, they run the most powerful dormitory networks in Turkey and the second-largest mosque network in Germany. Their dormitories are cleaner and more highly disciplined than those of the state and are equipped with up-to-date technology to meet the needs of the university students.

Features of the Movement

After the death of Tunahan, his followers claimed that he had the blessing of the Prophet (veraset-i nübüvvet) and was responsible for a spiritual renaissance in the Turkish nation. Like Sheik Khalid, Tunahan gave instructions to his followers to make a rabıta (spiritual bond) to himself rather than any other leader. This spiritual bond requires his followers to seek union with Tunahan through the interior visualization of his image in order to attain the supreme Reality—being absorbed in the sheik (al-fana fi al-sheikh) and God. According to his followers, he therefore represents the "seal of sainthood" (evliya), meaning that there won't be any similarly blessed leaders after Tunahan. The Süleymancıs have been very active in certain offices of the higher bureaucracy and actively involved in religious training throughout Anatolia. The movement singled out Turkish youth, in particular, from the outset. Tunahan was an early enthusiast concerning the importance and revolutionary role of the print media in opening up discursive spaces and liberating Islamic thought not only from Kemalist oppression but also from the weight of religious tradition. He supported Necip Fazıl's populist Islamic magazine Büyük Doğu and encouraged his followers to read it. According to his followers, he also stressed the need to restore pan-Islamic ties that had been sundered by the abolishment of the caliphate. He passionately supported the liberation movement of Algerian Muslims against French colonial rule and often was questioned by the police because of taking such a keen interest in international Islamic developments.

There are four characteristics that identify the movement of Tunahan. First, the movement has centered on traditional religious training, which was institutionalized after his death. The stress on traditional, memorized religious education differentiates the movement from the Nakşibendi and Nur movements. When the Kemalist state's policies shifted between closing all religious education and creating its own version of "enlightened religious scholar" (aydın din adamı), the movement created an alternative informal education to preserve and perpetuate traditional religious education. The movement stressed certain classical Islamic texts as essential and helped to transform this religious education into a social movement. For instance, the *Mektubat* has been the foundational text in the perpetuation of Nakşibendi-Süleymancı identity. This text is "read" but is not "discussed" to create an ideological movement; rather, it is used as an entry into the inner self of Muslims and as a way of building inner resistance against the corrupt influences of the consumer society. The text also plays the role of "symbolic recitation" to form a shared vocabulary among the followers of Tunahan.

Second, one might regard the movement as "passive civil resistance" to the Kemalist reforms that were aimed at creating a secular society and polity. By identifying religious training as its primary goal, the movement stresses communal discipline and Sunni-Hanefi-Ottoman orthodoxy as its main ideological boundary. In other words, the formation of the Süleymancı community through discipline and struggle to protect the "core" of Islam, that is, the Sunni-Hanefi vision of Islam, via religious training, is a response to the state policies of controlling religion and the inner life of its citizens. The Süleymancıs have carved a spiritual space to critique the state policies and also the impact of political Islam. In other words, the Süleymancıs participate in the modern market and politics by conserving Islamic orthodoxy. They prefer to live within a democratic and capitalist system but with an opportunity to build a set of inner walls within themselves against the corrupting influences of consumerism. In the process of building these inner walls, or immunization against consumerism, the communitarian nature of the movement always has been stressed, and individualism is looked down on as a form of egoism or a deviation.

Third, the movement struggles against religious innovations (*bid'at*) by trying to conserve Sunni-Hanefi Islamic tradition. However, at the center of this conservatism there is a traditional radicalism. The movement's ideas about the nature of the Nakşibendi sheik are radical and have gained some cultist characteristics centered around the personality of Tunahan. In a way, the movement simultaneously seeks to preserve Sunni-Hanefi tradition and engages a radical religious innovation in the Nakşibendi tradition. The Süleymancı identity therefore has been woven together by the duality of radicalism and conservatism. Radicalism in the interpretation of Nakşibendi tradition has been contained in terms of seeking to conserve the fundamental Sunni/Hanefi core of Islam. In other words, the Süleymancıs represented an attempt to modernize religious training under authoritarian premises by seeking to remold behavior and bodies to combat domestic decadence. The movement creates a distinct sense of identity and community as a result of its radical traditionalism. Its informal training networks are the most powerful and disciplined. These networks helped to create an impenetrable social capital, as it were, of trust in social relations but with very little room for free thought.

Fourth, its modern outlook, intense web of social networks, and commitment to electoral politics and the market system enhanced the communal characteristics of the Süleymancı movement. As far as the politics of the community are concerned, Sülemancıs always have been critical of political Islam in general, and Islamic intellectuals in particular. In addition, the Süleymancıs always have been critical of state-run education and religious activities. They prefer autonomous community-run religious education and criticize state religious education as state-centric. For instance, the movement has been critical of and distanced itself from the İmam Hatip schools.

The Süleymancı order has become one of the most powerful proselytizing movements among Turkish workers in Germany. One result, to the consternation of Turkish state authorities, has been that many religious Turks in Europe have become hesitant to follow the instructions of the state-controlled DİB. They reject the Kemalist version of secular Islam and, ironically, stress that secularism in the Western tradition means that the state has no right to interfere in the spiritual life of its citizens.[68] The followers of Tunahan during the Özal period warmly supported the "Turkish-Islamic synthesis." The movement dominated religious student hostels, and the Qur'anic courses opened at this time. In the past the Süleymancıs have sought to influence politics through their support of the AP of Süleyman Demirel (1964–1980), the ANAP of Özal (1983–1993), and the RP of Erbakan (1994–1998).[69] In the 2002 elections, two grandsons of Tunahan, Ahmet Denizolgun of ANAP and Mehmet Denizolgun of AKP, competed for a seat in Parliament. The election of Mehmet Denizolgun created a major power struggle between the brothers over the leadership of the Süleymancı community.

Conclusion

The Nakşibendi orders, along with their complex web of institutions and practices, successfully expanded their influence and created new social, cultural, and economic spaces that exist independent of state control. The Sufi orders have turned out to be the primary sources of the diverse interests and identities that have developed in the Turkish-Islamic scene. The discourse is led by figures such as Necip Fazıl Kısakürek, Nurettin Topçu, and Sezai Karakoç. This formation of a new urban-Islamic intellectual discourse indicates that Islamic acculturation goes hand in hand with accommodating different views and practices within conventional institutions. To a large extent, the long tradition of the Nakşibendis has been transmitted to the new urban culture through these Islamist intellectuals. The fact of having arisen within a Sufi tradition distinguishes Turkish Islamist intellectuals from Muslim intellectuals in other countries. The Turkish Islamists appreciate the role of history and tradition and argue that the understanding of Islam is conditional on a person's own spiritual quest. For this reason Turkish Islamic movements generally have tended to be liberal, open, and ready to reconcile differences within a democratic context, rejecting the slogans used by those who call for an "Islamic revolution" or an "Islamic state."

Empirical study of the Nakşibendi orders is very important for understanding that the Sufis' ability to adapt to new sociopolitical conditions also elucidates their power to shape society. From the examination of the Nakşibendi orders, it becomes apparent that Islam (as cultural and social signifier) should be understood not as a self-contained reality but rather as a historically evolving belief system. Islam, for various Nakşibendi orders, is an ongoing discovery of revealed knowledge; the different Nakşibendi orders compete to establish their own hegemonic, yet constantly evolving interpretation as the "authentic" one.

At the frontier of state-society interactions, the Nakşibendis display several features of great significance. The order articulates rapid social and economic changes in terms of shared Islamic idioms, thus building a common cognitive map on which to situate social changes. The Nakşibendis in the Turkish context have managed to reconceptualize the processes of modernity by reimagining Islam. The Nakşibendis have accommodated themselves to social, economic, and political changes. Expanding trade created a new middle class that became the basis of Islamic activism during the tenure of Özal. The Islamic movements of the 1980s had a strong middle-class dimension, and the revival of the Nakşibendi and Nurcu movements was a response to the ideological and political needs of the middle class.

The Nakşibendi orders, while serving as the matrix for the emergence of major Islamic movements, also witnessed a far-reaching transformation in religious discourse and associational life that came about with the economic developments of the country. The orders have undergone a transition from Sufi lodge–based communities to text-based ones as a result of the print and media revolutions. This transformation is seen most vividly in the life of the Nurcu leader Said Nursi.

Sufi orders all demonstrate a willingness to appropriate modernity on their own terms and for the benefit of the Muslim community with regard to democracy, human rights, and the market economy. These movements do not seek to project the past into the future but rather to read the past in terms of the needs of the present and the future. At the heart of all these movements in Turkey is the effort to articulate new identities as well as a new sense of community that provides Muslims with a sense of who they are and that they have intrinsic value which justifies their existence.

7

Print-Based Islamic Discourse

The Nur Movement

The Nurcu groups have evolved into the most powerful and effective sociopolitical communities in contemporary Turkey. The writings of Said Nursi, particularly his magnum opus, *Risale-i Nur Külliyatı* (*RNK*), constitute the base of this faith movement. Nursi's work has marked Islamic political discourse indelibly, offering original ideas for addressing political and sociocultural problems. By studying the Nur community, one can understand the dynamics of religion and state on the one hand and modernity and identity on the other. The Nur groups' dynamism as a social movement is rooted in their network of media, education, business, and publishing establishments. The text-based nature of the movement makes it unique; since Nursi's death in 1960, no one has succeeded him, and the movement remains very much centered around his writings. This focus has resulted in a new idiom of communication and a new message of moral and ethical renewal for society. The Nur movement's emphasis on text naturally has resulted in its involvement in the publishing and printing businesses.

The Life of Said Nursi

As a movement of resistance to the ongoing Kemalist modernization process, the Nurcu movement is forward-looking and proactive. Said Nursi offered a conceptual framework for a people undergoing the transformation from a confessional community (*gemeinschaft*) to a secular national society (*gesellschaft*). These concepts constitute a map of meaning and provide strategies for dealing with modern challenges by redefining Islamic folk concepts and practices to establish new solidarity networks and everyday-life strategies for coping with new conditions. Living during the collapse of the Ottoman state and the emergence of the new Republic, Nursi had to respond to the dominant debates of his time. To understand the shift in emphasis in Nursi's works, one needs to see the difference between the "Old Said" and the "New Said," as he referred to himself in different periods.[1] The New Said was the older Said who had turned more toward an examination of his own inner dimension.

Nursi was born in 1876 in the village of Nurs in Bitlis province of eastern Anatolia. He was first educated by his oldest brother, Molla Abdullah; then he continued to educate himself by participating in Sufi gatherings and followed the medrese cirricula.[2] Although Nursi was ambivalent about the role of the Sufi orders in revitalizing Islam and disapproved of the rigid relationship between the Sufi sheik and his disciples, his way of thinking and method of argumentation nonetheless were influenced by the Sufism of Anatolia.[3] Nursi himself admitted that the cultural dominance of the Nakşibendi order in this environment had a significant impact on him.[4] He not only developed close working relationships with prominent Nakşibendi sheiks but also eagerly read the works of the great Indian Sufi Ahmad Sirhindi during his transformation into the New Said.[5] However, Nursi remained critical of certain aspects of traditional Sufism, arguing that Sufi traditions, which are based on imitative learning and faith, only could play a limited role in social reforms during an age of modern skepticism. However, he realized the important historic role of Sufi orders in rejuvenating Islam and adapting to social changes in the Ottoman Empire. In his essay entitled "Telvihat-ı Tis'a" (The nine allusions), Nursi defended the orders against the attacks by the Kemalist regime.[6] Nursi also regularly read the works of the Nakşibendi sheiks Sirhindi and Ahmed Gümüşhaneli, although he fell under the spiritual protection of Abd al-Qadir Gilani, the founder of the Kadiri Sufi order. In his reading, even when concentrating exclusively on the Qur'an, Nursi always returned to the *Majmu'atu'l-ahzab* (Collection of parties) of Gümüşhaneli as a source of reflection. In the constitution of the New Said's spiritual consciousness and life, the writings of Nakşibendi sheiks played an important role. In its originality his thought, however, departed significantly from the Nakşibendi tradition. For example, Sufi orders stress inner cultivation of the self, while Nursi stressed the need to reconcile faith with reason and modern exigencies: "The future will be decided by reason and science. The Qur'anic interpretation, which addresses problems in the light of reason and science, will shape the future."[7]

Nursi's keen interest in current events and the media made him aware of European prejudices against Islam and the weaknesses of his society in confronting these prejudices. His own thought was catalyzed by the confrontation between European-based critical thinking and the traditionally more imitative thinking of Ottoman society.[8] This led him to stress the need for fostering open and critical thinking within the Islamic-Ottoman tradition.

In an effort to bring the natural sciences together with Islamic sciences, Nursi visited Sultan Abdülhamid II in 1907 to seek his support for a university in Van. However, the sultan rejected his proposal to reconcile scientific reasoning with Islam. Nursi was very critical of the absolutism of Sultan Abdülhamid II and the way Islam was reduced to a state ideology. Eventually, he joined the Young Turks and became actively involved in constitutional reforms. For example, he embraced the "Young Turk" revolution of the Committee for Union and Progress (CUP) and its call for the establishment of a constitutional state.[9] However, he quickly became an open critic on witnessing the CUP's oppressive policies, convinced that his commitment to the concepts of personal liberty and constitutionalism was at odds with the CUP's exploitative use of Islam and Turkish nationalism.[10] Nursi contributed essays to the pan-Islamic *Volkan*, a militant paper of the Society for Muslim Unity (İttihad-ı Muhammedi), sharply criticizing the policies of the government.[11] This newspaper argued that the disintegration of the Ottoman state along ethnolinguistic lines only could be prevented if the sharia were implemented, creating a protected space for Muslim society. As the oppression of the CUP increased, a revolt took place in April 1909 under the leadership of Sheik Vahdeti, the head of the İttihad-ı Muhammedi, who demanded the implementation of the sharia and restoration of Abdülhamid II's powers. The CUP-controlled Operation Corps entered Istanbul on April 9, arrested the leadership of the rebellion, hanged many people suspected of involvement in the revolt, and restored the CUP government. Although Nursi did not play any role in the instigation of the rebellion—he actually convinced a group of soldiers not to join the rebellion but to return to their barracks—he was arrested because of his involvement with the Society for Muslim Unity, which was accused of inspiring the rebellion. At this trial, Nursi delivered a long, complex speech defending the virtues of constitutionalism and freedom and subsequently was acquitted.[12] However, the rebellion, commonly known as *31 Mart isyanı* (because of the difference between the Ottoman and Gregorian calendars, March 31) became a defining event for state-society relations in the late Ottoman Empire and the Republican period. The CUP presented the rebellion, which was prompted by social and political discontent, as a "reactionary" (*irtica*) event against a progressive government. Since then, almost all anticentralization and anti-Westernization opposition has been framed as "reactionary." The discourse of "reactionary" became the popular tool for excluding religious people from politics and delegitimizing any form of religious entry into the public sphere. According to İsmail Kara, the most prominent scholar of late Islamic thought in the Ottoman Empire and the early Republic, the rebellion has been construed as a "framework" for representing any form of opposition against forced homogenization as "reactionary."[13] Indeed, this rebellion was "reconstructed" by Kemalist historians to establish one of the key features of Turkish political culture by creating a fixed dichotomy between the elite, with its "Kemalism, Westernism, and secularism," and the Islamic movement of the periphery.

Nursi's close brush with the executioner undoubtedly influenced his decision to leave the Ottoman capital for his home region, around the town of Van in eastern Anatolia. In southeast Anatolia, he delivered several speeches about the ideals of constitutionalism and freedom to the Kurdish tribes and local ulema who were critical of the new CUP government. He collected his lectures and conversation notes in a volume published as *Münazarat* (Debates),[14] in which he treats freedom and inquiry as an integral part of faith and identifies poverty, ignorance, and internal enmity as the problems of the Muslim community. An individual, for Nursi, requires freedom to realize the power of God, and through this realization, the individual will in turn be freed from manmade oppression and persecution. In short, democracy and freedom are treated as the necessary conditions for the existence of a just society.[15] After a year in Van, Nursi visited Damascus and delivered an acclaimed and controversial speech in the great Ummayyad mosque in support of constitutionalism and Islamic reform. He stressed the death of truthfulness in sociopolitical life, enmity, despotism, and egoism as the major sources of social and political decline in Muslim world.[16]

During World War I, Nursi wrote his most philosophically complex text, known as *İşaratül i'caz* (Signs of the Inimitable) in Arabic. He also participated in the war, organizing Kurdish tribes against Russo-Armenian advances in eastern Anatolia. He was captured in 1916 and spent two years in Kosturma, in the far west of the Urals, as a prisoner-of-war before returning to Istanbul. Back in Istanbul, he again became inner-oriented and found himself in deep spiritual crisis. During this period, Ahmed Sirhindi's *Mektubat* helped him to overcome the crisis and take the Qur'an as his guide and master. Sufism was the most powerful layer in the formation of his ideas and personality.

Nursi sharply attacked the British occupation of Istanbul, publishing an article, "The Six Steps," in newspapers. He mobilized religious opinion against the British and in favor of the emerging national movement led by Mustafa Kemal. In August 1922 he went to Ankara and became a strong supporter of the Turkish liberation struggle and the nationalist leaders around Kemal.[17] His enthusiasm only abated when he became aware of the radically anti-Islamic plans that the new Republican leaders intended to implement.[18] He took a train from Ankara to Van and later referred to this as the "transitional journey" from the Old Said to the New Said. During this journey in April 1923, he concluded that the rejuvenation of Islamic consciousness had to be carried out not at the state level but at the level of individuals. He shifted his emphasis to the inner dimension of individual spirituality and the development of a new, reflective Islamic consciousness. He saw the minds of the reformist elite as having been invaded by skepticism and positivist philosophy. In order to counter this skepticism, he sought to "bring God back" by raising Islamic consciousness in everyday life. He no longer believed in societal transformation through political involvement, saying that it was necessary to develop an "intellectually able group" to create a counterdiscourse of Islamic identity and morality. The goal thus became the construction of an Islamic consciousness and a new map of meaning to guide everyday life. Nursi's main struggle was not with modernity but rather with the positivist epistemology that sought to uproot human beings from their sacred origins. The New Said, therefore, was characterized by his withdrawal from politics and public life. This "internal emigration," or withdrawal into contemplation (*tefekkür*), marked his thinking and writings.

As a result of three years of contemplation in Van, Nursi finished his first essay, *Mesnevi-i Nuriye*, to set the conceptual framework of his lifelong work, the *RNK*. In order to carry out this goal, Nursi remained in Van, where he stayed until 1925, when he was accused of being involved in the Kurdish-Islamic rebellion that broke out the same year.[19] This rebellion was led by the Nakşibendi Kurdish tribal sheik Said and "the explicit aim of the rebellion was the establishment of an independent Kurdish state, where the Islamic principles, violated in modern Turkey, were to be respected."[20] After the rebellion, the government institutionalized a set of policies, including closure of the Sufi lodges and orders, to suppress such further incidents. Nursi was exiled to the village of Barla, near the city of Burdur.[21]

Nursi realized that the Kemalist reforms were meant to divorce the modern Turkish state and society from its Islamic heritage and, in a more general sense, reflected the profound crisis of religious faith itself in the face of the new positivist religion of the early twentieth century. Because of his continued activity, he was exiled to Isparta. During this eight-and-a-half-year period in exile, Nursi wrote almost 90 percent of the entire *RNK* collection.[22] Since all reading or discussion of his works was banned by the state, Nursi's commentaries were scribed by hand and distributed via a confidential network known as the postmen of the *RNK* (*Nur postacıları*). Those involved in the distribution and production of Nursi's commentaries formed a secretive solidarity network that became the foundation of "textual communities," the dershanes, that in turn became one of the embryonic forms of civil society in Turkey. His followers made more copies and distributed them widely throughout Anatolia.[23] When a core group of followers begun to emerge, Nursi was arrested and tried by the Eskişehir court on the charge of creating an illegal Sufi order and subsequently was imprisoned for 11 months. The court dubbed his followers "Nurcus."[24] In 1934 he was again arrested, allegedly for harboring antistate opinions, and was forced to live in the town of Isparta.

The mature Nursi of the Republican era saw his mission as safeguarding the Islamic religious and cultural underpinnings of Turkish identity. He also aimed to rejuvenate this identity by addressing some of the legitimate shortcomings that critics and intellectuals had pointed to in the late Ottoman period. The Kemalists' ultimate objective was to transform the consciousness of the new Republic's citizens by constructing a "secular *and* national" identity that was as devoid as possible of links to the Ottoman-Islamic past. In response to this project, Nursi struggled to create an alternative inner religious community, articulated in the household and formed through face-to-face relationships without requiring potentially hazardous outward demonstrations in the political sphere. To a large degree, this shift corresponded to the one Nursi underwent himself, from outward activism to withdrawal into the inner sanctum of a contemplative Islam. By stressing religious consciousness, which need not be manifested outwardly, Nursi sought to preserve an inner spiritual sphere free from the depredations of state policy. Nursi defined freedom in terms of his project of creating an inner community. He argued that the government only could prosecute an individual who actively broke the antireligious laws with his "hands" and "would find it difficult to interfere in the household, heart, and private realm of the individual citizen and believer."[25] His deliberate efforts to avoid politics, however, did not mean that the state ignored him. Between 1925 and 1949, Nursi was arrested several times and tried on charges of trying to organize an Islamic political party, although he always was acquitted by the courts.

Why did Nursi and his followers represent a threat to the Kemalist project? What made Nursi the "enemy" of the Kemalist project was his alternative conceptualization of science, identity, self, and the rule of law, which together would form a vernacular of modernity that was more appealing for common Muslims than the imitative top-down Westernization of the Kemalist state. Nursi rejected instrumental use of Islam as a national liberation movement or an ideology to empower the state. Religion, for Nursi, was the source of normative charter, a sort of "meta-norm" that can be used to form morality and identity. His conception of the state also differed from the Young Turk and Kemalist view in that the latter treated the state as the agent for determining what constitutes a good life and an instrument of modernizing and guiding the society. In other words, the official modernization project sought to empower the state and used all means to engineer a new "official" public sphere. Thus, this new "official" public sphere was based on binary oppositions of secular versus religious, ala franga (a European lifestyle and tastes in furniture and music) versus ala turca (an Islamically informed Turkish lifestyle, tastes in furniture and music, and ritual cleanliness), salon versus family room, science versus religion, and modern versus traditional. This in turn worsened relations between the state and society because the state tried to impose its exclusivist secularist ideology on the population.

The multiparty system facilitated Nursi's "return" to politics. He viewed "political parties as the pillars of democracy."[26] In his early writings, he argued that political parties were compatible with Islam as long as they promoted the unity and well-being of the nation.[27] He fully supported a multiparty system and did not hesitate to support the DP against the ruling CHP during the thaw of the 1950s.[28] He argued that parliamentary constitutionalism and the rule of law provided the best environment for the rejuvenation of Islam. Nursi saw political participation (meşveret) and the rule of law as the two pillars of social justice. He defended parliamentarianism and constitutionalism as the most reasonable means for the realization of a prosperous and just society. Nursi argued that, by nature, each citizen should be "concerned with the issues of homeland, nation, and government," but one "should not blindly subordinate individual will to collective will in the name of a nation or homeland."[29] By arguing that Islam cannot and should not be used for political goals, he said that religion ultimately had to occupy a realm above day-to-day power politics.[30] Nursi openly argued against the establishment of pro-Islamic parties because he believed Turkey's polarized society was not ready to tolerate them.[31] Nursi's followers also remained suspicious of nascent pro-Islamic parties, arguing that such parties were likely to harm Islamic interests by using Islam opportunistically for political goals. Nursi viewed the connection between Islam and politics as problematic. He believed that if the majority of society began to identify itself consciously with Islam, the antireligious policies of the Kemalist Republic would whither away.[32]

Nursi died in Urfa on March 23, 1960, only two days after arriving there. He wanted to spend his final days in Urfa, where different ethnic groups—Turks, Kurds, and Arabs—live together. Since the authorities required him not to leave Isparta, he asked his car driver to cover up the license plate as they drove from Isparta to Urfa via Konya.[33]

Nursi's Ideas

The writings of Nursi sought to create a conceptual bridge between Turkish society and Islam by addressing two perennial issues during the first half of the twentieth century: (1) the breakdown of religious authority, and (2) the dominance of scientific and political positivism. Nursi's goal was the survival of Islam as a living text, one embodied in daily experiences, without the support of political means and traditional pillars such as the Sufi lodges. As the Republican state began to treat religion as the main obstacle to national development, Nursi struggled to come up with a new interpretation and methodology of Islam. He stressed the study of the Qur'an to adapt Islam to modern conditions. Such study had to be undertaken by educated Muslims, for he realized that the traditional ulema, who claimed to possess a monopoly over the interpretation of religious texts, could not meet the challenges of a positivist age in which a new critical stance toward knowledge has developed. Nursi's writings thus profess three major objectives: first, to raise the consciousness of Muslims; second, to refute the dominant intellectual discourses of materialism and positivism; third, to recover collective memory by revising the shared grammar of society, Islam.[34]

Raising Muslim Consciousness by Faith

Nursi's understanding of Islam was based on his understanding of human nature. He believed that certain characteristics are innate to all human beings. Religious faith, for Nursi, is the outcome of man's intellectual weakness and failure to create permanent harmony in his life and society. He argued that individuals are in a state of constant tension between desire and reason, because humans have infinite appetites but limited resources. The only way to manage this tension is by developing a full connection with God. Nursi criticized positivist epistemology and its desire to control nature and man simultaneously. Since religion is innate to human nature, Nursi sees the lack of religion as the source of many conflicts and wars. He extended this concept of tension to the societal level, where the absence of God in public space is the source of man's problems. His goal, therefore, was to bring God back to the public space. This required a response to the dominant positivist epistemology. Connecting to God, for Nursi, meant introducing new conceptual resource tools, to shape and lead human conduct. Nursi's project offered a new "map of meaning" for Muslims to guide their conduct. He did not offer an "Islamic state" or "Islamic constitution" but rather a mode of thinking about reconnecting with God and forming one's personality.

Nursi contrasted the social, political, and cultural implications of living in a faithful versus a faithless society. He defined faith as understanding human life from birth to death in terms of Qur'anic concepts. He argued that by replacing faith through imitation (taklidi iman) with faith by inquiry (tahkiki iman), Muslims would be able to resist the forces of modern positivism, namely materialism and atheism. A Muslim must inquire why he or she is created and how one comes to exist. After becoming conscious of these questions, Muslims can construct a community with this consciousness. He argued that all virtues—justice, peace, honesty, integrity, and love—emanate from faith in a higher judge and religiously based moral precepts; whereas anarchy, egoism, oppression, and poverty are all outcomes of the lack of faith and moral precepts.[35] Faith, therefore, is the basis of a moral community and the source of knowledge concerning the phenomenal world. Nursi expressed his beliefs in terms of the concepts of faith (iman), and life (hayat) whereby faith is experienced in everyday practices, and the social order is shaped by Islam (sharia).[36] He argued that faith is formed through connections between the heart, the brain, and the spirit, whereas life is a zone where faith is expressed through behaving according to Islamic mores.

Nursi realized that in the modern era, dominated by the empiricism of the Enlightenment, faith could be sustained only if believers actively attempted to understand and interpret Islam. He made the text comprehensible to ordinary people in everyday language so that they could understand and contemplate. Nursi's approach, therefore, represents a turning point from an ulema/Sufi lodge–based imitative understanding of Islam to a more complex, reflective understanding. He argued that the Muslims of Turkey could not maintain their faith by mimicking their forefathers or Europe but only through critical and deliberative analysis.

Challenging Positivism

The main characteristic of positivism is its view that science is the only valid knowledge. The only way to achieve progress, then, is by using science to guide human conduct and society. The main target of Turkish positivists was Islam, which they viewed as a source of backwardness. The Republic used the new education system to institutionalize a "positive" religion in place of traditional theological religions. This divorce of man from his sacred roots was, for Nursi, the source of poverty, war, and animosity. Responding to the penetrating impact of positivism in the Turkish educational system and the total collapse of the Islamic educational system, Nursi tried to demonstrate the compatibility of science and religion; freedom and faith; and modernity and tradition. He updated the idioms of Islam in terms of the dominant universal discourses of science, human rights, and the rule of law. Although Nursi was reacting to this positivist philosophy, he also was constrained by the consequences of new socioeconomic forces that helped to expand public reasoning. This in turn resulted in the constitution of the abstracted self and dissemination of scientific reasoning by separating the laws of nature from the power of God. This epistemological secularization of public reasoning and the delinking of the self from the sacred was a major development.

By realizing the damaging impact of positivism and the erosion of religious authority in society, Nursi used the same new spaces of books and magazines to challenge the impact of positivism and propagate his own version of science. Nursi's sense that Islam was under the siege of positivism and skepticism motivated his writings. This sense of peril actually remained with him until the end of his life, motivating him to defend the Qur'an as compatible with human reason. According to Nursi, the Jewish, Christian, and Islamic revelations are the "word," and their interpretations can vary according to time and space. The meaning of the Qur'an, for Nursi, is changeable. Moreover, scientific discoveries reveal the depth of the Qur'an's message: "as times grows older," he said, "the Qur'an grows younger, its signs become apparent." Nursi, unlike other Islamists, treated scientific discoveries as an attempt to "further deepen understanding of the Qur'an."[37] As human knowledge expands in nonreligious areas, so does our understanding of Qur'anic revelation. By linking a better understanding of the Qur'an with scientific discoveries, Nursi sought to open a new and radical reading of the Qur'an.

Nursi argued that rigid imitation and rote learning may have sufficed in an earlier age but were no longer applicable in the modern age. He recognized that in an age of skepticism, there was a need for a new methodology to get people to believe in the existence of God. Nursi's target population was the urban and literate population because this group naturally would be the site where future hegemonic cultural forms would emerge. He stressed the importance of "evidence" or natural theology, to get educated people to believe in God without ignoring the role of revelation (*vahiy*). The goal was to prove the existence of God at the individual level. The Nur movement cultivated a new form of consciousness that demonstrated that science and technology were not incompatible with faith in God. Unlike many "fundamentalist" Islamist thinkers, Nursi did not present the Qur'an as the source for all major scientific discoveries. Instead, he considered scientific progress a sign and proof of God's purposeful plan for Creation.[38] Nursi's goal was to protect secular education from unbelief and religious education from fanaticism by reconciling faith and science.

According to his writings, there are three ways of acquiring Islamic knowledge: the Qur'an, the Prophet, and the universe, which he usually refers to as the "Grand Book of Universe." Nursi argues that nature as a "book indicates with utmost clarity, the existence of its scribe and its author, as well as His [God's] ability and accomplishments." In other words, nature should not be understood in itself, that is, *mana-yı ismi*, but rather in terms of its Creator, that is, *mana-yı harfi*. Almost every being in nature, including humans, reflects the artfulness of the Creator, the artisan and maker of them all. Nursi used the laws of nature to explain the power of the Creator. In response to the prevailing tendency toward skepticism and the discursive shift from a religious to a secular worldview,

Nursi attempted to develop a new conceptual terminology that would bring religion and science together. He stressed the multilayered meanings of the Qur'an
and taught that nature had no meaning in itself but rather signified *mana-yı
harfi*, the existence of order and the presence of God. In short, he regarded nature as the script of God and the Qur'an as God's word. Nursi's concept of knowledge is linked closely to the Qur'anic allegories. He tried to examine the laws of
nature as a manifestation of the many names of God. The knowledge of nature,
for Nursi, was illuminated in terms of the allegories from the Qur'an.

For Nursi nature by itself has no power, and it requires a transcendental power
of God to become action and thus take on meaning. Nature was the evidence of
the work of God and his omnipotence. Order in nature therefore is the reflection
of the names of God: eternal (*al-hayy*), giver of life (*al-Muhyi*), the ever self-existing
one (*al-qayyum*), the everlasting one (*al-baqi*), most holy (*ism-i Kuddus*), all-just (*ism-
i Adl*), and all-wise (*ism-i hakem*). In short, nature is a vision of God. Nursi wanted
his followers to feel God's presence by studying his words and continuous action.
By reading the verses of the Qur'an through the eyes of new scientific discoveries, he tried to free younger generations from the impact of positivism. However,
he did not reject the mechanistic understanding of the universe but treated this
mechanism and order as the design of the divine Creator. This theistic conception of the universe, that is, that God created the universe ex nihilo and that God
is separate from the universe but also continuously active in it, is one that Nursi
and his followers fully internalized and taught. In the case of Nursi, science and
sacred text mutually read to decode the other. Thus he advocated a relativistic
understanding of Islam, maintaining that neither a single cleric nor a religious
institution can claim to provide the true interpretation of religion. Since understanding Islam is dependent on time, space, and circumstance, competing paradigms must not be silenced. He also advocated the separation of religion and
politics—because the latter is bound to derogate or hinder free interpretation of
Islam. By allowing each person to interpret Islam according to his or her own
conditions, Nursi tried to socialize religion.

Personality and Memory

After identifying the enemies of Islam as ignorance, friction, and poverty, Nursi
presented education, hard work, and consensus as a solution. Nursi's Islam is
personal, with the goal of constructing microlevel morality by raising religious
consciousness. His writings constantly try to build a pious and modern Muslim personality, one that is tolerant but firm about the core virtues of Islam.
Nursi's books were his refuge, and they have become an avenue to fulfillment
for soul-searching Turks.

Nursi tried to protect the Muslim personality from the destructive impact of
the state's nationalism and positivism by carving an inner space of self-development and direction to cope with external events and pressures. The development
of this inner space was the major aim and challenge of his writings. The journey
of self-development only was possible through recognition of the power of the

inner self qua God. Like many Sufis, Nursi thought that the inner self is the only force capable of resisting and generating imaginative dissent against oppressive forces. This reflective and creative power of Muslims was Nursi's main capital in maintaining the journey of self-development. He knew the negative impact of capitalist forces and the ways by which the state and the market created the self as a stranger and a source of tension and problems. By stressing religious values, Nursi struggled to shape the self for power and to form the self with power to resist the "civilizing" policies of the state. He realized that the Kemalist project was producing persons short in collective memory and devoid of any cognitive map of action. He sought to offer an alternative reading of the self. He insisted that the fundamental goal of life is not the search for power but rather the search for knowledge to realize the power of God. Nursi treated Islam as a source of inner power to mobilize in confrontation with the state's positivist ideology and materialism. His concerns were very similar to those of modern theorists who say that rationalization threatens the self and society by depriving both of the capacity to posit anything but their own submission. He identified the sources of the autonomous self so as to resist its disempowerment by the bureaucratic system and positivism, which assigned all decisions to experts. He thus gave a central role to the concepts of *iman* (faith) and *insan* (person) rather than to the concept of power. Indeed, faith creates a capacity to initiate, resist, and alter power relations at the micro and macro levels.

To address these issues, Nursi sought to create a parallel inner space for the ordinary Muslim to contemplate faith in everyday experiences. His writing is a vehicle to translate Islamic forms and practices into the rhythms of everyday conventions. He realized that he could use the medium of print as a new means of constructing consciousness. He also realized that the ulema could not respond to these modern challenges. Therefore, he created a new locus for authority—the text itself—to give equal footing to all Muslims, allowing them to make sense of their faith according to their own encounters.

Nursi's ideas appeal to a large segment of Turkish society, partly because of his development of a new conceptual bridge for the transition from tradition to modernity, from oral to print culture, and from a rural to an urban environment. Nursi imagined a gradual transformation, beginning with the process of (1) raising individual Muslim consciousness, continuing to (2) the implementation of faith in everyday life, and then to (3) the restoration of the sharia. He sought to equip individual Muslims with the necessary tools to guide their lives in accordance with Islamic precepts. By a sharia-governed society, Nursi meant a law-governed, just society. In addition to his stress on the concepts of justice, identity, community, and the connection between science and religion, Nursi's extremely cautious attitude toward politics and the ideological state helped the movement to become more active in social and cultural spheres. Nursi's understanding of the state differed from that of the Young Turks and the later Kemalists, for he treated the state as the "servant" of the people and argued for a neutral state without any ideology. The state, for Nursi, should be molded according to the needs and desires of the people. He argued that citizens and communities are rivers and streams, whereas the state is the pool: a change in the quality and quantity of the "stream is going to have direct impact on the pool; if the problem is in the pool, it will not have an affect on the sources of the stream."[39] Since the state is a servant of the people, its employees, for Nursi, do not even need to be Muslims because their duty is to serve the people in accordance with the law.

Paradoxically, the success of the Kemalist reforms also resulted in the Nur movement's growth. The expansion of communication and universal education, the centralization of law, and the growing secularization and disenchantment of society were also products of the Kemalist revolution. Drawing a distinction between the positive and the negative consequences of Kemalism thus fractures my discussion because an analysis of the Nur movement involves a self-preserving dialogue within its internal and external boundaries. For example, the Nur movement first took hold and expanded in the western provinces of Anatolia; the literacy rate was higher there, and people there thus had a greater capacity for understanding the Nurcu message than did people in the eastern provinces, where the landowning elite, known as sheiks or *ağas*, controlled daily life. In fact, the western provinces of Anatolia have remained the center of the movement.[40]

As the attributes of modernity expanded to the periphery, individuals' needs for a symbolic structure and for religion were transformed. For example, although the urban environment tends to encourage skepticism, religion in the city becomes a form of identity and a network system that allows one to cope with urban problems. The rapid migration of rural populations to urban centers as a result of expanding capitalist conditions necessitated a new religious idiom that Nursi ably sought to provide. His project involved a break within Islamic tradition, one that could appeal to the rapidly evolving conditions of rural populations recently uprooted to urban centers.

With its textual characteristics, the Nur movement created new possibilities for those who had moved from rural areas to urban centers and desired to reconstruct their conception of Islam in a prevailing age of skepticism and secularism. These "textual communities" secularized Islam in an effort to make the secular functions of nature and life accommodate sacred concerns and understandings. The printed word became a vehicle for the formation of a Nurcu consciousness. Another main feature of the Nurcu movement is that it has stressed the significance of reason over miracles in religious understanding.

The Formation of Textual Communities as Dershanes

After Nursi's death in 1960, his inner circle transformed into "textual communities" and spread across Turkey. If Nursi's ideas gave meaning to the everyday life of his followers, it was this circle's organizational strategies that provided them with the institutional resources and the dynamism to become a leading social and religious movement. These "textual communities" got together to read out and interpret his texts in dershanes. The dershane is a special apartment or one-floor building where a congregation of people meets to read aloud and discuss Nursi's writings. Although his goal had been to present a book that did not need a teacher to understand its meaning, the spread of the work through its reading within the structure of dershanes has contributed to the formation of a communal Islamic-social political consciousness.

The *RNK* has become the tool that pulls diverse groups together. In dershanes, reading is evolving into a kind of large-scale community formation with a number of social activities that consolidate social ties. In the urbanizing society of Turkey, people are isolated and search for ways to connect with other people. Reading the same book and internalizing the same vocabulary play an important role in connecting people. Through collective readings, Nurcus learn a new normative charter of action that shapes their understanding of the world and serves as a basis for action. These beliefs inform what actions are good and desirable and what are to be avoided.

In order to understand the community-building impact of the *RNK*, one needs to explore the meaning of the reading in the Nur context. The mode of religious reading establishes certain relations between the reader and the writings of Nursi. As a result of this institutionalized reading, readers develop a certain cognitive and ethical attitude toward themselves, each other, and the whole community. This relationship between readers and what they read has not been examined fully. Some readers develop technical skills for extracting several competing meanings from the text. Nursi's Turkish narrative vernacular and metaphoric writing offers a rich and dynamic array of texts that can be tested out to understand contemporary challenges and the deep continuity in human relations. Moreover, new participants in these reading circles are encouraged to internalize a certain disposition in their approach to the *RNK*. The *RNK* empowers its reader by offering a worldview and a moral system for action. In a way, it becomes a treasure trove into which one can dig for deeper meanings in response to the human desire for meaning. Thus each gathering to read the *RNK* opens up new horizons, because there is no final act of reading when it comes to discovering the meaning of religious texts.

Nurcus believe that reading these texts is required to keep stability and a sense of community. In a way, reading becomes a way of understanding and discovering (not creating) the self and developing a moral position to cope with social issues and diversity. An act of reading becomes an act of self-discovery. The major difference between religious reading and regular reading of novels, magazines, and textbooks is that in the latter forms of reading one reads to get information, to be entertained, or to cultivate one's humanity with the goal of discovering a vocation in life; in the first form of reading, one seeks spiritual fulfillment. The *RNK*'s readers stress reading more than writing, and they even memorize some of the essays, which they recall during their debates and discussions to develop an argument.

Reading creates a community, and collective reading becomes a ritual activity to affirm this communal gathering. Readers not only are trained to think about the meaning of Qur'anic verses but also the world around them, because, according to the *RNK*, creation is the essential part of revelation. Thus God's power and grace is communicated not only through sacred texts but also through physical signs and the order in creation. People need to develop their eyes and hearts to capture the power of God. Nursi argued that the degree to which one can comprehend God depends on one's abilities (in terms of education, age, and positions) and willingness to understand God's power. When people comprehend the power of God and develop inner conviction, they then act in such a way that they feel the presence of God in their life. In other words, knowing requires conviction, and conviction, in turn, generates action. Nursi's RNK, then, forms the faith of these textual communities, but this faith also constitutes the meaning of the RNK. Some textual communities are more inspired to develop open-ended readings of the RNK. Individual understanding of the RNK always has been checked and examined by the understanding of the community. In a way, there is no communal authority to control the meaning and reading of the RNK other than the community of readers.

As a result of their devotion to these essential texts, Nurcus have developed a separate language and cognitive framework that sets them apart from other Islamic groups in Turkey. The main function of these textual-communities is to listen to and reflect on the texts and disseminate their meaning to society. Institutionalized as dershanes, the reading of the RNK has been transformed from a silent, inward process to an ultimately communal and interactive experience. The RNK, treated as knowledge bestowed by the grace of God, once read, creates shared attitudes toward the phenomenal world and social interactions.

Although Nursi invested the world with meaning, the Nurcus believe that Nursi's knowledge was not simply acquired but was bestowed by God. In fact he imposed religious meaning on the world and articulated regularities in life and nature as a manifestation of God. For a Nurcu, the act of knowing entails an effort to discover the power and presence of God in the universe. The Nurcu epistemological framework intermingles with metaphysics. Therefore, thought cannot be freed from metaphysical influence. Nursi's teaching and his attempt at discerning the truth are expressed through analogies that make the complexity of the world comprehensible.[41]

Nursi's books are written in allegorical comparisons and in narrative form. Knowledge about the Creator and the created is embedded in these narratives. His style thus is not disquisitional, and the stories are reenacted with the goal of telling the bigger story about the Creator. This new genre of literature has played a key role in the Islamization process as a discursive space for the formation and dissemination of ideas.[42] The traditional learning of the ulema, in contrast, stressed the memorization of certain texts, patterns of thought, and practices. Nursi was responding to the crises of the Islamic world and the inability of the traditional ulema to address this crisis, which was also apparent to such other prominent Islamic thinkers as Muhammad Abduh and Muhammad Iqbal. Nursi tried to cope with the problem by establishing the text itself as a source of authority and legitimation.

In Nursi's view, there is still an oral-textual connection but the text is freed from the hegemonic control of the ulema and opened to mass readership. The ulema had acquired their power from their monopoly on the interpretation of texts. When ordinary people raised questions with regard to social issues, the ulema traditionally responded that as guardians of the tradition they did not

have to provide an explanation or rationale for their decisions since their authority to make them was inherent in their traditional title and role. With the
empiricism of Republican education and the secularization of the law, Nursi
came to the conclusion that there was a need to explain religion to the masses
on a communal and personal basis and insisted that individuals must have
direct access to the understanding of religious beliefs. He declared his *RNK*
to be a space for teaching and producing knowledge that would counter positivist trends in formal education.[43] These "spaces of knowledge" thus were
transferred from the ulema and the Sufi lodges to the printed text. Oral discourse still has a function in Nurcu circles, but textuality and the print media
has become dominant.[44]

In attempting to understand the impact of literacy and print on Muslim
societies, it is important that one not equate literacy with print culture. Most
ulema were literate, but they were not part of print culture because they relied
not primarily on texts but rather on the oral mode of communication. Before
the 1930s, both the printing of books and general literacy in Turkey were quite
low. The trend in modern Turkey is not a straight shift from oral to print culture but rather a symbiosis of the two. If one examines the interactions between
oral and print culture, one sees that print culture gradually has become dominant. One of the main implications of this "print dominance" of Islamic discourse at the popular level is that oral exchange does not carry the same
legitimacy and authority as that of written exchange.

With the expansion of literacy and Nursi's insistence on the collective reading of the *RNK*, the need evolved for dershanes to carry out the activity of interpreting his texts. Gathering to study Nursi's work fostered certain practices
among Nurcus. The *RNK* and the institution of the dershane helped to form a
social space between the private sphere and the state in which Nurcus organized
themselves as a public pressure group. This public sphere, à la Jurgen Habermas,
was a counterpublic sphere vis-à-vis the one dominated by the secularist state
and its supporters.[45]

Placing Nursi's writings into the prevailing discourses of that period suggest a connection between the text and author. However, Nursi's followers read
the books to answer current questions. Nursi's message therefore is reproduced
within the challenges of the present time. This recoding of Nursi's narrative takes
place either in interpretive circles or in commentary books. Since mass production of books decontextualizes knowledge, the reading or listening audience
tends to give new meanings to what they read or hear. They engage in the complex process of recoding messages, through which internalization takes place.

The New "Folk" Club: Dershanes as Reading Circles

An open-door policy in the dershanes and weekly assemblies facilitated the dissemination of Nursi's ideas. These institutions are not only centers for reading
Nursi's works but also places to reaffirm a particular Islamic identity and exchange opinions on political issues. Through the dershane structure, the Nurcu

discourse assumed concrete expression in areas outside the strictly religious realm. The dershanes became socioeconomic and, indirectly, political networks with which upwardly mobile segments of the religious middle class established trust and connections and competed in the capitalist market economy. Cooperation in business relations has been one of the main social and economic achievements of these dershanes.

In order to understand more clearly the operation and significance of the contemporary Nurcu dershanes in Turkey, I will describe a visit to one in the Istanbul neighborhood of Tamirhane.[46] I was invited to attend an *iftar* (the evening meal to break the Ramadan fast) at a dershane located in a sixth-floor apartment. Six permanent residents, all students, shared the apartment, which had three bedrooms and a living room. Approximately 20 people were present, mostly owners of small retail establishments, with one university professor—of mechanical engineering. They all knew one another, and during their initial conversations most of the talk focused on the business and economic situation in Turkey. These dershanes thus are not confined only to religious issues but also are centers for business networking and sharing information about the market. After a half hour of conversation, everyone joined the iftar.

The person who leads the interpretive discussion tends to be the most educated person present and is given more respect than the others. The students living in the dershane call him *abi* (older brother). From their conversations and interactions it was easily discernable who the group leader was. The difference in status in the dershane is determined by who knows and interprets the *RNK* best. Knowledge and formal education become a source of power in this context. What is important here is the stress placed on formal education and its role in producing Islam. Neighborhood mosque functionaries (imams) are not regarded very seriously because they are assumed to be dogmatic in their approach and thus unable to have the same kind of interpretive ability as those with modern state educations. During prayer, it is not the elderly or those who have memorized the Qur'an better who lead the prayer but rather that person whose interpretation of the Nurcu texts generally is considered to be most authoritative. In this case, this person was Murat, the professor of mechanical engineering. Nonetheless, there is a hierarchy, according to age, in the way people sit in the room; young people sit closer to the door, and the interpreter sits in the center.

After the iftar, the interpreter leads the prayer and presents the lesson *(ders)*—a reading and interpretation of Nursi's work. The interpreter has a "dual" function: (1) to read Nursi's work aloud and to offer, in the process of recitation, a Turkish translation of Arabic, Persian, or Ottoman words; and (2) to interpret the text in terms of the prevailing social, economic, and political conditions. The interpreter inserts his ideas into Nursi's text, reflecting his own thinking and understanding. For example, in the lesson I witnessed, the interpreter turned Nursi into an environmentalist, claiming:

The essence of Islam is balance and justice in environment and
society. There is justice in this world and balance between nature

and human societies. This balance only can be maintained if the coexistence between humans and nature is maintained in balance. Nothing God has created is useless or extra in this world. Every thing has a function, even though we may not be aware of it. This also indicates the power of God; we still do not know enough about the place of each animal and natural event that God created. The order in nature proves that there is a God. Nursi brings the power of God to the forefront and renews our faith. Communists and atheists see nature as the source of power, but the order in nature points to the existence of a transcendent God.[47]

The interpreter constantly used the analogy of nature as an ordered system to prove the existence of God. Toward the end of his interpretation, a few people asked questions, but these were meant to facilitate interpretation rather than to challenge either Nursi or the interpreter. In his response, the interpreter gave examples from Istanbul and the neighborhood, saying "Look at our environment, there was a balance with God and we destroyed it with our hands and we are made to pay the price. Ten years ago there were more gardens in this street. Look at it now. You have more buildings."[48] The interpreter articulates Nursi's message in the modern context and within day-to-day experiences.

After the lesson, the listeners enjoyed some tea and again the discussion turned to business. In my conversation with the university students, I realized that they do not read any (nonacademic) book other than Nursi's. One student told me that the older brothers (abiler) do not want them to "distract their attention with fashionable books." I was introduced to an older brother (a graduate of the Middle East Technical University who worked at Faisal Finance), and he also interpreted a chapter.

The dershanes clearly are more than religious institutions. They also function as business channels and networks where employment and even the raising of investment capital among fellow Nurcus takes place. These dershanes also have a strong class dimension. Wealthier people tend to congregate in their own upper-class neighborhood dershanes. And interpretations of the RNK tend to vary according to the class makeup of each dershane. The Nurcu and Nakşibendi groupings that burgeoned in the second half of the 1980s and the 1990s did so among small-scale merchants and the expanding professional groups in Turkey. There are several reasons for this mushrooming of traditional and modern Islamic networks. A clublike arrangement of Nurcu dershanes as centers for the exchange of legal and business advice has contributed to the spread of the Nurcu dershane network throughout Turkey, particularly in those major cities experiencing economic growth, as can be seen in table 7.1.

The dershanes are more common in industrial areas than in rural areas or working-class communities. The Nurcus are mostly university graduates who either work for small companies or own small businesses. My interviews in Erzurum, Istanbul, Kayseri, and Konya indicated that the dershanes' social func-

TABLE 7.1. Growth in number of
dershanes in major Turkish cities

	1970	2000
Adapazarı	5	123
Bursa	5	94
Eskişehir	0	19
Erzurum	6	67
İstanbul	23	349
Kayseri	2	60
Konya	3	182
Van	1	8

Source: Derived from the subscription addresses of the most prominent Nurcu magazine, *Köprü,* to which almost all dershanes
subscribe.

tion tends to attract merchants and professionals, who obtain economic benefits by maintaining membership in such groups. Since the early 1990s, for
example, this socioeconomic solidarity has allowed Nur dershane networks to
dominate the distribution of certain household products such as detergents,
processed foods, and textiles. Through these religiously rooted and socially
shaped Nur networks, the Nurcus have sought to establish a sense of community within the secular state. The Nur dershanes have become the institutions
that integrate the individual into society. Dershanes are central to Nur identity
and facilitate the formation of multifaceted close networks of relationships
among followers, who are able to form a bond of trust and civility among themselves. As informal channels for the flow of ideas, capital, and people, dershanes
help to institutionalize a pattern of conduct in society.

The writings of Nursi helped the formation of new mechanisms of sociability (dershanes, foundations, magazines, philanthropic associations), intellectual exchange, and a raised consciousness about public opinion. The Nur
movements utilized the informal network of reading circles as a stepping-stone
in the construction of new counterpublics. By counterpublic sphere, I mean
spaces where people come together in public, without bracketing their Islamic
identities, and invent new shared meanings and ideas to critique the hegemonic
and officially sanctioned identities and public policies. In these counterpublic
spheres, Islamically oriented writers offer an alternative conception of the "good
life" with its own normative principles. Moreover, the counterpublic under certain conditions absorbs the "official" public because the goal of the counterpublic
is to change the normative foundations of the official public and the strategies
of framing social issues.[49] For instance, Turkish nationalism created an "official" national public in which any religious or ethnic discussion was marginalized
and forced to create its own illegal counterpublic. Only with the liberalization
and economic diversification of Turkey have religious and ethnic publics been
gradually integrated into the public sphere.

Dershanes are spaces for socialization in community-oriented virtues through conversational readings, discussions, and prayers. In the 1980s informal dershane networks, along with media networks, created several social outcomes. The development of the Nur public spaces in the late 1980s demonstrated three things. First, they showed how the diverse policies of the state, the new privatized market conditions, and communication opportunities helped to create counterpublics. These spaces, in turn, facilitated the emergence of the new politically conscious Muslim actors. Second, they showed how dershanes facilitate not only the formation of a global ethics of engagement with "interna/external others" but also the construction of a new religious consciousness. Third, they showed how these dershanes challenge the boundaries of public versus private, national versus transnational, and secular versus religious. The dershane circles demonstrate the role of normative foundations of mixed public and private spaces and the utilization of privately formed "social trust" to shape new public goods. Islamic ideals of responsibility and good work inform Muslim activism. Dershanes, as new religious public spheres, have played an important role in the circulation and crossfertilization of ideas and civil skills of activism. These are places where public opinion either is formed or critiqued through the utilization of religious ideas. Indeed, these spaces are not a Habermasian public sphere but, in terms of their consequences, they are vital for the formation of a larger public sphere.[50] The informal dershane networks and their role in the constitution of the public require a new understanding of the public. Privately built trust and a new cognitive map for understanding the meaning of the good life have social consequences in terms of constituting a framework of public discussions. Because of its consequences, coming together in dershanes to read Nursi's writings becomes a public act. In these dershanes, Islam becomes a source of solidarity and a chart of social responsibility in the constitution of Muslim self and community. In these dershanes, it becomes clear that being Muslim is never an exclusive identity but rather a moral foundation of tribal, ethnic, regional, and other forms of identities.

With the activation of the free market economy and the liberalization of the legal system to allow private broadcasting, the Nur movement used these opportunities to create new counterpublic spheres or transformed the "official" public sphere. By doing that, these Nurcu actors used the media to speak back to the state. Furthermore, the locally built social trust in dershane networks is translated into activities in education, media, the economy, and politics.

As mentioned, Nursi's message did not seek the abrupt transformation of the sociopolitical system; rather it sought to create a newly conscious religious society. The dershane networks shape a distinct Nur identity that differs significantly from the identity of other Islamic movements in modern Turkey. At the individual level, Nur identity offers a conceptual framework for understanding social interactions. At the communal level, this identity functions as a boundary in relation to other groups. For example, it is possible to recognize Nurcus in public places by their distinct manners and appearance. According to Yasin Aktay, a professor of Selçuk University, Nurcus set themselves apart from other Islamic groups

with [their] very orderly clothing of suit with necktie, daily shaved
face, almond moustache [*badem bıyık*] and short and neatly cut hair.
It is very rarely possible, if not impossible, to see a Nurcu smoking,
or eating or drinking at fast-food places, sitting at the coffee-houses,
and so on.[51]

The strong emphasis on appearance as an index of "modern" Islam is taken very
seriously by the Nurcus. Thus the *RNK* helps to develop a set of manners for
the people who gather together around a literate interpreter. In short, the
dershane is a venue for social and cultural activities and interaction. Since
dershanes are important places, where the Nurcus meet, they become sites where
wealth and status are displayed. Which dershane a Nurcu attends affects his
standing and reflects his position in the larger Nur community. This Islamic
system of ethics, which evolves from the structure of the dershane, stresses life
as a garden of faith to be cultivated; and hard work and good manners constitute features of congregational Nurcu brotherhood.

Political and Economic Opportunity Spaces: Centrifugal Pluralization

In the 1980s and 1990s, the formation and expansion of new opportunity spaces
in the market, education, and politics led to ongoing pluralization of the Nur
movement. By seeking to restore the lost unity and "authentic" interpretation
of the *RNK*, each group inadvertently has deepened the division further. New
socioeconomic changes motivate textually inspired interpretations that offer
diverse entries into the text of Nursi. There are presently three major splinter
groups—the community of Fethullah Gülen, the Yeni Asyacı, and the Yeni
Nesilciler—as well as dozens of other small groups. In Anatolia, almost every
town has a reading circle and even competing circles in a single neighborhood.
These groups constitute neither a political union nor a standard ideology of
political Islam. Indeed, one of the main characteristics of the Islamic movement
in Turkey is its fragmentation and pluralization. Having a common goal of raising Muslim consciousness and an imagined "external other" are not enough to
overcome the dynamics of fragmentation. Regional, ethnic, generational, and
socioeconomic loyalties permeate religious movements, providing the grounds
for fragmentation and improving the chances of shaping social and political
spheres. Moreover, these Nur groups compete over state patronage, and this
political proximity also generates fragmentation.

   There is no institutional religious authority to produce a single reading of
the Qur'an and hadith in Turkey. As groups increasingly become focused on
print, the conflict over interpretation becomes more vivid. As Muslims seek to
bring Islamic principles into day-to-day practices to create coherence and make
sense of them, they need to interpret these principles in the light of current ideas
and challenging problems. This interpretation, in turn, produces divergent viewpoints, because individuals interpret the texts on the basis of their own personal

experiences, interests, and previous knowledge of Islam. The Nur movement and its pluralization in the Turkish context demonstrate the power of institutional and material factors in shaping ideas. The very textuality of the Nur movement is the source of its pluralization and fragmentation. Textuality brings diverse readings and interpretations with itself and opens spaces for new group formation on the basis of different readings.

In addition to its textuality, economic liberalization and political democratization also played a determining role in this process of fragmentation. Each group organized its own journals and created its community of readers. The print and media opportunities allowed different groups to turn journals into new discursive spaces.

Nursi supported the act of interpretation, not rigid imitation, holding that a Muslim cannot say "This is what the Qur'an says" but rather must say "This is what I understand this verse to say in this context." Nursi perceived the Qur'an as an organic, dialectic, and ahistorical text. He saw no single, objective understanding of the Qur'an; all understandings are conditioned by one's socioeconomic position, and all interpretations, therefore, are partial. Nursi stressed neither translation nor memorization but rather reading and interpretation. Interpretation allows individuals to reproduce the meaning of Islam in their daily lives. This reproduction makes Islam part of daily life and a source of inspiration. Traditionally, there are two ways of interpreting the text: *zahiri*, that is, interpretation from outside as an objective entity; and *batıni*, that is, interpretation of the text in terms of its internal meaning and its relationship to the general conclusion of the text. The zahiri interpretation takes the word literally and pays no attention to its deeper meaning. The batini interpretation requires training in Islamic concepts and idioms and seeks to reinterpret the text in terms of its intentions and purposes.

It is not only Nursi's thinking that is reproduced but also his books. For instance, Nursi never provided Turkish translations of religious passages in Arabic or quoted the sources of the verses or hadith that appear in his writings. He always opposed providing literal translations of Qur'anic verses because this closes off the possible range of their interpretation. In contrast, new editions of his books carefully include citations in order to give the texts more authenticity. New commentaries on the *RNK* attempt to shape both Islamic identity and a broader moral code of conduct.[52] The issue for the second generation of Nurcus is thus not how to build an Islamic consciousness but how to bring this consciousness into everyday life in order to overcome the splintering of the self and of moral society. The writings of these second-generation Nurcu intellectuals focus on contemporary issues: spiritual emptiness, the quest for identity amid growing fragmentation, and the loss of a common shared code of meaning. However, no one has yet developed a precise political agenda based on Nursi's writings. One reason for this is that Nursi's own primary goal was not to transform Turkey's social and political system but rather to concentrate on shaping the inner consciousness of the individual Muslim. He assumed that political and social implications automatically would ensue from this revitalized Islamic consciousness.

The Struggle to Control the Production and Meaning of the *RNK*

The debate over oral culture versus written culture in the Nur movement has led to pluralization among its various branches. Turkish society was dominated by oral culture until the 1970s. There was, and still is to a significant extent, an oral cultural discourse in Turkey. Turkish written culture has followed this rich oral tradition closely; print culture is thus not an independent formation.

Turkey's rapid transition from use of the Arabic script to the Latin alphabet in 1928 limited the availability of written texts during the first period of the Republic. The *RNK* was written during these years. Nursi wanted to bring written culture to the forefront by stressing text-based discourse rather than the sheik-based oral tradition. The Nurcus stressed lessons (*ders*) over Sufi-based conversation (*sohbet*). This marked a significant shift in the development of Turkish Islamic political and social thought. Reading and interpreting a book and written information is more abstract than the memorization of spoken stories. Acquiring knowledge directly from a sheik is personal, as transmission is carried out in face-to-face interactions. Nursi also stressed reason and proof, rather than miracles, as the means to acquire knowledge. He sought to develop a text-based discourse, but this goal was circumscribed by the prevailing cultural patterns of the production and consumption of knowledge.

Nursi himself wrote in the Arabic script. After his death, debate centered around the issue of whether his books would be printed in the new Latin script or in the old Ottoman one, and it generated a split within the Nur group. A dividing line fell between the scribal group (Yazıcılar, who favored writing the text by hand) and those who supported mass production. By insisting that Nursi's works be reproduced in Arabic script, these more conservative Nurcus also wanted to perpetuate the use of the Arabic script as a form of resistance to Kemalist prohibitions. The Yazıcılar insisted on oral debate of Nursi writings, contending that this personalizes the messages they contain. Led by the calligrapher Hüsrev Altınbaşak of Isparta (1899–1977), they refused to use modern machinery and the Latin script for mass production. This attitude had little to do with the old orientalist view of traditional Muslims as opposed to technological innovation, a view also subscribed to by some modern Turkish scholars. Rather, the reasons went much deeper, as the Yazıcılar believed that the use of a machine devalues a text's authenticity and depersonalizes it. Although recopying by hand requires intense work and care, they believed that this process makes the book more authentic and personal and offers psychological satisfaction that closes the gap between author and readers. The Yazıcılar's restrictions on the mass reproduction of the *RNK* also may be viewed as a reflection of their piety, respect for the text, and concern with preserving its original content. However, these restrictions also are intended to monopolize and control the meaning of the *RNK*.

Following the death of Nursi, his followers sought a successor to maintain unity and to keep the community together. They were looking for a sheik-like figure to interpret and make Nursi's text understandable. Those who had studied

with Nursi insisted on the lesson system, in which his books were read and interpreted by his followers in a group. Those who did the reading and interpretation
gained a position of power within the community. The oral tradition was reproduced in part through these elder brothers, who are the elders in the dershanes.

In 1967, a small group of educated Nurcus (Zübeyir Gündüzalp, Bekir Berk,
Mehmet Nuri Güleç, and Mehmet Emin Birinci) decided to establish a publication house and journal. They founded Mihrab Publishing and started to publish the magazine *İttihad* (1968–1971) with Mustafa Polat as its first editor.[53]
The magazine was closed in 1971 by the military court. The group, under the
leadership of Gündüzalp (1920–1971), then decided to publish a newspaper in
1971 entitled *Yeni Asya* and founded Yeni Asya Publishing House. *İttihad*'s staff
was transferred to the new *Yeni Asya*. Printing became a way of reproducing
the Nurcu message and disseminating it throughout Anatolia. With the help of
printing technology and new means of distribution, publishing became a crucial institution in the renaissance of Turkish Islam. These developments ultimately would lead to the dominance of print culture in the formation of Islamic
discourse in contemporary Turkey. Those Nurcu "brothers" who held authority
and power through reading and interpreting Nursi's writings in the dershanes
were critical of such high-profile ventures into the mass publishing of journals
and magazines. They argued that the *RNK* did not need a second vehicle of dissemination, such as a magazine or a newspaper, to clarify Nursi's message.
Moreover, this opposition group feared the politicization of Nursi's teaching by
interpreting the *RNK* to address current events and controversies.

As owners of publishing houses that produced journals and newspapers,
the Nur groups were forced to cover public events and to get involved in the
day-to-day political life of the country. Publishing activities thus not only led to
debate within the movement but also inevitably further politicized it. Mesut
Toplayıcı, the editor of *Köprü*, argued that "printing was necessary to create
harmony in reading and interpreting Said Nursi's works."[54] Moreover, he argues that the newspapers helped to navigate political coalitions and gave certain parties a forum to address voters.

Political Factors: Party Politics and Ethnicity

As Turkish society diversifies and the Kemalist national ideology increasingly
loses its appeal, attempts by any one group or school of thought to fill the ideological vacuum inevitably have failed in the face of the forces of fragmentation
and pluralization. The sources of the fragmentation that have created these
groups are the increasing autonomy of the Islamic movement, ethnicity, party
politics, and class differentiation. With respect to the Nurcus, each group has
sought to invoke a different, "imagined" Nursi to promote its own purposes.
Some Nurcu groups even became active participants in the political conflicts
that became a dominant feature of urban Turkey after 1971.

In the early 1970s, the Islamic political movement, which had evolved
around the center-right of the DP and then within the AP, became an indepen-

dent force with the formation of the Nakşibendi-dominated MSP. A group of Nurcus supported the pro-Islamic MSP, and this created the first political division within the Nur movement. The Nur group's decision to become politically engaged was very much a reaction to the pro–big business policies of the AP in the late 1960s. Because of the political radicalization of the Turkish Left and its increasing dominance of art and culture, the followers of the Nur movement reluctantly decided to become involved in politics. A number of Nurcus took part in the establishment of the MSP and later entered Parliament. This group included A. Tevfik Paksu, Hüsamettin Akmumcu, Sudi Reşat Saruhan, and Gündüz Sevilgen, all of whom would become the major shareholders of the Turkish branch of the Saudi-based Faisal Finance in Istanbul.[55] As a result of political and ideological differences with the MSP chairman Erbakan and the policies pursued during the coalition government, the Nurcu parliamentarians left the MSP before the 1977 elections.[56] This break with the MSP, which was dominated by Nakşibendi members at the time, created a permanent strain between the MSP and the Nur groups. The Nur movement as a whole, moreover, distrusted Erbakan's MSP and even at this early stage supported instead the AP of Süleyman Demirel. According to some Nurcus, even dershanes were used for political purposes to support the AP.

During the Cold War, Turkey's Islamic movement was embedded within the communal-religious trend in Turkish nationalism; the Nurcu movement, centered around the *Yeni Asya* newspaper, became a "nationalistic-religious" (*milliyetçi ve mukaddesatçı*) front against the increasing dominance of leftist activities in the 1970s. The followers of Nursi argued that Islamic faith is an antidote against the leftist movement. Many prominent Nurcus joined the "Associations to Fight Against Communism" (Türkiye Komünizmle Mücadele Dernekleri), and this in turn transformed the Nurcu movement into a conservative-nationalist bloc. Bekir Berk (1926–1992), the leading lawyer defending Nurcus in the courts, played a key role in the nationalization of the Nurcu movement.[57]

Conflicting views about the 1980 military coup led to a second major political split within the Nurcu group. These internal quarrels continued until 1982. The first group, known as the Yeni Asya (or Gazeteciler), consistently supported Demirel and maintained a critical stance toward the military coup leaders. They decided to campaign against the military's proposed new constitution. However, two prominent leaders of the Nur movement, Mehmet Kırkıncı of Erzurum and Fethullah Gülen of Izmir, gave their blessings to the military coup and the 1982 constitution.

The 1982 constitution created a major debate within the Nur groups. Those who were against it argued that it was antidemocratic. The constitution, indeed, sought to create a more powerful state by shrinking the borders of society. It limited political rights and freedoms and put associational life under state supervision. These restrictions served to limit the activities of the Nur community as well as force it to reexamine its attitude toward the constitution after 1982. Some Nurcus wanted, via Nur group–owned media, to challenge the constitution and urged followers to vote no to its implementation. When the newspaper

Yeni Asya adopted this approach, many Nurcu readers became upset that the group was sparking a potential confrontation with the state and demanded that the Yeni Asya group stop publishing its newspaper. Military officers visited prominent Nurcus, such as Mehmet Kırkıncı, and "convinced" them to support the constitution or risk the closure of Nur dormitories and dershanes.

After the vote in favor of adopting the 1982 constitution, those who supported it also firmly supported the new Özal government. The journalists of *Yeni Asya*, however, opposed Özal, arguing that he was merely an agent of the military coup. Kırkıncı and Gülen openly supported Özal's ANAP and were able to contain the opposition of the dissidents in the movement. Such political disagreements facilitated the fragmentation of the movement, with dissident factions declaring their independence by establishing their own magazines and cultural foundations.

The influence of the Nur movement has increased even as the movement frequently has fragmented. This paradox indicates the flexibility and broad range of the Nur idiom. The fragmentation has led to fierce competition among Turkish political parties to court the followers of the various Nurcu groups. Thus, in western Turkey at least, individuality and pluralism has gained prominence over the authority of the *hocaefendi* (respected religious leaders such as Fethullah Gülen, Mehmet Kırkıncı, and Mustafa Sungur) or the so-called *abis* (first-generation Nurcus who had close ties with Nursi, including Emin Birinci, Mehmet Fırıncı, Abdullah Yeğin, and Hüsnü Bayram). As the cohesiveness of the religious communities has fractured, new voices and leaders have surfaced to articulate their own visions for Turkey qua Nursi's writings.

The case of Mehmet Kırkıncı demonstrates how, in the city of Erzurum, for example, patterns similar to the traditional disciple-master relationship were reproduced within an oral-dominated discourse. Kırkıncı asked his followers to support the 1982 constitution and was largely obeyed by the rank and file of the movement. The state was particularly effective in controlling those *hocaefendis* who managed to revive a mixed oral and print culture. In my own research in Erzurum and Bayburt, I came across similar Sufi order–like relationships among the Nur groups. Here the dershane performed the functions of a Sufi lodge, with the Nurcu *hocaefendi* replacing the traditional role of the Sufi *hocaefendi*. To a great extent, the charismatic role of Nursi as the founder of the movement was reproduced within the patterns of oral tradition. Therefore, the contribution of the *RNK* with respect to the promotion of individuality and pluralization was limited in Erzurum and eastern Turkey. In this region, the concepts of state and community still override individual concerns and rights. Regional conditions and political developments have led to diversity within the Nurcu movement. For example, in Erzurum, one Nurcu told me: "we had to support the army because we did not want to see the mosque compete with the barracks over authority, but rather see them work together and complement each other. Can you have a mosque without a powerful and disciplined army?"

The process of "going Turkish" and "statist" created another split, along Turkish-versus-Kurdish ethnic lines. This ethnic fragmentation also coincided with the rise of politicized Kurdish nationalism as a result of the PKK attacks on the Turkish state. In the early 1980s, the Kurdish Nurcus began to organize around Tenvir Publishing House (Tenvir Neşriyat). The group stressed education in Kurdish by defending Nursi's *Medresetü'z Zehra* project for a university in eastern Anatolia, which proposed education in Turkish, Arabic, and Kurdish in modern sciences and religious studies. Moreover, the group criticized the "Turkification" of the RNK by eliminating any reference to "Kurdistan" or "Kurd."[58] This group later organized as the Med-Zehra community under the leadership of Sıddık Dursun and began to publish *Dava* magazine in 1989. The magazine's articles regularly questioned the close connection between Turkish nationalism and the Nurcu movement and tried to construct a Kurdish Nursi. The attempt to maintain balance between Kurdish nationalism and Islamism led to a split within the Med-Zehra community; more nationalist Kurds, under the leadership of İzzettin Yıldırım, established the Foundation of Zehra Education and Culture in 1991 and began to publish the monthly magazine *Nubihar* in Kirmanca Kurdish in 1992.[59]

The Kurdish nationalist magazine *Yeni Zemin*, which was funded by Yıldırım, tentatively tried to present Nursi as "a Kurdish nationalist" by recalling the struggle of the younger Nursi against the Kemalist state. The editor of *Yeni Zemin*, Mehmet Metiner, argued, "I like the activist Said who struggled for the recognition of Kurdish identity. Said was a major step in Islamic thought but his contribution did not end there."[60] Metiner, also a Kurdish ex–political advisor to Tayyip Erdoğan, sees Islam as a means to challenge the state and to open political space for the expression of Kurdish nationalism. The ethnicization of Nursi is achieved by selectively reading his writings and life struggles. Some Kurdish intellectuals argue that the state constantly persecuted Nursi not only because of his Islamism but also because of his ethnic Kurdish identity. Although most Nurcu groups reject these attempts to transform Nursi into a Kurdish nationalist, the rise of Turkish and Kurdish nationalism has contributed to the creation of two separate ethnic groups among the Nurcus.

Class and Generational Differences in the Nurcu Groups

Since 1983, the Nur movement consistently has defended the free market and the withdrawal of the state from the economic and educational spheres. The new Anatolian-based bourgeoisie welcomed this position and used its financial means to open new dormitories and study houses. Since the 1980s, most of the new businessmen have allied themselves with the policies of the ANAP, as have most Nurcu groups. New expanding markets consolidated the position of this new bourgeoisie and the revival of a socially conservative, politically progressive, market-oriented Islamism. The most prominent contemporary leader of the group, generally known as the neo-Nurcus, is Fethullah Gülen, who navigated the movement among this new bourgeoisie and mobilized them to support his private high schools in Turkey and Central Asia.

In examining generational differences in dershanes, I realized that the world of the reader evolves from generation to generation. New communities of readers develop their own sense of identity and interpretation of the texts, and this practice differentiates them from Nurcus of earlier generations. Each new reading community complains that the older ones missed the real meaning of the *RNK*. As the reading habits and norms of Turkey's increasingly educated population evolve, so does the Nurcu understanding of the *RNK*. A new mode of publishing the text, which includes footnotes and modern citations, indicates the impact of modern education and the media.

The Nur movement has the largest number of educated people and the youngest clientele of any religious group in Turkey. It dominates teachers' colleges and some other higher educational institutions. The clientele of the Nur movement are either urbanized or in the process of being urbanized. Older Nurcus are either involved in small trade or are professional craftsmen or lower level civil servants. Although the Nurcus constitute a series of textual-communities, generational variation shapes interpretations and this, in turn, creates distinctions. The Nur community has three generational bodies. The first group includes those who knew Nursi and participated in his conversations. This group maintained its unity in spite of or because of the state's virulent efforts to suppress it. Its prominent members constituted the Board of Trustees (Mütevelli Heyeti), or collective decision-making body, that was chosen to lead the movement following Nursi's death and until the mid-1970s. The repressive policies of the Republic increased its cohesiveness and made trust a key value for members of the movement. There was very little internal debate or self-searching since they were united against a common enemy: the secularizing forces of the state.

The second-generational group was educated by the first generation of Nurcus and has been dominated by the journalist faction. This group stressed the role of science and technology in making Nursi's message relevant to the youth. It established journals and newspapers to mediate Nursi's message within the context of current affairs. The journalists took a very critical attitude toward the translation and dissemination of books by certain inflexible Islamist writers from other countries, such as Sayyid Abu'l al-Ala Mawdudi, Sayyid Qutb, or Hasan al-Banna. They argued that these books did not represent a very deep understanding of Islam and shed very little new light on how to cope with present challenges. İhsan Atasoy argues that "the translated books offered a blueprint for an Islamic state and economic system. They do not confront the question of renewing faith in the age of skepticism."[61]

The third generation of Nurcus dominates many of the university student bodies and controls large sections of the religious media and publishing in Turkey. The main characteristic of this new group of Nurcus is the hybridization of its ideas. University graduates dominate this group, and most are followers of Gülen. They see society as a field to be cultivated in accordance with Islamic teachings. This group is much more confident and activist in its approach to politics and society. However, it is still critical of those Muslim thinkers and movements that want to reduce Islam to a political blueprint and create an "earthly heaven" through the power of the state. Many Nurcus feel anxious when Qur'anic verses are made into political slogans. Some Islamists in Turkey criticize the Nurcus as "good readers and debaters but poor activists and even loyal crowds at state rallies." Many Nurcus argue that the use of these radical slogans could provoke state persecution and create an anti-Islamic and antidemocratic environment in Turkey.

Conclusion

Said Nursi's conceptualization of the self, community, and God had a powerful impact on Islamic movements in Turkey. The Nur movement had three major consequences. First, it undermined the traditional ulema and their authority once this new form of transmission of knowledge was introduced. Second, its print-based discourse challenged hegemonic voices and opened up public spaces for dissent and emancipation. Third, it made Islam relevant once again for the economic and social transformation of Turkey. Nursi's project indicates that ethical thought is necessary in order for a society to discover what it is and what it wants to be. Individuals define themselves in an urban environment in terms of their commitment to certain ideals. In a Muslim society, ideals of a just and free society are derived from Islamic precepts. People define their identity by virtue of membership in a community of shared values and meanings. A new moral discourse compatible with urban conditions thus has become the goal of Islamic revival, which therefore is concerned primarily with issues of community and identity within the modern context. The legacy of Nursi indicates that Islamic identity is not homogeneous but is a source of conflict between different groups. It is inevitable that political and social dynamics have an impact on Islamic political identity, and this in turn has some implications for the character of the state. The Nur movement is likely to fragment even further while its branches paradoxically expand their influence in Turkish society and their ability to shape state policies. The Nur movement has made it clear that ideas matter in planting the seeds of a social transformation. Indeed, Nursi adopted a different and highly original path in comparison to other religious authorities and charismatic renewers of the Islamic faith in his time. He did not think that the state could address effectively the many problems confronting Muslim countries at the time; rather, the focus should be at the level of the individual and the society. He brought textual or print-based discourse to the forefront and laid out the framework for others to follow, stressing the importance of interpretation, tolerance, and open discussion.

8

The Neo-Nur Movement
of Fethullah Gülen

Although there are more than 10 major Nurcu textual-communities
divided along class, regional, and ethnic lines, the most influential
one has been that headed by Fethullah Gülen, commonly referred to
as the "community of Fethullah Gülen." The Gülen-led neo-Nur
movement seeks to improve Turkish society by using the market,
education, and information opportunity spaces to raise a new
generation with heightened patriotic and moral consciousness.[1] As a
result of the opening and closing up of political and economic
opportunity spaces, the Gülen movement has evolved from a stress
on religious-conservative community-building to a stress on creating
a global, faith-inspired educational system. One can identify three
different cycles in the movement: the formative period (1966–1983);
the emergence into the public sphere (1983–1997); and the paradox
of persecution and forced liberalization (1997–present). Each cycle is
shaped by structural changes that reproduce a more contextual
framing process. The movement functions like a beehive with a
sense of loyalty and discipline. A vivid picture emerges of the
dershane's highly organized social life, revolving around the disciplined sharing of construction tasks, the collection of resources, and
the warding off of enemies. The movement is based on three
coordinated tiers: businessmen, journalists, and teachers and
students. Gülen's mission is to reactivate the inner driving forces of
Turko-Muslim culture through the use of collective memory.
Gülen's neo-Nur movement has distinguished itself from other faith
movements through its soft and conciliatory voice on most hotly
debated subjects, such as secularism, the Kurdish question, and the
headscarf issue.

Gülen, a bachelor and retired functionary of the state's Directorate of Religious Affairs, has emerged as the leader of the most dynamic, transnational, wealthy, and faith-based Islamic movement in Turkey. An examination of this movement reveals how new political and economic opportunities affected the internal secularization of Turkish Islam in terms of modernity, nationalism, and the global discourses of human rights. Under new sociopolitical opportunities, Nursi's ideas about and methodology of religious consciousness, society, and politics are reconstructed and popularized by a dynamic set of businessmen, journalists, and teachers, whom I refer as the "the neo-Nurcus," the engaged members of Gülen's movement.

In due time, the Gülen movement ceased to be another branch of the Nur movement and evolved into an autonomous faith-based societal movement. One of the main doctrines of this group is the idea that religious consciousness is formed and perpetuated through engaging in social practices and institutions. The neo-Nur movement seeks to realize religious consciousness in the world. Hegel's notion of religion is analytically helpful for understanding the overall objective of the Nur movement: making objective religion subjective. By "objective religion" Hegel means "universal truths, especially moral truths, that every religion worthy of the name should teach." "Subjective religion," for Hegel, "expresses itself in feeling and actions" of believers.[2] This motivates moral actions and shapes communal interactions. Therefore, the translation of objective religion to the subjective realm requires a set of institutions and education. Religion for the neo-Nurcus not only aims to educate people and ensure their salvation but also to externalize their Islamic consciousness for the moral and intellectual uplifting of human society. Education, therefore, is an investment in building moral character and identity.

The Life of Fethullah Gülen

Before examining the activities and impact of the Gülen movement, it is necessary to consider the distinctive resources that informed Gülen's political and social vision. There are several primary influences on Gülen's Islamic worldview that must be considered: the life story of the Prophet Muhammad and his companions; the Nakşibendi sheik Muhammet Lütfi Efendi, known as Alvarlı Efe, who inculcated broad and sophisticated cognitive and emotional skills into Gülen;[3] Said Nursi's understanding of Islam, and the Islamic intellectuals of the Republic. In addition to these ideational influences, Gülen is also the "activist thinker" of his period and a product of the unfolding evolution of the Kemalist project, in general, and Erzurum and its regional identity, in particular.

Gülen was born in the village of Korucuk, near Erzurum, an eastern Anatolian provice, on April 27, 1941. His father was a religious functionary in several villages. In his memories, Gülen identifies his family as the most influential foundation in the formation of his personality and thinking. The major moral narrative that shaped social interactions in the Gülen family was the narrative stories of the Prophet Muhammad.[4] The institution of family, as well as the regional culture, molded Gülen's personality and his understanding of Islam as national-statist. The Turkish Islam of eastern Anatolia is differentiated by its nationalistic and Sufi characteristics.[5]

Erzurum, formerly the eastern frontier of the Ottoman state, was a zone of conflict among the Russian, Iranian, and Ottoman empires. One of the main implications of this geocommunal position is that Islam came to be very much associated with the defense of the community. Furthermore, much of the population of this region is made up of immigrants who fled the Caucasus following the 1878 war with Russia. Moreover, this region experienced one of the bloodiest communal conflicts in recent history between Armenians and Muslims between 1877 and 1920. The memories of this communal conflict and Russian occupation still loom large here. The region was central in the organization of the national movement against the occupation of Anatolia during the War of Liberation. The dominant culture of this region is state-centric, and the people of the region, known by their regional identity as Dadaş, traditionally have given the state priority over religion. Regional Islam, which is marked by Dadaş identity, therefore, is punctuated by the culture of frontier conditions, which stresses security over other concerns and identifies Russia (and then communism) as the "other" of Turko-Islamic identity. As a result of their historical experience, the people of Erzurum tend also to feel that religion cannot exist if the state is not in a strong position to defend it.[6] In his memoirs, Mehmet Kırkıncı, another Nur leader of Erzurum, constantly stresses Nursi's heroism in the defense against the Russian and Armenian forces to legitimize the writings of Nursi in this nationalist region of Turkey.[7] In short, this frontier population treats the state as a sine qua non for a Muslim society and the survival of Islam. Gülen's conception of Islam is conditioned by this nationalism and statism.

After receiving his informal education in the zone of Dadaş Islam, Gülen was appointed in 1958 as a state-salaried preacher (vaiz) in Edirne, where a large number of Balkan Muslims live. In 1966, he was appointed as the official İzmir preacher of the DİB and also worked at the Kestanepazarı Qur'an School in İzmir. Combining his personal abilities with the social resources in this developed Aegean Sea city, Gülen laid the foundation of the most widespread dershane networks. Gülen did not limit himself to Nursi's writings but read the books of socially conservative and politically national-Islamist intellectuals such as Necip Fazıl Kısakürek, Nurettin Topçu, and Sezai Karakoç.

The Stages of the Neo-Nur Movement

In the first period (religious community–building, 1966–1983), Gülen used the Kestanepazarı Qur'an School to tutor a spiritually oriented and intellectually motivated core group of students about building an exclusive religious community in İzmir. Summer camps became spaces of secular education (history and biology) and religious tutoring. In these summer camps, Gülen developed a theology of religious activism and encouraged students who would later be the core group in the movement to engage in faith-motivated civic activism. The all-male camps included high school and university students, who had an opportunity to bring religious and secular ideas and skills of thinking and arguing together; daily prayers were performed regularly, and social and ethical issues were discussed from the perspectives of Said Nursi. One sees the process of deepening private religious consciousness and the development of new and narrow Islamic fraternization among the participants of the camps. The students lived together within an atmosphere of sincerity and were tutored in a shared language of Islamic morality to form a common map of action. These camps, along with dershanes, also known as ışık evler (lighthouses), were spaces for deepening inner consciousness for public use and were the networks of the formation of a powerful sense of religious brotherhood in order to bring Islamic values into the public. The first generation followers of Gülen internalized Islamic values of responsibility, self-sacrifice, and dedicating oneself to the collective good of the Muslim community.

Gülen's knowledge and charisma fascinated these young men and motivated them to render their time and knowledge to revitalize the nation's spiritual and intellectual capital, and this in turn Islamicized the public spaces and public debates. In other words, after the camps, the students were asked to forms their own fraternity network to "bring" Islamic values and practices into the public spaces. In the making up of this activism, Gülen evoked the life of the Prophet and also the founders of the Ottoman state. The Ottomans, for Gülen, were models to indicate the possibility of becoming "great." For Gülen, the Ottomans were great because they lived in accordance with a liberal interpretation of Islam; if Turkey wanted to become a "great nation" again, it was necessary to bring "God" back into life, institutions, and the intellect.

This was the embryonic period for the formation of the Gülen-centric religious-conservative community. During this period, Gülen wanted to preserve his community from active political involvement in an Islamic political movement and treated political activity as a challenge to his attempt to create a dutiful Muslim community. However, due to the ideological polarization of Turkey, especially the rise of radical leftist movements, the Gülen movement embraced an anticommunist rhetoric and adopted a conservative nationalist position. The movement avoided active politics but used all its means to get access to educational institutions, media, the market, and other urban public spaces by establishing its own institutions or through its followers. Informal ties were critical in the evolution and activities of the community-building movement. Due to state oppression and limited economic resources, Gülen employed tightly knit, informal networks of dershanes that consolidated solidarity and helped to create a shared moral orientation. Gülen tapped both the personalism and informality of Muslim societies to control the boundaries of religious community. These densely woven webs of dershane networks mobilized new resources and accumulated powerful social capital that came to be used in a more conducive social and political environment.

Even though Gülen avoided any involvement in political activities, during the 1971 military coup, he was arrested, along with some prominent Nurcus, because of involvement with the Nur movement in İzmir. This involvement was presented as the violation of article 163, which criminalizes "unwanted" religious expression and association; Gülen spent seven months in jail before being acquitted.[8] Subsequently Gülen avoided direct involvement in political activities, concentrating instead on establishing educational institutions, such as the Foundation for Turkish Teachers (*Türkiye Öğretmenler Vakfı*) in 1976 and the Foundation of Middle and Higher Education in Akyazı (*Akyazılı Orta ve Yüksek Eğitim Vakfı*). The major leap of Gülen's movement was the publication of *Sızıntı* magazine in 1979, which always includes a lead article by Gülen and a number of other essays on science, religion and history.[9] The goal was to give a Muslim orientation to a new generation of Turks to help them to cope with, benefit from, and if necessary resist the processes of modernity. In this period, Gülen remained very skeptical of political activism and critized Nurcu intellectuals, who were concentrated around the daily *Yeni Asya*, for their deep engagement in politics.[10]

The second phase witnessed the expansion of the public sphere and a loosening of the boundaries of the religious community (1983–1997). Due to a more stable and religion-friendly political environment in the early 1980s, the Gülen movement put its vision of creating a "golden generation" into practice by utilizing new political, legal, and economic opportunity spaces.[11] Gülen developed close ties with Özal, then prime minister, and worked closely with him to transform the sociocultural landscape of Turkey. The political opening of the system in the 1980s enabled the people around Gülen to put locally constructed "trust" into use and to form one of the most influential movements of Turkey. After 1983, Gülen emerged as one of the dominant figures on the Turkish Islamic scene. The movement developed close ties with state institutions and became involved in economic, cultural, and media activities. The entry into social, educational, media, and economic fields also transformed the movement itself. The movement stressed the significance of the media and market economy and tried to become more professional by establishing new foundations, broadcasting companies, publishing presses, and cultural foundations.

After 1983, the most important change took place in the field of education. The privatization of the education system opened it up to competition, and the movement capitalized on the need and desire to establish a better education system. This was also the period of preparation for a more activist and assertive movement. Gülen's religious lectures of April 1986, known as *vaaz*, were a turning point in terms of his utilization of the national religious networks to carve a space for himself. Then prime minister Özal played an important role in getting the 1980 coup ban on Gülen's public preaching lifted because he wanted to benefit from the ideas and activities of Gülen against extremist Islamist groups. Gülen was expected to become the "Muslim preacher of liberalism," and he never hesitated to meet that expectation since it also coincided with his own goals. Gülen's lecture in Valide Sultan mosque in Istanbul on May 6, 1989, focused on the ethical aspect of Islam and aimed to meet the religious and ethical needs of the middle classes and the new bourgeoisie. He avoided controversial issues and developed an inclusive language, urging people to participate in the economy, media, and cultural activities to create a new and confident Turkey. His emotional preaching style stirs up the inner feelings of Muslims and imbues his messages with feelings of love and pain. He targets people's hearts more than their reason, and this appeal to feelings helps him to mobilize and transform Muslims. Gülen's style is effective and forms a powerful emotional bond between him and his followers. He not only stirs up the emotions of the faithful but also exhorts them to self-sacrifice and activism. Thus he arms his followers with an emotional map of action to translate their heart-guided conclusions into action. His preaching style also is a way of transforming the self by carving an inner space to resist oppression and cultural alienation.

This shift from religious-nationalist to more inclusive language created bridges with secular liberals and atheists in Turkey. Gülen acquired a reputation as the moderate, emotional, and caring hocaefendi. Moreover, his inclusive and liberal interpretation of Islam as a religion of love, peace, and social responsibility helped him to add new circles to the movement. These newcomers constituted a sympathizer circle within and outside the movement. Because they had different backgrounds and expectations, their presence forced the movement to liberalize its language and recruitment practices further. The movement gradually shed its religious-ethnic communalism and anticommunist rhetoric. In short, Gülen's neo-Nur movement evolved into a more moderate and open movement as it participated in the cultural, economic, and social domains, becoming a national-level civil movement inspired by Islamic ideas of social responsibility. The Gülen movements attempted to bring "religion" into the production of public opinion on issues such as how we ought to live and how we ought to think about how to live. This in turn led to the objectification of a "religious worldview" as an autonomous category to frame social and political issues. The process of "going public" and trying to communicate within the normative domain of the public sphere in Turkey required the Gülen movement to moderate its voice and frame its arguments in terms of reason and interests. This slow yet profound attempt to "go public" has facilitated the internal secularization of religion by forcing Nur groups to compete with diverse worldviews and frame their arguments so that anyone could understand.

In the 1980s, the Islam advocated by Gülen emphasized tolerance and coexistence with other cultures. He drew much of his support from engineers, the new Anatolian bourgeoisie, academics, and other professionals. In his speeches, he carefully stressed the role of merchants and businessmen as the sources revitalizing Turkey as a regional power. The three sociopolitical conditions made the Gülen community "come out" in public and venture to reconstruct the external world with Islamic consciousness. The conditions that led to the "coming out" and eventual transformation of the movement were the relaxation of the state's policies toward society, particularly its religious aspects; the existence of a new conscious and economically powerful bourgeoisie to sponsor Gülen's projects, along with the new urban educated professionals and teachers to take part in his schemes; and a democratic environment and associational life to organize his activities. These conditions helped to unleash the potential power of the movement just as the "chick was in the egg and waiting to be hatched," and political conditions helped the "chick to hit its shell to come out."[12]

The Gülen movement is of great significance because of its financial resources, vast educational network, and media outlets both in Turkey and abroad.
The neo-Nur identity movement is the most ambitious and well-organized Turkish Islamic movement poised to effect developments not only in Turkey but also
in the Balkans and Central Asia. The followers of the neo-Nur movement seek
to bring cultural frames to the forefront by investing new meanings in them
with the political goal of building Turkey as a regional power. No religious leader
in Turkey stresses action (aksiyon) more than Gülen; he does so because he is
aware of the sociopolitical effects of globalization on Turkey, and he takes the
initiative to mold minds and hearts through the movement's financial, educational, and media empires.[13] Moreover, the movement has managed to form a
symbiotic relationship with the rising new Anatolian-Muslim bourgeoisie and
has used its enormous resources to challenge the assumptions of political and
cultural superiority held by those in the Kemalist-secularist establishment.

The Theology of Action: Hizmet, Himmet, and İhlas

An examination of the formation of a new prototype of a religious intellectual
and his transformation into a modern version of a hocaefendi reveals the modernization of traditional practices and institutions. Gülen, for example, is not a
traditional sheik but rather a new prototypical hocaefendi who has a series of
overlapping roles as a modern intellectual and religious scholar. Three main
characteristics differentiate Gülen from the traditional ulema. First, unlike the
ulema, whose references are the Qur'an and sunna, the reference points for
Gülen and the new class of Muslim intellectuals include rational reasoning and
European Enlightenment thought. Second, Gülen encourages independent
thinking (the ulema, in contrast, guide the community and seek to preserve tradition, whereas these new Turkish Muslim intellectuals seek to encourage critical
thought). Gülen, in fact, has managed to juggle a remarkable mix of these two
traditions, which accounts for his enormous popularity with middle-class and
urbanized Turks with religious sentiments. By realizing the power of ideas in
social change, Gülen stresses education for forming a class of Muslim intellectuals, who are rooted in the Turkish-Islamic tradition and able to breach the sharp
cleavages caused by the Kemalist revolution.[14]

Another major characteristic of this modern hybrid of ulema-intellectual is
his ability to interpret Islamic precepts within the context of modern social conditions. He recontextualizes Islamic knowledge across different social boundaries by making use of interpretation in an original and incisive fashion. For
example, Gülen is well versed in works of such world writers as Kant, Shake-
speare, Victor Hugo, Dostoyevsky, Sartre, and Kafka, and he uses their ideas to
reinforce his reinterpretations of Islam to meet contemporary needs.[15]

Gülen has a charismatic appeal that is derived from his intellectual abilities and leadership skills, as is evidenced by his ability to develop close ties with
the state, bourgeoisie, and international religious institutions. However, the
reasons for the growing influence of his movement go beyond his personal

charisma. First, it has reproduced a new vision of "contemporary Islam" that offers a set of options for people to be both Muslim and modern, European and Muslim, and Muslim and Turk, a national identity that is composed of national (Turkish-Ottoman) and religious (Sunni Islam) symbols. Second, his movement has adopted the global discourse of human rights and developed complex ties with the national bourgeoisie and the state. Finally, the movement has activated the inner mobilizing ideas of society by "inviting" Turks to take part in the construction of a new powerful Turkey.

Gülen wants to influence the full range of social and political processes pertaining to modern life. He therefore emphasizes the vital role of markets, education, and the media. A well-ordered ideal society, for Gülen, is based on a powerful state and vigorous market that, in turn, presupposes an adequately developed educational system, in which terbiye (building character) and talim (teaching modern sciences) are combined with discipline. This moral conviction to empower the Muslims of Turkey could only be derived from Islam, that is, the shared mental map of the Turks.[16]

In other words, the morality of conviction and the morality of responsibility create a sort of worldly activism that seeks to transform this world for the sake of the other world. This balance between conviction and responsibility in the construction of a new Muslim Turkey is realized in terms of the decisive quality of self-control and self-discipline under the purposive will to act in the name of religion that helps to (trans)form one's civilization. The goal of education, for Gülen, is to inculcate Turkish-Islamic values through terbiye and teaching scientific knowledge. Gülen's group differentiates itself from other Islamic movements by stressing the importance of ethics in education and the business world. In other words, Gülen moves his focus from Islam to public ethics and from identity to education; a well-ordered, disciplined society is a logical outcome. Gülen considers education and the media to be key instruments in the formation of this ethics and consciousness (şuur).

In order to achieve his goal, Gülen invokes three inner mobilizing concepts of Turkish society: hizmet (rendering service to religion and state); himmet (giving donations and protecting good work); and ihlas (seeking God's appreciation for every action). Gülen not only does mobilize the hearts and minds of millions of Turks but also succeeds in convincing them to commit to the mission of creating a better and more humane society and polity. By stressing social synergy—the willingness of Muslims to act from their ideals and conception of good life—Gülen is a religious modernist and a social innovator. The practice of hizmet, or religiously motivated labor, is used to restructure society according to Islamic ideals. Hizmet easily could be used for civic concerns in education, healthcare, media, and new sets of associations to build a public ethics of interaction. By employing people in its educational, media, and other activities, the movement teaches the way in which social capital is built and put into practice in the Turkish society. In short, hizmet functions as social capital by bringing people together for a collective goal in terms of rendering their time and resources to create a positive environment for the realization of specific goals. These hizmet activities also help to build interpersonal trust and a code of ethics.

In Gülen's conception of faith as an internal power to mobilize believers, the lasting piece of work that they create is called an *eser*. In a way, eser is the reflection of one's faith and a reservoir of one's pleasure and hard work. This eser, for Gülen, should reflect one's ability to realize one's potential, and its creation becomes a religious duty. In short, redemption becomes possible as a result of collective deeds to create a lasting work, eser. Gülen does not call people to build more mosques but rather schools, hospitals, and media corporations. His concepts of hizmet and eser lead to internal secularization of religion in terms of rationalization of social relations and dissemination of scientific epistemology through his educational system. Furthermore, congregational brotherhood circles help to free individuals and the community from the direct influence of the state and lead them to construct social networks that enhance civil society. In other words, Gülen's vision and networks help to "domesticate" and inculcate civic virtues among the youth by stressing cooperation, participation, and tolerance. The way of creating an ethical society, for Gülen, is not to offer courses in religion or ethics in schools but rather to set good examples, known as *temsil*, in one's daily life, as a teacher, policemen, businessmen, and journalist.

This formation of "activist pietism" is at the core of the neo-Nur movement, with the aim of molding this world in terms of Islamic ethics. Redemption through collective action becomes a way of inner salvation. Gülen offers a much-needed moral motivation for the evolving Anatolian bourgeoisie and educated classes. In the Gülen-led movement, the inner deriving forces of Turkish culture such as hizmet, himmet, and ihlas are utilized to shape the society according to the ideals of Islamic ethics. Through hizmet, one legitimizes one's social, educational, and economic activities as a way of realizing the power of God. In other words, the realization of God is an outcome of ongoing activity that is embedded in the Islamic ethos, and this unleashes social energy. Gülen's followers see themselves not as an interest group but rather as a community brought together by their religious commitment to create a more humane society. This community's mission is to realize, discuss, and bring the message of Islam to one's everyday life, to set the matrix of social and cultural action in a given society. The religious-economic practices are similar to those in Max Weber's thesis of the Protestant ethic: work inspired by religious belief produced the spirit of capitalism that affects rational capitalist action in Europe.[17]

With the rise of a well-developed, urban bourgeoisie, the social base of the producers and consumers of literacy has expanded. Before the emergence of printing and universal education, reading "circles," rather than the reading "public," were centered around the mosques and neighborhood. In other words, Gülen and those who follow him measure their spiritual success, to a certain extent, in terms of the worldly consequences of their actions. Believing that Gülen was trying to revive the Islamic faith and civilization under the leadership of Anatolian Turks, this newly urbanized group of intellectuals and merchants went into action to translate their worldly success into a heavenly mission.[18] For example, economic and social goals are manifested as a search for identity and justice. These goals are projected onto a spiritual quest to fulfill the will of God.

Religious ends are achieved through worldly actions rather than purely inward perfection. Gülen assumes that the inner transformation of individuals can only take place by exercising full control over modern processes. Indeed, Gülen's method of moving from the outer to the inner may be a reaction to the failure of previous Turkish-Islamic movements to move from inner-individual to the outer-public. When one sees the different emphases placed by Gülen on "action" and by Nursi on "belief," one can see the applicability of Alastair MacIntyre's view that the relationship between belief and action is internal and conceptual. MacIntyre argues that "it is because actions express beliefs, because actions are a vehicle for our beliefs that they can be described as consistent or inconsistent with beliefs expressed in avowal."[19] Islam, for Gülen, must be represented by actions, and these actions, in turn, are expressions of faith. However, the difference between Gülen and Nursi also is related to a newly evolving sociopolitical context within which Turkish Islam presently is embedded. Social factors that impinge on and influence this Islamic discourse set the direction of the neo-Nurcu movement.

Although both Nursi and Gülen expressed their views on social and political issues in terms of a perceived weakening sociopolitical consciousness during the Republican period, they both offered different remedies. Nursi, by forming a new religious consciousness, devalued the world in favor of certain spiritual ideals, whereas Gülen stresses praxis as the totality of all human activities through which a person seeks to transform nature into a "human world" (cemiyet)—of meanings, consciousness, technologies, and economic forces. One may conceptualize Nursi's understanding of Islam as from the "inside out" and Gülen's as from the "outside in." These different readings of the role of the Islamic religious tradition are responses to different conditions and needs. In the case of Nursi, the main task was the renewal of religious consciousness and the rejuvenation of faith in the midst of a militantly antireligious state campaign, whereas for Gülen reform of economic and social policy is the next important task.

The differences in stress on individual and community and religion and faith also differentiate Nursi from Gülen. Nursi wanted to free individuals as an object of the forces of materialism and utilitarianism. Nursi's goals were the reconstruction of faith in the age of skepticism and the cultivation of an ethically perfect self (insan-ı kamil). In Gülen's conception of the self, one is defined by, and matures through, membership in a community where one becomes fully aware of one's duty to the group and broader society. For Gülen, the constant theme has been action (aksiyon) and dominance over material conditions and control over the means of production and of ideas for the realization of a contemporary religious consciousness.[20] Gülen presents himself as a contemporary man of praxis as well as of spiritual contemplation. In the case of Nursi, however, the prevailing conditions of Kemalist persecution forced him to turn away from an externalized message of Islamic reform to an inner contemplative one. The incongruity between the inner and outer spiritual realms conditioned Nursi's understanding of modernity. According to Nursi, there is only one "home" where everyone can feel equal and free: the religious domain in which believers are fully conscious of the existence of God. Members of this inner community view each other as equals.

He sought to prevent the assimilation of Muslims into the external world and wanted them to return "home." One sees the perpetuation of this theme of "home" in the writings of other modern Turkish intellectuals. The notion of "home" was linked intricately with notions of memory, roots, and displacement within the secularizing and nationalizing Republic, where the new language of politics was introduced. This notion of "home" was an imagined and mostly invented mythical space for which Islamists yearned in response to their marginalization within the Republic. In the case of Gülen, however, "home" is a national-religious one where collective action is practiced.

Opportunity Spaces of Market, Media, and Education

The Gülen community consists of three circles. At the center of the movement is a core group of believers who lead the activities (hizmet) in a spirit of full and unconditional loyalty to the Gülen movement. This core group includes considerable numbers of university graduates who specialized in technical subjects and come from rural areas or small towns in Turkey. The main core of the movement consists of around 30 elder brothers (büyük abiler), some of them Gülen's closest friends and students, who are highly respected and regularly consulted on major day-to-day policies. Most of these elder brothers are fulltime activists who work as professionals with salaries at the Gülen movement's institutions. A large number in this core group have a Turkish nationalist background. There are some Kurds, but their number is limited, especially considering that Nursi himself was of Kurdish background.

The second circle of people support Gülen's religious-national goals and (in)directly participate in the creation of eser (good work) activities through charities, himmet. This circle includes esnaf (small and medium-sized merchants) and işadamı (businessmen) who constitute a board of trustees of the movement's numerous foundations of the movement. They support the movement's activities in their area through fundraisings organized by local volunteers.

Finally, there are those sympathizers who share Gülen's goals but do not participate in their realization. This group is very much involved in the protection of eser, whether the schools, newspapers, or dormitories. This last and biggest group includes many nominal Muslims, including agnostics and nonbelievers. Thus Gülen's community is less cohesive in its periphery but has a military-like discipline at the core.

The Gülen movement uses new opportunity spaces in the media, market, and education to transform ideas into action. A main question about it, and the Nur movement generally, is why it has appealed more to urban dwellers than to the traditional followers of Sufi orders. One explanation is their utilization of oral and print media in the dissemination of their ideas, media that are suited to facilitate the integration of recent migrants into large urban centers. These newcomers to the cities listen to Gülen's tapes or read his books rather than those of Nursi directly. Much of Gülen's appeal lies in his integrative and charismatic personality and his powerful presence as a television orator. He uses the television and radio as skillfully as any American televangelist to present Islam in the vernacular. His tremendous oratory and ability to project sincerity allows him to mobilize the masses through his sermons.

Gülen not only mediates between Nursi's *RNK* and its readers but also invests a new meaning into Nursi's works.[21] He makes use of lucid Turkish and, where appropriate, the local vernacular to appeal to a broad base of followers regardless of their background, education, or status. In his discourses on late Ottoman political and religious thought, Gülen examines these issues in terms of their contribution to the formation of national-religious consciousness and the state.[22] Gülen is also an accomplished poet; his poetry invokes a romantic nostalgia for the Ottoman past and elucidates its relevance for contemporary Turkish society.[23] Furthermore, his poetry seeks to construct an ethnoreligious (Turkish-Islamic) consciousness that calls for the mobilization of youth to realize a historical mission, namely the creation of a powerful and prosperous Turkey that once again will play a leadership role in the Islamic world as it did during Ottoman times.[24]

Media

The period 1983–1993 has been termed "the period of restoration" by some Nurcus. It is more appropriate, however, to treat this era rather as a time of invention and renaissance. In this period, Muslim intellectuals engaged in a novel reformulation of their Islamic beliefs vis-à-vis the contemporary social, cultural, economic, and political issues confronting Turkey.[25] They employed the print and the communications media widely to shape the exterior social world and manifest a plural (but not necessarily civic or democratic) Islamic discourse.

In the construction of neo-Nur communities, books and new means of technology played a formative and differentiating role. The cultural transformation of Turkey involved a revolution in the widespread dissemination of journals and magazines among the public. This process facilitated the expansion of the Gülen movement throughout Anatolia in the 1980s and 1990s and became an important ground for forming social and cultural associations and foundations. The expanding influence of the grassroots activities at dershanes prepared the necessary soil for the diffusion and construction of Islamic identity. These dershanes, interconnected by a shared code of ethics and social vision, are found all over Turkey and have spread to Central Asia, Europe, and the Balkan states as well. Moreover, the dershane networks have been an important matrix for the formation of a new intellectual class that has differentiated itself in terms of higher education and a more nationalistic outlook toward the state.

The development of a new pluralist and modern Islamic idiom through the electronic and print media also has played a key role in promoting the influence of Gülen's followers. The Gülen movement, with the support of the Özal, Demirel, and Çiller governments, purchased the newspaper *Zaman* and turned it into one of Turkey's leading dailies.[26] *Zaman* is unique among Turkish newspapers in that it is printed in 13 different countries that have large Muslim Turkic populations. It is a conscious effort to promote an "imperial Ottoman vision."[27]

Moreover, *Zaman* was the first Turkish newspaper to be available free through the Internet. It seeks to have all Central Asian newspapers and universities subscribe to its database. By 2002, the newspaper was the fifth largest in Turkey. It offers a distinctly Muslim voice on political and social issues. Nevertheless, not all of its views and positions are predictable. For example, the newspaper endorsed the idea of Turkey's integration with Europe[28] and did not react much to the partial closure of the controversial İmam Hatip schools, a demand of Kemalist hardliners in the military.[29]

In addition to the newspaper *Zaman*, the Gülen movement launched a national television channel, known as *Samanyolu*, and popular radio stations such as *Dünya* and BURÇ. The movement also owns *Sızıntı* (a scientific monthly), *Ekoloji* (an environment-related magazine), Yeni Ümit (a theological journal), *Aksiyon* (a weekly magazine), and *The Fountain* (an English-language religious publication). Gülen's activities are aimed at molding a cohesive and disciplined community through education, mass media, and financial networks. Gülen writes a long column once a month in *Sızıntı* and once every three months in *Yeni Ümit*; these essays are reprinted in *Zaman*. In these essays he deals with a wide range of issues. The pedagogical form of his essays indicates that his readers are familiar with print culture while still being receptive to the appeal of an oral cultural style of production. His form of argumentation is very allegorical and constantly refers to nature as "the book."[30] Gülen does not offer literal interpretation of the Qur'an but rather reads it through the lens of the phenomenal world. This literary interpretation softens the language of religion and makes it more amenable to practical life.

The Market

One of the main sources of controversy surrounding the movement has been its acquisition of financial resources. The movement's finances are collected from merchants and a smaller number of business groups. These groups collect religiously mandated alms (*zekat*), personal alms (*fitre*), and the hides of animals (*kurban derisi*) that are sacrificed during *Kurban Bayramı*, the Muslim festival of sacrifice. In a way his movement's reliance on domestic sources of funding forces Gülen to distance his group from political parties. After the death of Özal, the community diversified its support among a number of center-right and religious parties. For example, in Istanbul, many members tended to support Tayyip Erdoğan of the RP, in İzmir they supported Burhan Özfatura of the DYP, and in Ankara they supported Melih Gökçek of the RP at the municipal elections.

The typical neo-Nurcu member tends to be a professional or merchant, and his identity is a mixture of Islamic and national idioms. New merchants and small-scale industrialists support Gülen's missionary zeal for creating a powerful Islamic Turkey. For example, Gülen's wealthy followers established the Asya Finance Corporation in September 1996 to support social and educational activities inside Turkey and among Muslim populations in the Balkans, Caucasus, and Central Asia.[31] These pro-Gülen businessmen established the Association for Solidarity in Business Life (İSHAD), and the Businessmen's Association for Freedom (HÜRSİAD) to counter the pro-RP business association, MÜSİAD, which opposed Turkey's integration with the EU before 1997. This economic infrastructure is necessary to support 400 private high schools, universities and colleges, dormitories, summer camps, and over 100 foundations. Day-to-day activities are organized by a loosely structured local management on the basis of the tenets of charity, trust, obedience, and duty to the community. This structure is composed of businessmen, teachers, journalists, and students. Gülen is well aware of the opportunities available in a free market economy. His philosophy, therefore, is very much in tune with this growing business community. He stresses education and engagement in the market economy as an essential part of becoming a good Muslim.[32]

The Education of the Golden Generation

Islam, for Gülen, is first and foremost about morality (kişilik) and identity (kimlik). The connection between the two can be summarized in the idea that there is no identity without morality and no morality without Islam. Gülen, like Nursi, believes that free and democractic society requires public morality and this morality cannot be effective without religion. Religion offers the content of moral maxims and renders force to it by stressing divine judgment. Gülen's conception of identity and morality are interconnected but not a self-contained or closed system. Since morality translates into identity through conduct and collective action, "acting" and "engaging" in the public and private spheres are part of building the moral self. In short, morality and identity must be put into practice and reinterpreted on the basis of new challenges. "Islam by conduct" (hizmet and himmet) and "Islam by product" (eser) are the two key concepts of the Gülen movement. Since Islam, for Gülen, is the constitution of morality and identity, he stresses the role of education for the cultivation of the self. His education project is based on three principles: cultivation of morality, teaching of science, and the discipline of the self. In his faith-inspired education project, morality and discipline consist of sacrifice, responsibility to others, hard work, and idealism. In fact, this religiously motivated global education movement is a way of bringing God back into one's life through the ethic of self-sacrifice and hard work. Muslims constantly are reminded that avoiding sin is not enough; rather, engaging to change and create a more humane world is required. Salvation is not only to be "saved from" sinful activities but also to be engaged actively in the improvement of the world. In the first issue of his magazine Sızıntı, Gülen wrote:

> Our generation is humiliated and consumed by the oppressive forces
> of materialism. There is no sign that signifies the existence of an
> inner depth or lucid feelings and thought in our generation. Our
> mission should be the following: To breathe life into and raise the
> spiritual consciousness of a new generation that is cut off from its

spiritual and cultural roots and consumed by the wordly ideas of the world.... This new generation must be led by *tevhid* [the doctrine of absolute unity and idea that only God is worthy of worship and service] in thought and purpose in life.[33]

To overcome this ethical void and create a new modern Turkey, Gülen stresses the role of education in creating a new Islamic consciousness. Gülen believes in a cognitive transformation of society through education that is to be taught by an elite sensitive to Turkish history and traditions and the sentiments of the common people. His program, therefore, is aimed at raising this new elite, known as the "Golden Generation" (*altın nesil*), which is to reclaim the glories of the Ottoman-Islamic past while effectively adapting to modern conditions and needs.

Gülen effectively has exploited the opportunities provided by education through his extensive scholarships and dormitory network in every part of the country. For example, in Istanbul the movement operates many foundations, such as the Turkish Higher Education Youth and Specialization Foundation (*Türkiye Yüksek Tahsil Gençliği Öğretim ve İhtisas Vakfı*), which runs 37 dormitories, and the Marmara Education and Culture Foundation (*Marmara Eğitim ve Kültür Vakfı*), which runs 26 dormitories. Gülen's educational networks include over 6,000 teachers, who constitute the most important pillar of the movement. These teachers view pedagogical action rather than mere religious ritual as the road to consciousness. Since it is legally impossible to introduce a course on religion, the movement stresses the concept of "Islam by conduct," that is, presenting the essence of Islam by acting morally. Thus teachers in the classroom present Islam by conduct in terms of tolerance, respect, diligence, and commitment to the well-being of the community. In addition to informal educational networks, the Gülen movement also runs an elaborate chain of broader university preparatory courses, where money and supplies for poorer students are supported by donations.

One of Gülen's most remarkable and farsighted strategies has been the establishment of approximately 200 high schools and seven universities throughout Turkey, Europe, and the Turkic-Muslim republics of the former Soviet Union. Although these universities are very much at the level of community colleges, the high schools have acquired a strong reputation in the teaching of natural sciences and the English language. While Turkish is also taught, English is the primary language in the classroom.[34] The impact of these efforts has been quite profound in the educational system. In addition to high schools, Gülen's circle also has been very active in the Turkish educational system through its 79 university preparatory schools.[35] These preparatory schools have been very successful in achieving high marks for their students on university entrance examinations. In addition to these preparatory schools, Gülen's circle also controls over 50 private high schools in Turkey.[36] Financial supporters of these schools regularly are invited to visit the schools in Turkey and outside. The teachers at these schools usually come from the Middle East Technical University in Ankara or from Boğaziçi University in

Istanbul. They believe that they have a mission to fulfill, just like missionaries. Like American Protestant missionaries of the nineteenth century, the neo-Nurcu teachers are seeking to deliver God along with Turkish nationalism. These education networks are connected closely to conservative business circles. The combination of business interests with Gülen's ideas is powerful both inside and outside Turkey.

Students in the Gülen movement's high schools in Turkey consistently achieve superior results on university exams. Although these schools do a much better job than state schools, they still stress memorization and conservative values more than critical thinking. The Gülen movement's educational system does not necessarily promote free will and individualism but rather promotes collective consciousness. For the students who graduate from Gülen's schools, the sense of duty or fulfilling one's mission is a more important virtue than being different or thinking critically. This lack of critical thinking is an outcome of a cultural and educational system that discourages questioning of social and religious values. Being the same as and being "part of the group" and behaving in conformity with the group expectations are more important than carving a unique self.

In addition to these formal education networks, Gülen's community also has a widespread informal network of dershanes. The dershanes, inhabited by college students, are rooted in Islamic ethics and a sense of urgency to not only benefit from but shape the unfolding modernity. They have become spaces for multiple activities of education, sport, practical training, distribution of books, and conversation. Dershanes integrate religious and secular publicity together and remove the boundary between private and public space by arming the students against temptations and seductions of the modern world. Moreover, they are run according to a set of rules and seek to generate their own income by offering new services such as helping with students' homework, giving private lessons, or organizing athletic activities. These networks all seek to realize Gülen's goal of creating a Golden Generation of Turks to produce modernity and not just remain its consumers. The achievement of the dershanes lies in their institutional and conceptual ability to reconstitute the Muslim personality at the most subjective level. They offer necessary means for the self-realization of a Muslim personality. The religious ambience offered by the dershane structure encourages the internalization of the ideals (archetypes) as a map of action that would lead to the discovery of the richness of Muslim identity. In other words, people's interests are informed by their values and these values constitute the map of action. This shared cognitive map of ideals and action is at the core of the Gülen movement.

Islam in the Vernacular: *Türkiye Müslümanlığı*

Since Islam, for Gülen, is about morality (*kişilik*) and identity (*kimlik*), he has developed a historically rooted and politically sensitive identity with which Muslims can identify. Gülen redefines Turkish national identity as being essentially Ottoman and Islamic. By doing this, he aims to restore Islam to its historic role as the national religion of the Turks. To raise a new generation with an international vision, the Gülen movement stresses the role of bilingual (Turkish and English, not Arabic) education in Turkey and abroad.[37] Gülen's vision in the Balkans and Central Asia is akin to an Ottoman-imperial vision that seeks to integrate the Muslim populations of these regions into a coherent bloc.

In order to realize this mission, Gülen stressed the importance of investment in education and media to raise people's social and national consciousness. He has sought to reconstruct a new Turkish-Islamic identity through education and treated Islam as the foundation for a Turkish cultural and national renaissance. Gülen has argued that "ethnicity" does not determine a person's value before God. However, he has regularly stressed the positive role the Turks played in the defense of Islam and its positive interpretation.[38] There is a deep feeling among neo-Nurcus that contemporary Arab regimes and societies are wicked and too inept to understand and revitalize Islam. Gülen openly declared that "Turkey is the only country in which one can live freely and think as a Muslim."[39] Gülen rarely hesitates to express his views on Islam within his national and state-centered framework. He argues that the Turks have achieved the highest understanding of Islam and that this was manifested in Turkish-Ottoman culture and its tolerant state tradition. He does not hesitate to describe this "Sufi interpretation of Islam" as *Türkiye Müslümanlığı* (Islam of Turkey).[40] This interpretation of Islam consists of the Sufism of Anatolia and the pragmatic state-centric political culture of the Ottoman Turks.[41] By arguing that there are various understandings of Islam particular to each country and region, Gülen aptly serves the state's project of attempting to nationalize Islam. He argues: "I never thought my Turkish identity was isolated from my religious identity. I always thought it was side by side with my religion. I did not see them in contradiction."[42] In the same interview, Gülen argues that "the state and nation must be melded together."[43] Gülen's political thinking, influenced by the state-centric Ottoman culture and Turkish-Islamic nationalism, became very clear in his statements on the Alevi question and the Kurdish problem. As a solution to the Kurdish problem, he asked the state to employ "Muslim ulema to stress religious brotherhood between Turks and Kurds."[44]

Gülen and Mehmet Kırkıncı represent the degree of accommodation that has been attained by neo-Nur leaders with the Republican principles of the state.[45] They present Islam as a unifying bond to hold together diverse societal groups. Gülen supports the maintenance of the DİB because he sees the advantages in an institutional religious center closely tied to the state.[46] Religion becomes a framework for the unity of the nation and a source of state legitimacy. Islam in this context is subordinated to the existence of the nation-state and used as a repository for the construction of a well-ordered society.[47] Gülen and Kırkıncı therefore consistently have supported the state's policy of consolidating a Turkish-Islamic synthesis.[48]

Like Nursi, Gülen argued that there were three obstacles in the way of a Turkish national renaissance: ignorance, poverty, and dissension. It is interesting to note, however, that in his articulation of these three national problems, Gülen did not cite Nursi but rather Franz Kafka.[49] He rearticulated and projected

Nursi's ideas to a secular audience by utilizing Western intellectual discourse rather than specifically Islamic themes. Islam, for Gülen, is not only a ritual activity but also a cultural repository and a cognitive map of a national Turkish collective consciousness. His stress on a Turkish-Islamic synthesis indicates a vernacularization of the faith and a broad convergence with some of the goals of the Republican state.[50]

Gülen is first and foremost a Turko-Ottoman nationalist. His nationalism is an inclusive one that is based not on blood or race but rather on shared historical experiences and the agreement to live together within one polity. For Gülen, there should be no difference between a Bosnian and a Kazak. His first job as a preacher, in fact, was at the Üç Şerefeli Mosque in Edirne, where a large number of Torbes and Pomaks, both Muslim Slavs, live. Gülen hardly differentiates between ethnic and nonethnic Turks, treating both as Turks and Muslims.[51] He therefore has a more inclusive notion of identity, shaped by the Ottoman-Islamic legacy. Although the Arabs were part of the Ottoman Empire, Gülen, like other Nurcu groups, is critical of the Arab world and feels that Arab and Iranian Islamic movements have yet to arrive at a proper understanding of Islam. He also has accused Arab nationalists of collaboration against the Ottoman state and causing a negative image for Islam by reducing it to a political ideology. Moreover, he differentiates urban Ottoman Islam from tribal Arab Islam and expresses admiration for the Ottoman sultans and even—perhaps tactically—for Mustafa Kemal.[52]

Gülen, who seeks to restore the nation by "remembering" its past rather than "forgetting" it, calls on people to "rediscover the self [öze dönüş]" that has been "embodied within Islam and the Ottoman past." In his writings, the concept of ecdad (ancestors) is a key term in terms of forming or activating collective memory and teaching the heroic values of "our ancestors." The past is used as a quarry of cultural materials for didactic illustration, a moral tableau worthy of emulation. The past from which Gülen wants to derive the contemporary self is no longer just a past but rather a source to mold the present and the future. By reimagining the cultural content of the Turkish nation, the Islamic groups reconstructed the political nation as Muslim, Ottoman, and Turkish. This is an attempt to free the definition of the nation from the statist-Kemalist elite.

The Gülen movement, in constructing the present by "remembering" a past of their own choosing, operates simultaneously in modern and nonmodern times. Gülen argues that "returning to self means viewing yesterday, today, and tomorrow together holistically and selecting those ideas and practices that need to be preserved and eliminating those that do not fit into the perpetuation of the self."[53] These imaginative concepts and ideas, for Gülen, should be derived from religion and the traditions of the Ottoman state. His writings reveal that religion becomes a source to shape art, literature, education, and ethics with the aim of forming a national consciousness to meld religion with reason and the heart with the mind. This presents national consciousness as an important basis for the renewal and reform of Turkish society.[54] Nilüfer Göle argues that Gülen "declares the formation of a new Muslim self and a new civilization and creates his own elite."[55] Such ambitions are not without their problems, of course.

The attempt to construct a national consciousness from religious commitments has to come to grips with the reality of ethnic and sectarian divisions in Turkey, especially where Kurdish and Alevi identities are concerned. An in-depth analysis of how the followers of Gülen have responded to these ideas indicates that they support the reconciliation of religion and nationality in order to consolidate the state. By stressing the role of education and enlightenment to overcome social ills, however, Gülen also indirectly promotes the idiom of individuality, which may run counter to his more communitarian impulses.

A closer examination of the movement from the 1970s to 2000 reveals its constant evolution and adaptation to the new realities of Turkey. If one listens to Gülen's tapes from the 1970s, one encounters an obstinate preacher who sought to mobilize the emotions of people. His interaction with diverse groups and the government helped the movement to penetrate society but it also has been penetrated by diverse ideas and practices as well. The movement has shaped processes that in turn have shaped it. Moreover, as the movement became more institutionalized, it also became attuned to state policies and the need to maintain its relevance for the Turkish people. In order to carry religion to the public sphere, the movement has stressed tolerance, reconciliation, modernity, and democracy. For instance, Gülen argues that the female headscarf is a *füruat* (not an essential of faith), and one's veiling (*tesettür*) choice is also related to cultural understanding of Islam and therefore can be interpreted differently. Gülen said: "What is in the interest of the state and the nation: education or illiteracy? Each person should decide in her conscience on the issue of the headscarf. As far as I am concerned, she should prefer education."[56]

Gülen is attempting to construct a new social contract in which the multiculturalist Turko-Ottoman tradition plays a formative role. The movement has brought many diverse groups together to discuss the problems of Turkey and to present solutions. For instance, under the umbrella of the Foundation of Journalists and Writers of Turkey, the Gülen group has identified the major "divisive" political issues of Turkey, such as the relationship between Islam and secularism (1998),[57] religion and the state (1999), democracy and human rights (2000), pluralism and reconciliation (2001), and globalization and its implications. The group has brought many leading scholars, intellectuals, and policymakers together to discuss these divisive issues and author consensus charters, known as Abant Platformu. The first Abant Platformu, which came out of the most important of the five meetings, concluded that

> revelation and reason do not conflict; individuals should use their
> reason to organize their social life; the state should be neutral on
> beliefs, faith and the philosophical orientation of society; governance
> of the state cannot be based on religion and secularism, but should
> expand individual freedoms and rights and should not deprive any
> person from public participation.[58]

As a result of new opportunity spaces and the global discourses of human rights and multiculturalism, the Gülen movement is in the process of creating a "contemporary Islam" that is part of modern debate in Turkey. The goal of these activities and engagement with different intellectual groups is not to reorient the state in terms of Islamic precepts. Rather, the goal is to promote a state ideology that does not contradict Islamic teachings and opens spaces for different imaginations of Islam in the public sphere.

The State's Co-optation and Exclusion

In the 1980s, Gülen gained official protection during the late Özal's terms in office as prime minister and president. The center-right parties all backed Gülen, hoping to counterbalance the votes of Erbakan's RP in the general elections in 1991, 1995, and 1999. Gülen developed close ties with Özal and openly endorsed Özal's neoliberal policies. In an interview Gülen said:

> I had a close relationship with Turgut Özal when he was working on the State Planning Organization. He regularly visited my house and we had breakfast and dinner together on many occasions. He even attended my mosque and listened to my sermons. We held many conversations about social and political developments in Turkey. Just a week before the September 12 military takeover, he visited me and asked what I was thinking about the prevailing anarchy and chaos. I told him that as far as the future of Muslims was concerned, "I am positive." He responded, "[The] political situation is getting worse."[59]

The relations between Gülen and the state were based on a code of mutual interests. The governments of Özal and Çiller, and even the secular-Kemalist bureaucracy, regarded Gülen as a pliable countervoice to the Islamic RP's more overtly political role and more doctrinaire interpretation of Islam.[60] Despite criticism of his involvement in politics, Gülen did not hesitate to develop close connections with politicians. Indeed, as he became aware of his importance as a potential Islamist rival to the RP, Gülen regularly used his meetings with leading politicians to advance the interests of his community and its programs.[61] For example, he apparently perceived his meeting with Çiller, after she became prime minister, as being in this vein.[62]

His general popularity has grown as a result of his "progressive" interpretation of the Qur'an. For example, he argues that women can become judges and that the headscarf is not an essential attribute of a Muslim woman. In response to Gülen's broadminded interpretations, Mehmet Şevket Eygi, a columnist for the pro-Islamic *Milli Gazete*, argued that "the headscarf, like the boundaries of Turkey, is not open to disputation. It is the boundary set by God and cannot be discussed."[63] As a result of Gülen's ties with governing circles and his more tolerant Islamic attitude, some more puritanical RP supporters accused him of being an American agent. Ali Bulaç, a prominent Islamist intellectual, expressed a common suspicion with the following three questions to Gülen: "Where do you stand as far as Mustafa Kemal and his reforms are concerned? Will you try to stop RP from coming to power? And why do you invest in Central Asia but not the Middle East?"[64]

The rise of Gülen to public prominence shocked many Islamist intellectuals who expected to gain even further impetus in the 1995 general elections after successful local election results in 1994. Islamist intellectuals such as Mustafa Kaplan argue that the state supports Gülen in an effort to consolidate and expand its social basis and Kemalist ideology.[65] Gülen has argued that he had no intention of preventing the RP from coming to power, claiming there was a division of labor between the two movements. "The political sphere is managed by the RP and education by us." However, behind these public statements, there remained a deep rivalry between Gülen and the political Islam represented by Erbakan's Milli Görüş. By raising the issue of Central Asia versus the Middle East, Bulaç was trying to raise the issue of the role of state-promoted nationalism in Gülen's project.

Gülen has not hidden his cooperation with the State Intelligence Service (MİT). He said in an interview:

> In Erbil [an Iraqi town dominated by Kurds], we opened a school for
> the Turkmens [a Turkic seminomadic group]. I told the president
> that they need to open a school in this area to protect the Turks from
> assimilation by the Kurds.... We decided to open the school with the
> help of the State Intelligence Service.[66]

Gülen has always wanted to give the impression that he is working with and for the state to create legitimacy for the movement. Since most Turks share the state-centric and nationalist political culture, Gülen never wanted a confrontation with the state in general, or the military in particular. For instance, Gülen supported the anti-Iraqi coalition during the Gulf War and sharply attacked those who organized protests against the state. He also has expressed a rather dim view of some aspects of the Iranian Islamic Revolution and the Saudi Wahhabi interpretation of Islam, both of which, he thinks, promote a negative image of Islam.[67]

Gülen considers the importance of stability and security of the state to be above that of any particular faction, and this is seen as one of the principal conditions for the survival of Islam. As such, Gülen is aware of the need to maintain a balanced distance from any particular party that may be in power. He argues:

> We don't support every ruling party just because they are in power.
> There are ways in which they come to power and leave it. We need to
> control these ways and doors that play a key role to the walk to
> power.... We should respect the government and express our opposi-
> tion as is done in most developed Western countries.[68]

From his interviews, it seems that Gülen's ultimate goal is to become a political and cultural bridge between the state and the conservative middle class and upwardly mobile technocrats. Gülen also believes that the Islamic aspect of Turkish culture has been highlighted more following the 1980 military coup than at any previous time in Republican history. Gülen has claimed: "I am always on the side of the state and military. Without the state, there is anarchy and chaos."[69]

Although Gülen's thinking is more strongly shaped by the Ottoman tradition of statehood than any specific Islamic precepts, he strongly supports democracy. He argues:

> Democracy and Islam are compatible. Ninety-five percent of Islamic rules deal with private life and the family. Only 5 percent deal with matters of the state and this could be arranged only within the context of democracy. If some people are thinking something else, such as an Islamic state, this country's history and social conditions do not allow it.... Democratization is an irreversible process in Turkey.[70]

He similarly views democracy as a key means for promoting the Islamic dimension of national identity. He argues that "we need to find great brains and powerful individuals who would protect religion in the political domain."[71]

Gülen's main foreign policy objective is to create a powerful Turkey by organizing Muslim communities in the Balkans and the Turkic states in Central Asia.[72] He sees the Kurdish and Alevi upheavals as external plots aimed at preventing "the emergence of a major power from the Adriatic Sea to the Walls of China."[73] He sharply criticizes the state for not having a long-term strategy for integration with Central Asia and calls on the state to support private foundations in establishing schools and clinics in this arena.

Gülen particularly believes that he can shape the political and societal features of Turkey through his organizational abilities in education and the media. He now openly argues that the movement has moved from the period of internalization to that of the externalization of its ideas and vision. This new phase in the movement's history has been compared to the "birth of a child."[74] However, rival Islamic groups have sharply criticized Gülen's optimistic vision of Turkey's future and his leading role in it. His critics feel that his ideas are devoid of substance and authenticity and that his organization lacks an independent power base to play a significant role in the transformation of Turkey. Gülen's deft move toward supporting a liberal economy and politics compelled him to internalize the modern political discourse of human rights and nationalism. This in turn has limited his options and pulled him into controversy. For example, when Gülen was asked to comment on the confrontation between the military and the Erbakan-led government, he sided with the military, which was the ultimate locus of power, and said: "The government has failed to fulfill its functions and it should resign."[75]

According to some Islamist critics, Gülen's circle is not a religious community but rather an interest association. One young radical Islamist and critic in Konya said:

> The Nurcu circle constantly stresses the society and the individual. Fethullah Hoca and other Nurcus do not want the immediate control of the state. Instead, they prefer to cooperate with the state to gain legitimacy at the expense of other Islamist groups. They are too ignorant to understand that you cannot have an Islamic system through the "bottom." You need to control the state and then create it from the top down.[76]

The Gülen movement has been very careful to stress its distinctiveness from other Islamic groups, including the Milli Görüş, and its commonality with the more secular segments of Turkish society. Gülen's notion of politics cannot be considered liberal, since he gives priority to the community and the state over individual rights. Although Gülen makes political and social claims on the basis of religious distinctions, these are not based on mutual respect and responsibility to other political communities. Furthermore, he hardly questions the oppressive policies of the Turkish state. Gülen's project is a hybrid communitarian movement rooted in the Turko-Islamic state tradition. However, in comparison with the elitist and socially exclusive nature of Turkish intellectual life, Gülen, as a religious leader, is fairly tolerant of the "other." He is open to dialogue with all other groups in order to promote civility and democracy in Turkey.[77] The Gülen movement has reconciled itself with democracy and secularism without becoming either fully democratic or secular. Gülen's vision of Islam is based on discipline and dialogue. The first principle is stressed within the community, whereas the latter is an external principle for interaction with other non-Muslim groups. In order to promote his humanistic interpretation of Islam, Gülen stresses the role of dialogue and tolerance, and he has successes in this regard. For example, he met with Patriarch Bartholomeos, the head of the Orthodox Patriarchate in Istanbul, and other leaders of the Orthodox churches.[78] Gülen has also met with other Christian and Jewish religious leaders, including Pope John Paul II, in an effort to advance interfaith dialogue.[79]

In spite of its great influence, organizational abilities, and avowed aims, the Gülen movement may not be the best group for promoting democracy and civil society in Turkey. This movement, for example, presents private initiative and associational life as a way of consolidating the state, as opposed to creating autonomous civil spheres outside of its purview. The members of the movement are socially conservative and not very open to critical thinking. They seek to shape the souls of their followers through education in the values of a spiritual collective—a process of spiritual-intellectual formation that stresses loyalty to the state and a leader. The Gülen movement, by empowering community and raising the self-consciousness of Muslims as a way of achieving a well-ordered society, does not always promote the formation of a sense of individuality.

As far as gender equality is concerned, there is a gap between what Gülen teaches and how quickly the community follows his leadership. In his speeches, he advocates the integration of women into the workforce without clearly articulating equality for women. Gülen's community practices rigid gender segregation and does not permit women to work in high positions—in the movement's vast networks or in its media empire, for example. A decade ago, the members of this religious community were not even willing to allow their daughters to go to secondary or high schools. They preferred to send female students to Qur'anic courses or to the strictly female İmam Hatip schools. For years, Gülen publicly and privately encouraged the members of the community to educate all their children, regardless of gender. Gülen personally has expressed a desire to see women taking a more active role in the movement and occupy high position in it; he also has acknowledged that getting the socially conservative culture of Anatolia to accept a more active participatory role by women is difficult.[80] Before the 1997 coup, there were a number of all-girl schools, and sex-based segregation remained at the core of the Gülen movement. As a result of the 1997 coup, gender-segregated private and public education was ended, and all schools gradually became mixed. Thus, as far as gender equality is concerned, the Gülen movement is not proactive but rather reactive, and change comes as a result of state policies.

There is a deep-seated suspicion among some radical Islamic groups that the state seeks to use Islam to secularize it from within. Some even see Gülen's close ties with state authorities as having accomplished the nationalization of the RNK. Others, however, view this elaborate courtship between Gülen and the state as inevitably leading to the domestication of the state along Islamic lines. They argue that by gradually penetrating the state Gülen and others will be able to transform its Kemalist and antireligious foundation and render impossible any repeat of the "Jacobin" assault on Islam that Mustafa Kemal and his coterie carried out. In order to avoid attack in the 1997 coup, Gülen publicly defended the military crackdown against the RP government and did not oppose the suppression of peaceful Sunni Islamic groups in the country.[81] He has not been very consistent on the issues of democracy and human rights and has sought immunity by promoting his group's interest before the rights of civil society as a whole.[82] He regularly courted the state by supporting campaigns against radical Islamist groups and excused the military's intolerant policies against any manifestation of religion in public. Gülen and his community tried to present themselves as "soft" and "moderate" vis-à-vis other Islamic groups within Turkey. By stressing their differences from other groups as more "moderate," they tried to gain legitimacy from the Kemalist state. Moreover, Gülen and his followers offered little criticism of the oppressive state policies against nonviolent Kurds and many independent-minded journalists.

The Paradox of Persecution and Forced Liberalization (1997–2002)

Catering to state policies did not help the Gülen movement. On June 21, 1999, the state-guided media launched a fierce, orchestrated attack on Gülen and his activities as being "reactionary" and a "threat" to the secular nature of the Turkish state by broadcasting his speeches made in the late 1970s and early 1980s.[83] On the basis of these speeches, the Ankara State Security Court prosecutor requested an arrest warrant for Gülen on charges of plotting to overthrow the state by establishing a clandestine organization. The State Security Court rejected the request of the arrest warrant on August 28, 2000. On August 30, 2000, General Kıvrıkoğlu, then the chief of the General Staff, said publicly that Gülen "plans to undermine the State" and that he had supporters in the civil service, even in the judiciary, and "that's why his arrest warrant was rejected." On the basis of Kıvrıkoğlu's accusations, the state prosecutor indicted Gülen for "attempting to change the secular characteristics of the Republic" by allegedly trying to establish a theocratic Islamic state.[84] The prosecutor also alleged that "the organization of Fethullah Gülen, which is formed to destroy the secular nature of the state since 1989, wove the country with its legal and illegal networks that includes advisory boards, regional, city, neighborhood, hostel leaders."[85] As of January 2003, the prosecutor is seeking a maximum 10-year sentence based on Turkey's Anti-Terror Law. The prosecutor does not mention a single act of "crime" committed by Gülen but rather refers only to his destructive ideas. The indictment should be read within the political framework of the 1997 coup and its aim to criminalize alternative thinking. According to Çetin Özek, a leading legal scholar of secularism and criminal law in Turkey, the prosecutor's case is against freedom of thought. The state, for Özek, "should not criminalize alternative thinking if it does not fit into the state ideology." [86] Gülen's books, for Özek, make the following conclusions:

> The theocratic system cannot be reconciled with Islam; science and scientific reasoning are necessary for the understanding of religion; jihad does not mean violence or bloodshed but rather training of the human spirit and inner self; the dissemination of religious ideas by force is an anti-Islamic act; and a constant stress on brotherhood, tolerance, reconciliation and peace among humans.[87]

The anti-Gülen campaign forced Gülen to take refuge in the United States. This confrontation was one that Gülen always and judiciously had sought to avoid. Uncharacteristically, however, this attack was met with a sharp and hitherto unprecedented counterattack by Gülen's media outlets.[88] For his part, Gülen had learned the painful lesson that obsequiously catering to the center of military power can breed contempt as much as it does forbearance. Many journalists and members of Gülen's inner circle believed a radical group within the Turkish army is behind this attempt to further curtail civilian authority. The activities of the Gülen community have been under close scrutiny and are perceived as a source of fear for the secularist political elite for four reasons: Gülen's attempt to redefine nation, community, and identity in accordance with a religious-communal form of Turkish nationalism; his attempt to redefine secularism along the lines of Anglo-Saxon tradition rather than French Jacobinism; his attempt to create a dense web of networks to gain international legitimacy and translate this into suppport on the Turkish domestic scene; and fourth, his attempt to challenge the Kemalist monopoly on education and modernity. His better equipped and organized schools have become a source of the education of a new elite with multiple epistemologies, both secular and religious. Meanwhile, the Kemalist elite has feared losing control over education. The radical clique within the army has always worried that Gülen could use his networks to penetrate state institutions and co-opt some secular intellectuals.

State officials who are suspicious of Gülen's long-term goals refer to his tactics of "moving back and forth" in response to pressures from the state as betraying his long-term agenda, which is not consonant with that of the country's military-bureaucratic establishment. Even his statements apologizing for the military's draconian edict forcing observant Muslim women not to wear headscarves in public institutions and his liberal and pacifistic understanding of Islam are treated as tactical rather than the real positions that he is alleged to hold. One state official said that "his main goal is to move from the period of the 1997 coup process with least damage" to emerge as the most powerful Turkish Islamic group after the post–February 28 process.[89] Mehmet Kutlular, leader of the Yeni Asya Nurcu group, criticized Gülen for being a tool of the authoritarian state establishment and not being a sincere Nurcu concerned with the issue of human rights even if this would lead to prosecution. Kutlular argues that the state used Gülen against other Islamic groups and when it felt that it did not need him it decided to dispense with him and his movement.[90]

As a result of the 1997 coup, the public sphere and social spaces were shrinking, and the boundaries for critical thinking among Muslims were expanding. This paradox between the external pressure and internal expansion is the major characteristic of post-1997 Turkey. As people are pressured to give up their differences and become one, they become more sympathetic and supportive of diversity and cultural pluralism. This sympathy for difference is critical for the evolution of liberal thinking.[91] Since the 1997 soft coup, Gülen gradually has moved away from his previous nationalist and statist position to a more liberal and global perspective. This new Gülen has internalized the global discourses of human rights and democracy. He is less political and state-centric and more society and market oriented.

Conclusion

Gülen's ideas and activities have had a major impact on the political debate in Turkey over the role of Islam in state and society. Even though Gülen does not have a liberal imagination of Islam, his distinct conception of Islam vis-à-vis other Islamic groups promotes pluralism in Turkey. Leonard Binder argues that "without a vigorous Islamic liberalism, political liberalism will not succeed in the Middle East, despite the emergence of bourgeois states."[92] In the light of the Turkish experience, political and economic liberalism seem to be necessary frameworks for Islamic liberalism. Since political and economic liberalism helped to open new discursive spaces for diverse voices, intellectuals such as Gülen have appropriated Islam as a new bourgeois political identity rather than a counterforce against new openings in society.[93]

A close consideration of Gülen's mass educational strategy in Turkey and the ex-Soviet Turkic republics reveals that the program's motivation is a religious-national vision of Turkey and a belief that hard work and sacrifice to achieve this vision are in themselves an act of worship. One thus witnesses the paradox of Islam being in a sense secularized as it is harnessed for the practical needs of the state and the capitalist market. The Gülen movement also shows that civil society has developed several strategies to penetrate the state and also to neutralize its secularist hostility to Islam and traditional Turkish culture and identity.

An examination of the Gülen movement reveals not only the ideological diversity of the Islamic movements in Turkey but also the extent to which some

of them internalized aspects of the Republican reforms. This phenomenon occurred during the process by which they emerged as a part of modern consumer
society. Among the different Islamic groups, the Gülen movement has been
especially influential. Gülen's praxis-oriented worldview induced merchants and
educators to involve themselves in a project to create a new Turkey with a distinctly inclusive Turkish-Islamic identity. This new Turkey is seen as eventually reclaiming the country's historic role of leading the Turkish and Islamic
worlds once it makes peace with its Ottoman past.

9

The National Outlook
Movement and the Rise
of the Refah Party

Mehmet Zahid Kotku was the brainchild of the party. He wanted to
have a party where Muslims could feel at home. We were, in fact,
tired of being used by other center-right parties. I became involved in
this party because of Zahid Efendi. I remember that evening when
Zahid Efendi invited five people and told us that "you are all men
dedicated to the cause of protecting and advancing this nation. The
core identity [*kimlik*] and character [*kişilik*] of this wounded nation is
Islam. Your main heritage is Islam and as Muslims you can heal this
wound by listening to what our Turkish Muslim people want. What
they want is an Islamic sense of justice and the restoration of their
Ottoman-Islamic identity.

Lütfi Doğan, head of the Directorate
of Religious Affairs, 1968–1971

Mehmet Zahid Kotku, the renowned Nakşibendi leader of the
İskenderpaşa Cemaati, played a seminal role in the formation of
what would become the MSP, underscoring once again the position
of the Nakşibendi order as the matrix of most leading contemporary
Turkish-Islamic sociopolitical movements.[1] He understood
the connections between macro socioeconomic forces and microlevel ethical issues at the individual level. He set the coordinates
of the MGH by pinning down the search for identity and justice as
two principles animating vast sections of Turkish society.[2] The
Nakşibendi Iskenderpaşa order first mobilized a group of community leaders and merchants to get Necmettin Erbakan to the
Grand National Assembly from Konya in 1969. Soon after, Kotku
and his followers set the organizational model and necessary
networks for the formation and evolution of the MGH into the MSP,

the first avatar of Erbakan's Islamic political party. Advancing demands for justice and identity remained the two pillars of the movement. In modern Turkey, Islamic identity was first explicitly articulated in the political domain by the MGH. The MGH conveyed the voices of Islamist groups to the public sector, representing Islamist interests in Parliament, also allowing at this time more openly Islamist figures into the administration of local municipalities and the larger national bureaucracy. Consequently, the MGH played a vital role in integrating marginalized yet vast sections of Anatolian Turkish society into the political processes through presenting a more inclusive identity rooted in Ottoman-Islamic tradition.[3]

Many Turkish Muslims during the period of the early 1970s began using newly opened opportunity spaces for articulating formerly prohibited identities and demands for dealing with the challenges of secularism, industrialization, urbanization, and the popularization of knowledge through mass education and communication, and they supported the formation of the MSP to encompass and express this newly formed consciousness. After the closure of the MSP by the military coup leaders in 1980 and the RP in 1998, the same social groups re-formed as the FP.[4]

The changing names, from *Milli Nizam* (National Order) to *Milli Selamet* (National Salvation) to *Refah* (Welfare) to *Fazilet* (Virtue) to *Saadet* (Felicity) reflect both the pressures of the ongoing power struggle between the secular Kemalist center and the Turkish-Islamic periphery and also the main political platform of the party during each period.[5] National Order, for example, is synonymous in popular Turkish with the concept of a religiously rooted just order. *Milli* does not mean simply "national" but also connotes religious ethnos, and it continues to be articulated as an ethical signifier of justice, loyalty, and community. *Milli* easily could be used interchangeably with "religiously defined community,"[6] and it also was used because any form of religious designation for a party has been against the law.[7] In other words, the Islamic movement in Turkey always has managed to connect to society by skillfully utilizing religious symbolism. *Selamet* (salvation), *refah* (welfare), *fazilet* (virtue), and *saadet* (felicity) are symbolic vernacular concepts and are thus understood and carry meaning among ordinary Muslims.

The MNP and the MSP

As the secular Kemalist ideology began to be imposed by the center over much of traditional Anatolian social life, religion gradually was politicized and became the dominant counterhegemonic identity of the broad periphery. When the later internal power struggle within the secular sector made support from the periphery crucial, concessions such as allowing limited public manifestations of religion were made in order to harness this support. First the DP and then its successor, the AP, demonstrated a more sensitive attitude toward religious sentiments in a notable break from the militancy of the early Kemalist period.

As the emerging bourgeoisie in the 1960s sought to free itself from state bureaucratic controls, the AP began to support free initiatives and to subsidize industrial projects. Although it first used the support of the Muslim periphery to reduce the hegemonic power of the Kemalist bureaucracy, the AP subsequently began to sustain the dominance of the secular center through its ties to state-supported big business. At that point, the small merchants, craftsmen, and farmers began to search for new institutions and avenues to express their demands and opposition to the AP's pro–big business and state-centric policies.[8]

Erbakan and a coterie of friends left the AP prior to the 1969 elections and subsequently established the MNP on January 26, 1970. The founding declaration refers to the golden age of the Ottoman period. The charter of the party identified the imitative Westernization and disestablishment of the Ottoman-Islamic heritage as the root cause of the country's problems and offered a new identity respecting Ottoman-Islamic history and technology and industrialization as a cure.[9] The MNP socially and culturally was rooted in small Anatolian towns and villages and represented provincial interests. Five of the founding members were engineers, five were small businessmen, and the rest were lawyers and white-collar workers. The Nurcus and some Sufi orders also played an active role in the MNP's establishment, while the newspapers, *Bugün* and *Sabah* presented the party as the voice of the "oppressed Muslim masses"[10] and the party of conservative Muslims (*mukaddesatçı*).

On May 20, 1971, two months after the military coup, the Constitutional Court disbanded the MNP, claiming that the party wanted to alter the secular principles of the state and institute an Islamic order to replace the Kemalist system.[11] Erbakan, the MNP chairman, was forced to flee to Switzerland to avoid prosecution and stayed there until 1972. According to Süleyman Arif Emre, a prominent MNP member at the time,

> General Refet Ülgenalp, the General Secretary of the National
> Security Council, was against the decision for closing the MNP. Nuri
> Emre, an agent of the Turkish National Intelligence Service, showed
> me the report of Refet Pasha. In this report, Refet Pasha argues that
> there is a need to stress religious education in order to counter left-
> wing ideology and activities. Refet Pasha even sent an army official
> to the National Education convention to prevent any move against
> religious education.[12]

Emre's claim that the Kemalist army could use Islam to counter a perceived leftist threat to their power was one of the arguments used for reopening the MNP. In fact, there was a widespread belief that the decision of the Constitutional Court to shut down the party had made Erbakan and his friends victims of the state in the eyes of the populace and thus enhanced their popularity.[13]

The generals who were against the banning of the MNP and opposed to Süleyman Demirel's domination of the political spectrum asked some of Erbakan's friends to establish a new party, the MSP, which was founded on October 11, 1972. However, none of the founding members were from the original MNP, and Süleyman Arif Emre, also a member of the İskenderpaşa Nakşibendi order, became its first chairman. Erbakan only became a MSP member in May 1973, although the party actually contested the October 1973 national elections under the leadership of Emre. After the election, the MSP's administrative board appointed Erbakan as the chairman. Although the Turkish constitution did not allow a person to become a chairman if his previous party had been banned by the Constitutional Court, the generals wanted Erbakan to lead the new party because they hoped to weaken the AP in the next elections.

In its first election, the MSP won 48 seats in Parliament.[14] In addition, the party received 11.8 percent of the vote in the parliamentary election and 12.3 percent in the senatorial election, winning three seats in the Senate. Generally, the parties that were critical of military rule and had been shut down after the 1971 coup did well in the 1973 election. In contrast, the AP, which was accused of collaboration with the coup authorities, dropped from 46.5 percent of the total vote in 1969 to 29.8 percent in 1973; the Republican Reliance Party (Cumhuriyetçi Güven Partisi) dropped from 6.6 percent to 5.3 percent.[15]

The electoral success of the MSP was strongest in the eastern and southeastern provinces, owing to the sectarian religious divisions and tensions between the Sunni and Alevi communities, although the politicization of this sectarian division was caused by an underlying competition over economic resources and government jobs. Conservative groups and economically vulnerable farmers voted for the MSP. The fact that the MSP's program called for "rapid industrialization" rather then Islamization may be seen as evidence that many people in effect voted for electricity, not the sharia. However, after the closure of the MNP, the same leadership framed their new movement as one directed toward "salvation," using the Qu'ranic term for salvation and arguing that there were two types of salvation, ethical and material.[16]

The MSP joined the coalition government of the social democratic CHP on January 24, 1974. Erbakan became deputy prime minister, controlling six ministries (Interior, Trade, Justice, Food and Agriculture, Industry and Technology, and the State Ministry of Religious Affairs). The image of the MSP in the coalition government was of a party dedicated to the promotion of Muslim morality, Ottoman heritage, freedom of conscience, the modernizing of Turkey's economy through rapid industrialization, and concern for the "little man." This image, in turn, helped the MSP to restore calls for Islamic values as a potent force in Turkish politics and society.[17] The party considered the family to be crucial for molding the moral and spiritual character of the country's youth.[18] It also stressed social and economic justice and the equitable distribution of national wealth.

Both the 1973 and 1977 national elections indicated that the MSP's main source of support was in the rural areas. For example, in 1973 only 32.8 percent of the MSP's total vote came from urban centers, while 67.2 percent was from villages. In the 1977 national election, the MSP won 8.6 percent of the total vote, with 36.8 percent coming from urban centers and 63.2 percent from villages. Interestingly, in both the 1973 and 1977 elections, the MSP was most popular in Sunni Kurdish provinces, such as Elazığ, Bingöl, and Diyarbakır. This indicates that the Sunni Kurdish ethnicity was contained within the broader oppositional Muslim identity. According to Altan Tan, a prominent Kurdish-Islamist intellectual, the Kurds always supported the pro-Islamic parties, even on those occasions when the party did poorly in the western provinces. Tan offers two reasons: "the most serious organizational framework for the Islamic movement in Turkey is of Kurdish origin. The Kurdish region is where Islam traditionally is lived."[19] Tan argues that the "Kurdish negative reaction to this laic/Kemalist system is more religious than it is ethnic. . . . Both the MNP and MSP were based on this traditional opposition to the system."[20] By organizational framework, Tan means to highlight the role of the Nakşibendi Sufi orders and the Nur movement, in which Turkey's Kurds played a critical role.

In the provinces where there is a sizeable Alevi population and traditional conflict with Sunnis (e.g., Erzurum, Kahramanmaraş, Malatya, and Sivas), the MSP did better than in those provinces where there was no sectarian tension. Other provinces where the MSP regularly increased its vote were the Sunni Kurdish provinces of Elazığ, Adıyaman, Diyarbakır, and Bingöl. The identification of Alevi voters with the Kemalist CHP helped the MSP to emerge as the representative of Turkish and Kurdish Sunni Islam.

The main political challenge the MSP faced was the war over Cyprus in 1974. After occupying 40 percent of Cyprus and safeguarding the threatened Turkish minority, Prime Minister Bülent Ecevit and Deputy Prime Minister Erbakan became national heroes. As people began to call Erbakan *ghazi* (a warrior of the faith), Ecevit sought to erode the popularity of his rival and searched for an opportunity to end the coalition.[21] Although his plan for early elections failed, Ecevit eventually broke the coalition on September 18, 1974. However, the MSP joined the First National Front coalition government led by Süleyman Demirel (April 1975 to June 1977), and Erbakan became deputy prime minister; other MSP members became ministers of state, the interior, justice, food and agriculture, industry and technology, and construction.

In the early parliamentary elections of 1977, the MSP's share of the vote declined to 8.6 percent,[22] primarily because of the emergence of the MHP, which attracted popular support in the Sunni-dominated Turkish cities because of its radical strategies of opposing leftist Alevi and Kurdish groups. In addition, the Nurcu groups deserted the MSP in large numbers in 1977, taking with them 11 seats in Parliament.[23] The party did not offer any concrete solutions to the country's problems and was seen as being overly ideological.[24] The MSP joined the Second National Front Coalition, composed of the AP, the MSP, and the MHP, and held 24 seats in Parliament between July 21 and December 31, 1977. This government did not last long because there were profound political differences between the coalition partners. In January 1978, Bülent Ecevit, the leader of the CHP, established a new government by bribing 11 ex-AP deputies with ministerial posts. However, he failed to cope with rising inflation and terrorism. Moreover, the oil crisis greatly exacerbated the hard currency and trade deficits. The local elections on October 14,1979, revealed the unpopularity of the Ecevit government and forced him to resign. On November 12, 1979, the MSP supported a minority coalition government led by Süleyman Demirel; this lasted until the September 1980 military coup.

The MSP's main characteristics were its hybrid populism and representation of hitherto peripheral forces (new merchants, intellectuals, and shop owners) wanting an increased say in the affairs of the state. Its populism was based on a program of economic nationalism and cultural and religious mobilization, which was to be accomplished by invoking an Ottoman-Islamic ethos to provide moral stability and a framework for a society suffering from the dislocation caused by state-led industrialization and corporatization of economic activities. The MSP developed a new conservative ideology based on Islam to challenge the hegemonic forces and secular discourse in Turkish society. This campaign was articulated against the secular state, which was seen as becoming increasingly detached from society. However, the MSP never was able to develop an effective patron-client network, since it hardly benefited from the rewards of government office. The total period during which the MSP remained as a coalition partner in three different coalition governments was only two years.

MSP Identity and Ideology

The main ideological contribution of the MSP was the revitalization of the Ottoman-Islamic liberal reformist tradition that had been dominant in Turkish society until the radical Kemalist-positivist revolution of the 1920s. The Ottoman-Islamic reformers had posited that Turkish society could adapt European institutions and technology and at the same time preserve the many positive and vital aspects of its Islamic culture and religion. The MSP platform thus was a direct protest against the radical Kemalist project. Although the MSP was not the first political articulation of Islamic resistance to the Kemalist reforms, for the first time it institutionalized Islamic protest within a semidemocratic political system. The MSP formulated its social contract as the National Outlook (Milli Görüş), which was defined according to four pillars: culture, industrialization, social justice, and education.[25] Because of the Kemalist ban on overtly religious political platforms, subtle Islamic symbols and norms were interpreted and presented within the concept of culture rather than of religion. In this sense, the MSP played a key role in the diffusion of Islamic norms through shared cultural tropes. By cultural revival the MSP did not mean an explicit program of Islamic revival but rather the reconstruction of Ottoman-Turkish norms and associations to challenge the alienating aspects of the Kemalist project of radical positivism. When the MSP was a partner in the Ecevit-led coalition, it opened more İmam Hatip schools and added to the high school curriculum a new course on ethics that borrowed from Islamic principles.

With the National Outlook platform, the MSP expanded the boundaries of political debate in society and integrated Islamic discourses into the political sphere. This in turn fueled the democratization of society by integrating the previously marginalized voices of the periphery that could claim to represent the bulk of the country's population. In addition to its focus on culture, the MSP stressed the material dimension of society and brought the issue of industrialization to the forefront. However, the MSP did not have a detailed and concrete program of industrialization. Another pillar of MSP ideology was the invoking of Islamic motifs in society, especially those relating to the concept of social justice. The party defended small merchants and producers against big corporations that benefited from high tariffs and asked the state to regulate the economy to protect the interests of the common people and small merchants. Finally, the MSP stressed the role of education in reinstilling traditional values and culture in society.

New Ideological Space: The Co-optation of Islam and Nationalism

Since the 1980 coup, the Turkish state has pursued a dual-track policy of co-optation and containment by opening more options to Islamist groups to participate in political and economic processes. Consequently, Islamist political groups have been incorporated into the democratic process, and this in turn has softened and restructured Islamist policies and demands.

Although the 1982 constitution empowered the state to intervene in every aspect of social life, societal groups controlled the tempo of change with liberal agendas demanding an open civil society and the deregulation of the economy and education. This liberal campaign unleashed a new debate about the boundaries between the state and society and between the individual and society. However, the post-1980 political and economic setting clearly favored the social and political activities of those Islamic groups and Sufi networks that favored a sweeping program of liberalization. As prime minister, Özal pursued a policy of putting Islam in the educational system. For example, his minister of education, Vehbi Dinçerler, a member of a Nakşibendi Sufi order, prepared a new curriculum on national history and culture that constantly used the term *national* (milli) in the religious sense.[26] The Islamism of the 1980s differed from the Islamic movements of the 1960s and 1970s in its social basis, nature, and impact, because changes in Turkish society shaped the Islamist discourse. Indeed, the social and political basis of the Islamic movement had experienced a major transformation at the grassroots level, one that had major implications for the rhetoric and actions of the RP, the successor of the MSP. For example, the RP-led Islamic movement shifted from being an anti-global, market-oriented, small merchant and farmer's party to one that demands full integration into the global market and sees a reduced role for the state in the economy. Although the RP was not strictly an Islamic party—it attracted votes for a combination of social and economic reasons involving both self-interest and identity—it evolved in the 1980s by energetically claiming that it was the only representative of the "deeper Turkey." Abdullah Gül, then the RP's vice-chairman, defined this "deeper Turkey" as a dynamic "idea" of creating an honorable and powerful Turkey by linking the Anatolian bourgeoisie, Sufi orders, neighborhood associations, and foundations. Gül rejected the idea that the RP represented only the "needy and little man" of society, a notion that both the MNP and MSP had publicized in the 1970s.[27]

After the 1983 election, the political elite decided that Islamists had to be integrated into the system in order to pursue the goals of economic development and eliminate the threat posed by the Left. It was decided that this integration could be done only by accepting a "soft Islam," that is, an Islam that the state carefully domesticated and monitored. Subsequently, Islamist groups entered the system through the expansion of educational opportunities, economic activity, and party politics. The educational means by which this "domesticated" Islam was to help promote national unity included the opening of more İmam Hatip Schools and the introduction of Qur'anic classes. The government also granted permission for Islamic groups to build private colleges and high schools and to establish new foundations and associations for carrying out their social activities.[28] The economic sphere was penetrated by new companies owned by Islamist entrepreneurs and by the establishment of an interest-free Islamic banking system. Meanwhile, conservative groups found the new tolerance of Islamic idioms in Turkish political and social life ideal for the promotion of the RP. As the isolated periphery began to take part in the system and to shape the educational, political, and economic spheres with their own interests and values, the state became legitimized in their eyes in a way it never had been since the establishment of the Kemalist Republic. However, the "Turkish-Islamic synthesis," based on Sunni Ottoman traditions, led to a reactive politicization of left-leaning Kurdish and Alevi identities.[29] In the interaction between the newly legitimized Islamic groups and the Republican state, the process of interpenetration marked both sides. The Islamic groups were transformed from being purely marginalized social groups into sophisticated and complex organizations that were an amalgamation of state- and society-centered movements and interests. However, the relationship between Islamists and the state is dynamic and evolving. Therefore, the sociocultural and political processes by which Islamization is actualized can only be understood by examining the dynamics of the "top down" and "bottom up" processes.[30]

The RP, 1983–1998

The municipal elections of March 27, 1994, and national elections of December 24, 1995, marked a psychological break in Turkish history that was an outcome of the search for new state-society relations and the rearticulation of national identity. Some newspapers reported the news under such headlines as "The Other Turkey Wins the Election," "The Black Turks versus the White Turks,"[31] or "Fatih Won against Harbiye."[32] Both elections ended with the victory of the pro-Islamic RP. The results of the elections revealed a society sharply divided along secular versus Islamist sociocultural lines. In this context, the RP is one of the main avenues for political Islam to articulate its demands within the public sphere. It represents a platform for those who seek to change the secular system as well as for those who demand reforms *in* the system, that is, within the bureaucratic state structure. This competing, even conflicting, campaign to reorganize the political center and transform the bureaucratic system has mobilized large segments of the population that range from Kurdish groups to the new emerging Anatolian bourgeoisie, all in the name of *identity* and *justice.*

The conflict between the ruling secular elite and Islamist activists, who seek to redefine society and then the state, revolves around the question of identity and the control of public spaces. This indicates the limits of the Turkish experiment with political Islam within a functioning democracy. The electoral success of political Islam is an outcome of four factors. First has been the state policy of a Turkish-Islamic synthesis introduced by the leaders of the 1980 military coup. Second has been the political and economic liberalization accompanied by the emergence of the new conservative Anatolian bourgeoisie, represented by such organizations as MÜSİAD. The third factor has been the prominence of a new class of Islamist intellectuals based in the print and electronic media. The final factor has been the internal organizational flexibility of the RP and its ideological presentation of the Just Order (*Adil Düzen*) platform.

New Economic Opportunity Spaces and Their Implications

The RP's election victory in the 1995 general election had to do with the strategic use of Islamic symbols to frame worsening social, cultural, and economic conditions. After the local elections in March 1994, the RP mayors offered markedly better services than their predecessors had. Moreover, by most accounts, they significantly reduced, though they did not eradicate, corruption and nepotism in the municipalities. The RP also acted more professionally than the other parties on the left and right in responding to the needs and expectations of the people. The two main parties on the right, the DYP and ANAP, constantly accused each other of corruption and tried to prevent the other from enacting much needed legislation. They showed little interest in addressing the pressing problems of the country. Moreover, the main Sufi orders and Nurcu groups supported the RP because of its potential to form the government.[33]

One major reason for the strength of the RP was the expansion of the economy that resulted from Turkey's open-door trade policies. In the late 1980s and 1990s, Özal's free market policies came to be strongly supported by small-scale provincial businesses and the large city petit bourgeoisie consisting of merchants, contractors, restaurant owners, and relatively small-scale industrialists. This sector did not want state intervention in the economy in favor of large-scale industrialists traditionally tied to the Republican political elite and as a result was the main supporter of economic liberalization. This sector found Islamic symbols and ethics and the values of free enterprise the best weapons to galvanize public opinion against the state and big industrialists. Small to medium-sized companies benefited the most from this economic expansion and formed MÜSİAD, an association of Islamic capitalists to defend their interests against big business and its ties to ruling circles. The ideology of the emerging Anatolian bourgeoisie, while socially Islamic, was economically liberal.

In addition to the highly organized MÜSİAD, informal economic groups also identified themselves with Islamic activism. Because the political center still adhered to the laic identity, peripheral groups were all the more encouraged to identify with an oppositional Islamic identity. Moreover, Islamic Sufi orders played a key role in the development of business connections that facilitated their penetration of the economy. The struggle between secular and Islamic groups, therefore, has both deep historical roots and economic dimensions. Islam has come to play a leading role in the economic and political transformation sought by this segment of society. Islam is the identity of this new wave of the bourgeoisie and, by drawing on their strong sense of moral probity and their communal solidarity, they managed to overcome problems in finance and banking through an Islamic banking system. Özal reached out to the traditional groups of the periphery and accepted them as partners in opening the Turkish economy. These groups, in turn, reinterpreted Islam and Islamic society in a manner compatible with their own ideological needs as members of the provincial bourgeoisie and upwardly mobile technocrats. In the hands of the Anatolian bourgeoisie, Islam became an instrumental ideology for legitimizing business connections and profit-making. This economic expansion helped to create a new image of religious uprightness and worldly success. This in turn made a reexamination of Islamic identity and values appealing for those who also aspired to succeed in the capitalist market while retaining a sense of Islamic piety. While all this was proceeding, ordinary people simply stressed the value of religion in protecting their dignity and justifying their demands for social equity in the rapidly changing Turkish society of the 1980s.

Another reason for the strong showing of political Islam at the polls in 1995 was the development of "personal Islam." This inner Islam, in a manner akin to the return to religion seen in many advanced industrial societies, filled a spiritual void in the lives of many relatively educated and well-to-do Turks who sought something beyond the verities of Kemalist positivism. Because the official post-1980 coup policy of the state sought to identify personal religious devotion as "normal" and a sign of good "citizenship," the effect was to remove the onus that had long existed on the outward display of religion by those with access to economic and political power. This renewed respectability of religion in official circles, albeit circumscribed, led to a competition between the mainstream center-right parties and the religious Right over the representation of "Allah's bloc" in Parliament. This further politicized religion and moved Islam into the center of political debate. For example, a week before the 1995 election, the DYP-controlled Ministry of Education gave full status to 70 new religious high schools and opened 6,000 new positions for religious functionaries. The DYP also nominated Tayyar Altıkulaç, the ex-head of the Directorate of Religious Affairs, as its candidate from Istanbul. The ANAP, not to be outdone, allied itself with the conservative Sunni-Turkish nationalist party, the Great Unity Party (BBP: Büyük Birlik Partisi),[34] and Korkut Özal, the brother of Turgut Özal.[35] The center-right parties competed against the RP over representation of the Islamic vote. Political participation and electoral competition promoted the politicization of Islamic and other forms of identity. Power brokers invoked Islamic symbols to carry out their campaigns, and the center-right parties competed with the religious right in representing Islamic interests in parliament.

The Reification of Islamic Identity as the RP Identity

Although Islamic political consciousness also was expressed through the center-right ANAP and DYP, there was a tendency to reify Islamic identity in politics with the RP. As a result of this process, for many people an Islamic identity beyond strictly personal concerns was reduced to a political party identity and used interchangeably with that of the RP in opposition to the Westernized secular identity. Intellectuals especially have objectified the RP phenomena by giving the party a spatial dimension that extends from restaurants to shopping malls, from individual municipalities to the capital, and encompasses everything from cuisine to consumption to the ways people vote.

The secular reforms have had only a limited success in instituting in Islam's place a new and more rigid code of conduct or aesthetic for ordering everyday life. In contemporary Turkish society, epistemological differences are reified with a plethora of identity signs—rings, clothes, books, furniture, and music—that help to locate the individual in a culturally divided society. These identity markers structure interactions in public spaces and define interactions between the secular bureaucratic elite and the masses.

The RP played a key role in the political socialization of Islamic groups by mobilizing them to take part in the political process and thus facilitating political participation in Turkey. For example, the RP's voter registration drives and election services involving free transportation to the polls were borrowed from European social democratic parties but ignored by other parties in Turkey. Developed to integrate *vulnerable* and *excluded* groups into the political system, the RP helped to resolve one of Turkey's foremost problems by integrating the Islamically oriented "periphery" which makes up the bulk of society and a large segment of the Kurdish population, into the political system. This inclusion did not destabilize the Kemalist Republican order since the Islamic periphery did not request the immediate redistribution of political power. This measured inclusion was instead an outcome of the changing parameters of state-society relations in the post-1980 era, which involved an unprecedented economic and political liberalization in the country. This inclusion did not lead to a breakdown of the system because the demands made for inclusion coincided with the strategy of the state. This strategy called for the expansion of its social base by incorporating Islamic voices into the system and thereby co-opting them.

Unlike other parties in Turkey, the RP was an institutional expression of a modern social movement that strives to redefine sociocultural and economic relations through political means. It was based on a new form of consciousness created by mass education, the expanding impact of the Islamist print media, and the rise of an Anatolian middle class. The party ventured to discipline and institutionalize this social movement under its own leadership, but it had only limited success because most of the prominent Islamic groups and Sufi orders maintained a certain political distance from RP.[36] The party defined the "people" as Muslim—an organic, collective union—regardless of class or ethnic divisions. It highlighted Islamic solidarity to override ethnic or class differences. In other words, society, for the party, was composed of Muslims who were unified by their shared Islamic faith (iman) and objective practices (e.g., *namaz* [praying] and *oruç* [fasting]). This image of society was, needless to say, in opposition to the secular ethnic nationalism of the state.

Leadership, Ideology, and Organization of the RP

The political idiom, the organizational structure, and the clientele of the RP were based on those of its predecessor, the MSP (1973–1980). After the military leaders decided to allow the return to civilian rule, Ali Türkmen and his cohorts established the RP on July 19, 1983. The generals, however, strictly regulated the role of Islam in public life and banned the 27 founding members, including Erbakan, from participating in politics. Consequently, the party was not able to enter the first post-coup national elections in 1983. Nevertheless, the RP did manage to enter the local elections held on March 25, 1984, and won mayoral seats in Van and Urfa. The party received 778,622 votes, or 4.4 percent of the total vote. Its first General Party Congress on June 30, 1985, sharply criticized Özal's economic policies and stressed social justice and political freedom for the working classes.[37] Binnaz Toprak argues that this was a sign that the party wanted to expand its social base, but she assumes that the party was molding and forging the larger segment of voiceless Muslims.[38] In contrast, my interviews with the RP leaders indicate that they were responding to the trend toward Islamization that already was taking place in the squatter towns. They felt that this trend needed to be channeled into the political process.[39]

After the 1987 referendum that allowed formerly banned politicians to reenter politics, Erbakan and some of the previous cadres took over the leadership of the RP. In the next parliamentary election in the same year, the party won 1,717,425 votes, increasing its share of the total vote to 7.16 percent. Nevertheless, it was still short of the 10 percent threshold required to gain a seat in Parliament. When the party only won 9.8 percent of the vote in the 1989 local elections, its policy-makers grew doubtful about their chances of being able to pass the legal threshold of 10 percent. Therefore, in September 1991, they agreed on the RP forming a purely pragmatic electoral alliance with the Nationalist Work Party (MÇP: Milliyetçi Çalışma Partisi, later the MHP) and the Reformist Democratic Party (Islahatçı Demokrasi Partisi; see table 10.1).[40] Many Islamist politicians unrealistically expected that this alliance would become a union, but a month after it won 16.2 percent of the vote and gained 62 seats in Parliament in the 1991 general elections, 22 deputies belonging to the MÇP resigned and returned to their own party.[41] Meanwhile, the Islamically oriented Kurds and Turkish Alevi groups interpreted this alliance as an anti-Kurdish/Alevi formation.[42]

The RP made its biggest showing in the local elections of March 27, 1994, and became a major force in Turkish politics in its own right. The party won 19.7 percent of the national vote, and pro-Islamist mayors took control of 29 large cities, including Istanbul and Ankara.[43] Support for the RP continued to increase, and in the national elections of December 24, 1995, the party garnered 21.4 percent of the total vote and 158 of the 550 seats in Parliament. This dramatic rise in the political fortunes of an Islamic party exemplified both the role of cultural cleavages in Turkish politics and the collapse of the monopoly on power held by the Kemalist-dominated political and cultural elite, which no longer could claim a national consensus on the orientation of the country.

Keeping the Islamist Genie in the Bottle

Support for the RP was a reaction to (1) the dislocation of the rural population by mass migration; (2) the growth of shantytowns and ghettos; (3) import substitution strategies that favored big businessmen over small merchants; and (4) the global economic recession. The formation of the RP can be explained by the salient sociocultural divisions that have been exploited by the party. Although economic and social conditions are very important for explaining political Islam, they are contributors to rather than central causes of that multidimensional movement. For example, rural migrants to cities seek mobility but defend Islamic cultural norms as a common language in their new, alien environment. The RP's two main ideological concepts of the Just Order and Islamic identity express the intention of such migrants to seek both economic prosperity and the shared moral practices of the environment they left behind.

The spread of RP membership also is visible on the periphery of Istanbul. When Islam was forced out of the public sphere through secularizing dictates, those on the periphery, who still were not fully integrated into the capitalist center, continued to organize their own social life, space, and time in terms of Islamic rhythms. The disenfranchised segments of the Muslim population realized that they were excluded from the political and economic system before Özal's reforms integrated them into the economic market and the political domain.

Islamic political activism and the externalization of an Islamic identity cannot be explained solely by theories of economic deprivation. Those who are in the forefront of these movements are usually either middle- or upper-middle-class people. Cultural and political factors are often more important than economic ones in accounting for the support of Islamic political movements. Nevertheless, speculation and even sensationalism about the sociopolitical background of the RP's supporters has often ignored sound scholarship with respect to this issue. When RP supporters were asked in an ARAS survey what mobilized them on behalf of the RP, their replies included the following:[44] (1) many felt that the party is willing to meet them face-to-face and one-to-one; (2) it sincerely wants to solve problems if it comes to power; (3) the local party leadership is accessible and treats each individual seriously regardless of status differences; (4) the party respects local conventions and the Turkish-Islamic traditions. All these answers reflect the way the RP is socially rooted in a traditional network system within modern Turkey and manages to mobilize traditional groups, such as the Sufi orders, on its behalf.

Another major question asked by the ARAS survey had to do with the expectations of RP supporters of the contingency that their party came to power. The supporters said that they were not expecting the party to institute the sharia; for only 15.5 percent said that it would implement an Islamic criminal code and legal system if it came to power. Instead, nearly 73 percent of men and 61 percent of women held that the RP's program had nothing to do with implementing sharia. These responses are a further indication that the support for the RP was not based on purely religious sentiments, and a religious revival was not an adequate explanation for the political triumph of the party. The reason for its success was its ability to articulate socioeconomic issues through the common idiom of the masses. The party also enjoyed a reputation for opposing the dictatorial policies of the state and its supporters in the parties of the center while it espoused a more politically liberal ideology.

Although the RP built on the foundation of the MSP, its borders encompassed new socioeconomic solidarities. The RP's success, therefore, cannot be explained by the alleged rural and underclass nature of its electorate. The incorporation of new groups within the party became a reason for its success. Simply to label the RP as Islamic does not further understanding of its societal dynamics. Moral questions and values in Turkish politics largely have been articulated in Islamic terms because the Kemalist cultural revolution did not produce an alternative shared moral language, and Islamic references and idioms remained the depository for this moral debate. Instead, that which is Islamic and that which is secular is largely a contextual matter that determines, for example, whether the ANAP's criticism of alcohol and gambling will be considered by others as its "Islamization of social life." In other words, moral questions raised by the RP or any other political party always invoke the name of Islam. This area was not simply the domain of the RP. Furthermore, the ruling secular elite often has labeled popular antigovernment protests as "Islamic and reactionary" in order to delegitimize them. This tactic not only promoted the politicization of religion but also strengthened antirepublican sentiments throughout much of society. These political responses are a result of an erosion of public values and a sense of ethical crisis that Turkey has been experiencing for some time. In effect, the secular system has failed to produce a proper ethical code for the new level of social and economic development. Because the system and its political ideology did not seem capable of providing values for civil society, many in Turkish society began searching for a new moral framework. To resolve this conundrum Turkey needs to transform its concepts of the state, society, and individual.

The Political Appeal of the RP: Justice and Identity

The most critical factors in the strength of the RP are to be found in its discourses on identity and justice. Devout Muslims evoked Islamic symbols and institutions to express their discontent and, most important, to construct their own vision of modernity by reactivating Islamic tradition. The Turkish paradox is that a new conceptualization and a new phase of modernity has coincided with that of Islamization. The two are in a rather causal relationship, contrary to what some scholars imply when they suggest that Islamism is a reaction to the consequences of modernity. It is this correlative relationship that often leads scholars either to befuddlement or simplistic generalizations concerning religion and contemporary Turkey's sociopolitical conditions. The study of the rise of the RP requires a bottom up approach to the developmental issues and cultural representations of justice and identity.

The most appealing program that the RP presented was the Just Order platform (Adil Düzen), and most supporters identified social equity as the main objective of the Just Order system.[45] An analysis of the Just Order program reveals a hybrid ideological agenda that straddles the divide between a free-market and a state-led mixed economy with the aim of accommodating competing demands without offering concrete solutions to the contradictions between them. The Just Order is based on a theoretical charter that university professors under the leadership of Süleyman Karagülle and Süleyman Akdemir, who founded Turkey's first Muslim commune, the Akevler Kooperatifi in Izmir, introduced for the party in 1985. Its aim was the creation of a pluralistic, democratic, and free market–based civil society.[46] The charter envisioned a society consisting of communes and similar settlements that would cooperate on common issues and services. Advocating less state intervention and more individual responsibility, the charter was prepared by professional economists and social scientists on the basis of Islamic principles. It marked one of the first times a group of Muslim professionals used Islamic precepts to justify notions usually associated with liberal ideologies, namely pluralism, democracy, the free market, and individual responsibility. The charter thus exemplifies a lack of tension between Islamic beliefs and liberal ideals, demonstrating that Islam is compatible with modernity, even with some features of secularism as commonly understood in the West.

Erbakan gradually integrated the charter into the RP's program. It was presented and accepted as the Just Order Project for the 1991 parliamentary election with the publication of a booklet, *Just Economic Order*, under Erbakan's name.[47] This tract demonstrated the RP's commitment to economic growth, social justice, and national prosperity. However, its economic ideas often are confused, and it failed to address adequately the contradictions inherent in its promises of social justice and equity along with rapid export-oriented capitalist development. For example, Erbakan has argued that the Just Order will be realized by the cooperation of seven major "armies": (1) the devout people; (2) religious authorities and leaders who will be the architects of a greater Turkey; (3) scientists and university professors; (4) engineers and economists who will prepare the projects to turn natural resources into developed industries; (5) businessmen who will implement the projects; (6) guilds; and (7) labor, including workers, farmers, and white-collar workers. These "seven armies," according to Erbakan, will build a powerful industrially and technologically advanced Turkey that eventually will lead the Muslim world.[48] In addition, a stable, well-ordered society will emerge if Turkey achieves four objectives: a Milli Görüş philosophy that is not in conflict with its own past; a just order; an economically and militarily powerful country to lead the union of Muslim countries; and a new world order where Muslims have an important voice.

When I asked RP supporters what Just Order stands for, their answers included justice, a secure social and economic environment, an end to nepotism and corruption, cooperation between the state and society, protection of the unity of the state, and an end to undue Western influence over Turkey.[49] These common responses indicated that the Just Order is seen not as a way of bringing about an Islamic political system but as a way of addressing the immediate social and economic problems of Turkey. The protection of the state and its property also is an important objective of the Just Order, because many people believe that their economic and social welfare presupposes a powerful state. The Just Order program, contrary to common secular claims in Turkey, does not mean an interest-free economic system or a welfare state; it calls for the prevention of injustice and religious discrimination against devout Muslims. In this respect, Islam matters not so much as a religion but as a communication system and metaphysical basis for ideals of justice and harmony.[50] Indeed, the RP's leadership simply expressed the collective longing of many people in the country for these ideals in a language that they can understand.

While on the one hand the RP's policies are very conservative in form and are articulated in terms of Islamic concepts, on the other hand they are quite revolutionary in content. For example, when 172 people were asked to identify the RP's three most common characteristics, over 70 percent cited honesty (dürüstlük), justice (adalet), and equality (eşitlik).[51] Other commonly cited characteristics were resisting corruption and bribery, protecting traditional mores, helping the poor and needy, sincerity, unity, solidarity, and the elimination of prostitution and social immorality. Because the party was rooted in a search for a conception of community to cope with the collective problems of justice and identity, it sought to revise the shared understanding of "morality" at the same time that it addressed social and economic problems. For instance, the RP leadership seldom hesitated to invoke the popular understanding of the umma as an ideal model to restructure society in confronting problems of justice and identity. Thus the aims motivating RP supporters to become involved in politics were not solely religious but rather included the search for community, representation at the center, and relief from the skewed distribution of resources. Islam became a cultural depository for new models and ways of understanding Turkey's ethnopolitical and socioeconomic problems.

Identity and the RP

The modern nation-state controls every aspect of an individual's life. Through its institutions, it forces individuals to play different and conflicting roles that split their personalities and fragment their identity. As the state expands its power through new technologies, individuals searching for ways to protect their personal integrity are finding it in shelters constructed out of religious idioms. Islamic identity offers a flexible repertoire to accommodate diverse roles and identities. This was especially evident in the RP's use of Islamic idioms explicitly linked to the image of shelter. It also was evident in the consistent way that Erbakan and his inner circle used the word *milli* (meaning religiously rooted national community) as an adjective to indicate their Ottoman-Islamic sense of community. In addition, they used the word *hak* (the authentic, godly, sacred, and just system of Islam) to differentiate themselves from other political parties. The RP supporters I interviewed in 1997 were quite aware that the party represented both their political and religious idea:

> when you look at other parties you see them as an association of interests or an organization to distribute state-based goods and jobs. Whereas the RP is something more than that. It is an expression of our identity.[52]

This view is an indication that participation in RP activities facilitated the realization of personal identity within a web of sociopolitical networks. The pro-Islamic movement led by the RP drew heavily on the following sources: the grievances and discontent of the large Kurdish population; the prevalent religious-nationalistic ideas and beliefs in central and eastern Anatolia; the capacity to mobilize its supporters to act collectively for self-realization in a local and global context; and the opportunities to redefine the role of the state. For many of its supporters, the RP offered an answer to the basic questions "Who am I?" and "Where do I belong?" By defining Turkish nationality in terms of Islamic identity, the RP managed to exploit the keenly felt sentiments relating to identity politics in contemporary Turkey. Those who voted for the RP tended to be pious and sought to fulfil their personal and collective identities by joining activities and campaigns and eventually voting for those parties that manifested the realization of an Islamic identity, an identity that is all the more resonant because of the fierce persecution of the Kemalist era. This realization, in turn, involved a degree of tradeoff with other subnational and transnational identities and memberships.

In order to distinguish his party from rivals on the political scene, Erbakan constructed two diametrically opposed ideological categories: *Batıl* (the imitative, materialist, and colonial system of the West) and *hak*. In the fourth RP congress, Erbakan claimed that the West (Batıl) consists of the DYP, ANAP, DSP, and CHP, four parties that were pro-EU. Aspects of the West, for Erbakan, included the exploitation and oppression of those societies that are defined as non-Western, especially those in the Islamic world. On one occasion, as part of a general metaphor for the West, Erbakan said "the Cowboy, the United States, and *AT*, the horse [i.e., the European Community], create too many problems in the world."[53] He strongly rejected Western claims of possessing a higher and universal set of values and insisted that the West brazenly uses issues of human rights and democracy only selectively and self-servingly. For Erbakan the most glaring example of the West's hypocrisy was the way the architects of "the new world order" devastated Iraq for its aggression and ignored and actively covered up the far more brutal Serbian aggression and genocide in Bosnia one year later.

Erbakan defined the concept of *hak* as respect for human rights and the rejection of coercion and exploitation. He argued that society should stress liberty in political and economic matters while maintaining a communitarian responsibility for the less fortunate. Erbakan maintained further that the main features of hak were put into practice in the period of the Seljuk and Ottoman empires. Having a perspective on an imagined utopia is necessary for every society to transcend itself. Although some Islamic movements have as their utopic paradigm the era of the Prophet Muhammed, the RP in Turkey stressed instead the classical Ottoman period.[54]

The RP leadership turned Islam into a "storehouse of images" to determine what constituted unjust conduct and how a sense of community could remedy it.[55] In Erbakan's view, the concept of the Just Order was the key to the successful governance of both the Seljuk and the Ottoman empires, and "when the Ottomans began to imitate Batıl, their state disintegrated."[56] Erbakan's message was understood and internalized by the masses much better than that of the other parties or the militant Islamic groups that proposed to create an Islamic utopia on the basis of the Qur'an. This mode of thinking attaches a sacred quality to the state by presenting it as a *gazi* state, that is, defender of Islam against external threats, and requires a loyalty to the state. In Muslim societies new ideas as well as revived ones effectively are disseminated by evoking such a historical consciousness.

The RP sought to distinguish between Westernization and modernity.[57] Westernization, in the Turkish context, was a process of alienation from one's own cultural values and history and its replacement by an empty shell that only could be a pale shadow of the Other that it aspires to be. This weakness, in turn, was viewed as causing underdevelopment, the lack of political independence, the erosion of moral values, and the subjugation of the Turks in their own historical regions. Modernity, by contrast, was viewed as a necessity for survival, and its technological, scientific, democratic, and industrial elements were not seen as being incompatible with Islam. In having this view, the RP ideologues were very close to Ottoman liberals like Namık Kemal, who also thought that a prudent incorporation of Western attributes, such as democracy, liberalism, and industrialization, could be accomplished without compromising essential Islamic customs and values. The promotion of a liberal political and economic agenda, in fact, was cleverly used by the RP to assail the authoritarian aspects of the Kemalist tradition while increasing their popularity and credibility with those who were dissatisfied with the present system.

The RP proposed two solutions for Turkey's underdevelopment: revitalizing cultural bonds in order to ground modernity in authentic Islamic values and industrializing Turkey in order to secure political and economic independence. The party hoped to create a symbiotic relationship in which cultural values softened the negative impact of industrialization and ideally promoted its success, as was the case in east Asia. With its use of Islamic idioms and symbols, the RP provided a forum within which diverse ethnic and regional identities could flourish and coexist. The RP supporters' conception of Islamic identity brought fragments and subidentities together without negating them and created a more holistic understanding of identity.

Although the RP differentiated itself from other nationalist parties by stressing Islamic identity, an in-depth analysis of its rhetoric and practices demonstrates that it was an Istanbul-centered Islamic identity in which the Ottoman legacy played a formative role for the reimagination of the future orientation of Turkey. The RP leadership, for example, asserted that the Muslim countries could form a bloc only under Turkish leadership. This argument was supported by the historical role of the Ottomans, as well as Turkey's location and vibrant economy. In a way, Islamic identity and solidarity, for the RP, became an instrument for promoting Turkish national interest and a bargaining card vis-à-vis European exclusion. This neo-Ottoman vision of forming an Islamic bloc under Turkish leadership is a common theme among the RP leadership, who, unlike the party's supporters, believed that other subidentities and interests could be negated within an Islamic identity. This in turn would eliminate many sources of conflict in Turkish society. Thus, the RP leadership hoped to terminate intra-Muslim conflicts by negating other identities within an overarching Islamic one. Therefore, they proposed Islamic identity as a cure for restless Kurdish ethnonationalism.[58]

Although the leadership of the party viewed it as a higher identity to supersede diverse local identities, in practice the RP functioned as a mediator between or space-in-between different identities that also helped to negotiate political tradeoffs between competing loyalties. The RP, according to Erbakan, "has a network and associational abilities to bring 65 million Muslims of Turkey to create the 'leader' country among the Muslim countries."[59] The politically shaped and strategically deployed Islamic identity thus became a mobilizing tool in the hands of the party leadership. Erbakan conceived of the RP as a base for a supraidentity within which other ethnic, religious, and regional identities would be subsumed. He saw the party as an institution for building identity by negating the sources of difference. He demanded that newcomers accept the form and ideology of the party, which would act as a school to mold and shape its new pupils. When Erbakan called Muslims to "come" and "join the party," he expected party institutions to reconstitute them with new identities and interests. He claimed that "our party, unlike the other parties in the parliament, has faith at the core. Whoever joins us will be transformed in due time. I also believe that newcomers will create new frontiers for the expansion at the core of the faith."[60] Erbakan's main concern was the politics not of pluralism but of authenticity. He believed that there is an authentic Muslim identity and voice that should govern day-to-day politics. Within the context of Erbakan's authenticity, there seemed to be limited room for pluralism and tolerance.

Generational, Ideological, Regional, and Gender Cleavages within the RP

According to the RP leadership, there were three spheres of confrontation in Turkish society: ideological (left versus right and Islamist versus both Marxist and Kemalist); ethnic (Turk versus Kurd), and sectarian (Sunni versus Alevi). The liberal wing of the party sought to eliminate these three zones of conflict by opening public forums for the discussion of such differences in the hope that some of their sharpness could be blunted. One prominent liberal, Bahri Zengin, who had been kept at a distance by the Erbakan-led conservatives because of his liberal views, played a key role in the opening of such new channels of inter-action between the different segments of society.[61] Zengin ideally wanted the party to be a mediator of such differences. Such an idealist vision, of course, faced the difficulty of reconciling the RP's well-formulated Islamist agenda with its opponents who shared an opposite view of state and society. Undeterred, Zengin continued to emphasize the importance of bringing together different sections of society on a common basis of toleration and understanding:

> when I became vice-chairman of the party, as the one responsible for advertising and campaign management, I stressed two things: freedom of religion and ideas; and the development of a plan to meet the immediate social and educational problems of this society. We realized that the most important issue in this society is social peace. We therefore sought new ways to prevent further fragmentation in society and hoped to bring people together. We brought different women's groups together in 1983–84. For the first time, Western-ized "open" women and traditional "covered" women were brought together by our party. We told them, "We have to live together by respecting our differences." We were aware at the time that social peace also was threatened by the ideological division between the left and right. In this case, we searched for a common ground. In 1985–86, we organized meetings between Marxist intellectuals and Islamist ones. This brought them together to reexamine the prin-ciples of the state.[62]

However, the party's conservative core leadership, having been socialized in the authoritarian Kemalist tradition, reacted negatively to this openness, insisting that the Islamic principles of the party could not be compromised to accommo-date cultural and political cleavages in Turkish society.

The overall ideology of the RP may be described as a rather incoherent form of pragmatic liberalism, social conservatism, welfarism, and capitalism. One may treat the RP ideology as an eclectic and amorphous mixture of competing lifestyles, ideas, and politics based on different interpretations of Islam, nation-alism, and the state. The party did not see Islam as a fixed doctrine that would obviate the need for politics but searched for ways to integrate Islamic identity and symbols into the political sphere. The younger generation of the party was more open to such liberal views than Erbakan and his generation. This genera-tion wanted the RP to represent Islamic groups and views within the political domain but still believed that the political sphere would be autonomous from the purely religious one. The younger generation of intellectuals in the party, such as Abdüllatif Şener, Tayyip Erdoğan, and Abdullah Gül, did not seek to subordinate democracy to a particular interpretation of Islam. Rather they con-ceded that, in a democratic political system, Islam in various forms will be one voice among a number of competing visions. Not all of the party members, of course, are inclined to such liberal views, and a consensus or clearly articulated doctrine on these issues is lacking.

Erbakan's speech at the RP's Fourth Congress in 1993 carefully avoided equating Islam as a religion with the party. In fact, Erbakan tried to reach out to everyone, including nonpracticing Muslims. [63] He presented three solutions to three immediate problems of Turkish society: recognition of Kurdish identity within the concept of umma; establishment of the Just Order to address the problem of poverty and inequality; and "multilegal communities," that is, each community would be governed by its own laws and norms to create a civil society.[64] The conception of legal pluralism was concerned more with the autonomy of separate communities rather than individual freedoms. This proposal negated individualism in order to consolidate the authority of community. Erbakan's speech, which set the tone for the 1994 municipal elections, played a key role in the transformation of the RP's image from that of a potentially rigid fundamentalist party to one willing to compromise and work within the system.[65] In his speech, Erbakan differentiated majority democracy from pluralistic democracy and said that pluralism and diversity are a necessary framework for prosperity and a working democracy.[66] The speech demonstrated that Erbakan and the party leadership realized that they would have to temper their rhetoric and modify their views if they were to secure enough popular support to form a governing coalition. In fact, a group of liberal intellectuals, including Zengin, Ali Bulaç, and Mehmet Metiner, had prepared Erbakan's speech.[67]

Regional Identities

The 1994 local and the 1995 national elections transformed the political landscape. Some secular groups interpreted this transformation as a revolt against Kemalism, whereas Islamist publicists viewed it as the gradual democratization of the Republican political system. In fact, the election was a turning point in terms of bringing peripheral and marginal voices to the center of Turkish political discourse. The new pragmatism of the party, its long-term strategy to become a legitimate part of the system, and its organizational skills were the main factors in this process.

Erbakan, as the RP leader, was capable of orchestrating many of Turkey's diverse Islamic groups through his personality and leadership skills. His capable righthand man, Oğuzhan Asiltürk, aided him in this effort. They made Turkey's variegated Islam a source of strength that allowed the party to penetrate virtually every corner of society. In its leadership characteristics, the RP was similar to other Turkish political parties: The leader's personality dominated the institutions over and above the party itself. One of the major reasons for the RP's political success was its organizational flexibility and strategic use of modern means to mobilize traditional networks. The organizational structure of the party was known as the *tesbih* model (i.e., the provincial organizational committee has 33 members, modeled after the 33 beads of the traditional Muslim rosary). Each neighborhood (*mahalle*) had an organizer who in turn appointed street representatives to collect information about the age, ethnicity, religious origin, and place of birth of the residents on each street. At the district level, inspectors reviewed the work of the neighborhood organizers every week. In addition to the inspector, each district had a party *divan* (committee) consisting of 33 members. None of the other Turkish political parties was organized to communicate in this way with the neighborhoods that politically and socially are the basic, grassroots units of Turkish society. For example, the RP representatives always took part in communal ceremonial activities such as funerals and weddings, which reaffirmed communal links. The RP differed from other Turkish parties in having organic connections with hundreds of associations and foundations that helped to keep voters united. The RP used many associations and institutions to mobilize youth, and these associations even became means to shape RP policies. For example, the National Youth Foundation (Milli Gençlik Vakfi) had over two thousand offices spread throughout Turkey. Its functions ranged from offering scholarships to running private dormitories. According to İhsan Aktaş, the vice-chairman of the Foundation, these "dormitories in Istanbul serve four to five thousand students."[68] Aktaş defined the goals of the Foundation as promoting a new civilizational understanding of Islam and nurturing the spirituality of Muslim youth. The supporters of the party established close connections with the people of the neighborhood and, during elections, asked them to return their dues to the party in the form of votes. Jenny B. White has argued that the RP "also maintains many types of clubs that bring together potential voters. The RP's strategy relies on building interpersonal trust."[69] At the provincial level, there were several conferences and panels that regularly trained the neighborhood and district representatives, demonstrating the importance of internal party training as well as neighborhood organization.

Unlike other parties, the RP had the most intensive and highly organized connections with Turkish workers in Europe in general and with other Islamic groups in Muslim countries. The European National Outlook Organization (AMGT: Avrupa Milli Görüş Teşkilatı), with its headquarters in Cologne, Germany, was founded in the early 1970s.[70] It has a membership of over 70,000 and remains the most powerful Turkish expatriate organization, with close financial connections to RP. Through their religiously rooted and politically shaped networks, AMGT members are critical of their country of origin and able to mobilize their financial means and human skills to intervene inside and outside Turkey. Moreover, the RP used its Berlin-based International Humanitarian Help (IHH) organization to develop transnational connections with other Muslim communities in Bosnia, Chechnya, and even Myanmar. The members of AGMT are in constant move between Turkey and Germany and they carry financial means, skills, ideas, attitudes, and modes of action between the two countries. Thus Islamic networks in Europe are dense and very active in the flow of ideas and resources.

One of the main reasons for the RP's success was the relative autonomy of the district organizations in utilizing local resources, devising their own strategies, and adopting close relations and trust with their local communities. This was not the case for other parties that were centralized in terms of campaign strategies and lacked the flexibility to use verbal communications and face-to-face exchanges. For example, when representatives of the RP visited a family after a funeral, they introduced an element of human contact that differentiated the party from the impersonal and faceless image of other political parties. In the March 1994 local elections, the DYP organized only 12 coffeehouse meetings in the Maltepe neighborhood of Istanbul. In contrast, the RP held one or two meetings in coffeehouses or in private houses almost every night, hosting a total of 43 coffeehouse meetings alone. Moreover, after the elections, the RP's meetings continued on a bimonthly basis. An RP official's speech illustrated how the party critique of the system was informed by moral values. The RP's "new type of state," while not yet a fully developed concept, was similar to the "virtuous society" (*fazilet toplumu*), as was evidenced in his denunciation of the current system:

> This system rewards Manukyan, who runs the chain of prostitution motels in Istanbul. The system rewards someone who sells the bodies of Fatma and Ayşe. Therefore, those who vote for the ruling parties and the ANAP will be held responsible for their act in the presence of God.[71]

In using the names of Fatma, the daughter of the Prophet, and Ayşe, the wife of the Prophet, the lecturer was trying to convince Muslim individuals to distance themselves from the governing party.[72]

The RP did not see election campaigning as an activity to influence a few voters; rather, it considered campaigning an opportunity to convert and gain long-term member allegiance. The party's efforts continued after elections and made an impact on Turkish domestic life long after the campaign banners were put away. For example, the RP often utilized religious holidays to transmit its message in face-to-face interactions, effectively transforming such occasions into political events and spaces where public issues were discussed. Clearly, RP supporters perceived the political struggle as a war of cultural values. Politics, for the ordinary RP supporter, was not simply a mechanism for distributing goods or rulemaking but also a means for articulating communal values in the public space. Political participation, therefore, was an avenue for cultural self-realization.

The political map of Turkey was redrawn to correspond to the cultural and social landscape of a country that is marked by regional differences. The RP won local and national elections in Bayburt, Diyarbakır, Erzurum, Kayseri, Malatya, and Trabzon and in both Ankara (the capital of the reformist Republic) and Istanbul (the former Ottoman imperial capital). However, there were different reasons for each regional victory, especially for those in Ankara and Istanbul. One of the features of the *tesbih* (rosary) organizational structure was the RP's ability to understand and respond to local cultural characteristics. In the towns of central Anatolia (Çorum, Erzurum, Sivas, and Yozgat), the RP supporters were mostly middle-class workers, small merchants, and farmers; ideologically, they were conservative Sunni-Turkish nationalists who shared a state-oriented political culture.[73] In this region the party became an institutional expression of Sunni-Turkish identity vis-à-vis the Alevi identity. There were three reasons for the enormous increase in the vote for the RP in central and eastern Anatolia. First, by adopting a new policy of indifference to the Kurdish problem in the 1995 national election, the RP no longer was vulnerable to the accusation that it was pro-Kurdish. Thus the RP became acceptable to the *Turkish*-Sunni voters, who did not vote for the ultranationalist MHP because of that party's collaboration with the discredited governing parties. Second, RP candidates embraced certain anti-Alevi positions. Finally, the RP mayors of Ankara, Bayburt, Çorum, Erzincan, Kayseri, Konya, and Sivas, who had been elected in 1994, had performed better than was expected and with much less corruption than usual. The RP mayors, even by secularist accounts, not only curtailed the widespread corruption at the municipalities but also improved public services substantially. All these factors encouraged the Sunni-Turkish nationalist voters to opt for the RP and enabled the party to register a 9 percent increase in votes in central Anatolia and a 7 percent gain in eastern Anatolia.

In the Black Sea region, however, the RP strongholds were highly urbanized or involved in the market-oriented production of tea, hazelnuts, or tobacco. In the 1994 municipal elections, for example, RP mayors won elections in Trabzon and Rize, two main Black Sea ports where economic development was phenomenal, as a result of trade with the former Soviet republics. In both cities, the presence of Russian, Ukrainian, and Azeri women prostitutes prompted an "anti-Natasha" movement among local women's groups, which were led by RP candidates. Islam as a code of conduct and a cultural framework was most effective in combating such social ills in this region. In the 1999 national election, the party increased its votes in the Black Sea area by 2.95 percent.

In the Black Sea region Islamic activism has always been rooted in local religious seminaries.[74] When religious education was ignored during the first three decades of Kemalism, the informal Black Sea seminaries became the custodians of Islam and provided "religious service" to different regions of Turkey. The Black Sea region's seminaries, from Ottoman times, traditionally have been very active and have offered a more liberal interpretation of Islam than has been common in the rest of the country, and the Islam of this region remained more liberal and practical than in other regions of Turkey. Limited agricultural land often forced members of many families to move to different regions of the country. This economic pressure induced the people of this region to see "religion" as a service to be sold and a profession in which to be employed; the Islamic seminaries in Of, Rize, Sürmene, Caykara, and Trabzon thus became the main employment centers of the region. After their training, the new ulema the seminaries produced would work in different parts of Turkey. Thus, the religious training in these seminaries has always been "functional" and extremely pragmatic. The ulema of the region did not react negatively to the reforms of Mustafa Kemal and utilized the job opportunities created in the newly established religious bureaucracy—DİB. The seminaries remained pro-state and supported the sweeping Kemalist reforms. The Islam of the Black Sea region, unlike the Southeast Anatolian version, never became an oppositional identity and always allied itself with the state and this alliance, in turn, facilitated the implementation of Kemalist reforms. Moreover, the ulema of this region have always employed Islam to facilitate change and modernize everyday lifestyles and practices. One can view the ulema of the Black Sea region as the custodians of religious change and the agents of vernacularizing (popularizing and legitimizing) social and political change through Islamic ideas and practices.

The "Other Muslims": The Kurdish Question

Islamic movements always have found the southeastern Anatolian mountains fertile ground.[75] In the nineteenth century, Nakşibendi orders very much concentrated in this area and fulfilled educational, judicial, and integrative functions there. The Nakşibendi networks became sources of interpersonal trust and communication for the tribal Kurdish population. The orders and Shafi'i medrese structure protected the society from the centralizing policies of the state. During the early Kemalist period, the dense networks of Nakşibendi-Shafi'i medreses played a key role in organizing resistance against the attempted centralization and indoctrination of education by Ankara. Despite the general anti-religious oppression of the times, some medreses continued their educational activities until the late 1960s.[76] There were several reasons why it was difficult for the state to control the Kurdish medreses: they were located in geogaphically difficult areas; they were economically self-sufficient; and they managed to survive because of the contributions of major tribes in the area. Ironically, over the long run, the Kemalist educational system did not integrate the Kurds into Turkish society but rather helped to politicize Kurdish consciousness.

In southeast Anatolia (Adıyaman, Diyarbakır, Muş, and Van), the Sunni-Kurdish population regularly voted for the RP, whereas the Alevi-Kurds, who usually voted for the Social Democrats, supported the pro-Kurdish HADEP in the 1995 national election. The reason the RP (and earlier the MSP) had a strong constituency in this region was its antisystem rhetoric, which appealed to the largely disillusioned Kurdish population. The Kurdish scholar Hamit Bozaslan perceived the RP's victory in this region as being "different from other parts of the country where political Islam is on the rise . . . [because it was] linked to the centrifugal formation of a Kurdish political space and, in some cases, to the larger Kurdish protest."[77] Abdulbaki Erdoğmuş, one of the most prominent Kurdish deputies from Diyarbakır, explained the basis of the RP's regional strength as due to its being "the only political party that is outside the system, and it can fulfil the change we want . . . justice and freedom . . . [and] restructuring of the system."[78] The RP argued that Islamic identity and solidarity were the best means for diffusing ethnic conflict in the country.

As a result of the 1995 election, the RP's representation in Parliament included 35 Kurdish deputies. The most influential ones were Fuat Fırat, Fethullah Erbaş, and Haşim Haşimi, who openly called for the establishment of an independent Kurdish state in northern Iraq.[79] Fırat, a grandson of the Nakşibendi-Kurdish Sheik Said who had led the 1925 rebellion, argued that the severe conflict in southeastern Turkey could be solved by the deethnicization of the state and its separation from Turkish nationalism and the cultivation of Islamic solidarity. He called on the state and people to subordinate their particular identities and interests to a broader Islamic identity and interest.[80] In stressing Islamic identity, many Kurdish politicians argued that the sources of the politicization of Kurdish identity were the militant secularism and ethnic Turkish nationalism of the Kemalist Republic, which naturally led to the alienation of many Kurds. For example, Nurettin Aktaş, an RP deputy from Gaziantep, said: "if we don't openly question this established system [Kemalism], we cannot find a solution. Many mistakes have been made during the painful shift from an *umma*-based state to a nation-based state."[81] In his yearly reports, Fethullah Erbaş argued that the "disestablishment" of Islam was the main cause of this ethnic conflict. According to Erbaş,

> those generations who were raised during the Ottoman period had
> a common Islamic identity and values for coexistence. Those
> generations raised under the Kemalist educational system with the
> indoctrination of secularism and nationalism are nationalist and
> see themselves separate from the Turks. This Republican Kurdish
> generation first joined the Revolutionary Cultural Society of the
> East [DDKO: Devrimci Doğu Kültür Ocakları] and then the PKK.[82]

In addition to these cultural explanations of the problem, another group within the RP saw the Kurdish question as being mainly an economic one. For example, Ömer Vehbi Hatipoğlu, a prominent RP deputy, argued that the problem only could be solved if the economic disparity between the southeast and the west of the country were eliminated.[83]

The main problem for the RP was its dual self-declared goals: restructuring the political system and restoring state power. The first goal captured the desires and hopes of the Kurds and other discontented groups. With this goal in mind, the RP offered breathing room and a forum for Kurds to express their identity, interests, and goals. Turkey's Kurds sought the deethnicization of the state, but this objective was in conflict with the RP's goal of consolidating the "Turkish" state based on an "authentic" (Islamic) identity. Erbakan, for example, was conscientious in using the term *millet* (a group of people bound by Islam), not *ulus* (an ethnolinguistic nation in Kemalist terminology), for the people of Turkey without making any reference to its Turkish or Kurdish origins. He stressed the idea of fatherland and Islam as the bases of nationhood.

Beginning with the 1991 election, the RP began to distance itself from its formerly principled and inclusive approach to the "Kurdish question." To prove its Turkish nationalist credentials to secular critics, it did not nominate a Kurdish-Muslim-oriented candidate from the southeastern region. After the March 1994 local elections, the party sent a fact-finding mission to the region; under the chairmanship of Şevket Kazan, it published its report on August 21, 1994.[84] The report called on the state to open democratic spaces for Kurdish groups and associations, utilizing and consolidating religious networks as crosscutting bonds, allowing education in the Kurdish language, and giving more power to municipalities.[85] The RP leadership, however, totally ignored this report and its findings during the 1995 national elections. The (unstated) reason was to appease Turkish voters susceptible to state propaganda portraying any attempt to ameliorate the harsh conditions facing the vast majority of Turkey's Kurds as "concessions to terrorists." Equally important was the fierce hostility of the Kemalist military and bureaucracy to any cooperation between what they viewed as the two mortal threats to their power: politically active Turkish Muslims and ethnically conscious Kurds.[86] These political "realities" thus forestalled what would have been the most promising avenue for easing the terrible conflict in the southeast.

In the 1995 national election, a large number of Kurds who were disappointed with the faintheartedness of the RP leadership voted for the Kurdish nationalist party, HADEP. Nonetheless, some Islamist-Kurdish nationalists, especially among the Sufi orders in the southeast, still voted for the RP as an alternative to the state-imposed, secular ethnolinguistic Turkish nationalism. Ironically, many state officials in the region—who had little personal connection to Ankara—also voted for the RP. They did so because they viewed the party as having the best long-term prescription for derailing the PKK's program, which would create an unbreachable chasm between Anatolian Turks and Kurds.

In the Marmara region (Istanbul and Adapazarı), the RP appealed to urban Kurds (as well as to Turks) by presenting a social democratic image of itself. Ercan Karataş, a prominent social democratic politician, noted that "the RP filled the vacuum created by the collapse of social democrat parties in Turkey "[87] Altan Tan, a Kurdish-Islamist politician, argued that the RP in Istanbul emphasized justice and the distribution of benefits and responsibilities, thus becoming a "Muslim social democrat party."[88] The common theme here, whether in central, southeast, or western Anatolia, was the RP's ability to express each region's socioeconomic problems in vague Islamic terms that had broad appeal because the symbolic structure of Turkish society is Islam. Because there are different readings of Islam in Turkey, what makes Islam relevant is not its ostensible rigidity but rather its flexibility. For example, landowners and party bosses in southeast Anatolia invoked Islam to consolidate the old power structure, but in industrialized cities, Islam became a banner for rallying the oppressed lower classes around demands for justice and equality. In general, the RP's success derived from its appeal to four distinct social groups: Islamist intellectuals who demanded freedom of expression for religion in the public sphere; Sunni Kurds who sought either autonomy or a reorganization of the Turkish nation-state that would allow them to be recognized as a separate ethnic group; the *gecekondulular* (squatter town dwellers) who demanded social justice and integration into the capitalist economy; and the new bourgeoisie who wanted less state intervention, more liberalization, and the eradication of state subsidies for big corporations.

The RP represented a paradox for the Kemalist system. It was enemy and ally at the same time. On the one hand it was a major force that should be controlled carefully to maintain the secular nature of the state. On the other it was a necessary political force that contained and gave hope to Turkey's most dynamic and potentially destructive peripheral forces. The RP domesticated and educated these forces by incorporating them into the political system. Its political structure constituted a web of associations, networks, and relationships. It transformed rural values into urban values. Turkey's social stability owes a lot to the RP and other religious networks. Although it did not solve the Kurdish question, it prevented the radicalization of Kurdish nationalism. The RP's stress on Islamic symbols and networks helped to release the Kurdish nationalistic energies and prevented the dominance of solely ethnically based opposition to the Kemalist system. Some members of the military establishment recognized the constructive role of the RP. The PKK's activism, combined with the suppressive policies of the Turkish state, resulted in the secularization of the Kurdish identity and disengagement from the RP. Islamic political spaces-in-between Turkish and Kurdish identities were destroyed as the RP acquired more Turkish and conservative features after the 1991 elections. The pro-Kurdish HADEP emerged as the dominant agent to articulate secular and nationalist Kurdish identity claims.

Women's Role in the RP

Islamic groups want to maintain the distinction between themselves and secular groups by regulating Muslim women's sexuality. Women, for the Islamists, have been and still remain the icon by which social stability and the family is to be maintained.[89] After the mass rape of Muslim women in Bosnia, the Islamists became even more determined to confine symbolically Muslim women's bodies within the protective borders of the umma during the 1994 and 1995 elections. At the same time, politics, economic development, and the debate over modernity put women in a particularly difficult situation. Although some Islamic women's groups share in an antimodern disposition, their antimodernism does not necessarily make them traditional.[90] Opposed to a modernity that collapsed differences in gender roles, most of these women's groups redefined themselves, and their quest for a new community formed along religious lines, as is expressed in their support for the RP. However, the views of their urban cadres regarding the proper place of women in society was often quite different from what many men would like to have seen in the Islamic movements.

Women's groups played the most crucial role in carrying the party's message to the far corners of society. For example, Sibel Eraslan, the head of the women's group in Istanbul, claimed that there were women's groups in 22 counties, and each group consisted of 33 women. In addition, each neighborhood had a women's group that consisted of 14 women, under the control of its county group, and each street had a women's group of six that reported to the neighborhood.[91] There were, in all, around 250,000 women activists who claimed to work for Islamic principles. There were very few university graduates among these activists, although the number of graduates rapidly increased. Instead, the party managed to mobilize women through grassroots politicization, with the women's groups besieging neighborhoods and conveying RP's message to

women in individual households.[92] This was a revolutionary change in terms of their traditional role in society.[93] Traditionally, women did not participate in the public arena to promote their own interests, but now they aimed to become "conscious of the problems of Turkey and the world, to define womanhood and its role in society, and to fight for the rights of women."[94] The 1994 election reflected the success of these women more than that of the RP.[95]

The RP became an institutional tool for the mobilization and politicization of traditionally inclined women, bringing them out of their houses and neighborhoods and into the public arena. As women from different backgrounds and various parts of Istanbul met regularly with new people to pursue common goals, their political activities raised the consciousness of women and encouraged them to become active agents for change. The resulting new self-confidence of Turkey's women in their ability to shape society led the women's groups to demand official positions within the party.[96] In time, Sibel Eraslan believes, "there are and will be women nominees."[97] She explained that Muslim women, having exercised their right to vote, now would like to exercise their right to be elected. Consequently, when Süheyla Kebapçıoğlu, the chairwoman of the party's Commission on Women, resigned on September 14, 1994, she made her resignation public and argued that women wanted a larger role and more power in the party.[98] The influence of women's groups enabled the RP to carry its message into the households of Turkish cities and, through personal visits, made women in homes aware of the importance of everyone's vote.[99] "Conversation" is the term used for these face-to-face meetings, and it has been a key to the training of the RP's followers and the conversion of new members among the first generation of literate town dwellers who just a decade ago came from villages. Oral communication is still at the center of their culture, and the human voice and accompanying gestures can be as important as the words themselves used in conversation.[100] Indeed, the message of the party was embedded in these gestures.

External Others—Neo-Ottomanism

The external dimension of Islamic political identity relates to the RP's perception of and relations with the rest of the world. One of the main characteristics of the Turkish Islamic movement is its neo-Ottomanism.[101] Olivier Roy has argued that

> the Islamic movement in Turkey is first and foremost a nationalistic
> one. Islam is interlinked with the idea of homeland in Turkey, but
> this also includes the Turkish workers in Europe. The Turkish
> workers remain Turks and maintain their connection with Turkey.

In addition to the territorial dimension, Roy also mentions the role of history and the Ottoman legacy in the evolution of the Turkish Islamic movement.[102] Indeed, the problem of identity tends to dominate any discussion of foreign

policy issues. Gül, who played a leading role in formulating RP's foreign policy positions, said:

> Turkey is neither Luxembourg nor Bangladesh. History, geography and reality require Turkey to carry and fulfill a mission regardless of our desires. This mission or role may be the role of the Ottoman Empire. We therefore cannot remain indifferent to the developments in Palestine, Yugoslavia, and Albania due to our national interest.

He concluded that Turkey is "the cultural center of Islamic civilization in Europe. We [Turkey] therefore have to involve ourselves in the developments in the Balkans."[103]

From 1991 to 1995, the central concerns of Erbakan's foreign policy were Bosnia, Cyprus, the Middle East, and Azerbaijan. Because Erbakan did not rely on a speechwriter, he formulated the issues for his public addresses, which usually were printed after he had spoken. Consequently, Erbakan's foreign policy was based less on critical analysis and more on ambiguous appeals to populism. For instance, he claimed to be "against making any concessions" in Cyprus, Bosnia, and Azerbaijan. His party tended to share the view of most Turks that Ankara's foreign policy was an extension of Turkish-European relations.[104] According to Erbakan, the United Nations served as an instrument of Western imperialism. With respect to the conflict in Bosnia—which he and most Turks viewed as genocide against the Muslim population—Erbakan claimed that

> the major catastrophic event of the century is taking place at the heart of Europe. The double standard of the West became clear. What did they do to stop this carnage? The West only observed the massacre! They therefore want this carnage to go on because those who are killed and raped are Muslims. I want to know where is the United Nations which was established on the principle of no forceful acquisition of territory? What happened to the principles of the United Nations? The UN implements its principles only against the Muslims. If Muslims suffer, these principles have no value whatsoever. The UN has no moral face any more.[105]

Erbakan similarly judged NATO in terms of its role in the Bosnian crisis: "NATO does not want to help because its new enemy is Islam (Green) not communism (Red)."[106] Through the concept of an Islamic Union, the RP wanted to establish an Islamic UN, an Islamic NATO, an Islamic UNESCO, and an Islamic economic community,[107] in other words, an Islamic international system under the leadership of Turkey. Ultimately, Erbakan argued, the RP seeks to establish a new civilization that will revolve around "*hak* [divine justice] rather than force." Turkey, he said, "had to lead other Muslim countries in the establishment of a new civilization and just world order."[108] Erbakan sought to fly "the RP flag to unify 1.2 billion Muslims all over the world."[109] Nevertheless, when Erbakan listed the successes to date of his party's Milli Görüş, he mentioned Turkey's full membership in the Organization of the Islamic Conference, even though Turkey is only an informal member, not a fully accredited one.[110]

The RP preferred to focus its foreign policy on the European attitude toward the Bosnian Muslims, maintaining that the government of Tansu Çiller was a product not of Atatürkism (i.e., nationalism) but of Western-oriented subservience. Atatürk, according to the RP, was against the American and European mandate system and fought for full independence. As Erbakan put it, "Atatürk sought to establish industry and develop the country with its own national resources. Atatürk preferred an independent foreign policy to a dependent one."[111]

Erbakan's foreign policy platform was also characterized by anti-Zionism and concern for Islamic claims in Palestine, especially the old city of Jerusalem. He charged: "Zionists are seeking to assimilate Turkey and pull us from our historical Islamic roots through integrating Turkey to the European Economic Community."[112] Israel, for Erbakan, represented a major locus of anti-Muslim evil in the world. In his view, "Whenever the UN talks about human rights, it means the rights of the Jews but nothing else."[113] Furthermore, "since the European Community is a single state, Turkey's membership means being a single state with Israel. The goal is to create a Greater Israel by integrating Turkey to the Community."[114]

Erbakan also argued that Turkey already had been "colonized" by a banking system that is dominated by Israel. He claimed that the average Turk worked a half-day for Israel and a half-day for local compradors. Of the price of a loaf of bread, he maintained that one-third is paid toward interest on the national debt, which goes through the IMF and American banks to Israel; one-third is paid to taxes to subsidize foreign trade; and only one-third goes to the baker himself.[115] With respect to the 1993 Oslo Agreement between Israel and the Palestine Liberation Organization (PLO), Erbakan claimed that it was in accord with Zionism's goal to penetrate Muslim countries under the guise of helping them in order to get some Muslims (namely the PLO) to kill other Muslims (Hamas).[116] Erbakan also rhetorically asked on one occasion of America: "Are you a slave of Israel? You claim to be a superpower. What happened to you! You are a toy in the hands of the Jewish lobby. . . . You are a servant of Israel, your situation is very clear."[117] Given the role the Turkish-Israeli alliance played in the military's decision to overthrow his civilian government in 1997 and the support this action garnered among major Jewish organizations abroad, Erbakan's hostility toward the Israeli state is likely to have increased.

Conclusion

Since the 1980 coup, the state has pursued a dual-track policy of co-optation and containment of Islamist groups by gradually expanding the political system to allow limited participation. Turkey has succeeded in incorporating Islamists into the system, and this in turn has softened and restructured Islamic demands and voices. However, the Islamic political movements, which criticized the ideological position of the militantly secular state and demanded a more neutral state, have been resorting to electoral politics to Islamicize political institutions.[118]

The 1980s witnessed rapid economic development and the Islamization of Turkish nationalism as a result of the 1980 military coup. At first the growing bourgeoisie and craftsmen gained confidence and invoked religious idioms to carve a larger space for themselves vis-à-vis the big industrialists and rigid bureaucracy. As a vocal and well-organized Islamic movement began to crystallize, the RP took advantage of the new state-led ethnoreligious nationalism to mobilize the masses, using the issues of identity and social justice. Sufi and new cultural associations provided extra political scope for the Islamic movement to translate its growing appeal into policy decisions.

The main goals of the RP were the externalization of Islamic identity in the public domain and the construction of a community marked by Islamic morals and virtues (*ahlak ve fazilet*). Although the traditional networks and primordial identities bolstered the RP, its primary goal was to penetrate the political system and transform it from within. As a result, the RP was able to foster the externalization of Islamic identity in many ways. It acted as a conveyor of the voices of Islamist groups to the public sector. It represented Islamist interests in the Turkish Parliament; and it became a vehicle for Islamists to move into the administration of local municipalities and the larger national bureaucracy. By facilitating the formation of a common denominator for national (milli) solidarity, the RP tied Sunni Muslims together with the government while excluding the large Alevi population. However, paradoxically, the process of Islamicization promoted the process of the inner secularization of Islam. Islamic movements reconstituted the space between Muslim citizens and state institutions with diverse and overlapping associations and divergent Islamic discourses. This incorporated Sunni Muslims into government circles but shut out Alevi and secular communities. In a way, creative pluralism has been turned into communal division in modern Turkey without a neutral state and legally protective spaces. The dissidents and the heterodox are faced with an increasingly hostile political environment.

Erbakan and his associates reimagined the Islamic tradition as a modernist discourse to solve Turkey's contemporary problems of identity and justice. This radical conceptualization is influenced by European notions of modernity and industrialization, even though they are not fully internalized. The unfolding processes of Islamization and modernity have created a new synthesis in which Islam is radically rethought in terms of modern concepts and institutions. What has been going on in modern Turkey is the reconstruction of the Islamic tradition in terms of modern idioms to create a new Turkey that can become an exemplar of political, economic, and cultural success for Muslims around the world. While the Islamic political identity that this presents is a new notion of identity and loyalty among these religiously oriented social associations, this identity has an instrumental as well as intrinsic value, for its purpose is to externalize shared patterns of ritualized behavior in order to live a better life and communicate harmoniously using shared vernacular idioms.

10

The Securitization of Islam and the Triumph of the AKP

In the 1990s, Turkey's religious and Kurdish groups used new opportunity spaces to assert their own identity claims. Since identity-based political systems tend to subsume all forms of class and ideological divisions in identity categories, in the case of Turkey political debate became dominated by the themes of Islam versus secularism, Sunni versus Alevi, and Kurd versus Turk. The state establishment, mainly the military and civilian bureaucracy, reacted to these identity claims as security threats, and the "securitization" of Kurdish and Islamic identity claims further politicized Turkish society. By "securitization" I mean a concept articulated by Barry Buzan, Ole Waever, and Philippos K. Savvides whereby the state brands certain religious, ethnic, class, or ideological groups and movements as a national security threat justifying coercive and often extrajudicial measures against them. This process defines ethnic and religious identity claims "as an existential threat, requiring emergency measures and justifying actions outside the normal bonds of political procedure."[1] The assertive Kurdish and Islamic identity claims reinforced the "securitization" of domestic politics in Turkey and the institutionalization of a national security state, in which the military expanded its overseer role to include such civilian areas as the judiciary, economy, education, and foreign policy. In accordance with its endowing ideology of Kemalism, the Turkish military regards acknowledgment of ethnic or religious diversity as a potential threat and a precursor of disunity. In the 1990s, this fear of ethnic and religious diversity and its potential to undermine the political and ideological hegemony of the Kemalist establishment underpinned the state policy of denying individuals and groups the right to articulate religious and ethnic identity claims outside of the very narrow officially sanctioned space.

Following the 1995 national election, the main political goal was to exclude the RP, which had won a plurality of seats in Parliament, from government (table 10.1). In response to the pressures from the military, media, and major business corporations,[2] the two center-right parties formed a new coalition government on March 3, 1996. Tansu Çiller of the DYP and Mesut Yılmaz of the ANAP agreed on a rotating prime ministerial position, despite the traditional rivalry over their similar agendas and supporters. This development persuaded some RP followers that the institutional means of change were closed to them. The de facto closure of the system to the largest party in Parliament agitated a large segment of the electorate, and RP deputies became excessively restive.[3]

Moreover, by excluding the RP in the name of secularism, the Kemalist establishment—that is, the armed forces, big corporations that preferred state-protected markets, and some media sectors—alienated the most dynamic segment of the population, further narrowing its social base and unwittingly expanding the RP's base. Instead of seeking gradually to integrate (and thus co-opt) Islamic groups into the system, the political elite opted to prevent this "historic compromise" between the center and the periphery. Moreover, the TÜSİAD and its media networks, such as the Doğan and Sabah publishing conglomerates, constantly represented periphery and provincial bourgeoisie as "reactionary" so as to exclude them from the privatization process and governance.[4]

TABLE 10.1. Electoral results in national elections, 1987–2002

Parties	1987 %	1987 seats	1991 %	1991 seats	1995 %	1995 seats	1999 %	1999 seats	2002 %	2002 seats
Center-right										
DYP	19.1	59	27.0	178	19.2	135	12.0	85	9.55	—
ANAP	39.3	292	24.0	115	19.7	132	13.2	86	5.12	—
Center-left										
DSP	8.5	0	10.4	7	14.6	76	22.1	136	1.21	—
CHP	—	—	—	—	10.7	49	8.8	—	19.39	178
SODEP	24.8	99	20.8	88	—	—				
Nationalists										
MÇP/MHP	—	—	—	—	8.1	0	17.9	129	8.34	—
HADEP	—	—	—	—	4.1	0	4.7	0	6.22	—
Pro-Islamic										
R/F[a] SP	7.2	—	16.2[b]	62	21.4	158	15.4	107	2.46	—
AKP	—	—	—	—	—	—	—	—	34.26	363

[a]After the closure of the FP, two parties with roots in RP and FP have been formed. The AKP emerged as the most formidable force in the Parliament.

[b]In order to meet the required 10 percent threshold, an electoral pact among the RP, the MÇP, and a minor third party was formed. A single list of candidates ran on the RP ticket.

A dash indicates non-participation in election or no seat taken in the election.

Source: High Electoral Board of Turkey (Ankara, 2002).

The political rivalry between Yılmaz and Çiller opened a new window of opportunity for the RP. According to the coalition's rotation agreement, Yılmaz became prime minister first, and Çiller was to assume the post in January 1997. However, Yılmaz's main aim was to prevent Çiller from assuming the premiership, and thus he began to search for evidence of corruption allegedly carried out by the Çiller family. Hoping either to remove Çiller as head of the DYP or to divide the DYP, Yılmaz leaked some of the incriminating documents to the RP, the main opposition party in the Parliament. But the RP used these documents not to attack Çiller but rather to assault the coalition government.

There were three main corruption dossiers on Çiller. When the RP brought these charges to Parliament to establish a special investigation committee, about 30 ANAP deputies voted in favor of launching an inquiry into the scandals. The first inquiry, which opened on April 24, 1996, examined the claims that Çiller as prime minister during 1994–1995 had made money illegally by favoring certain private companies during the sell-off of the state-owned electricity firm TEDAŞ. The second investigation, which began on May 10, inquired into allegations that she meddled illegally in the bidding for the sale of state shares in TOFAŞ, a Fiat subsidiary automobile manufacturer. Although the RP brought the parliamentary motions to launch the investigations, the allegations against Çiller originally had been made by the ANAP. During the 1995 election, the latter party had promised to investigate the allegations of corruption during her tenure and similar allegations against her banker husband, Özer Çiller. Yılmaz used his office to expose the "Waterfront Villa Gang" (*Yalı çetesi*), named after Çiller's posh villa on the Bosphorus, and to publicize that it had used the government for personal gain. The last blow to the coalition government came when the RP deputy Şevket Kazan openly charged Çiller of misusing a secret prime ministerial fund by appropriating 500 billion Turkish lira ($6.5 million) before she had left office in March 1996. Parliament voted to investigate all these charges; had the committees found Çiller guilty, the Constitutional Court would have tried her. A guilty verdict in that body would have barred her from assuming the position of prime minister at the beginning of 1997; she would in effect be ousted from the political scene. During the parliamentary debate over corruption, however, the Constitutional Court ruled that the confidence vote that had allowed the Yılmaz-Çiller coalition to take office was invalid. Accordingly, Çiller ended this government in May 1996 by withdrawing her DYP and forming a new coalition with the RP; in return, the RP agreed to support an end to the investigations on the corruption cases in Parliament.

On June 28, 1996, for the first time, the Turkish Republic had a prime minister whose political philosophy was based on Islam. This marked a psychological turning point for different groups. For conservative Muslims, this was the end of their exclusion from the public spaces and recognition of their identity by the state. For the Kemalist bloc that controlled economic resources, this was the darkest moment for the Republican project. The Kemalists did not utilize this historic development as an opportunity to form a new social contract based on tolerant secularism, democracy, and the rule of law. Rather, they perceived the moment as one to "fear" and mobilized the secularist seg-ment of the population against the government. Moreover, Erbakan's initia-tives very much played into the hands of the military. These deepened the secular-versus-Islamic fault line because it is the military that decides "who should rule Turkey" and draws the boundaries of politics; these now were drawn against Erbakan. The military viewed the RP's increasing electoral vic-tories as ultimately threatening the very ideological basis and worldview of the Kemalist Republic.

The RP tried to overcome this fear during its Fifth Party Congress in October 1996, during which Erbakan demonstrated his readiness to compromise his anti-Kemalist establishment rhetoric by telling a cheering crowd: "We are the guaran-tee for secularism and obstacle to those who seek to move Turkey toward atheism and antireligion." During the convention the RP leadership carefully controlled the crowd so as not to give an anti–Republican establishment image.[5] The con-vention displayed the division between the activist RP supporters and the more reserved leadership, which wanted to give the impression in the media that it did not seek any radical overthrow of the Republican establishment, entrenched since 1923.[6] A modernist group, led by Abdullah Gül, tried to utilize the coalition gov-ernment to transform the RP party into a Muslim democratic party, along the lines of the Christian democratic parties in Europe. However, this ongoing transfor-mation would be interrupted by the coalition of external and domestic forces that supported the coup of February 28, 1997.[7]

Erbakan, who led the most conservative wing of the RP, not only had acted as opportunistically as Çiller in joining the coalition but also initiated new poli-cies that were viewed as attempts to undermine secularism. For example, he suggested lifting the ban on female students and civil servants wearing head-scarves; organized a fasting breakfast for the leaders of traditional Sufi orders at the residence of the prime minister; made plans to build a mosque on Taksim Square in Istanbul; and supported legal pluralism (including Islamic law).[8] Moreover, Erbakan did not control a small group of radical parliamentary depu-ties, such as Şevki Yılmaz and Hasan H. Ceylan, who made inflammatory state-ments about Mustafa Kemal.

Erbakan's government not only deepened the fault line between the secu-lar and Islamic groups but also further politicized the Alevi community.[9] The latter were disturbed by the appointment to the government of Şevket Kazan, the key lawyer of many accused Sunni Muslims in the 1993 Sivas incident, in which many prominent Alevis had been burned to death. Erbakan's government thus further solidified the boundaries of the Alevis as a separate "ethnoreligious community."[10] The Alevi elite was more concerned with the expanding role of the Sunni Islamic movement than other sectors of the population. Indeed, the Alevi community was the only sector of the Turkish population that welcomed the February 28 coup, because the conflicts in Sivas and Gazi had created a deep fear of the state and the Islamic political movement. These events and the in-creasing activism of the Alevi associations for the first time brought marginalized Alevi identity into the public sphere in a dramatic fashion.[11] State officials, the Kemalist elite, and major newspapers all became involved in the redefinition of

Alevism as the "ally of Kemalism" to protect secularism (against Sunni political Islam) and the unitary state structure (against Kurdish nationalism).[12]

Erbakan also vexed both secularists and Turkey's Western allies with a series of initiatives to shift Turkey's foreign policy eastward.[13] The new prime minister's first meeting was with the leader of Egypt's Muslim Brotherhood, the son of the late Hasan al-Banna.[14] This caused enough concern that President Hosni Mubarak paid a short visit to Ankara to stop Erbakan's "interference" in Egyptian politics. Erbakan also aroused concern among some Middle Eastern governments, while giving hope to Islamic movements throughout the region. His first official visit was to Iran, where he signed a $23 billion gas and oil deal. He then visited Libya, where he was humiliated by Muammar Qaddafi, who accused Turkey of being too pro-Western and oppressive of the Kurds.[15]

One of the critical external factors working against Erbakan was the Turkish-Israeli strategic relationship, which had started in 1994 with high-level visits. Some of Erbakan's speeches and policy initiatives deepened American and Israeli concerns about the ability of Muslim parties to lead "democratic" governments in the region. After Erbakan criticized certain Israeli policies, his government became the target of the Washington Institute for Near East Policy (WINEP), a pro-Israeli think thank that was trying to overcome Israel's isolation in the Middle East by helping to develop strategic relations between Turkey and Israel. In 1996, the Çiller government had signed a number of military agreements with Israel. The military was ready to join this strategic relationship with Israel for several reasons: to confirm Turkey's secular orientation; to counter regional support (primarily from Iran and Syria) for local Islamic and Kurdish groups; to gain a back door to Washington via Israel's good offices; and to secure a reliable new source of military technology not subject to human rights constraints. After the formation of Erbakan's coalition, the military used Turkish-Israeli relations to embarrass the government by exposing its powerlessness to halt an alliance it openly had opposed. Not only did the military totally ignore the government in dealings with Israel, but in May 1997, the military engaged in a massive military operation in northern Iraq without notifying the civilian government in advance.

Kemalism Strikes Back: The Coup of February 28

The immediate events leading to the coup took place on February 4, 1997, at a rally organized by the RP mayor of Sincan, a small town near Ankara, to protest against Israeli occupation of Jerusalem. At the rally, the Iranian ambassador delivered a speech asking Turks to obey the "precepts of Islam," and signs supporting Hamas and Hizbullah were displayed. Tanks rumbled through Sincan, and the military forced the government to arrest the mayor and expel the Iranian ambassador. The media then sensationalized the subsequent visit to the jailed mayor by the minister of justice, Şevket Kazan. Çevik Bir, who would lead the February 28 coup, defended the military's show of force in Sincan as "fine-tuning" to restore the status quo.[16] Indeed, when diverse identity movements make claims and upset the balance, the military historically has moved to reimpose the Kemalist equilibrium.

On February 28, 1997, the armed forces openly moved into politics via the NSC, on which top generals sit ex officio. The NSC declared the Islamic movement to be the number one internal security threat, placing it above the Kurdish separatism and external challenges, to the existence of the state and to the Republic and ordered the Erbakan government to implement a list of 18 directives (see appendix).[17]

After some resistance, Erbakan signed the "directives" on March 5, 1997, and asked the cabinet to implement them. President Demirel justified the directives by insisting that they were necessary to protect the secular nature of the Republic. Social democrats, such as Deniz Baykal, the head of the CHP, and the ANAP of Yılmaz supported the military's intervention in the political arena by presenting the army as another "pressure group" with progressive goals. However, when the military realized that the RP was not willing to implement its directives, it decided to force the government out of power.

The directives identified Muslim businesses, the Islamic education system, media, and religious activism as primary threats to the secular nature of the Turkish state.[18] The goal of the military was to roll back the Muslim sectors of civil society by closing off their opportunity spaces.[19] Because of the emergence of these new opportunity spaces, Kemalist hegemony had lost its control over national and municipal layers of the state. Pro-Islamic mayors had been winning and controlling large budgets, and these mayors were using the resources of municipalities to compete at the national level. Moreover, the Kemalist dominance over economic resources was coming under challenge as a result of the new bourgeoisie that was seeking a larger share in the market. In addition, the Kemalist control over the production of culture and norms was undermined as a result of the diversification of cultural networks. For instance, the state-led radio and television stations were forced to compete with private ones. Finally, organizational life, in terms of bourgeoning civil society groups and associations, did not allow any form of official ideology to become dominant. The military not only wanted these associations and foundations to be closed but also identified "19 newspapers, 20 television stations, 51 radio stations, 110 magazines, 800 schools, 1,200 student hostels and 2,500 associations" that it claimed were part of reactionary political Islam.[20]

The Securitization of Islam

A major characteristic of the 1997 coup was that judges and journalists, rather than bullets and tanks, supported and implemented it. The military authority used the mass media, as well as briefings, conferences, and regular public announcements to inform the judges and the public about the existential threat to the state stemming from political Islam and Kurdish ethnonationalism. In order to generate support from the secular sector of society, the military presented the Islamic presence in public spaces as a threat to the Kemalist lifestyle, which it claimed was the only legitimate one. The military also tried to mobilize women's associations, trade unions, and business organizations to oppose the sharing of public spaces with the emerging Islamic identity and lifestyle.

Since Islamic groups were criminalized and excluded in the name of national security, it is important to examine the way this concept of national security is constructed and utilized against the society. The political arena in Turkey has been designed in accordance with the Kemalist precepts of secularism and nationalism and closely guarded by the military. Four times in the past 50 years, in 1960, 1971, 1980, and 1997, the military intervened to "guard" the Kemalist system. The primary task of the military, according to article 35 of the Internal Service Act (1961), is to "safeguard and defend Turkish territory and the Republic of Turkey as designated by the constitution."[21] Since Kemalist doctrine in general, and secularism in particular, is enshrined in the constitution, the military's duty is to "look after" the Kemalist ideology as the guiding public philosophy within Turkey. Secularism, for the military officers, is the backbone of the regime, and if it collapses, the whole system fails. Moreover, article 85 of the Internal Service Regulation says that the "Turkish military shall defend the county against internal as well as external threats, if necessary by force." Thus the military has authority to define threats that present existential danger to the existence of the state and its founding ideology. Any issue can be securitized if it is regarded as "antisecular." In the worldview of the military officers, the connection between secularism and security is causal, that is, secularism creates security, and all antisecular acts are regarded as sources of insecurity. This military conception of secularism as the foundation of the "national unity" and "unitary state" structure would inform the decisions of the judiciary.

The failure of the ideologically rigid Kemalist state to cope with these new identity claims prompted the military-dominated state elite to define the identity claims of ethnic and religious groups as existential threats to the core values of the state ideology. These perceived threats have led the state to reduce major social, political, and economic problems to security issues.[22] This military viewpoint/policy position has resulted in the criminalization of identity groups. Thus, by framing Islamic and Kurdish identity challenges as security issues, the military believes it has the sole responsibility to deal with these threats with extraordinary means outside normal political norms.

In April 1997, the military changed its National Military Strategic Concept (MASK: Milli Askeri Strateji Konsepti) from targeting the Kurdish separatist and external threats of interstate war to "reactionary Islam" as the number one enemy to the country's founding ideology and unity. In order to focus on the new "enemy," the Office of the Chief of the General Staff established the West Working Group to monitor the activities of suspected Muslim organizations and businesses in all sectors of society.[23] This group also was used to inform academics, judges, and bureaucrats about the dangers of Islamism and

Kurdish ethnonationalism and the proper attitude they should have toward them.

The regular military interventions and briefings against Erbakan's pro-Islamic coalition government destabilized Turkey's domestic and foreign policy. For example, on April 29, 1997, General Kenan Deniz, the head of Internal Security and the Planning Department at the chief of staff's office, briefed journalists on the major security threats to Turkey: "Islamic fanaticism, the Kurdish Question, and Turko-Greek relations." Deniz identified Islamic radicalism as the number one threat to "national security," informing the journalists that "according to a new national security doctrine, the perception of threat had shifted from outside to inside."[24] The military's main target was the Muslim sector of civil society, and the goal was to cleanse Islamic voices from the public sphere by criminalizing Islamic associations, media, parties, companies, and politicians in the name of national security.[25] By stressing Republican authoritarianism over democracy, security over freedom, a rigid, fundamentalist secularism over tolerance toward religion, and state-led modernism over bottom-up social modernity, the military expanded its control in education, telecommunication, the legal system, business, and politics. This situation in turn resulted in the shrinking of political, economic, and cultural opportunity spaces.

During the coup, the military worked very closely with major media cartels such as the Doğan group, which publishes the dailies Hürriyet and Milliyet, and leading business and university administrators in justifying the need for military intervention and civilian purges because of alleged "national security threats." For instance, the Higher Educational Board (YÖK), an official body that oversees postsecondary education in Turkey, issued a new set of regulations to protect and preserve the Kemalist doctrine in higher education institutions by seeking to eliminate all forms of Islamic identity claims.[26] The new regulations empowered university administrations to fire those who "acted against the Republic and its values" and to strip professors and other faculty of their academic titles for expressing views contrary to the official Republican ideology.[27] They also could "lose their social security rights and face a life ban in state service."[28]

This virtual declaration of "war" against a broad section of Islamic groups extended to private business competitors of the state-supported oligopolists connected with the TÜSİAD. The army targeted 100 major Turkish companies whose only apparent transgression was to be run by conservative Muslims, many of whom in fact had supported political parties other than the RP. The army included the prominent Ülker biscuit company, the İhlas corporation, and the 36-company Kombassan conglomerate. Without the need for even cursory evidence, the army declared 19 newspapers, 20 national television stations, 51 radio stations, 110 magazines, and 1,200 student hostels as constituting the "reactionary sector." In response to the military's actions, 300,000 pro-Islamic demonstrators rallied in Istanbul against the closure of İmam Hatip schools on May 11, 1997. The armed forces responded to the increasingly bold and popular demonstrations by declaring their "readiness to use force against Islamic groups" on June 11, 1997. Erbakan, sensing a forceful military coup in the offing and seeking to avoid violence at all cost, resigned as prime minister on June 17, 1997.

In January 1998, the Constitutional Court (CC), under Chief Justice Ahmet Necdet Sezer, who became president of Turkey in 2000, assented to the wishes of the powerful military, closed down the RP, and banned Erbakan from political activity for five years on the basis of antisecularism.[29] The CC judges acted as the agents of Turkey's militarized ideology (Kemalism) rather than as the guardians of human rights. The CC, which is the watchdog of the regime, banned the RP for violating articles 68 and 69 of the constitution and becoming the center of antisecular activities. Indeed, the 1982 constitution draws the boundaries of democracy with the Kemalist principle of secularism. No party could be established "against the principles of the secular Republic" (article 68) and those parties that employ religious emotions, symbols and arguments "shall be banned" (article 69). To close the party, the CC seized on statements of parliamentarians within and outside Parliament that were critical of the Kemalist definition of secularism. The CC decision not only set back Turkish democracy but also reinforced the proponents of Kemalist ideology in their contest with religion.

Before handing down its decision, the CC redefined secularism as "the way of life."[30] By "the way of life," the court means that secularism is the only officially sanctioned "regulator of political, social and cultural life of the society."[31] The central goal of Kemalism was defined as being a political, social, and cultural system "free of any religious influence or presence."[32] Religion, for the CC, only can be tolerated in the private conscience of an individual, and any externalization or reflection of religiosity in the public domain is defined as an antisecular act against the principles of Kemalism. In order to justify its decision, the CC said that secularism is the basis of "national sovereignty, democracy, freedom and science, and as such is the contemporary regulator of the political, social and cultural life." The CC decision also alludes to "the different nature of secularism in Turkey on the basis of the unique characteristics of Islam and the sociohistorical context of Turkey."[33] Indeed, the court defines religion in opposition to secularism and argues that "religion regulates the inner aspect of the individual whereas secularism regulates the outer aspect of the individual."[34] Thus, Turkish secularism can be seen as different from democratic forms of secularism in terms of its "Jacobin," "militant and militarized," and "antireligious" features that impose a top-down Western lifestyle.[35] Secularism in the Turkish context is a state ideology and an instrument of othering and criminalizing opposition.

The CC used such the statements by the RP as "the headscarf must be free in the universities" and "the right to choose your own legal system, including sharia," as examples of antisecular activities. Only 2 of 11 justices dissented, arguing that laicism is a means to consolidate participatory democracy, which would ensure that neither the state nor a particular creed forced its views on the other.[36] The majority of the CC effectively accepted the principle of Kemalist ideological purity and the military's unchallenged right to interpret and defend it as a higher value trumping democracy and individual liberty.

The military also was instrumental in the removal from political life and jailing of Tayyip Erdoğan, the mayor of Istanbul and one of the most popular politicians in the country. The Kemalist generals particularly feared Erdoğan's popularity across a broad segment of Turkish society, his youthful charisma, and his honest and efficient running of Istanbul. Indeed, he emerged from the 2002 election as the leader of the new, transformed Islamic political movement. Under pressure from the military, the State Security Court sentenced Erdoğan to 10 months in prison and banned him from politics for reciting a poem by Ziya Gökalp, ironically a nationalist icon for early Kemalist leaders. The Gökalp verses he had recited were: "Turkey's mosques will be our barracks, the minarets our bayonets, the domes our helmets, and the faithful our soldiers."[37]

The process of securitization and criminalization of alternative lifestyles and identities has not strengthened but on the contrary has undermined the legitimacy of the Kemalist state in general, and the military in particular. Most of the Islamic and Kurdish actors allied themselves with the pro–European Union forces as the only option to contain the military and rid the state of its governing ideology.

Implications of the Coup: Europeanization and the Division of the MGH

Although its impact on different identity movements varied, the coup shrank public spaces, politicized the legal system, reduced the concept of what is political to management by the elite, and institutionalized the politics of fear. Nevertheless, the coup failed to eliminate political Islam from the Parliament. Yet it used the legal system and the media to divide political Islam and successfully regimented it in accordance with the needs of Kemalist doctrine. After the closure of the RP, the party elite failed to capitalize on this opportunity to redefine and reinvent the party and rather meekly preferred to surrender to the forces of Kemalist authoritarianism.[38] The RP's successor, the newly incarnated FP, became not an agent of change but rather a subject of change. The fear of being closed down again was the main context for the FP's politics, forcing it not to engage in politics but rather to become, ironically, in a sense an apolitical party. Recai Kutan, the FP leader, adopted a conciliatory tone toward the military. He acknowledged that the Turkish armed forces are an integral part of the Turkish nation and that the FP would address constructively the issues that are of concern to the military establishment. The FP distanced itself from the radicalism of Erbakan to demonstrate to the generals that Islamic politics no longer threaten Turkey's secularism.

In the 1990s, the attitude of political Islam toward the West in general, and the EU in particular, changed.[39] This discursive shift from the West as *the* foe of political Islamic identity to a friend is an outcome of a number of factors. The closure of the RP, systematic oppression of Islamic presence in the public sphere, and the establishment of the FP created an opportunity for the MGH to redefine itself in terms of global discourses of human rights, democracy, the rule of law and become the main advocate of Turkey's integration with the EU.[40] Some writers construe this shift as a survival attitude under the military, legal, and economic pressures to form an alliance with liberal groups.[41] More critical analysis, however, reveals four facts that prompted the Islamic groups to support Turkey's full integration into the EU: the rise of a new bourgeoisie from Anatolia with economically liberal and socially religious values; the belief that religious freedoms in Turkey would be protected better under the EU than under the Turkish constitution as interpreted by the CC and the military; the European National Outlook Movement's encouragement of Turkey's integration into the EU;[42] and the increasing influence of a new generation of Muslim politicians and intellectuals. Moreover, political conditions forced the FP to reconsider modernity, democracy, and multiculturalism as universal values rather than to treat these values as an extension of European domination. Indeed, the MGH leadership was responding to the new popular public discourse by advocating Turkey's integration with the EU.[43] Changed Muslim public opinion about Europe prompted the MGH leadership to make its own shift. The public realized that, to reduce the influence of the military and to establish a democratic state in Turkey, the European option had become the *only* option. In effect, the 1997 coup helped the MGH to rediscover Europe as a repository of democracy and human rights and to discard the long-held Islamist idea of Europe as a source of Kemalist authoritarianism.

The transformation of the FP's ideas about Europe did not prevent a Kemalist fundamentalist attack on its policies or members. For example, when Merve Kavakçı, who was elected to Parliament as an FP candidate in the April 1999 elections, attempted to take her oath of office wearing a headscarf, she was not allowed to do so; hundreds of secularist parliamentarians demanded her expulsion.[44] President Demirel accused Kavakçı of being an "agent provocateur working for radical Islamic states," and the chief prosecutor opened a case against the FP at the CC on May 7, 1999.[45] Since Kemalist state ideology criminalized all forms of identity claims, Kavakçı was presented first as the "other." She then was portrayed not as a woman but as a militant, not as a politician but as a member of HAMAS, and even not as a Muslim but merely as an ideological symbol. This criminalization of opposition became the politics of the Turkish state in the late 1990s. The chief public prosecutor accused the "FP of being vampires touring the country and gorging on ignorance."[46] He argued that "the FP has become the extension of a banned political party [the RP] and also is becoming a focal point for criminal activity against secularism."[47]

Despite the hysteria of the prosecutor's charges, the link between the RP and the FP was real. In fact, the FP was under the indirect control of Erbakan, who ran its everyday affairs through Kutan and Oğuzhan Asiltürk. This control angered the younger members of the party and turned into a rebellion. The reformist wing of the FP displayed its growing power at the first FP Convention on May 14, 2000. Even though its leader, Abdullah Gül, lost the party leadership to Kutan, the narrow margin of the conservative victory demonstrated that a pro-reform movement within the FP was fermenting. Meanwhile, the CC closed the FP on grounds that it had become the "center of antisecular activities."[48] Following the CC decision, the MGH split into two different parties. The conservative faction of the FP, under Kutan, founded the SP in July 2001.[49] More moderate leaders formed the Justice and Development Party (AKP: Adalet ve Kalkınma Partisi) in August 2001, thereby cementing the division in the Islamic movement.

The AKP has managed to redefine itself not as a "splinter group" of MGH but rather a dynamic force to incorporate center-right voters by stressing its socially conservative Muslim-Turkish and economically liberal project. The three prominent actors of the AKP, Erdoğan, Gül, and Arınç, all came from the nationalist background and were influenced by the writings of Necip Fazıl, Sezai Karakoç, and Rasim Özdenören. Moreover, there are prominent Nakşibendi intellectuals in the AKP, such as İrfan Gündüz of the Erenköy Nakşibendi order. The charisma of Erdoğan, his lifestyle, and his role as a generational bridge between younger and older voters make the AKP a party with potentially broad appeal. Nevertheless, the political future of Turkey will not be determined by how well the AKP or any other parties do at the ballot boxes but rather by a compromise between Kemalism and democracy.

The Politics of Fear: The Rise of the Nationalist Action Party (MHP)

After the resignation of Erbakan in 1997, a new coalition government was formed with Yılmaz as prime minister and Ecevit as deputy prime minister. The government's goal was to implement the 18 directives of the military. Many conservative and religious deputies from the center-right parties refused to support the necessary changes. Yılmaz only managed to implement the education "reform," which raised compulsory secular education from five to eight years; the goal was to cripple the İmam Hatip schools. The coalition government soon came under attack because of Yılmaz's close ties to underworld-linked businessmen bidding for state contracts. A vote of no confidence ended Yılmaz's government in November 1998. President Demirel nominated Ecevit, who had full military support, to be prime minister. Other party leaders, such as Yılmaz and Çiller, supported Ecevit's minority government, which had the task of preparing the country for elections in April 1999 (see table 10.1).

The major result of the April 1999 general elections was the serious erosion of the political center, a development that had grave implications for efforts to institutionalize Turkey's already weak democratic process.[50] The two parties that emerged with the largest number of votes from the general elections, the DSP led by Ecevit and the MHP led by Devlet Bahçeli, both espoused a militant and particularistic version of nationalism that is hostile to Turkey's diverse ethnic and religious groups. By making stunning gains in central and western Anatolia, these nationalist parties won a combined total of 40 percent of the popular vote, became the two largest blocs in the parliament, and joined to form a coalition government.[51] The DSP was created by Ecevit, but it is not so much a mass party as one dependent on his personal popularity and character.

The success of the MHP, in contrast, is much more significant because it is a long-established party with branches throughout the country. Yet prior to 1999, the MHP had not been able to attract more than a small fraction of the vote (see table 10.1). How was it possible for this inexperienced party to double its share of the vote to 18 percent of the electorate? Various explanations have been offered for this phenomenon;[52] the most likely is that the MHP's rising status is an outcome of the securitization of Kurdish and Islamic identity claims that further polarized the society. There are three discursive political parameters of the MHP: the state, the homeland, and the nation.[53] Since the state is necessary to protect the homeland, the nation should be in the service of the state. This authoritarian political culture does not assign any value to human rights and cannot facilitate a consolidation of democracy. Rather, it institutionalizes politics as a way of identifying the "friends and enemies" of the state and nation and calls on its Idealists (*ülkücü*) to sacrifice. The party defines the object and parameters of politics by the security concerns of the Turkish state. The MHP always sides with the state when there is any tension between state and society. Hence its parliamentarians are more likely to function as representatives of the state rather than civil society. In this ideology, Turkish identity is closely tied to the state and, in fact, cannot be separated from it. The state has become the engine of political change. It is recognized as a legitimate institution that controls the destiny of its citizens. Because of the MHP's statism, the military regards the MHP as a reliable and safe mechanism for maintaining the status quo.

The military's grip on society tightened, particularly after its February 28 directives undermined the rule of law and weakened political freedoms. Major social, political, and economic problems have been reduced to security issues; and the Turkish military, the self-appointed guardians of the Kemalist ideology, is intent on employing exceptional measures to cope with them. The securitization of the political landscape in Turkey, therefore, led to the politicization of the judicial system in dealing with the "existential threats" of competing identity claims by the Kurds and Islamists. The nationalistic revival is in good part a response to the military pressure to ensure control over domestic and foreign policy. The rise of nationalistic politics, both Kurdish and Turkish, and the securitization of the political landscape are mutually reinforcing. The results of the 1999 national elections did not remove the shadow of the Turkish military but rather has it looming ever larger over the new coalition governments.

The outcome of the April 1999 elections can be viewed as the institutionalization of the politics of fear. The military, with the help of the major media cartels, successfully "convinced" part of the public of internal threats. This fear translated into the political landscape in the April 1999 general election, resulting in the erosion of the two major center-right parties, the weakening of the FP, and increased support for the two nationalist parties. By concentrating all forces on hammering the pro-Islamic FP, the powerful military prepared the ground for the nationalistic takeover. In portraying the ethnic and religious identity claims as major threats, the NSC institutionalized a new framework for insecurity.

The politics of fear is an instrument to sustain the interests of the state. This process militarized domestic politics by setting the parameters of Turkish politics in terms of evoking nationalism to protect the Turkish state and nation. Largely as a result of the destructive conflict with the PKK, the MHP has managed to reactivate dormant Turkish ethnoreligious nationalism in central Anatolian provinces. As a result of the PKK insurgency, the MHP invented a new farewell ceremony to send soldiers off to southeast Anatolia, and the major connection between the MHP and ordinary people has been through these ceremonies. New soldiers are accompanied by male friends and close relatives, along with a convoy of taxies or minibuses, from their homes to the central bus stations. On the way, vehicle windows are opened, nationalistic songs are played, and horns are tooted. The people carry the party emblem of the MHP, the three-star flag, with the Turkish flag. On arrival at the bus station, the group plays two common Turkish musical instruments, the drum and pipe, to raise nationalistic emotions, the young men perform folk dances, and the new soldier is tossed into the air and caught by his male friends. These new ceremonies have turned Turkey's bus stations into centers of anti-PKK Turkish nationalism and have helped to establish MHP's place within the new Turkish identity.

Since military service is mandatory in Turkey, many men along with their families have been affected deeply by the Kurdish problem since 1984. The Ministry of Defense usually sends new conscripts to regions distant from their homes as part of its policy to increase national integration. For instance, soldiers born in central and eastern Anatolia usually are sent to the southeast, while those born in the southeast are sent to western parts of the country. Therefore, most of the soldiers who have been killed in the conflict with the PKK hail from central and eastern Anatolia. Their experience in the southeast, in turn, has led young men to search for security and authority, and the MHP has made large voting gains in the provinces of central and eastern Anatolia.[54] In the southern provinces with mixed Kurdish and Turkish populations and where there exists major tension between the Turks and Kurds, the MHP has also made major gains. Terrorist incidents, such as the bombing of the Blue Shopping Mall on March 13, 1999, in Istanbul, which resulted in the deaths of 13 people, also played a key role in the transformation of public opinion toward favoring the MHP's militant answer to the question of security.

In most of the provinces where the MHP became number one, the FP followed in second position. One might interpret this as nationalism assuming a primary role over Islam as the main source of political identification in the Turkish Anatolian heartland. However, in central Anatolia the relationship between Islam and Turkish nationalism is one not of contradiction and conflict but rather of mutual enhancement. These are the most conservative provinces, and both Islam and Turkism mark the political culture of this region. Moreover, the MHP's "macho" and state security–aligned image has also played a role in increasing support for the desired defense of a Turkish-Islamic lifestyle under severe threat from the Kemalist establishment. Many people believed that the

MHP could resolve the headscarf issue and send the military back to the barracks by removing the strict need for "national unity and security" from the purview of the military.

Many people did not vote for the FP because of its tension with the military and instead opted for the nationalist movement, which has a powerful religious component. The MHP undermined FP support by stressing constantly that even if the FP were elected, it would not be allowed to come into power. This message inclined some conservative Muslims to regard the FP as a party of "risk" and tension and therefore to switch their votes.[55] The MHP also presented itself as an untried party that deserved a chance, a powerful argument for undecided voters. Despite these attitudes, as well as pressure from the military and the media cartels, the FP did not do badly, capturing 15 percent of the national vote and emerging as the third largest party in parliament; more significantly, it retained control of the major municipalities, including Ankara and Istanbul.[56]

Alevi and Kurdish Identities after February 28, 1997

Since the 1997 coup, the state has been trying to reframe Alevi identity as a source of security for secularism. In furtherance of this project, it has sponsored conferences, opened Bektaşi lodges, promoted publications and movies, and even inaugurated a university center for Alevi studies. The goal is to present the Alevi understanding of Islam (as created by the state) as an authentic Turkish form of Islam.[57] For example, the 1998 budget for the first time allocated 425 billion lira for different Alevi associations. The Alevis are portrayed as the loyal supporters of Mustafa Kemal's secularizing projects, and Hacı Bektaşi Veli is depicted as the Turkish religious leader who used all means to Turkify and Islamicize Anatolia.

In addition to the Alevi community, the Kurdish nationalist movement also has been directly affected by the 1997 coup. The MHP, DSP, and other victorious parties do not operate in the Kurdish-populated southeastern Anatolia. After the arrest of Öcalan, HADEP emerged as the leading Kurdish political organization in Turkey. In January 1999, the public prosecutor asked the CC to ban the party on the basis of organic links with the PKK. Nevertheless, Kurds in the southeast voted heavily for HADEP, which stressed the value of constitutional citizenship, the recognition of Kurdish cultural rights, the consolidation of local governments, land reform for landless peasants, and a regional economic development plan that included a number of free-trade zones with Iran, Iraq, and Syria. However, HADEP failed to obtain any seats in Parliament in the April 1999 elections because it failed to get 10 percent of the total national vote, the threshold required for parliamentary representation. This 10 percent threshold defeats the purpose of proportional representation: the inclusion of all viable political entities in government. The people of this region, therefore, are denied national representation. The Turkish government imposes taxes in the region and expects loyalty without representation. HADEP secured key mayoral posts in the southeastern cities of Batman, Bingöl, Hakkari, Siirt, and Şırnak and the regional capital of Diyarbakır.

Since the military had the full support of Israel and the United States in ousting the Erbakan government, it decided to capitalize on this international support and pursue an assertive policy against Syria and the PKK. On September 16, 1998, the army commander, General Atilla Ateş, on an inspection tour of the Syrian border, warned that

> some of our neighbors, especially Syria, are misinterpreting our efforts and goodwill for having good ties. By supporting the bandit Abdullah Öcalan, the fugitive head of the PKK, they have helped plunge Turkey into the turmoil of terrorism . . . our patience is exhausted.[58]

In response to Turkey's determined position, the Syrian government forced Öcalan to leave for Moscow. From there he took refugee in Rome, and eventually the Turkish military brought him to Turkey from Nairobi, Kenya, on February 16, 1999. During his trial, Öcalan offered "to serve the Turkish state" and declared that "the democratic option . . . is the only alternative in solving the Kurdish question. Separation is neither possible nor necessary."[59] He praised Atatürk's attempt to create a secular and European state and sharply criticized "the Sheik Said uprising of 1925 and the traditional tribal system which promoted often despotic *ağas* [landlords]." Nevertheless, the court found Öcalan guilty of separatist treason and sentenced him to death. The Court of Appeals upheld his sentence on November 25, 1999.His lawyers took the case to the European Court of Human Rights (ECHR), to which Turkey belongs; the ECHR issued an interim measure asking Ankara to suspend the execution until it could rule on the appeal. The Turkish government agreed to wait for the final decision of that court.

The EU as a Disciplining Act—The New Hope: EU Membership

The Helsinki EU summit on December 10–11, 1999, declared that Turkey "is a candidate state destined to join the Union on the basis of the same [Copenhagen] criteria as applied to the other candidate states." At the EU summit in Copenhagen in 1993, the EU set broad political and economic standards for those countries wanting to join the Union. Those criteria require full implementation of democracy, human rights, the rule of law, and the protection of minorities. On the basis of the Copenhagen criteria, the EU asked Ankara to reform its legal system and to solve the Kurdish problem by peaceful means. This represented a turning point in Turco-EU ties, and it has created an optimistic environment to end the tragic conflict that has involved 30,000 deaths and a cost of more than $100 billion. On October 4, 2001, the Turkish Parliament adopted 34 constitutional amendments that lifted a ban on using "forbidden" languages to voice opinions and liberalize restrictions that had hindered the formation of voluntary associations. Subsequently, in August 2002, Parliament enacted new legislation that further expanded legal opportunity spaces. For example, one of the new laws authorizes the use of Kurdish for broadcasting and publishing material in their mother tongue. For the Kurds, as for the Islamic groups, full support of Turkey's entry into the EU is seen as a way to guarantee basic human rights. However, the military and the Turkish nationalists perceive freedom of expression and the recognition of Kurdish cultural rights as the process of weakening the "unitary state" structure and the nation-building ideology of Kemalism.

Turkey's political landscape increasingly is being restructured around new ideas about Europe and the resulting political cleavages. For instance, after the 1997 coup, the anti-EU military bureaucratic Kemalism divorced itself from the pro-EU Kemalism that defined Kemalism as a process of joining the EU. In other words, nation-state–oriented Kemalism has been in conflict with the globalization-oriented democratic version of Kemalism. After 1997, the military Kemalism began to divorce itself from the West and its own Westernization project. This shift from viewing the West as a trendsetter to imitate to seeing it as a hostile "enemy" to fight against has created an opposite effect on the Islamic movements. As some Kemalists are redefining the West as a negative force to be avoided, the Islamic groups are in the process of rediscovering Europe as a positive force and have been defending Turkey's full integration into the EU. What this transformation means is that Kemalism has become an ideology to insulate the state from democratic inroads. The major revolution in contemporary Turkey has been the cognitive transformation of the image of the West and Westernization. In contemporary Turkey, the new sociopolitical cleavages are shaped by what position one adopts on the EU and the 1997 coup. Those who support the 1997 coup and reject the EU constitute a very small group of nationalist and hardcore Kemalist intellectuals. The majority of the population supports Turkey's entry into the EU and rejects the 1997 coup.

The AKP utilized the winds of democratization blowing from the EU and helped to create hope for the implementation of democracy in Turkey. The goal of becoming a member of the EU and the obligations that came with it constrained the establishment's campaign against Muslim-oriented sociopolitical movements because official Kemalism's very *raison d'être* of Europeanizing Turkey had become intertwined with EU membership and its requirement of respecting human rights and democratic norms. Furthermore, the EU's critical reports about Turkey's domestic politics not only helped to pressure the elite but also informed the Turkish public about the serious shortcomings of Turkish semidemocracy and identified the "dual-track government" as the obstacle blocking Turkey's path to both genuine democratization and eventual EU membership.

In the 1990s, overwhelming popular support for EU membership even among radical Islamic groups critical of the Kemalist legacy also is directly a result of the popular perception that the "carrot" and "stick" of potential EU membership was proving to be the most persuasive mechanism for pressuring the Kemalist military-bureaucratic establishment toward reform. Especially critical was EU pressure to end the "dual-track government" system whereby the elected government must be subordinated to the prescribed Kemalist secularism and Turkish nationalism as defined and enforced by the military-dominated NSC. The AKP thus capitalized on EU pressure to curtail the "dual-track government" in the 2002 elections. Voters outside of the official establishment legitimated their claims of rights and recognition of identity by framing their demand in terms of the broader European discourse of human rights. However, one must be careful not to place too much emphasis on the electoral rise and fall of the Islamic parties, because doing so ignores the widespread and deep crossfertilization of Islamic and European ideas and practices in the everyday life of Turkey. The Islamic movement represents only one sector of such activities, but it is important to realize that it has changed the national agenda, introduced an index of being modern in an Islamic way, and brought Islamic ethics to the public sphere.

The AKP's Dual Electoral Revolution: Earthquake and Restoration

The 2002 election represents a historical break in terms of providing to a socially Muslim party an opportunity to restructure the political landscape and expand the public sphere. Among the 18 parties that competed for seats in Parliament, only two actually won seats because a party is required to obtain 10 percent of the nationwide vote to be able to send representative(s) to Parliament. The AKP came in first by winning 34.26 percent of the popular vote and 363 of the 550 seats in Parliament. The CHP also mustered almost 19.40 percent of the votes and 178 seats. Independent candidates won other nine seats. The election result represented a popular repudiation of the authoritarian political establishment. A large plurality of voters believed in AKP, or at least were willing to take a risk for broader political change. The elections swept away a generation of established politicians, giving the AKP a majority of seats and the right to form a government on its own. One also may see this election as a restoration of an Islamic movement that was forced out of power in the 1997 coup. Thus the elections significantly transformed the political establishment and brought the AKP to power with a clear mandate to redefine the political center in terms of societal values. In fact, a majority of the electorate was searching for a new social contract based on the global discourses of democracy, human rights, and social justice, the underlying ethical principles of such a contract.

The 2002 election thus was not about establishing an Islamic state or instituting Islamic law but rather about redrawing the boundary between the state and society, consolidating civil society, and reconstituting everyday life in terms of a shared vision of "the good life." A majority of voters hoped to create a morally justifiable modern and participatory life in which civil society is in charge of its own fate. The excluded and marginalized sectors of society, along with those who hope to expand opportunity spaces, want their leaders to make political decisions that inherently share their moral language referring to the meaning of the good life. The Muslim idea of an inner self that is capable of initiating resistance and generating imaginative dissent from social practices provides religious sanctions for civil values. Despite the inroads of Kemalist secularism, there is still a strong connection between Islam and an ethical ethos that informs everyday life in Turkey. Over time, a close affinity has developed between certain values and certain interests, and these class locations must be taken into account in the examination of the election results.

In the transformation of the Islamic movement in general, and the electoral victory of the AKP in particular, a "new" urban class, consisting of horizontally connected solidarity-based groups with rural origins and shared Islamic ethos, played an important role. This "new" urban class has been excluded culturally and economically by the Kemalist elite. The excluded segment of the population utilized Islamic idioms and networks to overcome their exclusion. Thus Islamic networks both facilitated this group's integration into modern opportunity spaces and offered it a hope for social mobilization.

Sociologically, the AKP appears to engage people of very diverse backgrounds, from teachers, policemen, vendors, traders, and new Muslim intellectuals to humble shopkeepers and businessmen. The AKP, however, was only formed in August 2001. Thus it was not so much the AKP that utilized traditional solidarity networks in neighborhoods to mobilize voters; rather, these religiously inspired networks mobilized themselves to redefine the political center of Turkish politics in terms of their values. In short, this is a bottom-up political change in which civil society wants to expand the boundaries of the public sphere and make the political instittutions representative of the people rather than of the official state establishment. The AKP utilized culturally rooted grassroots networks, personalities, and cultural frames to project itself as the party of a 99 percent Muslim electorate in a country where most support groups are inspired by religion yet are infused with the discourse of secularism and Westernism that has developed as a result of 80 years of Turkish experimentation. Furthermore, almost all Islamic groups offer some form of community service, making such activity more common than prayer groups. These religious groups act as the social base of Islamic identity and have very strong commitments to social justice and direct participation in communal outreach programs. The AKP became the favored party of these networks, and this translated into political support.

The electoral cleavage is determined by the normative value conflict between the secularist bureaucratic center and the Muslim values that constitute the societal center. As this book has shown, the history of modern Turkey is the story of the struggle between the values of the Kemalist state and the values of a Muslim society. In Turkey, the political center and the social center do not necessarily overlap and often have been in constant conflict. Elections can be attempts by society to socialize the political center in terms of its values and norms and to redefine the boundaries of the state to open more space for societal participation and values. Islamic groups can use electoral processes to create new political compasses in accordance with its values and to redraw the boundary between the state and civil society. This is what happened in the November 2002 elections. The elections created a new actor with the mandate to restructure the state-society boundary. The people want the state to become the servant of society rather than an arrogant "headmaster" that dictates orders. This cognitive shift of seeing the state as a servant of society and not a "headmaster" was started, in actual practice, during the Özal era.

Who among so many Turkish citizens voted for the AKP, and why? In order to understand what they voted "for," it is necessary to clarify what they voted "against." They voted against the "center-right" parties, the ANAP and the DYP, and the two nationalist parties (MHP and DSP). The AKP received votes from former supporters of the FP, the MHP, and the ANAP. Thus nationalist (Turkish), conservative (Muslim), and economically liberal voters voted for the AKP. The major flow of votes, in contrast to the 1999 election, came from the following parties: RP/FP (69 percent), MHP (29 percent), and ANAP (29 percent). Moreover, 29 percent of new voters also voted for the AKP. The center-right parties had been based on the balance between the state and society. Since the 1997 coup, however, this balance has been lost at the expense of civil society. By attacking the Sufi orders and Islamic networks, the coup eroded the social bases of the center-right parties. This in turn delegitimized the center-right parties, and they became simply agents of an oppressive state. The voters sought to recreate a new political center according to their social needs rather than the needs of the state. They voted "for" the AKP because of political, economic, and social reasons. For many, the AKP represents another attempt to retrieve the pioneering legacy of Özal in expanding the public sphere and bringing a shared code of moral values into the public sphere and in his efforts to close the chasm separating the Turkish state from the majority of Turkish society. It could economically expand opportunity spaces in order to create more jobs to restore the social peace and integrate Turkey into the EU.

One also needs to appreciate Erdoğan's identification and constant appeal to Özal's policies as a way for society to reactivate Özal's legacy and utilize it to promote his new policies. Erdoğan was the only leader who identified himself with the spirit of Menderes in the 1950s and Özal of the 1980s. Invoking Özal's legacy had a powerful resonance, since Özal had been successful in creating an index of modern lifestyles in which Islam was the lexicon from which coding and legitimization took place. Thus there was a model of public policy demonstrating the compatibility of worldly success and spiritual values by redefining Islamic identity. Many Sunni-Muslim Turks who voted for the AKP voted for the restoration of the Özal era (see chapter 4). In this way, the election was very much an act of restoration rather than a "political earthquake." Erdoğan's Özal-like reformist message resonated with certain segments of the population who believe in the expansion of opportunity spaces.

Özal initiated economic, social, and political liberalization, focused on the boundary separating the state and civil society, and used opportunities to empower civil society vis-à-vis the state. Özal carried out a peaceful revolution of opening opportunity spaces for the excluded (dışlanmış) sectors of Turkey's population. Since his untimely death in 1993, the process of liberalization not only has been interrupted but also was reversed by the February 1997 process. Moreover, the "dual-track government" expanded its power at the expense of the elected government. The military, along with the judiciary, used all available means to criminalize the opposition. Because of these developments, many Muslims witnessed the erosion of their rights and freedoms and the reduction of opportunity spaces by the establishment: the coalition of corrupt politicians, the media, businessmen, and some power-hungry generals. In August 2001, Mesut Yılmaz, then a deputy prime minister, boldly said that the military had orchestrated a so-called national security syndrome that was responsible for the slow progress of democratization and integration with the EU. The military responded to Yılmaz's "unfortunate speech" by issuing a sharp statement, noting that it was not the "national security concept" but "those [i.e., politicians] who did not fulfill their responsibilities or those who gave priority to personal gains rather than political stability in the face of such pressing issues as economic bankruptcy and widespread corrupt activities who were to blame."[60] The Ecevit government was ineffective, and consequently the political spaces gradually shrank so that all major decisions were made by the state bureaucracy in the name of the state and much of society was excluded from the political process.

The Nationalization and Westernization of Islamism

Although the electoral cleavages in Turkey are usually examined in terms either of the center-periphery framework or as merely being a religious protest vote against failed government policies, the AKP victory is a sign of the constitution of a new social center and the socialization of the political center with the new hybrid ideas of nationalism, Islam, and Westernism. There is a dominant tendency among Turkish scholars to treat the vote for Islamic parties as a protest vote. However, this approach ignores the "constructive" aspect of Turkish voting behavior. Many people voted for the AKP because they were unemployed, hungry, and marginalized and excluded from almost all economic and political processes. However, they also voted to reconstruct a new center of politics. Erdoğan is just one of those who was excluded and marginalized by the establishment. But as the state tried to exclude Erdoğan, his popularity increased and he became the symbol of the marginalized (*mazlum*, "persecuted"). His treatment cast him as the Nelson Mandela of Turkey's excluded majority. Given the evolution of the MGH since 1994, one can see the political transformation of political Islam, in general, and Erdoğan in particular. A self-made man, who sold lemonade as a boy to support his family, Erdoğan possesses working-class values and has enough pragmatism to keep an open mind when it comes to politics. However, like other political players who have graced the Turkish political landscape, he views himself as the embodiment of the party, a sultan and not just a member. In this respect, Erdoğan may make the same mistakes as Erbakan.

In addition to the leadership, the AKP includes a new generation of Muslim politicians, such as Hüseyin Çelik, Ömer Çelik, Abdullah Gül, Akif Gül, Murat Mercan, and Abdullatif Şener, who have risen to prominence because of the expansion of education and the media. They have university educations and have been exposed to new ways of accessing and using knowledge in the political market of ideas. This generation of Muslim politicians has been more exposed than previous ones to European ideas and also has a sense of clearly defined Islamic identity. They know how to promote their ideas in the competitive market of ideas and ideologies in Turkey. Although this competitive market of ideas has led some of them to view Islam as an objective system and a separate civilization, this objectification of Islam has remained transitional and has gradually been replaced with mixed ideas and the recognition that Turkey belongs to a complex world where modernity and tradition overlap. Since the majority of parliamentarians elected in 2002 have local political experience and are versed in global discourses of human rights and democracy as well, they represent the connection between the local and global. Their language is not one of exclusion but rather an inclusive blending and syncretism of the local and global.

In addition to its leader and a group of recognized Islamically oriented politicians in the AKP, the hybrid identity of the party also played an important role in its electoral success. The AKP's identity and ideology resembles a fabric that changes color depending on the light. This eclectic aspect of the party is the reason for its broad appeal. It is simultaneously Turkish, Muslim, and Western. This pluralist aspect is also very much a political necessity, given the diverse lifestyles in the country. It seeks to provide a framework of civic peace in which various groups can live together. The AKP's Islamism has a very heavy Turkish accent, rooted in the Turko-Ottoman ethos of communal life and a sense of leadership that requires full obedience to the party ruler, Erdoğan. Regionally, the RP was successful in Kurdish and Turkish areas of central and eastern Anatolia from 1987 to the 1999 election. That election clearly represented the autonomization of Kurdish nationalism from the MGH. In the 2002 election, Islamic identity was not a space in-between identities or a shared worldview that blended ethnic identities under the reformist leadership of the MGH but rather represented the nationalization of Islamism as Turkish Islam and the ethnicization of the Kurdish identity. The Kurdish ethnic party, the Democratic People's Party (DEHAP: Demokratik Halk Partisi), emerged the number one party in the 12 Kurdish provinces. This indicates the developing degree of autonomization of Kurdish nationalism from Islamism. This is not to say that Kurds will be unrepresented in Parliament. Because of the electoral structure, Kurds will be represented by Kurdish members of the AKP (Abdulkadir Aksu, a prominent Kurdish politician from Diyarbakır, appointed as the minister of the interior) and the CHP, although these were not the parties that Kurds voted for overwhelmingly. This could have major repercussions in the future, depending on how the AKP capitalizes on its electoral victory and how Kurds are represented within the new government.

The AKP emerged the number one party in Sunni Muslim and Turkish nationalist provinces. However, the AKP's nationalism, unlike that of the MHP, is not a state-driven, secularist, ethnolinguistic one but rather an ethnoreligious and society-centric nationalism. Ethnic and religious identity, for the AKP, are codeterminant. Indeed, the boundary between Turkish nationalism and

Islamism in central Anatolia is fluid, supporters share the same symbolic worldview, and transition between the two groups is very common. The boundary between "us" and "them," for the AKP, is defined in religious terms. Turkishness also is defined in terms of religion and "we" the "Turkish Muslims" who serve God and society and "they" who serve Atatürk and the state. In the electoral success of the AKP, Turkism and Islamism were conflated. For instance, the heartland of Turkish Islam, in such cities as Erzurum, Kayseri, and Konya, overwhelmingly voted for the AKP. Thus the normative base of the AKP consists of a Turkish-Islamic synthesis within new global discourses of human rights and democracy. The 2002 elections represent the nationalization (Turkification) and Westernization of Islamism in Turkey.

The AKP's understanding of Europe and stress on Turkey's membership in the EU is an outcome of its "Western" layer of identity. It is "Western" in terms of stressing human rights, the rule of law, economic liberalism, and respect for popular will as the guiding principles of public policy. Its Westernism differs from the Kemalist Westernism in that it stresses bottom-up modernization and respect for the popular will and recognizes civil society autonomous from the state. This is the direct opposite of the ossified Kemalism that exists in Turkey today. The AKP's understanding of secularism is not "negative" but rather a "positive" one. It attempts to rearticulate the Ottoman Islamic ethos as the spirit of tolerance, accommodation, and coexistence of faiths, cultures, and ideas. This modernist and Western-influenced Islam has also appealed to many secularized, urban, and well-to-do Turks who have felt that the party could provide a much-needed corrective to the prevailing corrupt and authoritarian political structure.

The Tension between State and Society

The secularist Kemalist establishment, even though it has limited mass appeal, enjoys the full support of the military and judiciary as it guides public policy. There will be a number of areas where the AKP will conflict with the military. The key question is how much the Turkish state is prepared to accommodate this dynamic new political Islam. After a century of struggle between the secular state and Muslim society, a reasonable compromise is a possibility within the framework of integration with the EU. The AKP's experiment with democracy reveals the failure of an authoritarian secularism that is informed by crude orientalist conceptions, like those of Bernard Lewis, that posit Islam as inherently opposed to democracy, pluralism, and modernity. Ironically, for many decades the main obstacle to full democratization in Turkey has not been Islam but rather the authoritarian secular ideology of an oppressive state elite, which found many apologists in Western circles.

Erdoğan's goal is to change this equation:

> My story is the story of this nation. Either this nation is going to win
> and come to power or the arrogant and oppressive minority group,
> who look at Anatolia with contempt and are alien to Anatolian

realities, will continue to remain in power. The nation has the
authority to decide. Enough, sovereignty belongs to the nation.[61]

Even though the AKP won 34.26 percent of the popular vote, it may not be able
to transform the system. The AKP government is expected to consolidate democracy, address the demands for recognition of Kurds and Alevis, and improve
the economy. The government wants to address the first two issues, which directly concern military-civilian relations and the redefinition of Kemalist concepts of nation and secularism, through the Copenhagen criteria. I am cautious
about the AKP's ability to redefine state–civil society relations and transform
state institutions. One of the reasons for this caution has to do with the search
for legitimacy. If the Kemalist establishment (the military-civilian bureaucracy)
continues to question the legitimacy of the AKP government, the AKP might
opt for an "American and European protective umbrella" vis-à-vis the state. This
dependence on "foreign powers" will undermine AKP's popular legitimacy and
will further make it a hostage to very unpopular U.S. pressure to use Turkey
only as a military base against neighboring Muslim countries. Erdoğan wants
to expand his legitimacy vis-à-vis the Turkish state by gaining acceptance in Europe; even before the opening of the Turkish Parliament, he visited Italy to campaign for Turkey's membership in the EU and also draw legitimacy for his
leadership. This search for legitimacy in Europe is a central strategy of the AKP
government to both gain legitimation vis-à-vis the Turkish state and Western
countries and to be a central pillar for far-reaching democratic reforms in the
Turkish political system. Moreover, given its syncretic identity and the fact that
it is a coalition of diverse groups with different demands, the AKP is having
difficulty harmonizing competing identities and interests. However, the party
is playing a significant role in terms of integrating excluded sectors of the population into new opportunity spaces, and this in turn will further lead to the
internal secularization of Islam. As Islam continues to become a part of modern opportunity spaces, it will go through a major secularization. Through
Islamic idioms and practices, modernity and the ideas of the European Enlightenment will be disseminated into the deeper layers of the Turkish cognitive map, and this will result in the revision of key Islamic principles in terms
of the global discourses of human rights and democratization. For instance,
one of the symbolic areas of confrontation between the secularist state and
Islamic movements is the question of headscarves. The AKP's ability to expand the public sphere and allow universal, national, and religious ideas and
lifestyles (such as the headscarf) to compete and fertilize each other would
help to constitute Islamic modernities. The Islamic movement in Turkey does
not want to assimilate to a Eurocentric modernity that denies difference but
stresses its own difference in terms of Islamic symbols and practices. The AKP
government empowers and promotes the return of Muslim actors with Islamic
ethics to the public sphere. These new actors of the "urban class" stress their
difference as Muslims in terms of new ways of living, consumer patterns,
music, and poetry, and they seek to objectify their Islam in modern means.

These new Islamically shaped public spheres and actors cannot be reduced to representing antimodernist or antiglobalist reaction but rather are products of these new social forces. A new, hybrid, national, Islamic, modern identity and roles are under construction.

Conclusion

The 1997 coup reminded society that it is not the owner of the state but rather that, in the Kemalist view, the state is the real owner of society. The entire Turkish constitutional system is based on protecting the state and imposing a specific lifestyle on society. Demirel, then president, argued that the 1997 coup originated in the "proclamation of the Republic" and added that this process "will continue."[62] Indeed, exclusion and persecution in the name of creating a secular nation-state has been the source of Turkey's numerous fault lines and constant instability. The 1997 coup sought to cleanse the Islamic presence from the public spaces of economy, education, the media and politics. In its anti-leftist campaign, the state had used Sunni Islam as a Turkish-Islamic synthesis after the 1980 coup, and in 1997 it used the Alevi community against Sunni political Islam. However, the 1997 coup brought forward a questioning of the army's role more than the 1961 and 1980 coups. In particular, many conservative Muslim Turks, who constituted the traditional backbone of the military and militarism, started to question the legitimacy of the army. These groups used to think of the army as the "hearth of the Prophet" (*Peygamber Ocağı*). Their questioning has been very positive in the long run in terms of challenging the guardian role of the military, strengthening civil society, and emphasizing the significance of human rights. Islamic groups all supported Turkey's entry into the EU as a way of controlling the excesses of the Kemalist army. The major impact of the 1997 coup was the Islamic rediscovery of Europe as a space and an idea to protect human rights and the rule of law. In other words, many conservative Muslims recognized that Europe was more liberal than a Turkish society regulated by the rigid military doctrine.

At the core of the contemporary crisis in Turkey lies the official state ideology, Kemalism. Kemalism does not see social, cultural, and political difference as an integral part of democracy but rather treats sociopolitical "difference" as a source of instability and a threat to national unity. The current ethnic (Kurdish) and religious (Sunni Islamic and Alevi) movements seek to redefine themselves as "Muslims," "Kurds," and "Alevis" through the means provided by globalization. These identity- and justice-seeking social movements are in direct conflict with the Kemalist project.

Turkey needs a new social contract. The realization that coexistence depends on shared rules and the recognition of differences helped to transform the Turkish citizenry's conception of Turkey from being the "home" of a specific group, particularly Sunni Turks, to being a "hotel" in which each group has its own room and they all have to create the shared rules of coexistence. Consequently, a deep search has developed for a new social contract in Turkey, with the EU being viewed as the facilitator of this new social contract. The founding principles of this contract should include secularism, the rule of law, and recognition of the multicultural nature of Turkey. Both Kurds and Turks and both secularists and Islamic groups need to be involved in this search for a new social contract.

I

Conclusion

Since 1923, Kemalism has sought to modernize society and to defend and consolidate the state. The Kemalist principles of nationalism and secularism succeeded in creating a modern society, but Kemalism as an ideology failed to modernize itself, and consequently it became authoritarian. This is because Kemalism as understood by the military failed to internalize two crucial aspects of modernity: democracy and a fully autonomous civil society. The reason behind this failure is the belief in the primacy of the state over society that is inherent in Kemalism. In effect, the state became more important than its citizens. Thus the state is to be protected against its enemies whether they are foreign or domestic. Especially since 1980, Kemalism has become the "security regime" that produces insecurity for its citizens by transforming itself into an ideology that insulates the state both internally and externally from new ideas and actors. Overall, then, Turkey's experiment of Westernization resulted in the formation of two conflicting sources of legitimacy: on the one hand there is an elected parliament of people's representatives who seek to develop a new social contract; on the other there is a nonelected military-bureaucratic elite that wields ultimate authority on the basis of Kemalism being a Westernizing and progressive ideology. But the history of modern Turkey is the story of conflict between democracy and Kemalism. Democracy brought people to the public space, but their identity claims have been perceived as a threat for the Kemalist system and the army regularly has intervened to eliminate these identity claims and close off opportunity spaces.

The most important identity claims have come from Islamic actors who have felt excluded on account of the Kemalists' excessive preoccupation with secularism as defining "modernity" and Islam as defining "backwardness." But in Turkey the Islamic movements have been neither antimodern nor backward. Rather they are identity and justice-seeking movements. Such movements seek to reclaim the Muslim "self," which is perceived as being robbed of its authenticity and identity. Islamic groups use "new opportunity spaces" where they can develop and experience novel lifestyles and identities. For example, Turkish Muslims utilize the printed page, television screens, and educational institutions to act in concert to rearticulate a new Islamic identity, ethics, and justice. These spaces signify differentiation, contestation, and multiple articulations of "self" and offer frames of reference. The growth of the modern media and the expansion of universal education, instead of weakening the role and influence of Islam, have led to its redefinition as a dynamic form of political and social consciousness.

These identity-oriented Islamic movements of Turkey are interconnected with the processes of political participation and economic liberalization. Indeed, the democratization process and Islamic movements have become so intertwined that it is almost impossible to determine where one begins and the other ends. This study of Islam in Turkey contrasts sharply with traditional studies of Islamic movements—usually focused on topics such as the Islamic Salvation Front in Algeria and the Iranian revolution—that have concluded that Islamically framed political movements constitute an obstacle to political participation. This erroneous conclusion is based on a set of problematic assumptions that religious ideas and institutions are in conflict with reform and compromise.[1] In this study, I have argued that the obstacle to the peaceful transformation of many Muslim societies is not religious movements but rather the lack of political and economic liberalization. Political and economic liberalization of the state and economy would prevent any hegemonic and totalistic views (Islamic or Kemalist) from dominating everyday life. Various Islamic sociopolitical movements are, of course, not only active in Turkey but also map and mark contemporary politics in many Muslim countries, from Bosnia to Malaysia and from Kazakhstan to Nigeria. Issues of social justice and demands for authenticity in terms of cultural and political identity remain the two major concepts around which these movements have evolved. This global phenomenon prompts scholars of comparative politics to ask: Do Islamic movements reveal something about the common conditions of Muslims and the role of religion in politics? By examining the processes of "framing sociopolitical issues," I have indicated that Islam as a repertoire of images and actions helps Muslims to form their conception of a good society and identity. These movements shape them and in turn help to shape the social world they inhabit. Thus Islamic movements become reactionary or radical if the state they operate in is authoritarian and does not allow room for economic liberalization.

The main Islamic social movements studied here shifted from their desire to resist and co-opt the state to more society-centric movements because of the opening of new opportunity spaces, changing state-society relations, and economic and cultural liberalization. These movements, therefore, are productive in that they are redefining and reproducing new social webs of interactions.

Islamic movements in Turkey, Egypt, Lebanon, Jordan, and other Muslim countries are involved in social services. They are providing education facilities, health care, media outlets, housing projects, publishing companies, and finance institutions. One detects a gradual and incremental constitution of society with its own indigenous institutions to fill the void created by the failures of the secular/nationalist state. By examining how social factors impinge on and influence the direction of religious discourses, I demonstrate that religious doctrine (Islam-in-principle) and practices (Islam-in-practice) have been subject to transformation by the changing configuration of state-society relations. Islamic identity therefore must be seen as a terrain of contestation rather than a fixed ideological or behavioral understanding across time and space. Islam as a discursive framework affects the way people reimagine and understand their private lives, and this process has public significance. For example, Muslims evoke Islamic-centered frames of reference to create categories that under some conditions transcend narrower frames such as hometown, regional, and ethnolinguistic loyalties. This evolving frame of reference is evoked to articulate the politics of community and difference.

The Turkish case indicates that in the construction and internalization of contemporary Islamic identity, three forces play a formative role: the legitimacy of the state, the resources of society, and the expanding capitalist market forces. Therefore, without understanding the dynamics of the state and society, one cannot comprehend fully the paradoxical processes of the secularization of religious authority and the rejuvenation of Islam as a political identity. The conception of secularism was defined and structured by the Republican elite within the logic of the state. By suppressing Islam, the state ruptured the formative ties between politics and culture, and this estranged the majority of the population from the state. One of the major political consequences of this was the equation of Islam with tradition and continuity and secularism with antitraditional and progressive forces.

When the state elite's perception of the threat to itself shifted from Islamic groups to communists and Kurdish nationalists, the state started to adopt a new accomodationist policy toward Islamic groups. To cope with societal anarchy and ideological polarization, the state elite promoted an official "Turkish-Islamic" synthesis to consolidate social unity under the direction of state authorities. However, the state's attempt to co-opt Islamic sentiment, coupled with the political and economic liberalization of the Özal era, led to profound societal transformations and allowed hitherto marginalized Nurcu and Sufi Islamic groups to carve out large opportunity spaces for the promotion of their ideas and programs through the novel use of new social networks, print technology, and the electronic mass media.

The state invoked the legacy of both Kemalism and Islam to preserve its authority. The state pursued this policy by increasing the budget of the Directorate of Religious Affairs and by appointing new attachés to Turkish embassies to regulate religious activities of Turks in Central Asia, Europe, and the United States. This Sunni-centered policy of intertwining religious and national identity politicized Alevi communal identity and, less directly, the ethnic consciousness of the Kurds. In the 1970s, the center-right and religious-right government coalitions recruited thousands of new functionaries into the state administration. Most of these people came to Ankara from largely rural and more traditional central Anatolia. This policy was maintained after the military coup in 1980. Since the Alevis were viewed as left-wing, the state remained very cool toward them, and in the process of the purges carried out against the Left, many Alevis were expelled from government and establishment positions.

The main forces that have marked Islamic political discourse in modern Turkey have been a combination of the newly emergent middle classes of traditional Anatolian background and a new genre of Islamic intellectuals who are replacing the traditional role of the state functionaries and ulema and charismatic Sufi leaders in articulating a modernist Islamic discourse to address pressing issues of national identity and state and society relations. The Turkish case indicates that the inclusionary context provided by political pluralism, upward social mobility, and an autonomous civil society creates conditions conducive for the interpenetration and mutual recognition of secular-statist elites and Islamically defined groups. The phenomena of upward social mobility and the widespread use of publishing and the electronic media differentiate Turkish Islamic movements from other Islamic movements in the region. With the help of these opportunity spaces, Turkish Islamic intellectuals for the most part have managed to bring a progressive and pluralist Islamic discourse into the mainstream of Turkish intellectual life. The new Islamic intellectual elite often makes use of Western writers and schools of thought as much as traditional Islamic ones in presenting a more eclectic conception of knowledge and in seeking to critique the implications of modernity and technology.

Within the opportunity spaces of the media and the market, the Islamic groups have managed to undermine the Kemalist ideology by destabilizing the old boundaries between the "modern" Kemalists and the "backward" Muslims. As Turkey has continued to develop politically and economically, such formerly rigid dichotomies have broken down. The spread of universal education, the creation of opportunity spaces through the print and electronic media, and the creation of a new class of Anatolian bourgeoisie have eroded old boundaries, making them permeable and preventing any single ideological construct— Kemalist or Islamic—from dominating the public sphere in Turkey. While new opportunity spaces helped to decrease the division of lifestyles between the Islamists and Kemalists by new Muslim actors' adopting new tastes and participating in consumer culture, the same spaces simultaneously led to the differentiation of separate Islamic groups. Those who "moved up" by being able to lead a more affluent lifestyle had to leave their old Islamic communal spaces and create new ones. Islamic groups are using opportunity spaces in the media, education, and the marketplace to carve a separate identity illustrated by new modes of dress, furniture, cuisine, and architecture. For example, the economically well-off Nakşibendi circle of İskenderpaşa differentiates itself from other Nakşibendi circles by its visibly affluent lifestyle, journals, radio stations, consumer patterns, and economic activities. Thus, the human desire to develop more emotionally attached smaller groupings has become more possible as a result of opportunity spaces, as has the establishment of difference and self-identity.

By opening new bilingual schools, publishing newspapers, and running national television and radio broadcasting stations, Islamic groups not only challenge the secular elites' hegemony over the economic, cultural, and educational spheres but also position themselves to compete with other rivals in the Islamic movement. The newly emerging bourgeoisie has sponsored yet more of the religiously oriented dormitories, educational institutions, and television and radio stations. In other words, the culturally formed and reified boundary between "civilized" secular Turks and "uncivilized" Muslim Turks has been fractured, and new forms of cultural markers are being reproduced within Turkish society.

The printed page and the television screen offer a place in between different groups to formulate a shared code of conduct and an overarching identity. Politics is available not only to all members of society as autonomous citizens but preferably as members of particular identity groups. Islamic groups and secular groups have not created a common code of coexistence; rather, each has declared its segmentary autonomy without recognizing the difference of the other. With the ethnification of the state, public spaces have turned into private spaces, and a particular attempt at forging a Sunni Turkish identity has come to dominate the center. The utilization of print illustrates that economic and political liberalism promotes religious pluralism and this in turn promotes civic pluralism.

Religion still provides, even in advanced industrial societies, a set of practices and beliefs for moral and ethical responsibility and a source of meaning to stabilize human existence in the face of the unknown. The mutually reinforcing relationship between Islam and nationalism in Turkey has attempted to counter centrifugal forces of uneven economic development and growing ethnic separatism. Mary Douglas indicates that modernity did not lead to the waning of religion but rather promoted religious sentiments and ideas. By following Karel Dobbelaere's conceptual classification, one detects the realization of the process of differentiation of political, educational, and scientific institutions from strictly religious ones and a process of internal secularization, that is, the process by which religious ideas and organizations undergo adaptation and evolution to conform to irreligious ideas and practices.[2] Said Nursi, for example, came to explain the existence of God in terms of scientific epistemology.[3] According to Nursi, miracles in the Qur'an are a sign of the direction of scientific discoveries. This is a clear indication of the rationalization of religious dogma. In other words, religion is explained through a positivist epistemology and rationality. The Nurcus, Nakşibendis, and newly emerging merchants have been instrumental in this internal secularization of Islam.

The first part of this study indicated that the context has defined the nature of Islamic political discourse. The two chapters on state and society implicitly demonstrate that the Turkish nation is constructed by the state, and, even as the state attacked the religious context of the millet, it kept its spirit in forging a modern

Turkish nation. At the grassroots of society, one also observes a gradual move away from national solidarity to communal solidarity. This move has been fostered by the diminishing role of the state, due to its fiscal and ideological problems, but this communal solidarity has not completely displaced the notion of "nation."

The dynamism of Islamic movements in contemporary Turkey should not be viewed as a reaction to the failure of the state's developmental policies and structural adjustment programs. Social and political despair has not forced people to take refuge in imagined religious-ethnic communities. Rather, these communities have become a means for upwardly mobile segments of the population to move from the margins to the center of social and political life. Thus it has not been the most marginalized sectors of society that have been politicized by Islam but, on the contrary, it has been the most upwardly mobile ones who led the current wave of social and political Islamization.

The spread of print Islam and modern associational life has helped to diversify the epistemological sources and interpretations of Islamic discourses. The Nur movement founded by Said Nursi has been the main force behind the pluralization of sources in the debate on the relevance of Islamic values and traditions in contemporary Turkish life. Nursi, for example, sought to accommodate a religious worldview with modern science and rationality. In other words, in this flexible and evolving religious understanding, not only the natural sciences but also democracy and pluralism can be reconciled with revelation. Attempts at such intellectual reconciliation of reason and revelation have not produced a simple, stable, and coherent Islamic discourse but rather have led to further destabilization and intellectual hybridism. The internal fracturing of the Nur movement, for instance, indicates that different voices constantly are heard and produced, as a result of the opening up of discursive spaces through the print and media revolutions, and that it is impossible in present-day Turkey for any single ideology, either Islamic or secularist, to impose its effective hegemony on society and the state.

In the case of Turkey, the Kemalist revolution, in the process of seeking to overthrow tradition, inadvertently promoted both its transformation and its perpetuation. Because of this pressure "from above," one sees the emergence of an Islamic enlightenment in terms of the new emphases on human dignity, civic virtue, and social justice. The Islamic movements seek to form their own modernities in terms of drawing on their own traditions and values. In other words, the Nur movement and the Nakşibendi groups do not mimic Western patterns and forms of modernity, but they are not able either to reify a particular Islamic tradition in their struggle to create their own multiple discourses. One witnesses a distinctly posttraditional discourse and an implicit tension with modernity. By examining competitive Islamic identities within society and between Islamic groups, one sees that Islamic identity does not amalgamate ethnic, class, regional, and sectarian identities into one seamless Islamic construct. Interactions between Islamic and secular ideologies create more pluralistic images and options for identity and ideology in contemporary Turkey.

The construction of Islamic political identity has led to the fragmentation and pluralization of Islamic social and political movements. The rise of a print culture has promoted diversity in the hermeneutical understanding of sacred texts and has displaced the role of both the traditional ulema and charismatic leaders of Sufi groups, which had been organized around the basis of an oral tradition. In Turkey this void is filled by the emergence of Islamic intellectuals, concentrated in journalism and the mass media. This group of Islamic intellectuals, with close ties to the new urban bourgeoisie of Anatolian extraction, includes individuals such as Nurettin Coşan, Ali Bulaç, Rasim Özdenören, and Fethullah Gülen. The Turkish example is also of broader importance for scholars studying the emergence of Islamic movements worldwide which at present are the dominant social and political discourses in the vast majority of Muslim countries.

How are Islamic images of justice and community framed and translated into popular action via shared experiences? This interaction between ideas and lived sociopolitical experience has transformed Islam and the sociopolitical landscape in different Muslim countries. In order to understand this transformation, one needs to examine religiously rooted and politically shaped ideas and networks such as those of the Nakşibendi and Nurcu groups. Some Islamic movements, such as the Nurcus in Turkey, do not necessarily demand the immediate control of the state but rather undertake a project of building a new Muslim self, while other movements seek revolutionary change through all means to fulfill God's order. Governments in Muslim countries adopted different strategies ranging from brutal oppression to co-optation to deal with these powerful Islamic political movements that stress identity and justice.

The Muslim Brotherhood of Hasan al-Banna in Egypt, the Jamaat-i Islami of Abu'l al-Ala Mawdudi in Pakistan, and the Malaysian Islamic Youth Movement in Malaysia emerged within the modern sector of society.[4] In the mid-1970s, Muslim countries experienced growing interconnections via transnational Islamic movements, yet each had its own national characteristics. For example, the Nahda in Tunis, the Islamic Salvation Front in Algeria, the National Islamic Front in Sudan, and the RP in Turkey are movements largely confined within a nation-state. Each movement is shaped by the regime's policies, by the demands of a new bourgeoisie, by the internal dynamics of the movement, and other political forces and ideologies. Yet there are important similarities and interactions among these movements. These similarities can be reduced exclusively to Islam as such but rather to similar opportunity spaces. They challenge routine ways of doing politics and offer new projects for reimagining society and politics to create a more inclusive and harmonious society. They open new spaces for different ideas and lifestyles and generate new ideas to mobilize social groups to challenge established patterns of interactions. Thus Islamic movements in Turkey seek to expand the boundaries of public spaces and frame new issues in vernacular idioms. They challenge the established boundaries between the state and society to realize a more just society in which participatory channels are wide and identity is externalized freely. The goal is the liberation of the oppressed and recognition of the marginalized traditional sections of society that make up the vast majority of the population. This is a way of reconceptualizing Islam from a position at the margins and redefining the meaning of the social code within new webs of interactions.

Islamic movements create a critical space to translate new conceptions of justice and community into social and political action. Participation helps the processes of the externalization of Islamic political identity. In the Turkish case, democratization and liberalization have brought Islam closer to the center of politics. The history of political participation, therefore, is also the history of the carving of public spaces for Muslim voices in politics. The relationships between democratization and Islamic movements are not causal but rather constitutive. Islamic political movements and the expansion of public space need to be fully articulated. One of the main shared characteristics of Islamic social movements has been attempts to deprofessionalize the role of ulema expertise and democratize the interpretation of the Qur'an. The Turkish case indicates that democratization processes play a key role in the reproduction of Islam. While democratic processes localize national and international issues and ideas and bring cultural identities into the public sphere, they offer a dynamic framework of connection between universal and particular symbols. This changed debate becomes a dominant process in the formation of hybrid identities. The case of the MGH shows that the RP identity was a space-in-between diverse ethnic and religious identities.

Having examined the diverse and complex landscape of Islamic movements in Turkey, I conclude that these movements are not retrograde but rather a positive source of dynamism if they are integrated fully into an open, democratic, and constitutional system. The goals and strategies of Islamic movements vary from case to case as a result of the political milieu in which movements unfold, their organizational characteristics, and their ability to frame sociopolitical issues in a popular language. I stress that Islamic social movements are not dominated by a single voice but rather are a site of contestation and of multiple interpretations of "the good life."

When these collective efforts become patterned to challenge the hegemonic code of life and politics, they constitute a countercultural movement. The new Islamic movements of the 1980s primarily evolved around questions of cultural politics, lifestyles, and identities and secondarily around the distribution of income and state policies. The construction of an Islamic political identity in Turkey is a case in which excluded, marginalized groups invoke popular religious idioms to challenge the status quo. The primary goal of these Islamic movements is not to create an Islamic state but rather the reconstitution of everyday life by means of transforming personal identity and consciousness through microinteractions in the contexts of the Sufi order, the media, printed texts, households, and neighborhoods. In a way, the construction of Islamic political identity is the story of the transformation of the macrosystem through a series of microinteractions.

Studies of Islamic movements in Turkey have generally focused on the control of the state and ignored everyday life. This study shows the fundamental shift in modern Turkish history: the Republican elite used politics to create a new national-secular culture, whereas the more current society-centered movements use culture to redefine the meaning and role of politics. Politics, for some dominant Turkish Islamic groups, has become an arena to be shaped through cultural means. Therefore, the role of Islamic movements should not be assessed in terms of their immediate political consequences, in the manner of Olivier Roy. Alberto Melucci, a prominent Italian scholar of new social movements, argues that the success of social movements should be measured by their ability to redefine and transform the "internal landscape" of humans rather than by their immediate external political impact.[5]

Turkish Islam

Pluralism is the major characteristic of Turkish Islam. This pluralism has been the major sustainer and support base for the democratization movement in Turkey. It is possible to identify several key characteristics of Turkish Islam; they could be described as follows.

1. It is a frontier Islam that is in constant evolution as a result of the tension between heterodox and orthodox Islams. Turkish Islam is a Sufi Islam with dense Sufi networks that transmit the flow of ideas, practices, and leaders, helping to link local and universal versions of Islam. Sufi networks were major intellectual foundries for Turkey's earlier Republican Islamic intellectuals. The most prominent such intellectuals were tied in particular to the Nakşibendi order. These Muslim intellectuals were neither from the ulema nor engineers and medical doctors as is often the case in Muslim countries like Egypt and Pakistan. Rather they were poets, philosophers, and novelists. Thus, while bringing novel Islamic perspectives, they were also an integral part of Turkey's expanding literary public spaces. These writers, unlike Mawdudi or Qutb, were not didactic in their writings but rather narrative in style and eclectic in terms of sources and openness to divergent viewpoints.

2. Europe never became the "other" in the construction of the Turkish identity because there was no colonial legacy or long period of occupation. In the construction of Turkish identity, the "other" was "imperial and communist" Russia. Muslims of Turkey supported Turkey's entry into NATO and other European institutions as a safety measure against Russian expansionism. The conditions of the Cold War further consolidated Turkey's positive identification with Europe. When the communist movement became powerful in the 1960s and 1970s, the state used Islamic groups as an antidote to leftist ideology and activism. Moreover, the short and swift War of Liberation was carried out not by local militias but by a regular army. Thus the violence of national liberation did not set a pattern of opposition, as it would do in Algeria. And thus there never developed a deep sense of siege among the Turks. The 1974 Cyprus operation further consolidated the self-confidence of the Turks, as it was a very important moment in the articulation of Turkish identity and consolidation of the military.

3. Islam in Turkey serves as a "melting pot" to integrate diverse ethnic groups. During the War of Liberation, Islam served to bring diverse groups together against the occupying forces. It was the in-group symbol against the occupation forces. Atatürk's vision of a modern Turkey and understanding of Islam was ambivalent and shaped by social events.

4. Turkey has no oil, and it is a tax-based economy. The opportunity spaces shape the character and evolution of Islamic demands and activism. The market conditions and the formation of the middle class are essential for the formation of a civil society, and these factors are also necessary for the evolution of a liberal version of Islam. These conditions do exist in Turkey. Turkish Islam, rooted in Sufism, particularly Nakşibendi Sufi orders, and punctuated by the frontier conditions of Turkey, is pluralistic and liberal.

The old Republican Turkey we have known has become passé, and a new Turkey is unfolding in a troubled and uncertain fashion. The exact trajectory of state and society may be unclear but it is certain that the country has come to a crucial crossroads. The old Turkey was based on a conscious attempt to forget the Islamic-Ottoman past. The new Turkey, in contrast, is evolving on the basis of remembering and building on the deep-rooted legacy of the Ottoman-Islamic past. Turkey has been evolving from a state-centric society, where homogeneity and obedience were the imperative, to an associational society in which diversity is becoming a fact of everyday life, along with the anxious emergence of a civic culture.

Appendix

The 18 Directives of February 28, 1997

According to NSC decision no. 406, the Erkaban government was instructed to implement the following 18 directives:

1. The principle of secularism should be strictly enforced and laws should be modified for that purpose, if necessary.
2. Private dormitories, foundations, and schools affiliated with Sufi religious orders must be put under the control of relevant state authorities and eventually transferred to the Ministry of National Education (MNE).
3. An eight-year uninterrupted education system must be implemented across the country and necessary administrative and legal adjustments should be made so that Qur'anic courses, which children with basic education may attend with parental consent, operate only under the responsibility and control of the MNE.
4. National education institutes charged with raising enlightened clergy loyal to the republican regime and Kemal Atatürk's principles and reforms must conform to the essence of the Law on Unified Education.
5. Religious facilities built in various parts of the country must not be used for political exploitation and such facilities must be built in coordination with local governments and relevant authorities.
6. Activities of religious orders banned by law no. 677, as well as all entities prohibited by said law, must be ended.
7. Media groups that oppose the military and depict its members as inimical to religion should be brought under control.
8. Personnel expelled from military service because of fundamentalist activities, disciplinary problems, or connections with illegal organizations must not be employed by other public agencies and institutions or otherwise encouraged.

9. The measures taken within the framework of existing regulations to prevent infiltration of the military by the extremist religious sector should also be applied in other public institutions and establishments, particularly in universities and other educational institutions, at every level of the bureaucracy, and in judicial establishments.

10. Iran's efforts to destabilize Turkey's regime should be closely watched and policies to prevent Iran from meddling in Turkey's internal affairs should be adopted.

11. Legal and administrative means must be used to prevent the dangerous activities of the extremist religious sector that seeks to create polarization in society by fanning sectarian differences.

12. Legal and administrative proceedings against those responsible for incidents that contravene the constitution and laws of the Turkish Republic should be concluded in a short period of time and firm measures should be taken at all levels not to allow repetition of such incidents.

13. Practices that violate the attire law and that may give Turkey a backward image must be prevented.

14. Licensing procedures for short- and long-barrel weapons, which have been issued for various reasons, must be reorganized on the basis of police and gendarmerie districts.

15. The collection of (animal) sacrifice hides by anti-regime and "uncontrolled" (unregulated) organizations and establishments for the purpose of securing financial resources should be prevented.

16. Legal proceedings against private bodyguards dressed in special uniforms and those responsible for them should be concluded speedily and all such should be disbanded.

17. Initiatives that aim at solving Turkey's problems on the basis of the concept of "ummet" [religious worldview] rather than the concept "nation" [or a secular worldview] and that encourage the separatist terrorist organization [meaning the PKK] by approaching it on the same basis [means the Islamization of Kurdish nationalism] should be prevented by legal and administrative means.

18. The law (no. 5816) defining crimes against Atatürk, including acts of disrespect, must be fully implemented.

I

Notes

INTRODUCTION

1. The 1997 military coup is commonly known either as the "soft coup" or the "February 28 process." It is called a "soft coup" because the military mobilized the major business associations, media cartels, university rectors, and judiciary long subservient to its commands to engineer an anti-RP drive to force the recently elected Erbakan government to resign. Behind this public campaign was the unmistakable message that the recently elected Erbakan government would "voluntarily" resign or be forced out by the generals. The coup posed Islamic identity as a national threat and proposed a number of directives to cleanse the Islamic presence in public spaces where it had been present even in the most reactionary period of Kemalist zeal. It is also known as the "February 28 process" because the coup was not limited only to the removal of the RP-led government but also was a process of monitoring, controlling, and criminalizing all Islamic activism as a security threat and institutionalizing a permanent legal framework for ostracizing devout and active Turkish Muslims from the market, educational, and political spheres.

2. See, for example, Tarık Zafer Tunaya and Niyazi Berkes, who present modern Turkish history as the story of conflict between secularism and religion, progressive forces and reactionary (religious) forces. Both interpreted almost all social movements opposing state control as "reactionary" threats to the modernizing reforms of the state. Tunaya, İslamcılık Akımı, 2nd ed. (Istanbul: Simavi Yayınları, 1991); the first edition of this influential book was printed in 1962. Berkes, The Development of Secularism in Turkey, 2nd ed. (New York: Routledge, 1998); 1st ed. 1964. The Turkish version of this book caters more rigidly to Kemalist expectations than the English edition.

3. Daniel Lerner concluded that the emergence of the "new Turk" (secular Turk) was inevitable and this "new Turk" chose "mechanization"

(modernity) over "Mecca" (religion); see Lerner, *The Passing of Traditional Society: Modernizing the Middle East* (New York: Free Press, 1964), 128, 165, 398–412.

4. Edmund Burke III, "Islamic and Social Movements: Methodological Reflections," in *Islam, Politics, and Social Movements*, ed. Edmund Burke and Ira M. Lapidus (Berkeley: University of California Press, 1988), 19.

5. Ira M. Lapidus, *A History of Islamic Societies* (New York: Cambridge University Press, 1989), 899.

6. Benedict Anderson, *Language and Power* (Ithaca, N.Y.: Cornell University Press, 1990), 94.

7. John Waterbury, "Export-Led Growth and the Center-Right Coalition in Turkey," *Comparative Politics* 24, 2 (January 1992): 127–144; see also a special survey of the *Economist*, "Turkey: The Star of Islam," *Economist*, December 14, 1991, 1–18.

8. See Ömer L. Barkan, "Türkiye'de Din-Devlet İlişkileri," In *Cumhuriyetin 50. Yıldönümü Semineri* (Ankara: TTK, 1975), 49–97.

9. Benedict Anderson, *Imagined Communities: Reflections on the Origins and Spread of Nationalism* (London: Verso, 1991).

10. Nilüfer Göle, *The Forbidden Modern: Civilization and Veiling* (Ann Arbor: University of Michigan Press, 1996); Elizabeth Özdalga, *The Veiling Issue: Official Secularism and Popular Islam in Modern Turkey* (Richmond, Surrey, England: Curzon, 1998); and Emilie Olson, "Muslim Identity and Secularism in Contemporary Turkey: The Headscarf Dispute," *Anthropological Quarterly* 58, 4 (1985): 161–72.

11. My interview with Erol Göka, a liberal Muslim intellectual who has written several books on hermeneutics and Islam, Ankara, April 23, 1995.

12. Anthony Giddens, *Central Problems in Social Theory* (London: Macmillan, 1979), 3, 202.

13. Giddens, *Central Problems*, 204.

14. Giddens, *Central Problems*, 201.

15. On the roles of ulema and sheik, see Ernest Gellner, *Muslim Society* (Cambridge, England: Cambridge University Press, 1983); Michael Gilsenan, *Saint and Sufi in Modern Egypt* (Oxford: Clarendon Press, 1973); Dale Eickelman, *Moroccan Islam* (Austin: Texas University Press, 1976); and Clifford Geertz, *Islam Observed* (Chicago: Chicago University Press, 1968).

16. See Şerif Mardin, *Religion and Social Change in Modern Turkey: The Case of Bediuzzaman Said Nursi* (New York: State University of New York Press, 1989); and Ibrahim M. Abu-Rabi, ed., *Islam at the Crossroads: On the Life and Thought of Bediuzzaman Said Nursi* (Albany: State University of New York, forthcoming).

17. For figures on the number of Nurcus, see Şahin Alpay, "'Ufuk Turu,'" *Milliyet*, August 1, 1996.

18. See, for example, his controversial statements about the RP in his interview with Yalçın Doğan on the television station Kanal-D in "Bir Belge: Fethullah Gülen'in Kanal D'deki Konuşması," *Umran*, May–June 1997, 1–15.

1. ISLAMIC SOCIAL MOVEMENTS

1. I base these categories on the writing of Crawford Young; see Young, ed., *The Rising Tide of Cultural Pluralism: The Nation-State at Bay?* (Madison: University of Wisconsin Press, 1993).

2. For concise statements of these different approaches, see Daniel Pipes, *In the Path of God: Islam and Political Power* (New York: Basic Books, 1983); Elie Kedourie,

Democracy and Arab Political Culture (Washington, DC: Washington Institute for Near East Policy, 1992); P. J. Vatikiotis, *Islam and the State* (London: Croom Helm, 1987); and Bernard Lewis, "The Root of Muslim Rage," *Atlantic Monthly*, September 1990, 50–57.

3. Bernard Lewis, *The Political Language of Islam* (London: University of Chicago Press, 1988); by far the best critique of the "orientalists" is Maxime Rodinson, *Europe and the Mystique of Islam* (London: University of Washington Press, 1991).

4. Bassam Tibi, *Islam and the Cultural Accommodation of Social Change*, trans. Clare Krojzl (Boulder, CO: Westview Press, 1991).

5. Tibi, *Islam*, 120.

6. Bernard Lewis, preface to Gilles Kepel, *The Prophet and Pharaoh: Muslim Extremism* (London: Al Saqi Books, 1985), 13.

7. Ernest Gellner, *Postmodernism, Reason and Religion* (London: Routledge, 1992), 6–22.

8. Emmanuel Sivan, *Radical Islam: Medieval Theology and Modern Politics* (New Haven: Yale University Press, 1990), 3.

9. Sivan, *Radical Islam*, 138.

10. See Ibrahim M. Abu-Rabi, *Intellectual Origins of Islamic Resurgence in the Modern Arab World* (Albany: State University of New York Press, 1996).

11. For the critique of this literature, see Leonard Binder, *Islamic Liberalism: A Critique of Development Ideologies* (Chicago: University of Chicago Press, 1988), 225.

12. Daniel Lerner, *The Passing of Traditional Society: Modernizing the Middle East* (New York: Free Press, 1964), 405.

13. See, for example, Niyazi Berkes, *The Development of Secularism in Turkey*, 2nd ed. (New York: Routledge, 1998); Binnaz Toprak, *Islam and Political Development in Turkey* (Leiden: Brill, 1981); "The State, Politics and Religion in Turkey," *State, Democracy and the Military: Turkey in the 1980s* (New York: de Gruyter, 1988), 119–35; and "Islam in Politics: The Case of Turkey," *Government and Opposition* 18 (1983): 421–41; and İlkay Sunar and Sabri Sayarı, "Democracy in Turkey: Problems and Prospects," in *Transitions from Authoritarian Rule*, ed. Guillermo O'Donnell, Philippe C. Schmitter, and Laurence Whitehead (Baltimore: Johns Hopkins University Press, 1986), 165–86.

14. Frank Tachau, *Turkey: The Politics of Authority, Democracy, and Development* (New York: Praeger, 1984).

15. Sibel Bozdoğan and Resat Kaşaba, eds., *Rethinking Modernity and National Identity in Turkey* (Seattle: University of Washington Press, 1997).

16. Sami Zubaida, *Islam, the People and the State* (London: Routledge, 1989); Michael Gilsenan, *Recognizing Islam* (London: Tauris, 1990); Edward Mortimer, *Faith and Power* (London: Faber, 1982); Aziz al-Azmeh, *Islams and Modernities* (London: Verso, 1993); and Nazih Ayubi, *Political Islam: Religion and Politics in the Arab World* (London: Routledge, 1991).

17. For discussions of relative deprivation theory, see James Davies, *Human Nature and Politics: The Dynamics of Political Behavior* (New York: Wiley, 1963); Özay Mehmet, *Islamic Identity and Development: Studies of the Islamic Periphery* (London: Routledge, 1990); Feroz Ahmed, "Politics and Islam in Modern Turkey," *Middle Eastern Studies* 27, 1 (1991): 2–21, and "Islamic Reassertion," *Third World Quarterly* 10, 2 (1988): 750–70.

18. Mehmet, *Islamic Identity and Development*, 26.

19. Mehmet, *Islamic Identity and Development*, 51.

20. See Darius Shayegan, *Cultural Schizophrenia: Islamic Societies Confronting the West*, trans. John Howe (London: al-Saqi, 1992).

21. Clifford Geertz, *The Interpretation of Cultures* (New York: Basic Books, 1973), chaps. 8 and 10.

22. See Olivier Roy, *The Failure of Political Islam* (Cambridge: Harvard University Press, 1994).

23. Gabriel Ben-Dor, *State and Conflict in the Middle East* (New York: Praeger, 1983); Philip S. Khoury and Joseph Kostiner, eds., *Tribe and State Formation in the Middle East* (Berkeley: University of California Press, 1990); Raymond A. Hinnebusch, *Authoritarian Power and State Formation in Ba'thist Syria: Army, Party, and Peasant* (Boulder, CO: Westview Press, 1990); Eric Davis and Nicolas Gavrielides, eds., *Statecraft in the Middle East* (Miami: Florida International University Press, 1991).

24. Theda Skocpol, "Bringing the State Back In: Strategies of Analysis in Current Research," in *Bringing the State Back In*, ed. Peter Evan, Dietrich Rueschemeyer, and Theda Skocpol (New York: Cambridge University Press, 1985), 20.

25. Simon Bromley, *Rethinking Middle East Politics, State Formation and Development* (Cambridge, England: Polity Press, 1994), 169.

26. Giacomo Luciani, "Allocation vs. Production States: A Theoretical Framework," and Hazem Beblawi, "The Rentier State in the Arab World," both in Luciani and Beblawi, *The Arab State* (Berkeley: University of California Press, 1990), 65–84 and 85–98, respectively.

27. Eric Davis, "Theorizing Statecraft and Social Change in Arab Oil-Producing Countries," in Davis and Gavrielides, eds., *Statecraft*, 8.

28. Lisa Anderson, "Absolutism and the Resilience of Monarchy in the Middle East," *Political Science Quarterly* 106,1 (1991): 1–15, and "The State in the Middle East and North Africa," *Comparative Politics* 20, 1 (October 1987): 1–18.

29. Alan Richards and John Waterbury, *A Political Economy of the Middle East: State, Class and Economic Development* (Boulder, CO: Westview Press, 1990), 185.

30. Richards and Waterbury, *Political Economy of the Middle East*, 2.

31. Peter L. Berger and Thomas Luckman, *The Social Construction of Reality* (New York: Anchor Books, 1967).

32. Fazlur Rahman, *Islam and Modernity: Transformation of an Intellectual Tradition* (Chicago: University of Chicago Press, 1982); John L. Esposito, *Islam: The Straight Path*, 3rd ed. (New York: Oxford University Press, 1998), and Talal Asad, *The Idea of Anthropology of Islam*, occasional paper series (Washington, DC: Georgetown University Center for Contemporary Arab Studies, 1986).

33. John R. Gillis, ed., *Commemorations: The Politics of National Identity* (Princeton: Princeton University Press, 1994), 5.

34. Crawford Young, *The Politics of Cultural Pluralism* (Madison: University of Wisconsin Press, 1976), 65.

35. Lerner, *Passing of Traditional Society*, 128.

36. Sidney Tarrow, *Power in Movement: Social Movements, Collective Action and Politics* (New York: Cambridge University Press, 1994), 3–4.

37. Alberto Melucci, "The Symbolic Challenge of Contemporary Movements," *Social Research* 52, 4 (1985): 793, and *Nomads of the Present: Social Movements and Individual Needs in Contemporary Society* (Philadelphia: Temple University Press, 1989), 35; Alain Touraine, *Beyond Neoliberalism* (Malden, MA: Blackwell, 2001), 45–73.

38. See Craig Calhoun, "The Problem of Identity in Collective Action," in *Macro-Micro Linkages in Sociology*, ed. Joan Huber (London: Sage, 1991), 51–75.

39. Melucci, "Symbolic Challenge," 35.

40. Charles Tilly, "Social Movements as Political Structure" (July 1997), unpublished ms. (*www.ciaonet.org/wps/tic03/*).

41. Hank Johnson and Bert Klandermans, "Identities, Grievances, and New Social Movements," in *Social Movements and Culture*, ed. Hank Johnston and Bert Klandermans (Minneapolis: University of Minnesota Press, 1995), 7.

42. Marco Giugni, Doug McAdam, and Charles Tilly, eds., *How Social Movements Matter* (Minneapolis: University of Minnesota Press, 1999).

43. Charles Tilly defines the "repertoire of action" as a set of means that challengers use to make different claims on different groups and institutions. Tilly, *The Contentious French: Four Centuries of Popular Struggle* (Cambridge: Belknap Press, 1986), 4.

44. Michael Meeker, "The Muslim Intellectual and His Audience: A New Configuration of Writer and Reader among Believers in the Republic of Turkey," in *Cultural Transitions in the Middle East*, ed. Serif Mardin (Leiden: Brill, 1994), 153–88.

45. Ziya Öniş, "The Political Economy of Islamic Resurgence in Turkey: The Rise of the Welfare Party in Perspective," *Third World Quarterly* 18, 4 (1997): 748.

46. On the social construction of identity through social movements, see Ron Eyerman and Andrew Jamison, *Social Movements: A Cognitive Approach* (Oxford: Polity Press, 1991); Aldon Morris and Carol Mueller, *Frontiers of Social Movement Theory* (New Haven: Yale University Press, 1992); and Enrique Larana, Hank Johnston, and Joseph R. Gusfield, eds., *New Social Movements: From Ideology to Identity* (Philadelphia: Temple University Press, 1994).

47. Bert Klandermans uses the concept of "supply and demand" to explain the transformation of discontent into collective action in *The Social Psychology of Protest* (Oxford: Blackwell, 1997), 207.

48. Ernest Gellner, "Kemalism," in *Encounters with Nationalisms* (Oxford: Blackwell, 1994), 81–91.

49. See David C. Rapoport, "Comparing Militant Fundamentalist Movements and Groups," in *Fundamentalisms and the State*, ed. Martin E. Marty and R. Scott Appleby (Chicago: Chicago University Press, 1993), 429–61.

50. See Erbakan's speech, *Milli Gazete*, August 27, 1980.

51. M. Hakan Yavuz, "Political Islam and the Welfare (Refah) Party in Turkey," *Comparative Politics* 30, 1 (October 1997): 63–82.

52. Reşat Kasaba, "Populism and Democracy in Turkey, 1946–1961," in *Rules and Rights in the Middle East: Democracy, Law, and Society*, ed. Ellis Goldberg, Reşat Kasaba, and Joel S. Migdal (Seattle: University of Washington Press, 1993), 43–68; and Cem Eroğlu, *Demokrat Parti (Tarihi ve İdeolojisi)* (Ankara: Siyasal Bilgiler Fakültesi, 1970).

53. Menderes Çınar, "Republican Aspects of Islamism in Turkey from the Perspective of 'the Political'" (Ph.D. diss., Bilkent University, Ankara, 1998).

54. Paul Lubeck, "The Islamic Revival: Antinomies of Islamic Movements under Globalization," in *Global Social Movements*, ed. R. Cohen and S. Rai (London: Anthlone, 2000), 146–64.

55. March Bloch, *Feudal Society*, trans. L. A. Manyon (Chicago: University of Chicago Press, 1964), 148.

56. M. Nazif Shahrani, "Local Knowledge of Islam and Social Discourse in Afghanistan and Turkistan in the Modern Period," in *Turko-Persia in Historical*

Perspective, ed. Robert L. Canfield (New York: Cambridge University Press, 1991), 182.

57. Shahrani, "Local Knowledge," 182.

2. THE ENDURING OTTOMAN LEGACY

1. Engin Akarlı, "Osmanlılarda Devlet, Toplum ve Hukuk Anlayış," in *Osmanlılarda ve Avrupa'da Çağdaş Kültürün Oluşumu 16–18 Yüzyıl*, ed. Engin Akarlı (Istanbul: Metis Yayınları, 1986), 24–25.

2. Bernard Lewis, *The Emergence of Modern Turkey*, 2nd ed. (New York: Oxford University Press, 1969), 11.

3. V. L. Menage, "Devshirme," in *The Encyclopedia of Islam* (Leiden: E. J. Brill,1965), 210–13.

4. See Benjamin Braude and Bernard Lewis, eds., *Christians and Jews in the Ottoman Empire: The Functioning of a Plural Society* (New York: Holmes and Meier, 1982).

5. One of the better studies on the millet system is N. J. Pentazopoulos, *Church and Law in the Balkan Peninsula during the Ottoman Rule* (Thessaloniki: Institute for Balkan Studies, 1967); see also Theodore H. Papadopoulos, *Studies and Documents Relating to the History of the Greek Church and People under Turkish Diplomacy* (Brussels: Bibliotheca Graeca aevi posterioris, 1952), and İlber Ortaylı, "Osmanlı İmparatorluğun'da Millet," in *Tanzimat'tan Cumhuriyet'e Türkiye Ansiklopedisi* (Istanbul: İletişim Yayınları, 1985), 4:996–1001.

6. See Will Kymlicka, "Two Models of Pluralism and Tolerance," *Analyse und Kritik* 13 (1992): 33–56; and Halil İnalcık, "The Status of the Greek Orthodox Patriarch Under the Ottomans," *Turcica* 21–23 (1991): 407–37.

7. See Gabriel Baer, *Egyptian Guilds in Modern Times* (Jerusalem: Israel Oriental Society, 1963), and "Monopolies and Restrictive Practices of Turkish Guilds," *Journal of the Economic and Social History of the Orient* 13 (1970): 145–65, and "The Administrative, Economic, and Social Functions of Turkish Guilds," *International Journal of Middle East Studies* 1, 2 (1970): 28–50. For a criticism of Baer's arguments, see Halil İnalcık, "Critica," *Archivum Ottomanicum* 1 (1969): 317–19.

8. Şerif Mardin, "Power, Civil Society and the Culture in the Ottoman Empire," *Comparative Studies in Society and History* 11, 3 (1969): 279.

9. Halil İnalcık, "The Nature of Traditional Society: Turkey," in *Political Modernization in Japan and Turkey*, ed. Robert E. Ward and Dankwart Rustow (Princeton: Princeton University Press, 1964), 44.

10. Şerif Mardin, "Religion and Politics in Modern Turkey," in *Islam in the Political Process*, ed. James Piscatori (Cambridge, England: Cambridge University Press, 1986), 139.

11. Halil İnalcık, *The Middle East and the Balkans under the Ottoman Empire* (Bloomington: Indiana University Press, 1993), 85–86.

12. İnalcık, *The Middle East*, 81.

13. İnalcık, *The Middle East*, 100.

14. See Ergun Özbudun, "The Ottoman Legacy and the Middle East State Tradition," in *Imperial Legacy: The Ottoman Imprint on the Balkans and the Middle East*, ed. L. Carl Brown (New York: Columbia University Press, 1996), 133–58.

15. See Halil İnalcık, "Tanzimat'ın Uygulanması ve Sosyal Tepkiler," *Belleten* 27 (1964): 624–90, and Ahmet Hamdi Tanpınar, *19'uncu Asır Türk Edebiyatı Tarihi*, 3rd ed. (Istanbul: Cağlayan, 1967).

16. İlber Ortaylı, *İmparatorluğun En Uzun Yüzyılı* (Istanbul: Hil Yayınları, 1983), 170–73.

17. Tanpınar, *19'uncu Asır*.

18. Bernard Lewis, "Watan," *Journal of Contemporary History* 26 (1991): 526–33.

19. Şerif Mardin, "Modernization of Social Communication," in *Propaganda and Communication in World History*, ed. Harold D. Laswell, Daniel Lerner, and Hans Speier (Honolulu: University Press of Hawaii, 1979), 381–443.

20. Mim Kemal Öke, "'Şark Meselesi' ve II. Abdülhamid'in Garp Politikaları (1876–1909)," *Osmanlı Araştırmaları Dergisi* 3 (1982): 266.

21. Mujeeb R. Khan, "External Threats and the Promotion of a Trans-National Islamic Consciousness: The Case of the Late Ottoman Empire and Contemporary Turkey," *Islamic World Review* 1, 3 (1996): 115–28.

22. See James Tilio Maccaferri, "Ottoman Foreign Policy and the British Occupation of Egypt: The Hasan Fehmi Pasha Mission of 1885" (Ph.D. diss., University of California, Los Angeles, 1983), 1–25.

23. See M. Hakan Yavuz, "Islam and Nationalism: Yusuf Akçura and Üç Tarz-ı Siyaset," *Oxford Journal of Islamic Studies* 4, 2 (July 1993): 175–207.

24. B. Abu-Maneh, "Sultan Abdülhamid II and Shaikh Abdulhuda Al-Sayyadi," *Middle Eastern Studies* 15 (1979): 139.

25. See H. A. R. Gibb, "Lutfi Pasa on the Ottoman Caliphate," *Oriens* 15 (1962): 287–95, and "Some Considerations on the Sunni Theory of the Caliphate," in *Studies on the Civilization of Islam*, ed. Stanford J. Shaw and William R. Polk (Boston: Beacon, 1962), 141–50; and Halil İnalcık, "Islamic Caliphate, Turkey and Muslims in India," in *Shari'ah, Ummah and Khilafah*, ed. Yusuf Abbas Hashmi (Karachi: University of Karachi, 1987), 14–34.

26. For more on education policies in this period, see Stanford J. Shaw and Ezel Kural Shaw, *History of the Ottoman Empire and Modern Turkey* (New York: Cambridge University Press, 1977), 112–13.

27. Kazım Karabekir, Orhan Hülagü, Ömer Hakan Özalp, *Türkiye'de ve Türk Ordusunda Almanlar* (Istanbul: Emre, 2001); Colmar von der Goltz, *The Nation in Arms* (London: Hodder and Stoughton, 1914).

28. D. A. Rustow, "Politics and Islam in Turkey 1920–1955," in *Islam and the West*, ed. R. N. Frye (The Hague: Mouton, 1957), 73.

29. Cevat Dursunoğlu, *Milli Mücadelede Erzurum* (Ankara: Ziraat Bankası Matbaası, 1946), 151–52.

30. M. Kemal, "Mutarekeden meclisin açılışına kadar gecen olaylar," in *Atatürk'ün Söylev ve Demeçleri*, vol. 1 (Istanbul: Maarif Matbaası, 1945), 28.

31. M. Kemal, "Türk Milletini Teşkil Eden Müslüman Öğeler Hakkında (May 1, 1920)," in *Atatürk'ün Söylev*, 74.

32. Seha Meray, *Osmanlı İmparatorluğu Çöküş Belgeleri: Mondros bırakışması, Sevres andlaşması ve ilgili belgeler* (Ankara: SBF Yayınları, 1977).

33. The Kemalist conception of secularism was derived from Auguste Comte's notion of positivism, a doctrine that seeks to replace religion with science and create a new society by using technology. See Ali Fuat Başgil, *Din ve Laiklik*, 6th ed. (Istanbul: Yağmur Yayınevi, 1991); Bülent Daver, *Türkiye Cumhuriyetinde Laiklik* (Ankara: Son Havadis, 1955); and Nur Vergin, "Din ve Devlet İlişkileri: Düşüncenin 'Bitmeyen Senfonisi," *Türkiye Günlüğü* 29 (1994): 5–23.

34. Ali Haydar, *Milli Terbiye* (Istanbul: Milli Matbaası, 1926), 21–23.

35. Haydar, *Milli*, 23.

36. For example, article 4 of the Law of Settlement argues that "only those who belong to Turkish ethnicity and culture" should be allowed to settle permanently in Turkey. The Turkish government, however, labeled the ethnically non-Turkish Bosnians, Albanians, Torbesh, Pomaks, and Montenegrin Muslims as Turks and helped them settle in Turkey.

37. David Kushner, *The Rise of Turkish Nationalism: 1876–1908* (London: Cass, 1977), 102.

38. See Ilkay Sunar and B. Toprak, "Islam in Politics: The Case of Turkey," *Government and Opposition* 18 (Autumn 1980): 426–27.

39. Law Number 432, 1924, "Concerning the Abolishment of the Caliphate and the Expulsion of the [Members of] the Ottoman Dynasty from Lands under the Jurisdiction of the Republic of Turkey," says that "since the [notion of the] caliphate is in principle included in the concept and the meaning of a Republican government, the office of caliphate is annuled." This law was presented by Mehmet Seyyid Bey, the minister of justice, who eventually wrote a booklet to justify the abolishment of the office of caliphate. See İsmail Kara, *Türkiye'de İslamcılık Düşüncesi, Metinler, Kişiler* (Istanbul: Risale Yayınları, 1997), 256–308.

40. Article 1 of the 1965 law recognized the duties and functions of the DİB. As of 2001, the DİB owns 75,002 mosques, and 64, 157 out of its 88,506 civil service personnel work within mosques; see *Diyanet İşleri Başkanlığı 2000 Yılı İstatistikleri* (Ankara: DİB, 2001).

41. Article 136 of the 1982 constitution says: "the Department of Religious Affairs, which is within the general administration, shall exercise its duties prescribed in its particular law, in accordance with the principles of secularism, removed from all political views and ideas, and aiming at national solidarity and integrity."

42. Ahmet H. Akseki, *Müftü ve Vaizlerin Ödevleri Hakkında Gerekli Açıklama,* (Ankara: Diyanet İşleri Başkanlığı, 1945), 3–22. This booklet lays out the functions of the DİB and its personnel.

43. For the text of the report, see Sadık Albayrak, *Şeriattan Laikliğe* (Istanbul: Sebil Yayınları, 1977), 333–37; or Osman Ergin, *Türk Maarif Tarihi,* 5 vols. (Istanbul: Eser, 1977), 1958–1967.

44. Ergin, *Türk Maarif Tarihi,* vol. 5, 1959.

45. Dücane Cündioğlu, *Türkçe Kur'an ve Cumhuriyet İdeolojisi* (Istanbul: Kitabevi, 1998); Necdet Subası, *Türk Aydınının Din Anlayışı* (Istanbul: YKB, 1996).

46. Ahmet Eskicumalı, "Ideology and Education: Reconstructing the Turkish Curriculum for Social and Cultural Change, 1923–1946," (Ph.D. diss., University of Wisconsin–Madison, 1994).

47. Geoffrey Lewis, *The Turkish Language Reform: A Catastrophic Success* (New York: Oxford University Press, 1999).

48. Halide Edip, *Turkey Faces West: A Turkish View of Recent Changes and Their Origins* (New Haven: Yale University Press, 1930), 235.

49. *Atatürk'ün Söylev ve Demeçleri* (Ankara: MEB, 1956), 20.

50. On the Turkish History Thesis see Afet İnan, "Atatürk ve Tarih Tezi," *Belleten* 3, 10 (1939): 243–45; on the Sun Language Theory see A. Dilaçar, *Atatürk ve Türkçe, Atatürk ve Türk Dili* (Ankara: Türk Dil Kurumu, 1963), 47–49.

51. For more on the Sun Language see Uriel Heyd, *Language Reform in Modern Turkey* (Jerusalem: Israel Oriental Society, 1954), 33–34, and Zeynep Korkmaz, *Türk Dilinin Tarihi Akışı İçinde Atatürk ve Dil Devrimi* (Ankara: Ankara Üniversitesi DTCF, 1963), 65–68.

52. See the articles in *I. Türk Dil Kurultayı: Tezler, Müzakere Zabıtları* (Istanbul: Maarif Vekilliği İstanbul Devlet Matbaası, 1933). At the end of this first Language Convention, a study project was accepted by the Convention and the first article called for more comparative work on Turkish and other Indo-European languages.

53. Eric Hobsbawm and T. Ranger, eds., *The Invention of Tradition* (Cambridge: Cambridge University Press, 1983), 13.

54. Hobsbawm and Ranger, *Invention of Tradition*, 13.

55. See Metin Toker, *Şeyh Sait ve İsyanı*, 2nd ed. (Ankara: Bilgi Yayınevi, 1994); Robert Olson and W. F. Tucker, "The Shaikh Sait Rebellion in Turkey," *Die Welt des Islams* 28 (1978): 195–211; Yaşar Kalafat, *Şark Meselesi Işığında şeyh Sait Olayı, Karakteri, Dönemindeki İç ve Dış Olaylar* (Istanbul: Boğaziçi Yayınları, 1992), 101–319; and Halil Simşek, *Şeyh Sa'id İsyanı ve PKK* (Istanbul: Harp Akedemileri, 2000).

56. Naci Kökdemir, *Eski ve Yeni Toprak İskan Hükümleri Uygulaması Kılavuzu* (Ankara: Yeni Matbaa, 1952), 166–71.

57. Mete Tunçay, *Türkiye Cumhuriyeti'nde Tek-Parti*, 245–56.

58. Fethi Okyar, *Üç Devirde Bir Adam* (Istanbul: Tercüman Yayınları, 1980).

59. Tarik Zafer Tunaya, *İslamcılık Akımı*, 2nd ed. (Istanbul: Simavi Yayınları, 1991), 174; Cevat Rifat Atilhan, *Menemen Hadisesinin İç Yüzü* (Istanbul: Yaylacık Matbaası, 1968); Kemal Üstün, *Menemen Olayı ve Kubilay* (Istanbul: Çağdaş Yayınları, 1977).

60. For an interesting account of this trip, which revealed the widespread discontent of the periphery, see Ahmed Hamdi Başar, *Atatürk'le Üç Ay ve 1930'dan Sonra Türkiye* (Istanbul: Tan Matbaası, 1945).

61. *Dersim: Jandarma Genel Komutanlığı'nın Raporu* (Istanbul: Kaynak, 1998). This official report reflects the military's view on the Alevis. For more on the execution of Seyyif Rıza, the leader of the Dersim rebellion, see İhsan S. Çağlayangil, *Anılarım* (Istanbul: Güneş, 1990), 45–50.

62. The People's Houses were opened on February 19, 1932, and Dr. Reşit Galip (1893–1934) played a key role in the articulation of the policy of the Houses. See A. Şevket Elman, *Dr. Reşit Galip* (Ankara: Türkiye Matbaacılık ve Gazetecilik, 1955). By 1950, 478 People's Houses were open to disseminate the Kemalist revolution. See Cevat Dursunoğlu, "Halkevlerinin 18. Yıldönümü konuşması," *Ülkü* 3, 27 (March 1949): 2. After his visit to Russia, Falih Rıfkı Atay (1893–1971), a close loyalist of Atatürk, defended more popular ways of disseminating the principles of the Kemalist revolution by training the people. He initiated the idea of "Narodni dom" (*Halkevleri*) as a way to domesticate the periphery according to the principles of Kemalism. See F. Rıfkı Atay, *Yeni Rusya* (Ankara: Hakimiyet-i Milli Matbaası, 1931). It was H. Suphi Tanrıöver who argued that the idea and name came from Russian experience through F. R. Atay's visit; see Tanrıöver's speech in the Turkish Parliament on this issue: *T.B.M.M. Tutanak Dergisi*, 16/1, Session 8, B: 52, (25 February 1949), 608. According to Şükrü Kaya, the minister of home affairs, "the People's Houses were established to disseminate, expose, and internalize the principles of Atatürk's Revolution among the people. Therefore, the People's Houses are the cultural institutions of protecting and disseminating the ideals of the Revolution." Şükrü Kaya, "Halkevleri'nin Açılış Konferansı," *Ülkü* 11, 61 (March 1938): 9.

The Village Institutes were founded in 1940, although the debate started in 1936, when Atatürk was alive. They sought to recruit village youth after their five-year primary education in their own village school. They provided five years of training in practical and theoretical issues. Teachers were trained not only in how to teach but also in how to improve agriculture, build new houses, and change the patterns of manners.

They were asked to modernize living standards and agriculture. In turn, the graduates were appointed as teachers in villages. The graduates of these schools had a progressive and emancipatory ideology. They were the main instrument for challenging the traditional networks in rural areas and became agents of the state. Due to their emancipatory ideology and left-wing leanings, the DP closed these institutes in 1954 for political reasons. See F. A. Stone, "Rural Revitalization and the Village Institutes in Turkey: Sponsors and Critics," *Comparative Education Review* 28 (1974): 419–29; Andreas M. Kazamias, *Education and Quest for Modernity in Turkey* (Chicago: University of Chicago Press, 1966), 124–25 and 197–98.

63. Yusuf Sarınay, *Türk Milliyetçiliğinin Tarihi Gelişimi ve Türk Ocakları (1912–1931)* (Istanbul: Ötüken, 1994), and Füsun Üstel, *İmparatorluktan Ulus-Devlete Türk Milliyetçiliği: Türk Ocakları (1912–1931)* (Istanbul: İletişim, 1997).

64. Samet Ağaoğlu, *Babamın Arkadaşları*, 3rd.ed. (Istanbul: Baha Matbaası, 1969), 149; see Mustafa Baydar, *Hamdullah Suphi Tanrıöver ve Anıları*, (Istanbul: Menteş Yayınevi, 1968), 70–74.

65. See, for example, Bernard Lewis, "Islamic Revival in Turkey," *International Affairs* 28 (1952): 38–48, and Howard A. Reed, "Revival of Islam in Secular Turkey," *Middle East Journal* 8, 3 (summer 1954): 267–82.

66. Muhammed Arkoun "Imagining Islam," in *Rethinking Islam: Common Questions, Uncommon Answers* (Boulder, CO: Westview Press, 1994), 6–14. Arkoun derives imagination from Cornelius Castoriadis, *The Imaginary Institution of Society*, trans. Kathleen Blamey (Cambridge, England: Polity Press, 1987).

67. Alex Honneth, *The Fragmented World of the Social: Essays in Social and Political Philosophy* (New York: State University of New York Press, 1990), 177.

68. C. Pellat, "Mahalle," in *The Encyclopedia of Islam*, 2nd ed., 5 vols. (Leiden: E. J. Brill, 1978), 1222.

69. In the Ottoman Empire, some Sufis usually focused on the private aspects of religious life and became a buffer between the ruler and the ruled.

70. *Hijra* means "migration" and refers to the Prophet Mohammed's migration from Mecca to Medina in 622.

71. My interview with Mehmet Kırkıncı, Istanbul, September 25, 1995.

72. My interview with Mehmet Kırkıncı, Istanbul, September 21, 2000.

3. THE TEMPERING OF THE KEMALIST REVOLUTION

1. See İlkay Sunar, "Demokrat Parti ve Popülizm," *Cumhuriyet Dönemi Ansiklopedisi*, 8 vols. (Istanbul: İletişim Yayınları, 1986), 2076–86.

2. Ergun Özbudun, *Political Change and Political Participation in Turkey* (Princeton: Princeton University Press, 1976), 52.

3. See R. Salim Burcak, *Türkiye'de Demokrasiye Geçiş: 1945–1950* (Ankara: Cam Matbaası, 1970), and *Yassıada ve Ötesi* (Ankara: Cam Matbaası, 1976).

4. Reşat Kasaba, "Populism and Democracy in Turkey, 1946–1961," in *Rules and Rights in the Middle East: Democracy, Law, and Society*, ed. Ellis Goldberg, Reşat Kasaba, and Joel S. Migdal (Seattle: University of Washington Press, 1993), 59.

5. Mustafa Erdoğan, "Türk Demokrasisinin Doğum Tarihi," *Yeni Forum* 278 (1992): 39–42.

6. Eşref Edib, "Celal Bayar, Gladistondan mı ilham aldı," *Sebilürreşad* 2, 39 (April 1949): 220–21.

7. For more on the Tijani order, which originated in North Africa in the late eighteenth century and became popular in Turkey in the 1940s, see Jamil Abu-Nasr,

The Tijaniyya: A Sufi Order in the Modern World (London: Oxford University Press, 1965). For more on the Turkish Tijani order, see "Ticani Tarikatı Hakkında Tetkikat," *Sebilürreşad* 4, 87 (September 1950): 185, and "Ticani Tarikatının Esasları," *Sebilürreşad* 4, 89 (October 1950): 218.

8. *Vatan*, July 11, 1952.

9. In 1962, the Constitutional Court actually declared this law unconstitutional; see Şevket Süreyya Aydemir, *II. Adam III* (Istanbul: Remzi Kitabevi, 1975), 2nd ed., 136.

10. For the decision of the Court of Afyon, see Avukat Bekir Berk, *İthamları Reddediyorum* (Istanbul: Yeni Asya Yayınları, 1972), 313–15.

11. For more on the movement see chapter 6.

12. This argument is made by Feroz Ahmad, "Politics and Islam in Modern Turkey," *Middle East Studies* 27, 1 (January 1991): 11, and "The Islamic Assertion in Turkey: Pressures and State Response," *Arab Studies Quarterly* 4, 1–2 (1982): 97.

13. See Walter F. Weiker, *The Turkish Revolution: 1960–1961* (Washington, DC: Brookings Institute, 1965).

14. Rona Aybay, "Milli Güvenlik Kavramı ve Milli Güvenlik Kurulu," *Siyasal Bilgiler Fakültesi* 33 (March–June 1978): 59–82.

15. *Milliyet*, July 26, 1960. When O. Nuri Çerman defended a major reform in Islamic rituals in his book (*Dinde Reform ve Kemalizm*), the junta denounced Çerman; see *Sebilürreşad* 13, 323 (April 1961): 355.

16. Quoted in Feroz Ahmad, "The Islamic Assertion," 98, citing *Cumhuriyet*, October 25, 1960.

17. Hikmet Özdemir, *Kalkınmada bir Strateji Arayışı: Yön Hareketi* (Ankara: Bilgi, 1986).

18. For election results and socioeconomic analyses of vote distribution, see Nermin Abadan Unat, *Anayasa Hukuku ve Siyasi Bilimler Acısından 1965 Secimlerinin Tahlili* (Ankara: Sevinç Matbaası, 1966), and Paul J. Magnarella, "Regional Voting in Turkey," *Muslim World* 57 (1967): 224–34 and 277–87.

19. Ergun Özbudun, *The Role of the Military in Recent Turkish Politics* (Cambridge: Harvard Center for International Affairs, 1966), 7.

20. W. H. Sherwood, "The Rise of the Justice Party," *World Politics* 20, 1 (October 1967): 54–65.

21. Arnold Leder, "Party Competition in Rural Turkey: Agent of Change or Defender of Traditional Rule?" *Middle East Studies* 15, 1 (1979): 91.

22. İsmail Engin and Erhard Franz, eds., *Aleviler/Alewiten I–IV* vols. (Hamburg: Orient Institute, 2001).

23. Erdal Gezik, *Alevi Kürtler* (Ankara: Kalan, 2000).

24. See Colin H. Imber, "Persecution of the Ottoman Shi'ites According to the Muhimme Defterleri 1565–1585," *Der Islam* 56 (1979): 245–74, and Tord Olsson and Elisabeth Özdalga, eds., *Alevi Identity* (London: Curzon Press, 1998).

25. İ. Metin, *Aleviler'de Halk Mahkemeleri*, 2 vols. (Istanbul: Alev, 1994).

26. See İsmail Engin, "İzzettin Doğan: Türkiye'de Bir Alevi Önder," in *İzzettin Doğan'ın Alevi İslam İnancı, Kültürü ile İlgili Görüş ve Düşünceleri*, ed. Ayhan Aydın (Istanbul: Cem Vakfı, 2000), 16–26.

27. *Hemşeri* is someone coming from the same region, city, or village. For more, see chapter 4.

28. The symbol of the party was a lion, which was understood to represent Ali, the son-in-law of the Prophet Muhammed, an object of devotion by Shi'is worldwide. In 1973 the party changed its name into the Unity Party of Turkey (Türkiye Birlik

Partisi). The retired general Hasan Tahsin Berkmen was the first chairman of the party. In 1967 Hüseyin Balan became the chairman.

29. *Cumhuriyet*, June 13, 1967.

30. Martin van Bruinessen, "Kurds, Turks and the Alevi Revival in Turkey," *Middle East Report* 26, 3 (1996): 8.

31. İzzettin Doğan, *Alevi-Islam İnancı, Kültürü ile İlgili Görüş ve Düşünceler* (Istanbul: Cem, 2000), and Reha Çamuroğlu, "Alevi Revivalism in Turkey," in Olsson and Özdalga, *Alevi Identity*, 79–84.

32. See *Cumhuriyet*, *Milliyet*, and *Hürriyet*, September 7, 1980.

33. See Mehmet Ali Birand, *The Generals' Coup in Turkey: An Inside Story of 12 September 1980* (New York: Brassey's, 1987), 173–89.

34. *Milliyet*, September 12, 1998.

35. My interview with Ahmet Çetin, deputy director of the Propagation Department, March 30, 1995.

36. My interview with Arif Soytürk, March 29, 1996.

37. See Mehmet Kırkıncı's April 1982 letter to President Kenan Evren, in Mehmet Kırkıncı, *Mektuplar Hatıralar* (Istanbul: Zafer Yayınları: 1992), 84–93.

38. Evren, *Türkiye Cumhuriyeti Devlet Başkanı Orgeneral Kenan Evren'in Söylev ve Demeçleri: 1985–1986* (Ankara: Başbakanlık, 1986), 221.

39. The first book, *Atatürkçülük: Birinci Kitap, Atatürkün Görüş ve Direktifleri* [Ataturkism: First Book, Atatürk's Views and Orders], includes Atatürk's statements on diverse issues, including the state, the nation, religion, the economy, and the army. The second book, *Atatürkçülük: İkinci Kitap, Atatürk ve Atatürkçülüğe İlişkin Makaleler* [Ataturkism: Second Book, Articles on Atatürkism and Atatürk], includes a number of articles written by scholars and statesmen on Atatürk's views in regard to the state, nation, economy, and religion. The third book, which is the most important one since it offers the military's ijtihad on Atatürk's ideas and ideology, is entitled *Atatürkçülük: Üçüncü Kitap, Atatürkçü Düşünce Sistemi* [Ataturkism: Third Book, Atatürkism: Ataturkian Thought System]. The section on religion develops an argument for "enlightened Islam," 225–41. These three volumes were first published by the Publishing Office of the Chief of Staff in 1983. They were reprinted by the Ministery of Education (*Atatürkçülük*, vols. 1–3 [Istanbul: Milli Eğitim Bakanlığı Basımevi, 1984]) and distributed to all schools in Turkey as the sourcebook on Kemalism.

40. *Atatürkçülük: Birinci Kitap*, 465–67.

41. Following the 1980 coup, the military became actively involved in the development and dissemination of enlightened Islam. A course on Islam was introduced to all military academies. The textbook of the course constantly stressed the necessity of Islam for the development of moral society in which people are responsible and duty-oriented toward their state and society. Osman G. Feyzioğlu, ed., *Askerin Din Bilgisi* (Ankara: Kara Kuvvetleri Komutanlığı Basımevi, 1981). The book is written from a Hanefi-Sunni Muslim perspective and offers little information on Alevi interpretations of Islam.

42. İbrahim Kafesoğlu, *Türk-İslam Sentezi* (Istanbul: Ötüken, 1999).

43. See Decision 1982/614 of the Higher Military Court in Mustafa Tuncel, *163. Madde hakkında kesinleşmiş kararlar* (Istanbul: Yeni Asya, 1983), 13.

44. See the founding charter of the Intellectuals' Hearth Association, *Aydınlar Ocağı Derneği Tüzüğü* (Istanbul: Aydınlar Ocağı Yayınları, 1989), 7; see Mustafa Erkal, "21 Yüzyıla Doğru Milli Kültürlerin Geleceği ve Bazi Çelişkiler," in *İslamiyet, Millet Gerçeği ve Laiklik* (Istanbul: Aydınlar Ocağı, 1994).

45. Erkal, "21 Yüzyılda," 52.

46. See Istar B. Tarhanlı, *Müslüman Toplum, "laik" Devlet: Türkiye'de Diyanet İşleri Başkanlığı* (Istanbul: AFA, 1993).

47. *Danışma Meclisi Tutanak Dergisi*, B: 140 (January 9, 1982), 276–84.

48. See Abdurrahman Dilipak, *Bu Din Benim Dinim Değil* (Istanbul: İşaret Yayınları, 1990); Hüseyin Hatemi, "İslamı Kullanıyorlar," *Cumhuriyet*, April 23, 1987; Ali Bulaç, *Bir Aydın Sapması* (Istanbul: Beyan Yayınları: 1989), 156–58 and 173–77; and İsmet Özel, *Tehdit Değil Teklif* (Istanbul: İklim Yayınları, 1987), 139.

49. Özer Özankaya, *Atatürk ve Laiklik: Türk Demokrasi Devriminin Temeli* (Istanbul: Tekin, 1983); Emre Kongar, *12 Eylül Kültürü* (Istanbul: Remzi Kitabevi, 1993).

50. *Milli Kültür Raporu* (Ankara: State Planning Organization, 1983).

51. See İbrahim Kafesoğlu, *Türk-İslam Sentezi* (Istanbul: Aydınlar Ocağı, 1985).

52. On the Turkish-Islamist synthesis and its long-term implications, see Bozkurt Güvenç, *Dosya Türk-İslam Sentezi* (Istanbul: Sarmal Yayınları, 1991).

53. F. Birtek and B. Toprak, "The Conflictual Agendas of Neo-Liberal Reconstruction and The Rise of Islamic Politics in Turkey: The Hazards of Rewriting Modernity," *Praxis International* 13, 2 (1993): 195.

54. See Nevzat Bölügiray, *Sokaktaki Askerin Dönüşü* (Istanbul: Tekin Yayınları, 1991), 203–205.

55. Muhsin Batur, *Anılar ve Görüşler: Üç Dönemin Perde Arkası* (İst: Milliyet, 1985), 187. He identifies the threat to secularism and nationalism as the two principles that would bring military intervention.

56. Ümit Cizre Sakallıoğlu, "The Anatomy of the Turkish Military's Autonomy," *Comparative Politics* 29, 2 (1997): 151–66.

57. K. Haluk Yavuz, *Siyasal Sistem Arayışları ve Yürütmenin Güçlendirilmesi* (Ankara: Seçkin, 2000).

58. See The Higher Education Law, No. 2547, enacted November 4, 1981, and the Emergency Rule Law, No. 1402.

59. Binnaz Toprak, "The State, Politics and Religion in Turkey," in *State, Democracy and the Military*, ed. Metin Heper and Ahmet Evin (Berlin: de Gruyter, 1988), 131–32; Jeremy Salt, "Nationalism and Rise of Muslim Sentiment in Turkey," *Middle East Studies* 31, 1 (January 1995): 16.

60. *Nokta*, June 16, 1985, 20–22.

61. *Resmi Gazete* (hereafter *RG*), April 12, 1991, 8.

62. *RG*, October 22, 1983, 27–28.

63. On April 30, 1993, ÖZDEP's founding members resolved to dissolve the party voluntarily while proceedings still continued at the Constitutional Court (CC). Nevertheless, on July 14, 1993 the CC issued an order dissolving ÖZDEP on the basis of trying to "undermine the territorial integrity and secular nature of the State and the unity of the nation" and ordered ÖZDEP's funds transferred to the Treasury and its leaders banned from holding similar offices in other parties.

64. *Sabah*, February 17, 1994.

65. M. Hakan Yavuz, "Değişim Sürecindeki Alevi Kimliği/Die alewitische Identitaet in Veranderungsprozess," in *Aleviler: Identitat und Geschichte*, vol. 1 (Hamburg: Orient Institute, 2000), 75–95.

66. The first act of Alevi "coming out" was *Alevilik Bildirgesi* [The Manifesto of Alevism], which was printed and promoted by the leftist-Kemalist daily *Cumhuriyet*, May 15, 1990. The manifesto includes all the different redefinitions of the Alevism.

67. See İsmail Kara's articles in *Dergah* magazine, especially "Müslüman Kardeşler Türkçe'ye Tercüme Edildi mi?" *Dergah* 21 (November 1991): 14–15.

4. THE POLITICAL ECONOMY OF ISLAMIC DISCOURSE

1. Subidey Togan, "Trade Liberalization and Competitive Structure in Turkey during the 1980s," in *Economy of Turkey Since Liberalization*, ed. S. Togan and V. N. Balasubramanyam (New York: St. Martin's Press, 1996), 5–51.

2. See the OECD report *Regional Problems and Policies in Turkey* (Paris: OECD, 1988); *Milliyet*, September 3, 1994.

3. See M. N. Danielson and R. Keleş, *The Politics of Rapid Urbanization: Government and Growth in Modern Turkey* (New York: Holmes and Meier, 1985), and *Göç Veren Yöreler Bölgesel Gelişim Araştırması* (Istanbul: Ticaret Odası, 1996).

4. Danielson and Keleş, *Politics of Rapid Urbanization*, 86–87.

5. Sevil Cerit, "Türkiye'de İller Arası Göçler 1950–1980," *Turkish Journal of Population Studies* 8 (1986): 97.

6. *Statistical Yearbook of Turkey* (Ankara: State Institute of Statistics, 1993), 54.

7. Michael E. Meeker, "Oral Culture, Media Culture, and the Islamic Resurgence in Turkey," in *Exploring the Written: Anthropology and the Multiplicity of Writing*, ed. Eduardo P. Archetti (Oslo: Scandinavian University Press, 1994), 39.

8. Cerit, "Turkiye'de İller," 87–88.

9. Ruşen Keleş, "Konut Politikalarımız," *Siyasal Bilgiler Fakültesi* 44, 1–2 (January–June 1989): 88.

10. Keleş, "Konut," 65, and "Urban Turkey in the Year 2000: A Pessimistic Scenario," in *Turkey in the Year 2000*, ed. Ergun Özbudun and İlter Turan (Ankara: Siyasi İlimler Derneği, 1988).

11. See Azimet Köylüoğlu, then the minister of human rights, quoted in *Cumhuriyet*, October 10, 1994; and Kamer Genç, an Alevi-Kurdish deputy of the True Path Party, quoted in *Cumhuriyet*, August 6, 1995.

12. I thank Engin Akarlı for helping me to determine a proper translation of *hemşerilik* as "hometown solidarity."

13. Reşat Kasaba, "Cohabitation? Islamic and Secular Groups in Modern Turkey," in *Democratic Civility*, ed. Robert W. Hefner (New Brunswick, NJ: Transaction, 1998), 277.

14. Robert Kaplan, "The Coming Anarchy," *Atlantic Monthly* (February 1994): 44–76; see Kaplan, *The Ends of the Earth* (New York: Vintage Books, 1997), 132–34.

15. Yusuf Ziya Özcan, "Ülkemizdeki Cami Sayıları Üzerine Sayısal Bir İnceleme," *Journal of Islamic Research* 4, 1 (1990): 5–20; Özcan, "Mosques in Turkey: A Quantitative Analysis," *Intellectual Discourse* 2, 1 (1994): 19–40.

16. See N. Güngör, *Arabesk: Sosyokültürel Açıdan Arabesk Müzik* (Ankara: Bilgi, 1990).

17. Cinuçen Tanrıkorur, *Müzik Kimliğimiz Üzerine Düşünceler* (Istanbul: Ötüken, 1998), 108.

18. When Ferdi Tayfur sings "Recreate me my Lord" [Tanrım beni baştan yarat] and "Let the world sink down" [Batsın bu dünya], music constitutes a new communication among listeners, telling them they belong to a larger identity of "strangers." In the 1960s and 1970s, the bestsellers were "Comfort Me" [Bir teselli ver]," "This Is What I Am" [Ben buyum] or "Let Them Say" [Desinler bee], and "You Are in Love My Friend!" [Sen aşıksın arkadaş]. The beats of these songs were a genuine attempt to reflect the pain and hardship of modernization, as experienced by the vast and yet

marginalized sectors of Turkey's nascent capitalist economy. These songs articulated the feeling newcomers had that they were "strangers" within their own country. When Orhan Gencebay, the star of Arabesque music, sings "You Are a Stranger" [Yabancısın sen], he not only expresses this alienation but also offers avenues for escape from it.

19. Meeker, "Oral Culture," 32.

20. Korkut Boratav, "Kemalist Economic Policies and Etatism," in *Atatürk: Founder of a Modern State*, ed. A. Kazancıgil and E. Özbudun, (Hamden, CT: Archon Books, 1981), 167.

21. See Hakkı Nezihi, *Elli Yıllık Oda Hayatı* (Istanbul: Sanayi-i Nefise Matbaası, 1932); M.S. Hoel, "The Ticaret Odası: Origins, Functions, and Activities of Chambers of Commerce in Istanbul, 1885–1899" (Ph.D. diss., Ohio State University, Columbus, Ohio, 1973), and E. Zeytinoğlu and N. Nur, *Istanbul Ticaret Odasının 100. Yılı (1882–1982)* (Istanbul: ITO, 1982).

22. Ziya Öniş, "The Evolution of Privatization in Turkey: The Institutional Context of Public-Enterprise Reform," *International Journal of Middle East Studies* 23, 2 (May 1991): 164.

23. Öniş, "Evolution," 38.

24. Massoud Karshenas, *Structural Adjustment and Employment in the Middle East and North Africa*, working paper no. 50 (London: School of Oriental and African Studies, University of London, 1994), 77.

25. See T. Arıcanlı and D. Rodrick, eds., *The Political Economy of Turkey* (London: Macmillan, 1990), and Alan Richards and John Waterbury, *A Political Economy of the Middle East: State, Class, and Economic Development* (Boulder, CO: Westview Press, 1990), 30 and 246–49.

26. Rüştü Saracoğlu, "Liberalization of the Economy," in *Politics in the Third Republic*, ed. Metin Heper and Ahmet Evin (Boulder, CO: Westview Press, 1994), 69.

27. *Adjustment Lending: An Evolution of Ten Years of Experience* (Washington, DC: World Bank, 1988); and *Turkey: Towards Sustainable Growth* (Washington, DC: World Bank, 1988).

28. Sallama Shaker, *State, Society, and Privatization in Turkey, 1979–1990* (Baltimore: Johns Hopkins Press, 1995).

29. Tuncer Bulutay, "A General Framework for Wages in Turkey," paper presented at the Seminar on Employment, Unemployment and Wages, Ankara, October 1992.

30. Ayşe Buğra, "Class, Culture, and State: An Analysis of Interest Representation by Two Turkish Business Associations," *International Journal of Middle East Studies* 30, 4 (1998): 531–39.

31. For more on these new Anatolian small and medium-sized companies, see the series of articles in *Milliyet*, June 3–23, 1996, and Kemal Can, "Tekkeden Holdinge Yeşil Sermaye," *Milliyet*, March 11–18, 1997.

32. My interviews with Korkut Özal and Ersin Gürdoğan, Istanbul, May 25, 1997 and December 12, 1998.

33. Mustafa Özel, *Müslüman ve Ekonomi* (Istanbul: İz, 1997), 66–70.

34. Nail Güreli, *Gerçek Tanık: Korkut Özal Anlatıyor* (Istanbul: Milliyet Yayınları, 1994), 27–33.

35. Vural Arıkan, "Vergi Paketiyle İslam Bankacılığı Teşvik Ediliyor," *Yeni Gündem*, November 1–14, 1985.

36. Korkut Boratav, "Inter-Class and Intra-Class Telations of Distribution under 'Structural Adjustment': Turkey during the 1980s," in Arıcanlı and Rodrick, *The Political Economy of Turkey*, 224.

37. C. Keyder, "The Rise and Decline of National Economies in Periphery," *Review of Middle East Studies* 6 (1994): 10.

38. M. L. Karaman, "Sivil Toplum Kavramı ve Türkiye Üzerine Değerlendirmeler: Bir Yeniden Bakış," *Türkiye Günlüğü* 10 (1990): 9–10.

39. *Cumhuriyet*, July 12, 1997, and July 21, 1998.

40. Ayşe Güneş-Ayata, "Gecekondularda Kimlik Sorunu, Dayanışma Görüntüleri ve Hemşerilik," *Toplum ve Bilim* 51–52 (1991): 89, 91, 99, and 100.

41. *Türkiye'de Dernekler ve Vakıflar* (Ankara: Emniyet Genel Müdürlüğü Güvenlik Daire Başkanlığı Dernekler Şube Müdürlüğü, 1999), and Yalçın Doğan, "Vakıflara gözaltı," *Milliyet*, August 28, 1997.

42. Ayşe Buğra, "Class, Culture, and State," 533, and Guy Sorman, interview, "Asıl kapitalist MÜSİAD," *Yeni Yüzyıl*, October 29, 1998.

43. Huner Sencan, *İş Hayatında İslam İnsanı (Homo Islamicus)* (Istanbul: MÜSİAD, 1994).

44. For more on the conference and presentations, see Özel, *Müslüman*, 71–72.

45. Adem Esen, *Orta Anadolu Girişimcilerinin Sosyo-Ekonomik Özellikleri İşletmecilik Anlayışları ve Beklentileri Araştırması* (Konya: Konya Ticaret Odası, 1999), 88–97.

46. Esen, *Orta*, 66.

47. W. H. Swason, "Enchantment and Disenchantment in Modernity: The Significance of 'Religion' as Sociological Category," *Sociological Analysis* 44 (1983): 321–38.

48. Mehmet Zahid Kotku, *Tasavvufi Ahlak* (Istanbul: Seha, 1987); see also Özel, *Müslüman*, 51.

49. Kemal Can, "Tekkeden Holdinge Yeşil Sermaye," *Milliyet*, March 11–18, 1997.

50. Birol Uzunay, "Anadolu Kaplanları "marka" İçin Çalışıyor," *Aksiyon*, July 1998, 12–16.

51. For the list of major Turkish Muslim companies, see *Radikal*, June 13, 1997; "İslamcı Sermayeden Tefeci Faizi," *Milliyet*, June 7, 1997; and *Hürriyet*, June 6, 1997.

52. See "DGM'den MÜSİAD'a kapatma davası," *Cumhuriyet*, May 25, 1998.

53. Ahmet Taşgetiren, "Kapris'ten Çeçenistan görünüyor mu?" *Yeni Şafak*, August 16, 1996; Ali Bulaç, "Dinlenmek ve Tatil Kültürünü Tüketmek," *Yeni Şafak*, July 3, 1996.

54. Bahadır Saraçgil, "Islami Giyimde moda ve tüketim," *Yeni Zemin*, August 1993, 74–76.

55. For more on methodological issues of allowing marginalized groups a "voice," see Rosalind O'Hanlon, "Recovering the Subject: Subaltern Studies and Histories of Resistance in Colonial South Asia," *Modern Asian Studies* 1 (1988): 189–224.

56. Clifford Geertz, *Islam Observed: Religious Development in Morocco and Indonesia* (New Haven: Yale University Press, 1968), 69.

57. Cihan Aktaş, "Örtülü Kimlik Size ne Kadar Yabancı," *İzlenim*, January 15, 1994, 38–39.

58. Based on my conversations with students in Ankara, May 10, 1995, and April 12, 1996.

59. Lila Abu-Lughod, "Movie Stars and Islamic Moralism in Egypt," *Social Text* 37 (1996): 53.

60. See Nazife Şisman and Ayşe Böhürler, "Egemenlik ya da Ego-Menlik," *İzlenim*, August 1993, 16–27.

5. THE ROLE OF LITERACY AND THE MEDIA IN THE ISLAMIC MOVEMENT

1. Ron Eyerman, "Modernity and Social Movements," in *Social Change and Modernity*, ed. Hans Haferkamp and Neil J. Smelser (Berkeley: University of California Press, 1992), 52.

2. The İskenderpaşa order publishes three journals: *İslam* [Islam], *Kadın ve Aile* [Women and family], and *İlim ve Sanat* [Science and art].

3. Esad Coşan, *Yeni Dönemde Yeni Görevler* (Istanbul: SEHA, 1993), 31–32, 84.

4. Coşan, *Yeni Dönemde Yeni Görevler*, 32.

5. Coşan, *Yeni Dönemde Yeni Görevler*, 31.

6. See the special report of the Ministry of Interior in "Radyolarda Ideolojik Gölge," *Milliyet*, April 21, 1994, and Ayse Öncü, "Packaging Islam: Cultural Politics on the Landscape of Turkish Commercial Television," *Public Culture* 8 (1995): 51–71.

7. Robert Hefner, "Islam, State, and Civil Society: ICMI and the Struggle for the Indonesian Middle Class," *Indonesia* 56 (October 1993): 1–33.

8. For the history of printing in Turkey, see Orhan Koloğlu, *Basımevi ve Basının Gecikme Sebebleri ve Sonuçları* (Istanbul: Gazeteciler Cemiyeti Yayınları, 1987); Osman Keskinoğlu, "Türkiye'de Matbaa Tesisi," *İlahiyat Fakültesi Dergisi* 15 (1967): 121–39; Alpay Kapacalı, *Türk Kitap Tarihi* (Istanbul: Cem Yayınevi, 1989); and Nuri Inugur, *Türk Basın Tarihi* (Istanbul: Gazeteciler Cemiyeti, 1992).

9. Michael E. Meeker, "Oral Culture, Media Culture, and the Islamic Resurgence in Turkey," in *Exploring the Written: Anthropology and the Multiplicity of Writing*, ed. Eduardo P. Archetti (Oslo: Scandinavian University Press, 1994), 62.

10. Meeker, "Oral Culture," 62.

11. Brinkley Messick, *The Calligraphic State: Textual Domination and History in a Muslim Society* (Berkeley: University of California Press, 1993), 17.

12. Messick, *Calligraphic State*, 17.

13. Francis Robinson, "Technology and Religious Change: Islam and the Impact of Print," *Modern Asian Studies* 27, 1 (1993): 246.

14. The Egyptian social scientist Leila Ahmed has presented the similar phenomenon of shaping mainstream culture as "democratization," since social groups rather than the state are shaping the culture. I prefer to call this process *communalism* rather than democratization of the mainstream culture. See Leila Ahmed, *Women and Gender in Islam* (New Haven: Yale University Press, 1992), 225.

15. My interview with Murat Gül, Ankara, March 23, 1994.

16. Koray Calışkan, "İslami Romanlar Üzerine Bir İnceleme," *Birikim* 91 (November 1996): 89–95; and Ahmet Kekeç, *Yağmurdan Sonra* (Istanbul: şehir, 2000).

17. Rasim Özdenören, "İslami Edebiyat Tartışmaları," in *Ruhun Malzemeleri* (Istanbul: Risale, 1986), 37.

18. Şerif Mardin, "Modernization of Social Communication," in *Propaganda and Communication in World History*, ed. Harold D. Laswell and Daniel Lerner (Honolulu: University Press of Hawaii, 1979), 381–443.

19. Daniel Bougnoux, "New Ways of Being Together," *Courier*, February 1995, 10.

20. Jack Goody and Ian Watt, "The Consequences of Literacy," in *Literacy in Traditional Societies*. ed. J. Goody (Cambridge, England: Cambridge University Press, 1968), 44.

21. Francis Robinson, "Knowledge, Its Transmission and the Making of Muslim Societies," in *The Cambridge Illustrated History of the Islamic World*, ed. Francis Robinson (New York: Cambridge University Press, 1996), 208–49.

22. Ernest Gellner, "Nationalism," lecture given in Madison, Wisconsin, on February 11, 1993.

23. *Tezkire* is the most theoretically sophisticated Islamic journal. It was established by a group of young intellectuals, Ahmet Çiğdem, Nuray Mert, Yasin Aktay, Erol Göka, and Ercan Şen, in 1991. It focuses on the relationship between Islam, modernity, Qur'anic hermeneutics, and democracy.

24. Mehmet Metiner, editor of *Girişim*, and Osman Tunç, two prominent Kurdish intellectuals, founded *Yeni Zemin* to support Turgut Özal's "Second Transformation" program; it was funded by a pro-Kurdish Nurcu community, Med Zehra.

25. *İzlenim, Bilgi ve Hikmet* and *İktisat ve İş Dünyası* are published and funded by the İz Publishing House.

26. Scott Thomas, "The Global Resurgence of Religion and the Study of World Politics," *Millennium: Journal of International Studies* 24, 2 (1995): 298.

27. Şerif Mardin, *The Genesis of Young Ottoman Thought* (Princeton: Princeton University Press, 1962).

28. Zeki Coşkun, *Aleviler, Sunniler ve Öteki Sivas* (Istanbul: İletişim Yayınları, 1995), 358; For İsmet Özel's endorsing reaction to the burning, see "Ya Müslüman Türkiye veya Hiç!" *Milli Gazete*, July 6, 1993.

29. Ali Haydar Aksal, "Dönüşümler Kavşağında Büyük Doğu," *Yedi İklim*, May 1993, 60–62.

30. Şerif Mardin, "Culture Change and the Intellectual: A Study of the Effects of Secularization in Modern Turkey," in *Cultural Transitions in the Middle East*, ed. Mardin (Leiden: Brill, 1994), 189–213.

31. S. Seyfi Öğün, *Türkiye'de Cemaatçi Milliyetçilik ve Nurettin Topçu* (Istanbul: Dergah, 1992); Muamer Çelik, *Nurettin Topçu ve Bügünkü Türkiye* (Istanbul: Ülke, 2000); and Mustafa Kök, *Nurettin Topçu'da Din Felsefesi* (Istanbul: Dergah, 1995).

32. Şakir Diçlehan, *Sanat ve Düşünce Dünyasında Sezai Karakoç* (Istanbul: Piran, 1980), and Turan Karataş, *Doğu'nun Yedinci Oğlu: Sezai Karakoç* (Istanbul: Kaknus, 1998).

33. *Hareket Dergisi* was published intermittently between 1939 and 1974. For more on the influence of Blondel's writings on Nurettin Topçu, see Ali O. Gündoğan, "Blondel'in Felsefesi ve Türkiye'deki Etkisi" (Ph.D. diss., Atatürk University, Erzurum, 1991).

34. Nurettin Topçu, *Milliyetçiliğimizin Esasları* (Istanbul: Degah, 1978); *İsyan Ahlakı* (Istanbul: Dergah, 1995); and *Ahlak Nizamı*, 3rd ed. (Istanbul: Degah, 1997).

35. Öğün, *Türkiye'de*, chap. 2.

36. Abdullah Uçman, "Necip Fazıl ve Agaç Dergisi," *Mavera* 80–82 (July–September 1983): 86.

37. Kısakürek overcomes his ontological "emptiness" by developing spiritual ties to a Nakşibendi sheikh. In his book *He and I* [O ve Ben], 6th ed. (Istanbul: Büyük Doğu, 1990), he examines his interactions with his Sufi sheikh, Abdülhakim Arvasi. This book consists of three sections: the first explores his moral emptiness until he meets with the Sufi leader (1904–1934); the second part explains his transformation as a result of establishing a spiritual and moral tie with Arvasi and rediscovering his inner realm (1934–1943); and the third section describes his voyage to Turkish politics and literature without spiritual guidance (1943–1983).

38. Sezai Karakoç, *Diriliş Neslinin Amentüsü* (Istanbul: Diriliş Yayınları, 1979), *Kıyamet Aşısı*, 5th ed. (Istanbul: Diriliş, 1979), *İnsanlığın Dirilişi*, 4th ed. (Istanbul: Diriliş, 1987), *Yitik Cennet*, 4th ed. (Istanbul: Diriliş, 1979), *Ruhun Dirilişi*, 4th ed.

(Istanbul: Diriliş, 1979), and *İslam Toplumunun Ekonomik Strukturu*, 7th ed. (Istanbul: Diriliş, 1980).

39. *Sebilürreşad* [The Straight Path] was published between 1908 and 1966. It presented a religiously traditional and politically activist stand. It favored the Ittihad-ı İslam and supported the War of Independence. Its editor was Eşref Edip (Fergan) (1882–1971); Mehmet Akif (Ersoy), and Ebu'l-Ula Mardin, who also published *Sırat-ı Müstakim* in 1908, were assistant editors. The magazine became very popular in the 1950s. *Sebilürreşad* followed a religious-nationalistic path and supported democracy.

40. *Serdengeçti* was founded by Osman Yüksel Serdengeçti and was published between 1947 and 1952. It was reprinted in 1956 and 1958 without success. This magazine was very critical of the reforms.

41. *İslam* was published between 1956 to 1965 by a group of prominent scholars. It mainly dealt with religious institutions and the life of the Prophet Mohammad. It avoided political issues.

42. Topçu also made his spiritual commitment to Abdülaziz Bekkine. See also Mustafa Kutlu, "Nurettin Topçu İçin Bir Biyografi Denemesi," *Hareket Dergisi* (January–March 1976). In 1977, *Hareket*'s publisher changed its name to Dergah

43. Ersin Gürdoğan, "Kitlesel Üretim ve Edebiyat," *Mavera* 97 (December 1985): 23.

44. Michael Meeker, "The New Muslim Intellectuals in the Republic of Turkey," in *Islam in Modern Turkey*, ed. Richard Tapper (London: St. Martin's Press, 1991), 189–222; Binnaz Toprak, "İki Müslüman Aydın: Ali Bulaç ve İsmet Özel," *Toplum ve Bilim* 29/30 (1985): 143–51; İsmet Özel's response, "Hem Peruklu Hem Fadul," *Kitap Dergisi* 9 (1986): 10.

45. İsmet Özel, *Cuma Mektupları I*, 2nd ed.(Istanbul: Çiğdem Yayınları, 1990), 139.

46. Özel, *Cuma Mektupları III* (Istanbul: ÇiğdemYayınları, 1990), 168.

47. Özel, *Cuma Mektupları I*, 139.

48. My interview with Ali Bulaç, Istanbul, April 23, 1994.

49. Özel's essays on this theme appeared regularly in *Yeni Devir*; they have been collected in his edited volume, *Zor Zamanlarda Konuşmak* (Istanbul: Risale, 1986).

50. Bulaç's model of the *Medine Vesikası* dominated the intellectual debate in both Islamic and secular circles in the second half of the 1990s; see Ali Bulaç, "Medina Document," in *Liberal Islam*, ed. Charles Kuzman (New York: Oxford University Press, 1998), 169–78.

51. My interview with Ali Bulaç, Istanbul, March 22, 1994.

52. Ali Bulaç, *Islam and Fanatizm* (Istanbul: Beyan, 1993), 63.

53. My interview with Bulaç, Istanbul, March 24, 1994.

54. Quoted in Recep Kocak's interview with Rasim Özdenören, in "Rasim Özdenören'le 1980 Sonrasi Kültür Değişimi Üzerine," *İlim ve Sanat* 26 (1989): 11.

55. My interview with Özdenören, Ankara, June 12, 1999.

56. David Swanson, "Secular Turkey Teeters over Plan to Close Islamic Schools," *Christian Science Monitor*, June 12, 1997.

57. See Osman Ergin, *Türk Maarif Tarihi*, 5 vols. (Istanbul: Eser Matbaası, 1977); İlhan Başgöz, *Türkiye'nin Eğitim Çıkmazı ve Atatürk* (Ankara: Kültür Bakanlığı, 1995), 74–80; and İhsan Süngü, "Tevhid-i Tedrisat," *Belleten* 7–8 (1938): 21–45.

58. See Vergin's fascinating distinction between *laiklik* (laic/secularization) and *laikcilik* (laicism/secularism as an ideology) in "Mulakat," *Türkiye Günlüğü* 27 (March 1994): 5–12.

59. On the role of schools in the transmission of hegemonic culture, see Pierre

Bourdieu, "Systems of Education and Systems of Thought," *International Social Science Journal* 19, 3 (1967): 341.

60. *Yeni Yüzyıl,* March 17, 1997.

61. See Mustafa Öcal, *İmam-Hatip Liseleri ve İlk Öğretim Okulları* (Istanbul: Ensar Yayınları, 1994), and "Kuruluşundan Günümüze İmam-Hatip Liseleri," *Din Eğitimi Araştırmaları Dergisi* 6 (1999), 200-254.

62. Osman Ergin, *Türk Maarif,* 5:1735-42.

63. Ömer Okutan, *Cumhuriyet Dönemi Milli Eğitimimiz* (Istanbul: M. E. B. Yayınları, 1983), 416.

64. Beyza Bilgin, *Eğitim Bilimi ve Din Eğitimi* (Ankara: İlahiyat Fakültesi Yayınları, 1988), 52; Öcal, *İmam-Hatip,* 33.

65. For the memories of A. Hamdi Akseki, who was the deputy head of the Directorate of Religious Affairs, see *Sebilürreşad* 12, 284 (1959): 144.

66. *C. H. P. Yedinci Kurultay Tutanağı* (Ankara: C.H.P., 1948), 457.

67. Bilgin, *Eğitim Bilimi,* 56.

68. *Her Yönüyle Tevfik İleri* (Ankara: Diyanet İşleri Vakfı Yayınları, 1995).

69. Howard Reed, "Revival of Islam in Secular Turkey," *Middle East Journal* 8, 3 (1954): 271-73.

70. Okutan, *Cumhuriyet,* 420.

71. Halis Ayhan, *Din Eğitimi ve Öğretimi* (Istanbul: DİB Yayınları, 1985), 66-68.

72. Quoted in Süleyman Hayri Bolay and Mümtazer Türköne, *Din Eğitimi Rapory* (Ankara: Diyanet Vakfi, 1995), 131.

73. *İmam Hatip Liseleri Öğretim Programları* (Ankara: Milli Eğitim Basımevi, 1985).

74. On the opening of the *İmam Hatip* Schools by year and by government, see Ahmet Ünal, "*İmam Hatip*'lere Millet Teveccühü," *Zaman,* February 27, 1994.

75. Halis Ayhan, *Kuruluşunun 43.Yılında İmam-Hatip Liseleri* (Istanbul: Ensar, 1995).

76. Necmettin Erbakan, *Milli Görüş* (Istanbul: Dergah, 1975), 101.

77. On a survey by PIAR-Gallup on the students of *İmam Hatip* schools, see *Yeni Yüzyıl,* April 1, 1997.

78. Necmettin Erbakan, *Yeni Oluşum: Büyük Değişim* (Ankara: Refah Partisi, 1993), 15.

79. Interview with Beşir Ayvazoğlu in "İslamcı aydınlar 'İslami Aydınlanma' yı tartışıyor," *Nokta,* 26 June-2 July 1994, 18.

80. *Milli Görüşün İktidardaki Hizmetleri (1974-1978)* (Ankara: Refah Partisi, 1995), 5.

81. For more on the social and political attitudes of the *İmam Hatip* high school, see Bahattin Akşit, "*İmam Hatip* and Other Secondary Schools in the Context of Political and Cultural Modernization of Turkey," *Journal of Human Sciences* 5, 1 (1986): 38.

82. Kenan Evren, "Dini Siyasete Alet Etmedim," *Milliyet,* May 1, 1990.

83. *MEB Din Öğretimi Dergisi* 30 (1991): 25.

84. For example, the Association of Turkish Industrialists and Businessmen (TÜSİAD) prepared several reports on the *İmam Hatips* and called the state to close these schools; see Zekai Baloğlu, *Türkiye'de Eğitim* (Istanbul: TÜSİAD Yayınları, 1990).

85. Abbas Güçlü, "RP'nin 2. Kalesi, Okullar," *Milliyet,* February 19, 1994.

86. For the new law, see "The 4306 Education Law," *RG,* August 18, 1997.

87. *Milliyet,* July 22, 1997.

88. Ecevit's speech is in *Zaman*, July 30, 1997.

89. "İmam Hatiplere BaşvuruYüzde 95 Düştü," *Zaman*, September 11, 1998; for an interesting analysis by Halil Hayıt, former general director of religious education at the Ministry of Education, see "Anadolu Cezalandırıldı," *Aksiyon*, 152 (November 1998).

90. Mustafa Öcal, "Cumhuriyet Döneminde Türkiye'de Din Eğitimi ve Öğretimi," *Uludağ Üniversitesi İlahiyat Fakültesi Dergisi* 7, 7 (1998): 241–68 (*http://www.meb.gov.tr/Stats/Apk2002/64.htm*).

91. A. H. Akseki, *Askere Din Kitabı*, 3rd ed. (Ankara: D.İ.B., 1980). *Religious Instructions for Soldiers* is still the major textbook in the military schools.

92. A. H. Akseki's *İslam Dini* (3rd ed.; Ankara: Güzel Sanatlar Matbaası, 1954) was the most important textbook of Turkish divinity schools. It originally was published in 1933. Akseki wrote a detailed report to explain the situation of religious instruction and asked the government to improve the education level of the religious functionaries as a bulwark against religious fanaticism within Turkey, Islamic radicalism from outside, and the expanding influence of communism. For the full text of the report, see "Din Tedrisatı ve Dini Müesseseler Hakkında Bir Rapor," *Sebilürreşad* 100–105 (April–June 1951), 100: 387–88, 101: 4–5, 102: 19–20, 103: 36–38, 104: 52–53, and 105: 67–68.

93. Okutan, *Cumhuriyet*, 423.

94. Okutan, *Cumhuriyet*, 423.

6. THE MATRIX OF TURKISH ISLAMIC MOVEMENTS

1. Hamid Algar has developed the framework for Nakşibendi studies; see especially Algar, "The Naksibendi Order: A Preliminary Survey of Its History and Significance," *Studia Islamica* 44 (1976): 123–52, and "The Naksibendi Order in Republican Turkey," *Islamic World Report* 1, 3 (1996): 51–67; see also Martin van Bruinessen, *Agha, Shaikh and State: The Social and Political Structure of Kurdistan* (London: Zed Books, 1992), 222–65.

2. See Annemarie Schimmel, *Mystical Dimensions of Islam* (Chapel Hill: University of North Carolina Press, 1975); and J. Spencer Trimingham, *The Sufi Orders in Islam* (New York: Oxford University Press, 1971).

3. Yaşar Nuri Öztürk, *The Eye of the Heart: An Introduction to Sufism and the Tariqats of Anatolia and the Balkans* (Istanbul: Redhouse, 1988), chap. 1.

4. Ferit Aydın, *Tarikatta Rabıta ve Nakşibendilik* (Istanbul: Ekin, 1996).

5. See Mehmet Ali Aynı, *Tasavvuf Tarihi* (Istanbul: Kitabevi Yayınları, 1992), and Mahir İz, *Tasavvuf* 5th ed (Istanbul: Kitabevi Yayınları, 1990), 73; Mustafa Kara, *Tasavvuf ve Tarikatlar* (Istanbul: Dergah Yayınları, 1985); Erol Güngör, *İslam Tasavvufunun Meseleleri* (Istanbul: Ötüken Yayınları, 1992); Mustafa Kara, *Günümüz Tasavvuf Hareketleri* (Istanbul: Dergah, 2002).

6. E. Abdülhakim Arvasi, *Tasavvuf Bahçeleri* (Istanbul: Büyük Doğu Yayınları, 1983), 16–17.

7. For more on *bid'a*, see Vardit Rispler, "Toward a New Understanding of the Term *Bid'a*," *Der Islam* 68, 2 (1991): 320–28; and Maribel Fierro, "The Treaties against Innovations [*Kutub al-bid'a*], *Der Islam* 69, 2 (1993): 204–46.

8. Hamid Algar, "A Brief History of the Nakşibendi Order," in *Naqshbandis: Historical Developments and Present Situation of a Muslim Mystical Order*, ed. Marc Gaborieau and Alexander Popovic (Istanbul: ISIS, 1990), 3–45.

9. For more on Sirhindi, see Hayrettin Karaman, *İmam-ı Rabbani ve İslam*

Tasavvufu (Istanbul: Nesil Yayınları, 1992); İbrahim Edhem Bilgin, *Devrimci Sufi Hareketleri ve İmam-ı Rabbani* (Istanbul: Kültür Basın Yayın Birliği, 1989); Fazlur Rahman, *Selected Letters of Sirhindi* (Karachi: Iqbal Akadami, 1968); and Yohanan Friedmann, *Shaykh Ahmad Sirhindi: An Outline of His Thought and a Study of His Image in the Eyes of Posterity* (New Delhi: Oxford University Press, 2000).

10. Sajida S. Alvi, "The Mujaddid and Tajdid Traditions in the Indian Subcontinent: An Historical Overview," *Journal of Turkish Studies* 18 (1994): 1–15.

11. Jo Ann Gross, "Khoja Ahrar: A Study of the Perceptions of Religious Power and Prestige in the Late Timurid Period" (Ph.D. diss., New York University, 1982).

12. Ali Kadri, *Tarikat-ı Nakşibendiye Prensipleri* (Istanbul: Pamuk Yayınları, 1994), 80–87.

13. Martin van Bruinessen, "Sufis and Sultans in Southeast Asia and Kurdistan: A Comparative Survey," *Studia Islamika* 3, 3 (1996): 12.

14. Alvi, "The Mujaddid and Tajdid Traditions."

15. Hamid Algar, "Devotional Practices of the Khalidi Nakşibendis of Ottoman Turkey," in *The Dervish Lodge: Architecture, Art, and Sufism in Ottoman Turkey*, ed. Raymond Lifchez (Berkeley: University of California Press, 1992), 209–27.

16. See Mevlana Halid-i Bağdadi, *Risale-i Halidiye ve Adab-i Zikir Risalesi* (Istanbul: SEHA Neşriyat, 1990).

17. Butrus Abu–Manneh, "The Naksibendiyya–Mujaddidiyya in the Ottoman Lands in the Early Nineteenth Century," *Die Welt des Islams* 22 (1982–84): 14.

18. Albert Hourani, "Sufism and Modern Islam: Mavlana Khalid and the Nakşibendi Order," in *The Emergence of the Modern Middle East* (Oxford: Macmillan, 1981), 80.

19. İrfan Gündüz, *Osmanlılarda Devlet-Tekke Münasebetleri* (Istanbul: Seha, 1984), 243.

20. For a detailed description of the establishment of a *rabita* between *hocaefendi* and *mürid*, see Ersin Gürdoğan, *Görünmeyen Üniversite* (Istanbul: İz Yayıncılık, 1991), 36–39.

21. Kasım Kufralı, "Nakşibendiliğin Kuruluş ve Yayılması" (The establishment and diffusion of Nakşibendis) (Ph.D. diss., Istanbul Üniversitesi Türkiyat Enstitüsü, 1949), 102–12.

22. Algar, "Devotional Practices," 210.

23. Abu-Manneh, "Naksibendiyya-Mujaddidiya," 32.

24. Hourani, "Sufism," 76.

25. Martin van Bruinessen, "The Origins and Development of the Naksibendi Order in Indonesia," *Der Islam* 67 (1990): 151, and "The Origins and Development of Sufi Orders (Tarekat) in Southeast Asia," *Studika Islamika* 1, 1 (1994): 15, 16.

26. Algar, "A Brief History," 30.

27. See Butrus Abu-Manneh, "Shaykh Ahmed Ziyauddin el-Gumushanevi and the Ziya'i Khalid suborder," in *Shi'a Islam, Sects and Sufism: Historical Dimensions, Religious Practice and Methodological Considerations*, ed. Frederick de Jong (Utrecht: M. Th. Houtsma Stichting), 105–17.

28. Abu-Manneh, "Naksibendiyya–Mujaddidiyya," 12; Albert Hourani, "Sufism and Modern Islam: Rashid Rida," in *The Emergence of the Modern Middle East* (Oxford: Macmillan, 1981), 95.

29. On Nakşibendi participation in the Kuleli Incident, see Uluğ İğdemir, *Kuleli Vak'ası Hakkında Bir Araştırma* (Ankara: TTK, 1937), 30, 60–64.

30. Şerif Mardin, "The Nakshibendi Order of Turkey," in *Fundamentalism*, ed. Martin Marty and S. Appleby (Chicago: Chicago University Press, 1990), 205.

31. Algar, "The Nakşibendi Order," 149.

32. See Clarence Richard Johnson, *Constantinople Today: A Study in Oriental Social Life* (New York: Macmillan,1922); and Osman Ergin, *Türk Maarif Tarihi*, vols. 1–2 (Istanbul: Eser Matbaası, 1977), 240–41.

33. Algar, "Naksibendi Order in Republican Turkey," 54.

34. See Kadir Mısırlıoğlu, *Kurtuluş Savaşında Sarıklı Mücahitler* (Istanbul: Mizan, 1969), 263–73.

35. See Mısırlıoğlu, *Kutuluş*, 262–73, and Cevat Dursunoğlu, *Milli Mücadele'de Erzurum* (Ankara: T. C. Ziraat Bankası, 1946).

36. The Kemalists presented the Nakşibendis as "backward" and obstacles to change; see, for example, İlhan Selçuk, "Son Yüzyılda Nakşilerin Kilometre Taşları," *Cumhuriyet*, August 3, 1994.

37. See Reşat Halli, *Türkiye Cumhuriyeti'nde Ayaklanmalar (1924–1938)* (Ankara: Genel Kurmay Yayınları, 1972).

38. See *Menemen İrtica Hadisesi* (Ankara: Hariciye Vekaleti Matbuat Umum Müdürlüğü, 1931), and Mustafa Müftüoğlu, *Menemen Vak'ası* (Istanbul: Risale, 1991).

39. My interviews with A. Taşgetiren, Istanbul, April 12, 1995, March 15, 1996, and July 13, 2000.

40. Fahrettin Altay, *10 Yıl Savaş ve Sonrası* (Istanbul: İnsel Yayınları, 1970), 437.

41. A. Selahattin Kınacı, *Seyyid Muhammed Raşid Erol (K.S.A.)'nın Hayatı* (Adıyaman: Menzil Yayınları, 1996); N. Fazıl Kuru, "Menzil Nakşiliği Merkez Cemaati Üzerine Sosyolojik Bir Araştırma," M.A. thesis, University of Erciyes, Kayseri, 1999).

42. Emin Yaşar Demirci, "Modernisation, Religion and Politics in Turkey: The Case of the İskenderpaşa Community" (Ph.D. diss., Manchester University, U.K., 1996); M. Hakan Yavuz, "The Matrix of Modern Turkish Islamic Movements: The Naqshbandi Sufi Order," in Naqshbandis in Western and Central Asia, ed. Elisabeth Özdalga (Istanbul: Numune Matbaası, 1999), 125–42.

43. See Esad Coşan, "Thoughts on the Elections," *İslam*, October 1991, 1–2; and Mehmet Sayoğlu, "Vefatının 15. Yılında Mehmet Zahid Kotku," *Yeni Safak*, November 12, 1995.

44. Algar's note from his private conversation with Kotku, "Political Aspects of Naqshbandi History," in Gaborieau and Popovic, *Naqshbandis*, 143.

45. Halit İlhan, "Bağımsızlığa Teşvik Etmiştir," *İslam*, November 1992, 43.

46. Mehmet Sayoğlu, "Mehmet Zahid Kotku: Kafkasya'dan Bursa'ya," *Yeni Safak*, November 12–14, 1995.

47. Serdar Ömeroğlu, "Mehmet Zahid Kotku," *Milli Gazete*, November 13–18, 1988.

48. "Mehmet Zahid Kotku Hocaefendi Rahmetle Anıldı," *Zaman*, November 30, 1994.

49. Coskun Yılmaz, "Mehmet Zahid Efendi (K.S.) ve İktisadi Hayat," *İslam*, November 1994, 26.

50. During my interview on October 21, 1996, in response to my question, Lütfü Doğan, then parliamentarian of the RP, at his office in the Grand National Assembly said, "By 'one Mazda,' they mean an economically up-to-date Turkey since Mazda was the best car in the market in the 1980s. Moreover, you should note that Mazda is a Japanese car, and there is admiration of Japan for what they have achieved without giving up their tradition."

51. Kotku's books are published in Istanbul by Seha, and most do not list a date of publication. His major works include *Tasavvufi Ahlak*, 5 vols. (Istanbul: Seha

Neşriyat, no date); *Nefsin Terbiyesi*; *Ehl-i Sünnet*; *Mü'minlere Vaazlar*, 2 vols.; *Hadislerle Nasihatler*, 2 vols.; *Alim* (Istanbul: Seha Neşriyat, 1985); *Mü'minlerin Vasıfları*; *Cihad*; *Namaz*; *Zikrullah'ın Faydaları*; *Tevhid*; *Tevbe*; *İman*; *Sabır*; *En Güzel Ameller*; *Oruç*; *Zekat*; *Hac*; *Cömertlik*; *Yemek Adabı*; *Zulüm*; *Faiz*; *Korku ve Ümit*; *İçki*; *Ölüm*; and *Özel Sohbetler*.

52. See Seyfi Say, "Mehmet Zahid Kotku'yu Anarken," *İslam*, November 1991, 40–47.

53. Esad Coşan, *Yeni Dönemde Yeni Görevlerimiz* (İstanbul: Seha, 1993), 119.

54. Coşan, *Yeni*, 163.

55. H. Kamil Yılmaz, "M.Es'ad Erbili," *Altınoluk*, November 1994, 33–34.

56. This book is published in modern Turkish as well; see *Kenzü'l-İrfan* (Istanbul: Erkam, 1989).

57. Esad Efendi, *Divan* (Istanbul: Erkam, 1991).

58. *Mektubat* (Istanbul: Erkam, 1983).

59. In Istanbul, he wrote *Risale-i Es'adiyye*, a collection of short essays on the significance of Sufism and the norms of joining. It is published in modern Turkish (Istanbul: Erkam, 1989).

60. My interview with Ahmet Taşgetiren, editor of the monthly magazine *Altınoluk*, of the Erenköy order, Istanbul, May 31, 1999.

61. Sadık Albayrak, *Şeriat Yolunda Yürüyenler ve Sürünenler* (Istanbul, Medrese Yayınevi, 1979), 231–34, and Mete Tunçay, *Türkiye Cumhuriyeti*, 293–95.

62. Sadık Dana, *Mahmut Sami Ramazanoğlu* (Istanbul: Erkam, 1991).

63. My interview with Ahmet Taşgetiren, Istanbul, May 31, 1999.

64. Mahir İz, *Tasavvuf* (Istanbul: Rahle, 1969). İz's book very much reflects the thought of Ramazanoğlu.

65. Nazif Gürdoğan, "Bir Görünmeyen Üniversitenin Hicreti," *Yeni Safak*, July 26, 1999.

66. For the activities of the Süleymancıs, see Hızır Yılmaz, *"Süleymancılık" Hakkında Bir İnceleme* (Cologne: n.p., 1977); Vehbi Vakkasoğlu, "Süleyman Hilmi Tunahan," *Tercüman*, December 11, 1986; *Nokta*, December 19–22, 1993, 12–16. A more comprehensive work is Ahmet Akgündüz, *Arşiv Belgeleri Işığında Silistreli Süleyman Hilmi Tunahan* (Istanbul: Cihan Matbaası, 1997); see also Mustafa Özdamar, *Üstaz Süleyman Hilmi Tunahan* (Istanbul: Kırk Kandil, 1997); M. Ali Kırman, "Türkiye'de Bir 'Yeni Dini Cemaat' Örneği Olarak Süleymancılık" (Ph.D. diss., Ankara University, 2000). On the religious persecution of Tunahan, see the official file on Tunahan in Diyanet İşleri Başkanlığı, Sicil No: 23–0383 Süleyman Hilmi Tunahan Dosyası.

67. Mustafa Arıkan, "Büyük Müceddid İçin Ne Dediler," *Ufuk Gazetesi*, September 20, 1978.

68. For an example of the Süleymancı conception of secularism, see Ahmet Özcan, *Yeni Bir Cumhuriyet İçin* (Istanbul: Bakış, 1997).

69. Mustafa Ünal, "Tunahan Hazretleri'nin Torunu (Arif Ahmet Denizolgun) Mecliste," *Aksiyon*, March 1, 1996, 10–11. This article examines the Süleymancı support for the RP in the 1995 national elections.

7. PRINT-BASED ISLAMIC DISCOURSE

1. On Nursi's life and his ideas, see İhsan Işık, *Bediüzzaman Said Nursi ve Nurculuk* (Istanbul: Ünlem Yayınları, 1990); Nevzat Köseoğlu, *Bediüzzaman Said Nursi: Hayatı-Yolu-Eseri* (Istanbul: Ötüken, 1999); Mustafa Karacoşkun, "Nurcu

Cemaatine Mensup Kişilerin Dini Düşünce Duygu ve Davranışları" (M.A. thesis, Marmara University, Istanbul, 1991); and Abdullah Albayrak, *Sosyal Değişim Sürecinde Risale-i Nur Hareketi* (Istanbul: Nesil, 2002).

2. For the Turkish collection of Said Nursi, see *Risale-i Nur Külliyatı*, 2 vols. (Istanbul: Nesil, 1996) (hereafter *RNK*). These two volumes include all Nursi's writings.

3. "Mektubat," *RNK*, 1:355–57, 359; and Bilal Kuşpınar, "Bediüzzaman Said Nursi'nin Tasavvuf Değerlendirmesi," *Uluslararası Bediüzzaman Sempozyumu III* (Istanbul: Yeni Asya, 1996), 452–62.

4. "Mektubat," 1:220–578; "Şualar," *RNK*, 1:1001, 1002, 1097; and Abdullah Badıllı, *Bediüzzaman Said-i Nursi-Mufassal Tarihçe-i Hayatı* (Istanbul: Timaş, 1990), 102.

5. See more about his method of reading *Mektubat* in "Sözler," *RNK*, 1:95, 317; "Mektubat," 1:511–64; "Barla lahikası," *RNK*, 2:1467–94.

6. "Telvihat-ı Tis'a," *RNK*, 1:561–69.

7. My interview with Fethullah Gülen about the connection between the Nakşibendi order and Said Nursi, Istanbul, May 27, 1997. Some parts of this interview were published in *Milliyet*, August 10–13, 1997.

8. "Tarihçe-i Hayat," *RNK*, 2:2130–31.

9. See his essays "Hürriyete Hitap," *RNK*, 2:1932–36; "Yaşasın Şeriat-ı Ahmedi," *RNK*, 2:1930; and "Divan-ı Harb-i Örfi," *RNK*, 2:1920–28.

10. See Mevlanazade Rıfat, *31 Mart-Bir İhtilalin İçyüzü* (Istanbul: Pınar, 1996); Mustafa Baydar, *31 Mart Vak'ası* (Istanbul: Milli Tesanüt Birliği, 1955); İsmail Hami Danişmend, *31 Mart Vak'ası* (Istanbul: Kitabevi, 1961); Şinasi Akşin, *Seriatçı Bir Ayaklanma: 31 Mart Olayı* (Istanbul: İmge, 1994); and Sadık Albayrak, *31 Mart Vak'ası Gerici Bir Hareket mi?* (Istanbul: Bilim-Araştırma, 1987).

11. His defense at the court, "Divan-ı Örfi," *RNK*, 2:1917–35.

12. "Divan-ı Örfi," 2:1917–35.

13. My interview with İsmail Kara, Istanbul, August 4, 2001.

14. "Münazarat," in *RNK*, 2:1937–59.

15. One of the best analyses of the political philosophy of Said Nursi is Safa Mürsel, *Bediüzzaman Said Nursi ve Devlet Felsefesi* (Istanbul: Yeni Asya Yayınları, 1995).

16. His speeches were published in Arabic under the title "Hutbe-i Şamiye"; for Nursi's own translation of this work into Turkish, see "Hutbe-i Şamiye," *RNK*, 2:1959–85.

17. Nursi wrote his famous essay "Hutuvat-ı Sitte" (*RNK*, 2:2055–58) against the occupation.

18. "Tarihçe-i Hayat," *RNK*, 2:2137–39.

19. On Said Nursi's activities in stopping the rebellion, See Necmettin Şahiner, *Bilinmeyen Yönleriyle Bediüzzaman Said Nursi* (Istanbul: Yeni Asya Yayınları, 1974), 238–42.

20. Martin van Bruinessen, *Agha, Shaikh and State: The Social and Political Structures of Kurdistan* (London: Zed Books, 1992), 265.

21. "Tarihçe-i Hayat," *RNK*, 2:2140.

22. He wrote some of his best work in jail; for instance, *El-Hüccetü'z-Zehra* (*RNK*, vol. 1, 1116–52) in Afyon Prison (1948–1949) and *İsm-i Azam* (*RNK*, vol. 1, 797–827) in Eskişehir jail in 1935.

23. Since Nursi wrote all his commentaries in Arabic script, his followers insisted on copying the writing by hand to perpetuate Arabic alphabet education in Turkey.

24. *Nurcu* literally refers to the followers of the *RNK*. The Eskişehir Court named those who were arrested for possesing Nursi's books *Nurs*.

25. "Şualar," *RNK*, 1:1024.

26. "Sünühat," *RNK*, 2:2051.

27. Mesut Toplayıcı, "İslam ve Demokrasi," *Köprü* 50, (1995): 56–69.

28. For his support, see a letter to the president and prime minister in "Emirdağ Lahikası," *RNK*, 2:1904–905; for Nursi's criticism of Adnan Menderes's policies, see "Emirdağ Lahikası," *RNK*, 2:1882–83.

29. "Kastamonu Lahikası," *RNK*, 2:1585. In other words, Nursi is saying that a person should sacrifice the private sphere for the public/political sphere.

30. "Hutbe-i Şamiye," *RNK*, 2:1965.

31. "Beyanat ve Tenvirler," *RNK*, 1:24, 25–27.

32. For example, Said Nursi asked the state to publish his works in order to fight the atheism and nihilism that threaten society; see "Emirdağ Lahikası," *RNK*, 2:1720–21.

33. Şahiner, *Bilinmeyen*, 403–404.

34. M. Hakan Yavuz, "Being Modern in the Nurcu Way." *ISIM Newsletter* (October 2000): 7 and 14.

35. "Emirdağ Lahikası," *RNK*, 2:1729 and 1841–42; according to Nursi, his writings do not use Islam for political goals but promote social order and peace "by challenging atheism, nihilism and anarchism, at the bottom, and oppression on the surface," 1729.

36. "Kastamonu Lahikası," *RNK*, 2:1606, 1631, 1641.

37. "Mektubat," 1:362 and 485–86.

38. "Mektubat," 1:520–21; "İşaratü'l-İcaz," *RNK*, 2:1222–23 and 1260–61.

39. "Münazarat," *RNK*, 2:1947.

40. The largest number of Nurcu publications are still sold in the cities of western Turkey.

41. Ali Mermer presents the characteristics of the Nurcus in "*Aspects of Religious Identity: Nurcu Movement in Turkey Today*" (Ph.D. diss., University of Durham, U.K., 1985), 388–90; Fahri Çakı, "New Social Classes and Movements in the Context of Politico-Economic Development in Contemporary Turkey" (Ph.D. diss., Temple University, Philadelphia, PA, 2001).

42. New literacy, that is, mass literacy in which everyone is a reader, has been key in the formation of Islamic political consciousness.

43. For more on formal and informal education and the role of Nursi, see my "The Assassination of Collective Memory: The Case of Turkey," *Muslim World* 89, 3–4 (1999): 193–207.

44. The printed text helped to form new social organizations. As a result of becoming print-oriented, people start to put their experiences on paper and reflectivity is encouraged. This in turn creates a close relationship between literature and life. Although people usually signify their experiences, later literature starts to shape social life; from my interview with Nazif Gürdoğan on the role of print and books, May 9, 1997.

45. Geoff Eley, "Nations, Publics, and Political Cultures: Placing Habermas in the Nineteenth Century," in *Habermas and the Public Sphere*, ed. Craig Calhoun (Cambridge: MIT Press, 1992). In this article Eley criticizes Habermas's conception of public space and introduces the idea of "competing publics," 306.

46. During my fieldwork, I visited 23 Nur dershanes in Ankara, Bayburt,

Erzurum, Eskisehir, Istanbul, and Konya in 1994–2001 and 18 dershanes in Germany and Holland in August 2001.

47. From my notes of a visit to a Nurcu dershane, February 20, 1994.

48. From my notes of my visit of February 20, 1994.

49. Nilüfer Göle, a prominent Turkish sociologist, was instrumental in stressing the connection between privately formed practices and their utilization in the public sphere. She was the first scholar to unpack the "official Turkish public sphere" and stress the positive role of religion in the strengthening of civil society. My understanding of the counter- and "official" publics is very much informed by the Turkish experience and also by participating in discussion groups organized by Göle in Germany that examined the role of Islam in the public sphere, Essen (Germany), May 13–14, 2000.

50. Jürgen Habermas, "The Public Sphere: An Encyclopedia Article," in *Media and Cultural Studies: Keyworks*, ed. Meenakshi Gigi Durham and Douglas M. Kellner (Oxford: Blackwell, 2001), 102–107.

51. Yasin Aktay, "Body, Text, Identity: The Islamic Discourse of Authenticity in Modern Turkey" (Ph.D diss., Middle East Technical University, Ankara, 1997), 195.

52. *İslam Dünyasında Kimlik Problemi ve Bediüzzaman Said Nursi* (Istanbul: Yeni Asya, 1992).

53. *İttihat* was first published on October 24, 1967, and 186 issues were published, until 1971. Its circulation varied between 20,000 and 21,000.

54. My interviews with Toplayıcı, Istanbul, March 15, 1995, and August 2, 2001.

55. This group of Nurcu became successful bankers in the 1980s and 1990s. See Ruşen Çakır, "Demirel'in Kozu Nurcular," *Nokta*, May 3, 1987, 12–23.

56. M. Gündüz Sevilgen, *MSP'de Dört Yıl (1973–1977)* (Ankara: İstiklal Matbaası, 1979). This book examines the reasons that the Nurcu group split from the MSP.

57. Berk published several books to defend the connection between nationalism and Islam: see *Hakkın Zaferi İçin* (Istanbul: Yeni Asya, 1972); *Zafer Bizimdir* (Istanbul: Yeni Asya,1971); *İthamları Reddediyorum* (Istanbul: Yeni Asya,1972); and *Türkiye'de Nurculuk Davası* (Istanbul: Yeni Asya, 1971).

58. Malmisanij, *Said Nursi ve Kürt Sorunu* (Istanbul: Doz, 1991); and the response to this book, Latif Salihoğlu, *Bediüzzaman'dan Tesbitlerle Türk-Kürt Kardeşliği* (Istanbul: Gençlik, 1994).

59. Hizbullah, a radical Kurdish-Islamist organization, killed İzzettin Yıldırım along with a group of Nurcu businessmen in 2000; for coverage of the killing, see *Milliyet*, January 20–23, 2000. Hizbullah was a mainly urban phenomenon and targeted Kurds who had a history of being harassed and ill treated by the Turkish police. There is enough evidence to suggest that Hizbullah was used by the Turkish state against Kurdish nationalists; see Human Rights Watch, "What Is Turkey's Hizbullah?" February 16, 2000 (New York).

60. My interviews with Mehmet Metiner, May 18, 1994.

61. My interview with İhsan Atasoy, Istanbul, March 16, 1995, and July 27, 2001.

8. THE NEO-NUR MOVEMENT OF FETHULLAH GÜLEN

1. The early Gülen was a devoted Nurcu, a follower of Nursi. After the mid-1970s, the gradual differentiation of Gülen and the movement from the traditional

Nur movement is apparent. However, this detachment should also be seen as a response to the secularist accusation that Gülen was the Nurcu leader who had the intention of Islamicizing public life. Rather than seeking to change the misunderstanding of Nursi, the Gülen movement shied away from its intellectual connections with Nursi and present itself as an "education movement." See Gülen's interview in *Aksiyon,* June 6, 1998, and his written legal defense at the Ankara State Security Court, file no. 2000/124 E (November 6, 2001).

2. For Hegel's view on religion, see G. W. F. Hegel, *Three Essays,* trans. P. Fuss and J. Dobbins (Notre Dame, IN: Notre Dame University Press, 1984), p. 79; there is more on Hegel's division of objective and subjective religion in H. S. Harris, *Development toward the Sunlight 1770–1801* (Oxford: Oxford University Press, 1973); and Elie Kedourie, *Hegel and Marx: Introductory Lectures* (Oxford: Blackwell, 1995), 77–90.

3. Latif Erdoğan, *Küçük Dünyam,* 38th ed. (Istanbul: Ad, 1995), 27–37, 40; Eyüp Can, *Fethullah Gülen Hocaefendi ile Ufuk Turu,* 13th ed. (Istanbul: AD, 1996), 93; and Ahmet Ersöz, *Alvarlı Efe Hazretleri* (İzmir: Nil, 1993).

4. Erdoğan, *Küçük Dünyam,* 25.

5. This Anatolian Sufi Islam embraced a telos that entails (trans)formation of the self by shielding the autonomy of the inner self and the realization of justice.

6. I have examined the implications of this regional culture in the rearticulation of the teachings of Said Nursi in my "Türkiye'de İslam Çoğulcu," *Milliyet,* September 18, 1996.

7. Mehmet Kırkıncı, *Bediüzzaman'ı Nasıl Tanıdım?* (Istanbul: Zafer, 1994), 21–22 and 35–37.

8. Gülen's memoirs are in *Zaman,* November 25, 1996.

9. For more on the role of *Sızıntı* by Latif Erdoğan, a close associate of Fethullah Gülen, see "Sızıntı Dergisi Üzerine," *Zaman,* November 26–December 3, 1994.

10. "Fetullahçılar Sessiz ve Derinden," *Nokta,* December 28, 1986, 23.

11. During the 1980 coup, the military issued an arrest warrant for Gülen for allegedly violating article 163. Gülen remained a fugitive and kept a low profile, and this warrant was removed by Özal in 1983.

12. Can, *Ufuk Turu,* 16.

13. Can, *Ufuk Turu,* 16–17.

14. For an analysis of Fethullah Gülen's *Ufuk Turu* see Nilüfer Göle, "Muhafazakarlığının Manalandırdığı Modernlik," in Can, *Ufuk Turu,* 207.

15. His interview in *Sabah,* January 29, 1995; Can, *Ufuk Turu,* 111.

16. My interviews with Gülen, Istanbul, April 25, 1997, and Philadelphia, April 12, 2000.

17. Max Weber, "The Protestant Sect and the Spirit of Capitalism," in *From Max Weber: Essays in Sociology,* ed. H. H. Gerth and C. Wright Mills (New York: Oxford University Press, 1958), 302–22.

18. Many of Gülen's followers believe that he is guided by God through dreams and other events. Radical Islamist groups, who defend a more scripturalist and rationalist approach to the Qur'an, sharply attacked him. See the exchange between Gülen's lawyer and other Islamists in Sükuti Memioğlu, "Mistik hezeyanlar ve yeni bir kutbu azam," *Tevhid,* May 1992, 60–65, and "Tekzip hakkında bir kaç söz," *Tevhid,* June 1992, 74–75.

19. Alastair MacIntyre, "A Mistake about Causality in Social Sciences," in *Philosophy, Politics, and Society,* ed. P. Laslett and W. Runciman (Oxford: Oxford University Press, 1967), 52.

20. Can, *Ufuk Turu*, 25.

21. Fethullah Gülen, *Asrın Getirdiği Tereddütler I–IV* (İzmir: TOV, 1994).

22. Fethullah Gülen, "Düşünce ve Aksiyon İnsanı," *Zaman*, November 27, 1994.

23. M. Abdülfettah Şahin, "Beklenen Geçlik I, II," *Çağ ve Nesil: Zamanın Altın Dilimi IV* (İzmir: TÖV, 1992), 125–32.

24. M. Abdülfettah Şahin, "Dünya Muvazenesinde Bir Millet," *Çağ ve Nesil I* (İzmir: TÖV, 1992), 88–92.

25. Safa Mürsel, *Bediüzzaman Said Nursi ve Devlet Felsefesi* (Istanbul: Yeni Asya, 1995); Yavuz Bahadıroğlu, *Bediüzzaman Said Nursi* (Istanbul: Yeni Asya, 1993); İbrahim Canan, *İslam Aleminin Ana Meseleleri: Bediüzzaman'dan Çözümler* (Istanbul: Yeni Asya, 1993).

26. The newspaper *Zaman* first appeared on November 3, 1986.

27. In Germany in Turkish, Azerbaijan (8 pages, and only one page is Turkish), Uzbekistan (6 pages; 2 Turkish and 4 Uzbek), Kazakstan (8 pages; 6 Kazak and 2 Turkish), Kyrgyzstan (8 pages; 6 Kyrgyz and 2 Turkish), Turkmenistan (6 pages; 1 Turkish and 5 Turkmen), Tatarstan (4 pages; 1 Turkish and 3 Tatar), Boshgortastan (5 pages; 4 Baskurt and 1 Turkish), Bulgaria (16 pages; 12 Turkish and 4 Bulgarian), Romania (16 pages in Turkish) and Macedonia (8 pages; 6 Turkish and 2 Macedonian).

28. Nuriye Akman's interview with Gülen, *Sabah*, January 28, 1995.

29. For the critique of Gülen's position on the soft coup and the İmam Hatip Schools, see Ahmet Taşgetiren, "Menderes ve İmam Hatipler," *Yeni Safak*, July 20, 1997.

30. See, for example, his essay "Tahrib edilen tabiat," *Zaman*, June 25, 1994.

31. "İşte Fethullah Gülen Imparatorlugu," *Aktüel Para*, September 22,1996, 18–25. This essay examines Gülen's financial and educational networks.

32. Elisabeth Özdalga, "Worldly Asceticism in Islamic Casting: Fethullah Gülen's Inspired Piety and Activism," *Critique* 17 (2000): 83–104.

33. M. Abdülfettah Şahin, "Neslin Beklediği Kurtarıcı El," in *Çağ ve Nesil* (İzmir: TÖV, 1992), 14–15.

34. For more debate on these schools, see *Yurt Dışında Açılan Özel Öğretim Kurumları Temsilcileri İkinci Toplantısı* (Ankara: MEB, 1997).

35. The most prominent ones are: FEM (Istanbul), Anafen (Istanbul), Körfez (İzmir), Maltepe (Ankara), Işık (Adana), Söz and Sur (Diyarbakır, Hakkari, Elazığ), and Çağlayan (Van-Bitlis).

36. The most prominent ones are: Fatih (Istanbul), Yamanlar (İzmir), Samanyolu (Ankara), Yıldırımhan (Mersin), Aziziye (Erzurum), Serhat (Van), Server Gazi (Denizli), Nilüfer (Bursa), Otlukbeli (Erzincan), Ertuğrul Gazi (Eskişehir), Selahattin Eyyubi(Bitlis), Işık (Sakarya), and Fatih Sultan (Aydın).

37. Emine Kaplan, "Milli Eğitimde dış kuşatma," *Cumhuriyet*, March 12, 1995.

38. Interview with Gülen by Oral Calışlar, *Cumhuriyet*, August 21, 1995; and Can, *Ufuk Turu*, 34.

39. Interview with Gülen by Hulusi Turgut, "İslam sadece Türkiye'de özgürce yaşanıyor," *Sabah*, January 26, 1996.

40. Can, *Ufuk Turu*, 33.

41. Can, *Ufuk Turu*, 35.

42. Interview with Gülen by Ertuğrul Özkök, *Hürriyet*, January 23–30, 1995.

43. Interview with Gülen by Ertuğrul Özkök, *Hürriyet*, January 25, 1995.

44. Gülen, "Fethullah Gülen Hocaefendi Güneydoğu ve terror hadisesini Zaman'a değerlendirdi: Çare insan ve kültür," *Zaman*, November 5, 1993.

45. Ruşen Çakır, "Devlet Babanın Nurcu Oğlu: Kırkıncı Hoca," *Artıhaber* 1 (December 20, 1997): 19.

46. For Gülen's views on the Directorate of Religious Affairs, see Can, *Ufuk Turu*, 137.

47. Ahmet İnsel, "Yeni Muhafazakarlık ve Fethullah Gülen," *Yeni Yüzyıl*, April 27, 1997, and "Altın Nesil Eşittir Beyaz Türkler mi?" *Yeni Yüzyıl*, May 4, 1997.

48. Kürşad Oğuz, "Turkiye'nin birliğini Nurcular sağlayacak," *Aktüel* 190 (1995): 40–44.

49. Fethullah Gülen, "Hizipcilik ağından kurtulmamız gerekiyor," *Zaman*, February 6, 1996.

50. See interview with Gülen by Yalçın Doğan, *Umran* 37 (May–June 1997): 1–15.

51. Erdoğan, *Küçük*, 50–62.

52. For more on Gülen's views of Iran and Arabs, see interview with Gülen by Nevaal Sevindi, *Yeni Yüzyıl*, July 19–28, 1997.

53. Gülen, "Öze Dönmek," *Sızıntı* 80, 7 (1985): 283.

54. Gülen, "Milli Ruh Düşüncesi," *Sızıntı* 83, 7 (1985): 402–404.

55. Göle, "'Muhafazakarlığın," *Zaman*, August 27, 1995.

56. For Gülen's statement and its implementation in his schools, see *Yeni Yüzyıl*, September 16, 1998. Gülen defended his "education first" over headscarves policy during my interview with him on September 20, 1998, in Istanbul; see also Ali Ünal, "Başörtüsü Meselesi," *Zaman*, September 30, 1998.

57. For more on the debate over the Abant Declaration, see Kerem Çalışkan, "Fethullah Hoca ve Laiklik," *Yeni Yüzyıl*, July 21, 1998. Some scholars criticized the Declaration as a sign of the politicization of Islam, see Yakup Kepenek, "Abant Bildirgesi," *Cumhuriyet*, July 27, 1998. Some Islamists sharply criticized the Abant Declaration; see Ahmet Taşgetiren, "Abant'in Çözemediği Sorun," *Yeni Safak*, July 27, 1998.

58. Mehmet Gündem, *Abant Toplantıları I: Islam ve Laiklik* (Istanbul: Yazarlar ve Gazeteciler Vakfı, 1998), 269–72.

59. See interview of Fethullah Gülen by Nuriye Akman, *Sabah*, January 24, 1995.

60. The pro-RP newspaper *Milli Gazete* argued that Gülen was made popular by the state because of his critical attitude toward the RP. See Zeki Ceyhan, *Milli Gazete*, February 19, 1995; the Islamist intellectual Ali Bulaç argued that Gülen was used by the state to divide the Islamic movement and present the RP as radical; see Ali Bulaç, "Fethullah Hoca," *Yeni Safak*, February 8, 1995, and "Fethullah Hoca ve Refah Partisi," *Yeni Safak*, February 11, 1995. Bulaç believed that the United States was encouraging "moderate" Islamic groups to divide Muslims; Ali Bulaç, "İslam kuşatma altında," *Yeni Safak*, February 22, 1995.

61. On Gülen's meeting with Bülent Ecevit, see Ahmet Taşgetiren, "Fethullah Hoca-Ecevit," *Yeni Safak*, March 27, 1995. Tasgetiren asks whether the politicians are seeking to co-opt Islam into the system, which Taşgetiren thinks is corrupt.

62. Derya Sazak, "Tarikat krizi," *Milliyet*, December 23, 1994, and Ruşen Çakır, "Çiller and Fethullah Hoca," *Milliyet*, December 23, 1994.

63. Many moderate and radical intellectuals criticized this statement; see Mehmet Şevket Eygi's response in *Milliyet*, February 18, 1995.

64. Ali Bulaç, "Fethullah Hoca"ya Üç Soru: Bir: Mustafa Kemal," *Yeni Safak*, July 11, 1995; "İki: Refah"ın Önünü Kesecek misiniz?" *Yeni Safak*, July 12, 1995; and "Üç: Niçin Ortadoğu değil de Orta Asya," *Yeni Şafak*, July 13, 1995. In addition, some

leftists criticized Gülen as a U.S. agent; for the accusation of İlhan Selçuk that Fethullah is an American agent, see *Cumhuriyet*, February 19, 1995.

65. Mustafa Kaplan, an ex-Alevi and convert to be the Nurcu, sharply criticizes Gülen in *Cumhuriyet*, August 26, 1996.

66. Interview with Gülen by Oral Çalışlar, *Aktüel Para*, September 15, 1996, 22–23.

67. Interview with Gülen by Özkök, *Hürriyet*, January 28, 1995.

68. Interview with Gülen by Nuriye Akman in *Sabah*, January 27, 1995.

69. Interview with Gülen by Akman in *Sabah*, January 27, 1995.

70. Interview with Gülen by Akman in *Sabah*, January 27, 1995.

71. Interview with Gülen by Şemseddin Nuri before the general elections in 1991, *Zaman*, October 18, 1991.

72. Gülen, "Milli Öfke," *Çağ ve Nesil IV: Zamanın Altın Dilimi*, 146–49.

73. Interview with Gülen by Latif Erdoğan, *Zaman*, March 14, 1994. For more about his call to become a regional power see "Çare insan ve kültür," *Zaman*, November 5, 1993.

74. Can, *Ufuk Turu*, 34.

75. For the summary of Gülen's interview on D-TV, see "Beceremediniz artık gidiniz," *Hürriyet*, April 18, 1997.

76. My interview with Sezgin Koçak in Konya, May 12, 1994.

77. Fethullah Gülen, *Hoşgörü ve Diyalog İklimi* (Istanbul: Merkur Yayıncılık, 1998).

78. "Diyalog için cesur adım," *Aksiyon*, April 13–19, 1996.

79. "Fethullah Gülen Met with Pope John Paul II," *Turkish Times*, March 1, 1998.

80. My interview with Gülen, Philadephia, October 12, 2000.

81. Gülen gave an interview to Yalçın Doğan on D-TV and sharply criticized Erbakan—the RP leader—and political Islam. He called on the Erbakan-led government to resign; see "Hocaefendi'den güncel yorumlar," *Zaman*, April 16, 1997.

82. For more on the shortcomings of Gülen's position on democracy, see Gülay Göktürk,"Devletin inayetiyle," *Sabah*, June 25, 1999.

83. For more on the media attack, see *Milliyet*, June 21–28, 1999; *Sabah*, June 21–29, 1999; *Turkish Daily News*, June 21, 1999.

84. For more on the speech of Kıvrıkoğlu, see *Milliyet*, August 31, 2000.

85. For the court documents, see the file of 2000/124, Second State Security Court in Ankara.

86. Çetin Özek, "Hukuksal Görüş," April 4, 2001, in the file of 2000/124 of the Second State Security Court in Ankara, 10. I thank the court for providing all documents for my review.

87. Özek, "Hukuksal Görüş," 10.

88. For more on the court case, see *Zaman*, June 21–27, 1999.

89. My interviews with state security officers in Ankara, June 15, 1999.

90. Ruşen Çakır, "Fethullah'ı Kullanıp Attılar," *Milliyet*, June 26, 1999.

91. My interview with Gülen, Philadelphia, October 12, 2000. He said: "by visiting the States and many other European countries, I realized the virtues and the role of religion in these societies. Islam flourishes in America and Europe much better than in many Muslim countries. This means freedom and the rule of law are necessary for personal Islam. Moreover, Islam does not need the state to survive but rather needs educated and financially rich communities to flourish. In a way, not the state but rather community is needed under a full democratic system."

92. Leonard Binder, *Islamic Liberalism: A Critique of Development Ideologies* (Chicago: University of Chicago Press, 1989), 19.

93. Binder rightly argues that "the resurgence of Islam is both a threat and a promise, so the task of the moment is to appropriate religion as part of a new bourgeois ideology before it is appropriated by some rival force." *Islamic Liberalism*, 17.

9. THE NATIONAL OUTLOOK MOVEMENT AND THE RISE OF THE REFAH PARTY

1. My interviews with Lütfi Doğan—who served as the head of the Directorate of Religious Affairs in 1968–1971—on October 21, 1996, and August 10, 1998. On the role of Kotku, see Korkut Özal, *Gerçek Tanık Anlatıyor* (Istanbul: Milliyet, 1994), and Süleyman Arif Emre, *Siyasette 35 Yıl* (Istanbul: Akabe, 1990), 185–86.

2. The MGH founded five parties: the MNP (January 26, 1970–January 14, 1972); the MSP (October 11, 1972–October 16, 1983); the RP (July 1983–January 16, 1998); the FP (December 17, 1997–June 22, 2001); and the SP (June 20, 2001–).

3. During my interview with Erbakan, December 12, 1997, he identitified A. Yesevi, B. Nakşibend, and Yunus Emre as the intellectual fathers of Islamic identity and Fatih Sultan and Abdülhamid II as its practitioners.

4. Serdar Şen, *RP Partisi'nin Teori ve Pratiği: RP Partisi, Adil Düzen ve Kapitalizm* (Istanbul: Sarmal Yayınevi, 1995).

5. The founding charter of the MGH argued that "the task of the party is to carry welfare, felicity/prosperity [saadet] and salvation [selamet] to all corners of Turkey." *Milli Nizam Partisi Kuruluş Beyannamesi* (Ankara: MNP, 1970), 7. All these goals became the names of the *Milli Görüş* movement–led parties in Turkey.

6. Bernard Lewis, *The Political Language of Islam* (Chicago: University of Chicago Press, 1988), 38–39.

7. Fehmi Yavuz, "Milli sözcüğü yerine 'Dini' Sözcüğü," *Yankı*, September 22–28, 1975, 9.

8. Ahmet Yücekök, *100 Soruda: Türkiye'de Din ve Siyaset*, 3rd ed. (Istanbul: Gerçek Yayınevi, 1983), 80.

9. The founding charter of the party very much reflects the views of Mehmet Zahid Kotku, and articles 1, 3,5, 19, and 49 directly deal with the question of identity and justice. See *Milli Nizam Partisi Kuruluş Beyannamesi*. The goal of Islam, for Kotku, "is to bring salvation [selamet], prosperity [saadet] and welfare [refah] to every corner of Turkey." My interview with Nazif Gürdoğan, Istanbul, August 23, 2001.

10. M. Gündüz Sevilgen, *MSP'de Dört Yıl (1973–1977)* (Istanbul: İstiklal Matbaası, 1979).

11. Necdet Onur, *Erbakan Dosyası* (Istanbul: M. Yayınevi, 1996), 104–105.

12. S. A. Emre, *Siyasette 35 Yıl I* (Istanbul: Akabe, 1990), 237.

13. Anonymous, *Niçin Milli Nizam Partisi Kapatıldı?* (Ankara: Vesika Yayınları, 1990).

14. For one of the earliest studies, see Jacob M. Landau, "The National Salvation Party," *Asian and African Studies* 2, 1 (1976): 1–56, and see Ali Yaşar Sarıbay, *Türkiye'de Modernleşme Din ve Parti Politikası: MSP Örnek Olayı* (Istanbul: Alan, 1985).

15. *14 Ekim 1973 Milletvekili Genel Seçimleri* (Ankara: State Statistic Institute, 1974), and *Milletvekili Genel ve Cumhuriyet Senatosu Üyeleri Yenileme Seçimi Sonuçları* (Ankara: State Statistic Institute, 1977).

16. Sadık Albayrak, *Türk Siyasi Hayatında MSP Olayı* (Istanbul: Araştırma Yayınları, 1989).

17. Mehmet Zahid Kotku played an important role in the formation of certain policies; see "Politikada Nakşibendiliğin Parmağı ve Şeyh Mehmet," *Devir* 82, May 27, 1974, 12–13.

18. Binnaz Toprak, "Politicisation of Islam in a Secular State: The National Salvation Party in Turkey," in *From Nationalism to Revolutionary Islam*, ed. Said Amir Arjomand (Albany: State University of New York Press, 1984), 119–33.

19. Interview with Altan Tan by Hüseyin Akyol, in *Başlangıcından Günümüze RP'ın Tarihsel Gelişimi* (Istanbul: Pelikan Yayınları, 1996), 100.

20. Akyol, *Başlangıcından*, 100–101.

21. For more on the Cyprus operation and the internal coalition politics, see K. Özal, *Gerçek Tanık*, 59–80; and S. A. Emre, *Siyasette 35 Yıl*, 2 vols. (Istanbul: Milsan, 1991), 154–68.

22. "Seçim 77'den Ne Çıktı," *Cumhuriyet*, June 15, 1977.

23. G. Sevilgen, *MSP'de Dört Yıl*, 242–51.

24. Cahit Orhan Tütengil, "MSP'nin Aradığı Taban," *Cumhuriyet*, May 22, 1977.

25. Necmettin Erbakan, *Milli Görüş* (Istanbul: Dergah, 1975).

26. Binnaz Toprak, "The State, Politics and Religion in Turkey," in *State, Democracy and the Military*, ed. Metin Heper and Ahmet Evin (Berlin: de Gruyter, 1988), 131–32.

27. My interview with Abdullah Gül, Istanbul, June 10, 1994.

28. Mustafa Öcal, *Imam-Hatip Liseleri ve İlk Öğretim Okulları* (Istanbul: Ensar Nesriyat, 1994).

29. Ali Coşkun, *Öteki Sivas* (Istanbul: İletisim Yayınları, 1994).

30. Vali Nasr, *Islamic Leviathan* (New York: Oxford University Press, 2001), 23.

31. "Black Turk" is used to designate those Anatolians and Rumelian (the Balkans) who were excluded from the political and economic system, whereas the "White Turks" are those who have been dominating the system. See Mehmet Ali Soydan, *Dünden Bugüne ve Yarına Türkiye'nin RP Gerçeği* (Erzurum: Birey Yayıncılık, 1994).

32. Fatih is one of the major conservative quarters of Istanbul, whereas Harbiye is populated by Westernized and cosmopolitan people. *İzlenim*, April 2–9, 1994; the cover page reads "The Other Turkey Wins [Öteki Türkiye Kazandı]"; For evaluation of the March 1994 election, see Saffet Solak, "Son Seçimler ve bazı gerçekler," *Zaman*, April 23, 1994; Abdurrahman Dilipak, "RP'nin Başarısında Gözardı Edilen Birkaç Nokta," *Milliyet*, April 22, 1994; and Ümit Cizre Sakallıoğlu, "Alacakaranlık kuşağı seçimleri," *Birikim* 81 (January 1996): 26–30.

33. My interview with İsmail Kara, Istanbul, February 14, 1996.

34. My interview with Muhsin Yazıcıoğlu, Ankara, January 10, 1996.

35. My interview with Korkut Özal, Istanbul, June 11, 1997.

36. Ismail Kara, "RP hareketi ve cemaatler," *Yeni Safak*, October 14, 1995.

37. See *Milliyet* and *Cumhuriyet*, July 1, 1985.

38. Toprak, "The State, Politics and Religion," 129.

39. My interview with Oğuzhan Asiltürk, Ankara, June 13, 1995.

40. For more on the justifications of this alliance by Hasan Hüseyin Ceylan, the ex-editor of the Nakşibendi magazine *Islam* and a member of the RP's Administrative Board, see special issue on "Islamic-Nationalist Alliance," *Bizim Dergah* 43 (October 1991); for more on the "Alliance" see Ruşen Çakır, "52 Günlük İttifak," *Cumhuriyet*, November 24–30, 1991.

41. The MHP is an extreme right-wing entity with links to groups that are ready

to use violence to promote ethnic Turkish nationalism. However, in recent years, the party became a site of power struggle between two competing visions and definitions of identity: *Islamist*-Turkish versus *Turkish* groups. The Islamist-Turkish members resigned under the leadership of Muhsin Yazıcıoğlu and established the Greater Unity Party (BBP).

42. Altan Tan, "İttifak sürecinde Türkiyeli Müslümanların siyasal mücadele alternatifi," *Tevhid* 23 (November 1991), 19–22, and Fehmi Çalmuk, *Erbakan'ın Kürtleri: Milli Görüş'ün Güneydoğu Politikası* (Istanbul: Metis, 2001), 37–64.

43. Jenny B. White, "Islam and Democracy: The Turkish Experience," *Current History* (January 1995): 7–12.

44. *Rapor: RP Partisi* (Ankara: ARAS, 1994). This research, carried out from September 1 to 24, 1994, was conducted in 24 provinces and towns and covered 5,182 people, 728 of whom claimed they had voted for the RP in the last election. The questionnaire used included 52 questions, and there were 172 in-depth interviews. On the expectations of RP supporters on sharia discussed in the following paragraph, see pages 21–22.

45. Menderes Çınar, "Islam ekonomisi ve RP'ın adil ekonomik düzeni," *Birikim* 50 (1994): 21–32; for Necmettin Erbakan's speech see "MÜSİAD II. Büyük İstişare Toplantısındaki Konuşma," June 19, 1994 (Ankara: RP, 1994).

46. Ruşen Çakır, "İslam Komunu: İbadetten Eğlenceye Ortak Yaşam," *Nokta*, July 17, 1988, 28–35; interview with Süleyman Karagülle, *İzlenim*, September 1993, 38–42; and Arif Ersoy, "Adil Düzen," *İzlenim*, October 1993, 56–59.

47. According to one story, the booklet was written by Karagülle and printed under the name of Erbakan. N. Erbakan, *Adil Düzen* (Ankara: RP, 1991).

48. Erbakan, "MÜSİAD II. Büyük İstişare Toplantısındaki Konuşma."

49. These answers were elicited in the interviews carried out by me in Konya and Kayseri between April and June 1994.

50. Bünyamin Duran, "Tevhid-Duyarlı Siyasetin Önemli İlkesi: Adalet," *Köprü* 58 (Spring 1997): 37–53.

51. *RP Partisi* (Ankara: Araş, 1994).

52. My interview with a group of RP supporters in Maltepe, Istanbul, June 12, 1997.

53. Interview with Necmettin Erbakan, Ankara, June 10, 1994. "AT" is the abbreviation in Turkish for "European Community," and "at" is the Turkish word for "horse."

54. In the speeches of Abdullah Gül, deputy from Kayseri, the Ottomans are the reference point.

55. For more on "repertories of action," see Charles Tilley, *From Mobilization to Revolution* (Reading, MA: Addison-Wesley, 1978).

56. Necmettin Erbakan, "Kahramanmaraş Belediye Binasında Basın Toplantısı," June 28, 1993, in *Erbakan'ın Konuşmaları Haziran 1993* (Ankara: RP, 1993), 211.

57. This differentiation was made clear in my interviews with Abdullah Gül and Lütfü Doğan, Ankara, July 12, 1995.

58. Ömer Vehbi Hatipoğlu, *Bir Başka Açıdan Kürt Sorunu* (Ankara: Mesaj, 1992).

59. From the speech Erbakan delivered on February 2, 1996, in Ankara during the İftar dinner organized by the pro-RP ESAM Foundation, which I attended.

60. My interview with Necmettin Erbakan, Ankara, June 8, 1994.

61. For the debate between Renewalists and Conservatives, see "Yeni Dönemde

RP," *Yeni Zemin*, January 1993, 28–41; "RP Kitle Partisi Olma Yolunda," *Yeni Zemin*, May-June 1994, 38–47.

62. My interview with Bahri Zengin, Istanbul, May 9, 1994.

63. *RP Partisi 4. Büyük Kongre Genel Başkan Erbakan'ın Konuşması* (10 October 1993) (Ankara: RP, 1994).

64. The idea of multilegalism originally was formulated by Bahri Zengin, then a member of the Parliament, as a solution to the problems of Turkey. See Zengin, *Özgürleşerek Birlikte Yaşamak: Hukuk Toplulukları Birliği* (Istanbul: Birleşik, 1995); Ali Bulaç, *İslam ve Demokrasi: Teokrasi-Totaliterizm* (Istanbul: Beyan, 1993), 167–80.

65. Mehmet Metiner, "RP'nin Yeni Söylemi Üzerine," *Yeni Zemin*, November 1993, 44–45.

66. Zengin played a key role in the formulation of the Fourth Congress's Declaration. See more on Zengin in "Devlet Nedir?" *Nehir*, June 1995, 31, 34–36.

67. Both Bulaç and Zengin told me that they incorporated "multilegalism" and the comments on the Kurdish question into the speech.

68. İhsan Aktaş's statement is in Oral Calışlar and Serpil Gündüz, "95 Milliyetçi İslamcı Gençlik Ne İstiyor?" *Cumhuriyet*, February 6, 1996.

69. White, "Islam and Democracy," 11.

70. My interview with Mehmet Erbakan, the head of the European National Outlook Movement, Cologne, July 11–12, 2001.

71. Remarks made during my visit to the RP Maltepe Office, Istanbul, March 20, 1994.

72. Prostitution is a thriving business, making Mathilde Manukyan the country's leading Turkish-Armenian businesswomen through her ownership of brothels in Istanbul. In fact, Turkey's biggest single taxpayer for three consecutive years was Manukyan. She paid $616,300 to the tax office in 1995 alone. The lecturer at the local RP conference hall argued that by awarding Manukyan a ceremonial plaque, the government constructed its own stereotypical Western role model for Turkish women. The RP used this incident to attack and shame the ruling parties by portraying them as degenerate and lacking morality.

73. Ruşen Çakır, "Bir Sistem Partisi olarak RP Partisi," *Birikim* 81 (January 1996), 31–35; Ömer Laciner, "Şecim Sonuçları Üzerine," *Birikim* 81 (January 1996): 36–42.

74. Sadık Albayrak, "1914 Trabzon Medreseleri ve Caykara'da İlim Hayatı," *Caykara Aylık Eğitim Kültür ve Fikir Gazetesi*, August 4–September 1, 2002.

75. Burhanettin Duran, "Approaching the Kurdish Question via Adil Düzen: An Islamist Formula of the Welfare Party for Ethnic Coexistence," *Journal of Muslim Minority Affairs* 18, 1 (1998): 111–28.

76. İsmail Kara, "Kürt Medreseleri Gündeme Gelmeyecek mi?" in *Şeyh Efendinin Rüyasındaki Türkiye* (Istanbul: Kitabevi, 1998), 69–72.

77. Hamit Bozaslan, "Turkey's Elections and the Kurds," *Middle East Report*, April-June 1996, 16–19.

78. *Milliyet*, November 27, 1994.

79. Ali Bayramoğlu, "Çözüm Kuzey Irak'ta Kürt Devleti," *Yeni Yüzyıl*, July 22, 1996.

80. Interview with Fuat Fırat, "Çözüm İslam Kardeşliğindedir," *Değişim*, December 1996, 33.

81. Nurettin Aktaş, "Sistemin tabularıyla sorun çözülemez," *Değişim*, December 1996, 35.

82. Fethullah Erbaş, *Rapor I, September 15, 1993*; and *Rapor II, August 16, 1995* (Ankara).

83. Ömer Vehbi Hatipoğlu, "Terör ve Güneydoğu Sorunu," *Ekonomi*, October 1996; this report was issued as a separate booklet accompanying the journal.

84. Interview with Şevket Kazan on his fact-finding mission in "Kürt-Türk husumetini din alimleri kaldırır," *Milli Gazete*, September 7, 1994.

85. Ruşen Çakır, "RP Güneydoğu'da yürüdü," *Milliyet*, August 22, 1994.

86. Ruşen Çakır, "RP Partisi İstanbul'u alırsa darbe olur," *Pazar Postası*, February 5, 1995.

87. Ercan Karataş, "RP Sosyal Demokrat mı?" *Milliyet*, January 31, 1993; İsmail Cem argues that it was the RP that used the slogans of the social democratic party in "Türkiye Solu Nereye Gitmiyor," *Pazar Postası*, December 17, 1994.

88. Altan Tan, "RP Değişiyor," *Yeni Zemin*, May-June 1994, 65.

89. Cihan Aktaş, *Tesettür ve Toplum* (Istanbul: Nehir, 1992), and *Suya Düşen Dantel* (Istanbul: Nehir, 1999).

90. Aynur İlyasoğlu, "Islamcı Kadın Hareketinin Bugünü Üzerine," *Birikim* 91 (November 1996): 60–65; C. Aktaş, "Islamcı Kadının Hikayesi," in *Osmanlıdan Cumhuriyete Kadın Tarihi Dönüşümü*, ed. Yıldız Ramazanoğlu (Istanbul: Pınar, 2000), 171–87.

91. Sibel Eraslan, "RP'li Hanımlar Geliyor," *Nehir*, March 1994, 27.

92. There was also a special issue on women and politics, "Islam and the Politicization of Women," *Yeni Zemin*, July 1993, 8–35. See also Sibel Eraslan, "Refahlı Kadın Tecrübesi," in Ramazanoğlu, *Osmanlıdan Cumhuriyate*, 211–133.

93. Cihan Aktaş, "Kadin Politikacilar ve RP Partisi," *Nehir*, February 1994, 38–39.

94. Eraslan, "RP," 27.

95. Muyesser Yıldız,"'Yukarıdakiler-Asağıdakiler: RP'ta Kadınlar Savaşı," *Nokta*, September 25–October 1994, 29.

96. Hülya Aktaş, "Kadına aktif siyaset yolu acılmalı," *Yeni Zemin*, May-June 1994, 36.

97. Eraslan, "RP," 28.

98. *Sabah*, September 15, 1994.

99. Eraslan, "PR," 28.

100. Bahri Zengin told me in my interview with him that he has sent veiled women to conservative mahalles and modern-looking ones to well-developed areas.

101. Heinz Kramer, "Turkey under Erbakan: Continuity and Change towards Islam," *Aussenpolitik* 47, 4 (1996): 379–88.

102. Interview with Olivier Roy by Ruşen Çakır, "Türk İslamcılarının projesi Osmanlıdır," *Yeni Yüzyıl*, July 8, 1996.

103. Abdullah Gül's speech at the Turkish Parliament Committee on Planning and Budget, February 17, 1992.

104. Erbakan, "Kıbrıs Konusundaki Son Gelişmelerle İlgili Basın Toplantısı, June 12, 1993," in *Erbakan Konuşmaları*, 7–32.

105. Erbakan, speech at the Ankara Organization of the RP, June 20, 1993, in *Erbakan Konuşmaları*, 82.

106. Erbakan, speech at the Ankara Organization of the RP, June 20, 1993, 175.

107. Erbakan, *Türkiye'nin Meseleleri ve Çözümleri: Parti Proğramı* (Ankara: RP, 1991), 32–34.

108. Necmettin Erbakan, speech at the Grand National Assembly, *T.B.M.M. Tutanak Dergisi*, vol. 46, 38th session, December 8, 1993, 47.

109. Erbakan, *Erbakan Konuşmaları* (Ankara: RP, 1993), 52.

110. Erbakan, *RP Partisi 4. Büyük Kongre*, 5.

111. *T.B.M.M. Tutanak Dergisi*, vol. 46, 38th session, 1993, 50.

112. Erbakan, "Kahramanmaraş Konuşması, June 26, 1993," in *Erbakan Konuşmaları*, 146, 155, 174.

113. Erbakan, "Kahramanmaraş Konuşması, June 26, 1993," 174.

114. Erbakan, *Türkiye'nin Gerçek Durumu, Sebebleri: Teşhis* (Ankara: RP, n. d), 18.

115. Erbakan, *Teşhis*, 28, 32.

116. Necmettin Erbakan, "RP Ankara Il Kongresi'nde yapılan Konuşma," in *Erbakan Konuşmaları*, 22; 153.

117. Necmettin Erbakan, "RP Partisi TBMM Grup Toplantısı Konuşması, Eylül 15, 1993," in *Erbakan Konuşması*, 72.

118. Mustafa Erdoğan, "RP'nin histerisine kapilmak çok yersiz," *Yeni Yüzyıl*, February 23, 1996.

10. THE SECURITIZATION OF ISLAM AND THE TRIUMPH OF THE AKP

1. Carsten Bagge Laustsen and Ole Waever, "In Defence of Religion: Sacred Referent Objects for Securitization," *Millennium: Journal of International Studies*, 29: 3 (2000): 705–739; Ole Waever, "Securitization and Desecuritization," in *On Security* ed. Ronnie D. Lipschutz (New York: Columbia University Press, 1995), 46–86; Philippos K. Savvides, "Legitimation Crisis and Securitization in Modern Turkey," *Critique*, 16 (Spring 2000), 55–73. Quote in Barry Buzan and Ole Waever, and Jaap de Wilde, *Security: A New Framework for Analysis* (Boulder,CO: Lynne Rienner, 1998), 23–24.

2. The TÜSİAD made its position on the RP very clear with advertisements in the press, asking the two center-right parties to ally their forces against possible Islamic involvement in the government.

3. I examine the negative implications of this exclusion on Turkish politics and indicate the advantages of inclusion in "Refah Partisi: Modernleşmenin İçinde, Batılılaşmanın Dışında; Sistemin İçinde, Hükümetin Dışında," *Türkiye Günlüğü* 38 (January 1996): 45–50.

4. For more on the media, see Andrew Finkel, "Who guards the Turkish Press? A Perspective on Press Corruption in Turkey," *Journal of International Affairs* 54 (2000): 147–66.

5. Erbakan quote from "ANAP İltihak Etsin," *Hürriyet*, October 14, 1996; for control of the crowd, see Zülfikar Doğan, "İktidarda terbiye!" *Milliyet*, October 14, 1996.

6. Derya Sazak, "İki Ayrı RP," *Milliyet*, October 14, 1996.

7. My interviews with Abdullah Gül, Ankara, August 13 and 15, 2001.

8. Erol Özkasnak, *Radikal*, November 7, 2000.

9. "Basına ve Kamuoyuna," *Hacıbektaş* 25 (September 1996): 14.

10. İsmail Üzüm, *Günümüz Aleviliği* (Istanbul: ISAM, 1997).

11. "Aleviler Adlarını İstiyor," *Nokta*, August 16–22, 1998, 34–36, and "Alevi Örgütlerinin Ortak Bildirisi," *Hacıbektaş* 41 (September 1998): 19.

12. Alevis has been trying to become more secure in the eyes of the state by becoming more secularist. In other words, the changing sociopolitical challenges forced the state to shift its image of the Alevi community—from being a source of "insecurity" and the basis of "communism" to being a source of security for secularism and Turkism.

13. Philip Robins, "Turkish Foreign Policy under Erbakan," *Suvival* 39, 2 (Summer 1997): 82–100.

14. *Yeni Yüzyıl*, October 14, 1996.

15. For more on the visit and the debate in the parliament, see *T.B.M.M. Tutanak Dergisi*, 8th session, October 16, 1996.

16. After his retirement, Bir became the representative of Israeli military industries to sell arms to the Turkish military; see Mehmet Barlas, "Emekli generaller silah satıcısı olur mu?" *Yeni Safak*, July 28, 2000.

17. *Sabah*, March 19, 1997; *Sabah*, August 23, 2000, in FBIS-WEU-2000-0826; and Hikmet Çiçek, ed., *Irticaya Karşı Genelkurmay Belgeleri* (Istanbul: Kaynak, 1997). For the full text translation, see David Shankland, *Islam and Society in Turkey* (Huntingdon, U.K.: Eothen Press, 1999), 204–208.

18. See *Umran* 78 (February 2001), special issue "28 şubat Süreci" on the 1997 coup.

19. See şevket Kazan, *Öncesi ve Sonrasıyla 28 Şubat* (Ankara: Keşif Yayınları, 2001).

20. Hugh Pope, "Turkish Military Tightens Noose on Pro-Islamic Regime," *Wall Street Journal*, June 13, 1997.

21. Türk Silahlı Kuvvetleri İç Hizmet Kanunu, no. 211 [The Law (211) on the Regulation of the Domestic Duties of the Turkish Armed Forces], *RG*, January 9, 1961; Haluk Yavuz, *Türkiye'de Siyasal Sistem Arayışı ve Yürütmenin Güçlendirilmesi* (Ankara: Siyasal, 2000), 358–59; Metin Öztürk, *Ordu ve Politika* (Ankara: Gündoğan Yayınları, 1993), 114–16.

22. Ole Waever, "The EU as a Security Actor," in *International Relations Theory and the Politics of European Integration: Power, Security and Community*, ed. Morten Kelstrup and Michael C. Williams (London: Routledge, 2000), 251.

23. See interview with Güven Erkaya (chief of the navy in the 1997 coup) by Taner Baytok, in *Bir Asker Bir Diplomat* (Istanbul: Doğan, 2001), 260; Güven Erkaya, "Meral Akşener 28 Subat ve BÇG'yi Anlatıyor," in *28 Şubat-Belgeler* (Istanbul: Pınar, 2000), 497; and Hakan Akpınar, *28 Şubat: Postmodern Darbenin Öyküsü* (Ankara: Umit, 2001).

24. Bilal Çetin, "Genelkurmay'dan 5 önemli mesaj," *Yeni Yüzyıl*, April 30, 1997; and Derya Sazak, "Askeri brifing," *Milliyet*, April 30, 1997; *Radikal*, June 12, 1997.

25. Yalçın Doğan, "Vakıflar gözaltı," *Milliyet*, August 28, 1997; in 1923–1980, there were 544 foundations; in 1980–1997, the number jumped to 3,806 foundations. The military asked the government to examine and close some of these foundations.

26. Burton Bollac, "A Ban on Islamic Head Scarves Unsettles Turkey's Universities," *Chronicle of Higher Education*, April 24, 1998, 39–40.

27. For the new regulations by the Higher Education Council, see *RG*, November 7, 1998, 22–23.

28. *Turkish Daily News*, November 11, 1998.

29. The court issued its decision in January and published the decision in February. For the decision of the Constitutional Court, see *RG*, February 22, 1998, 31–345.

30. *RG*, February 22, 1998, 255.

31. *RG*, February 22, 1998, 256.

32. *RG*, February 22, 1998, 34–35.

33. *RG*, February 22, 1998, 256. This interpretation is not only problematic but also potentially very destructive.

34. *RG*, February 22, 257.

35. Mustafa Erdoğan, *Liberal Toplum, Liberal Siyaset* (Ankara: Siyasal, 1993), 193, 195, 229; Ali Fuat Başgil, *Din ve Laiklik*, 4th ed. (Istanbul: Yağmur, 1979), 169.

36. Sacit Adalı and Haşim Kılıç, both of whom were appointed by Turgut Özal.

37. "Tayyip Erdoğan Dosyası," *Hürriyet*, September 23, 1998.

38. Mustafa İslamoğlu, "Fazilet çizgisi Türkiyeleşti mi?" *Yeni Şafak*, July 30, 1999.

39. Hasan Kösebalaban, "Turkey's EU Membership: A Clash of Security Cultures," *Middle East Policy* 9, 2 (June 2002): 130–46.

40. *Günışığında Türkiye: 18 Nisan 1999 Seçim Beyannamesi* (Ankara: FP, 1999), 45.

41. Ziya Öniş, "Political Islam at the Crossroads: from Hegemony to Co-existence," *Contemporary Politics* 7, 4 (2001): 281–98.

42. My interview with Mehmet Erbakan, the head of NOM in Europe, August 13, 2001.

43. *Günışığında Türkiye: 18 Nisan Seçim Beyannamesi* (Ankara: FP, 1999), 45.

44. Mehmet Sılay, *Mecliste Merve Kavakçı Olayı* (Istanbul: Birey, 2000).

45. Şahin Alpay, "Merve ve Fitne," *Milliyet*, May 4, 1999.

46. Vural Savaş, *İrtica ve Bölücülüğe Karşı Militan Demokrasi* (Ankara: Bilgi, 2000), 338.

47. Savaş, *İrtica ve Bölücülüğe Karşı Militan Demokrasi, 338.*

48. Mustafa Erdoğan, "Fazilet Partisi'ni Kapatma Kararı Işığında Türkiye'nin Anayasa Mahkemesi Sorunu," *Liberal Düşünce Dergisi* 23 (2001): 36–40. The Constitutional Court viewed the fact that Merve Kavakçı became a deputy and that she was brought to the Parliament to take an oath "as a severe violation of the principle of laicism." *RG*, January 4, 2002.

49. *Saadet* has three meanings: prosperity, felicity, and happiness. "Prosperity" captures the meaning of *saadet* better than "felicity" or "happiness."

50. Paul Kubicek, "The 1999 Elections," *Mediterranean Politics* 4 (1999): 186–92.

51. Almost everyone in the media was surprised by the victory of the MHP, including the leadership of the party. Devlet Bahçeli told journalists: "I never expected this much of the vote"; *Zaman*, April 20, 1999; Yalçın Doğan, "Türkiye sağa doğru," *Milliyet*, April 19, 1999.

52. Some scholars seek to explain the MHP's rise in terms of its leadership. I would argue that if the MHP leadership had one outstanding talent, or perhaps one should say instinct, it was an unerring sense of other parties' weaknesses: their weak leadership and corruption.

53. M. Hakan Yavuz, "The Politics of Fear: The Rise of the Nationalistic Action Party (MHP) in Turkey," *Middle East Journal* 56, 2 (2002): 200–221.

54. "MHP şehitli illerde fark attı," *Star Gazetesi*, April 21, 1999. The provinces that lost the largest number of troops are Niğde, Çankırı, Yozgat, Amasya, Aksaray, Kırşehir, Sivas, Tokat, Karaman, Kastamonu, and Çorum. Within these 11 (out of 12) provinces, the MHP became the number one party. In Çankırı, which lost the second largest number of troops, the MHP received 38.2 percent of all votes. There is a close correlation between the number of troops killed and the high percentage of MHP votes.

55. For more on the "risk" factor, see Ali Bulaç, "İlk sonuçlar," *Zaman*, April 20, 1999.

56. In municipal elections, the FP still emerged as the number one party. Those who voted for the FP in municipal elections voted for the MHP in national

elections. This indicates that the two parties compete for the same identity–based voters.

57. The Turkish state has been sponsoring the annual festival to remember Hacı Bektaş Veli, the patron saint of the Bektaşi order and of Alevis. The state prefers to promote Hacı Bektaş against Pir Sultan Abdal, whose poetry has been a source of revolutionary ideas. Hacı Bektaş is promoted as the religious leader who Turkified and Islamicized Anatolia. Since 1997, the state has regarded Alevism as the "indigenous" Anatolian faith system. For instance, the state reactivated the Turkish Culture and Hacı Bektaş Veli Research Institute at Gazi University in Ankara.

58. *Hürriyet*, September 17, 1998.

59. Abdullah Öcalan, *Declaration on the Democratic Solution of the Kurdish Question*, trans. Kurdistan Information Centre (from the Turkish original) (London: Mesopotamian, 1999), 18.

60. *Yeni Şafak*, August 8, 2001.

61. *Yeni Şafak*, October 25, 2002.

62. *Hürriyet*, February 29, 2000.

CONCLUSION

1. See, for example, Daniel Pipes, *In the Path of God: Islam and Political Power* (New York: Basic Books, 1983), 144–47; and Elie Kedourie, *Democracy and Arab Political Culture* (Washington, DC: Washington Institute for Near East Policy, 1992).

2. Karel Dobbelaere, "Secularization: A Multi-Dimensional Concept," *Current Sociology* 26 (1978): 1–21, and "Secularization Theories and Sociological Paradigms: A Reformulation of Private-Public Dichotomy and the Problem of Societal Integration," *Sociological Analysis* 46 (1985): 377–87.

3. İsmail Kara, "İslamcılar, mucizeler, bilim ve positivizm," *Dergah* 6 (August 1990): 18–19.

4. For a detailed analysis of the UMNO (the United Malay National Organization), see Özay Mehmet, *Islamic Identity and Development: Studies of the Islamic Periphery*. (London: Routledge, 1990), 110, 201; and Nasr, *Islamic Leviathan*, 105–29.

5. Melucci, *Nomads of the Present* (Philadelphia: Temple University Press, 1989).

I

Selected Bibliography

WORKS IN ENGLISH

Adıvar, Halide Edip. *Turkey Faces West: A Turkish View of Recent Changes and Their Origins.* New Haven: Yale University Press, 1930.

Ahmad, Feroz. *The Making of Modern Turkey.* New York: Routledge, 1993.

Akarlı, Engin D., and Gabriel Ben-Dor, eds. *Political Participation in Turkey: Historical Background and Present Problems.* Istanbul: Bogazici University Publication, 1975.

Anderson, Benedict. *Imagined Communities: Reflections on the Origin and Spread of Nationalism.* London: Verso, 1983.

Andrews, Peter A., ed. *Ethnic Groups in the Republic of Turkey.* Wiesbaden: Reichert, 1989.

Arıcanlı, Tosun, and D. Rodrick. *The Political Economy of Turkey.* London: Macmillan, 1990.

Arkoun, M. *Rethinking Islam.* Washington, DC: Georgetown University Center for Contemporary Arab Studies, 1988.

———. *Rethinking Islam: Common Questions, Uncommon Answers.* Boulder, CO: Westview Press, 1994.

Asad, Talal. *The Idea of an Antropology of Islam.* Washington, DC: Georgetown University Center for Contemporary Arab Studies, 1986.

Ayubi, Nazih. *Political Islam: Religion and Politics in the Arab World.* London: Routledge, 1991.

Baumann, Gerd. *The Written Word: Literacy in Transition.* Oxford: Clarendon Press, 1986.

Berger, Peter, and Thomas Luckmann. *The Social Construction of Reality.* New York: Anchor Books, 1967.

Berkes, Niyazi. *The Development of Secularism in Turkey.* New York: Routledge, 1998.

Bianchi, Robert. *Interest Groups and Political Development in Turkey.* Princeton: Princeton University Press, 1984.

Binder, Leonard. *Islamic Liberalism: A Critique of Development Ideologies.* Chicago: University of Chicago Press, 1988.

Birand, Mehmet Ali. *The Generals' Coup in Turkey: An Inside Story of 12 September 1980*. New York: Brassey's Defense, 1987.

———. *Shirts of Steel: An Anatomy of the Turkish Armed Forces*. London: Tauris, 1991.

Braude, Benjamin, and Bernard Lewis, eds. *Christians and Jews in the Ottoman Empire: The Functioning of a Plural Society*. New York: Holmes and Meier, 1982.

Bromley, Simon. *Rethinking Middle East Politics, State Formation and Development*. Cambridge, England: Polity Press, 1994.

Burke, Edmund, III, ed. *Global Crises and Social Movements: Artisans, Peasants, Populists and the World Economy*. Boulder, CO: Westview Press, 1988.

Burke, Edmund, III, and Ira M. Lapidus, eds. *Islam, Politics, and Social Movements*. Berkeley: University of California Press, 1988.

Calhoun, Craig, ed. *Habermas and the Public Sphere*. Cambridge: MIT Press, 1992.

Cohen, Jena. "Discourse Ethics and Civil Society." In *Universalism versus Communitarianism*, ed. David Rasmussen. Cambridge: MIT Press, 1990.

———. "Strategy or Identity: New Theoretical Paradigms and Contemporary Social Movements." *Social Reseach* 52, 4 (1985): 663–716.

Danielson, M. N., and R. Keleş. *The Politics of Rapid Urbanization: Government and Growth in Modern Turkey*. New York: Holmes and Meier, 1985.

Darnovsky, Mary, ed. *Cultural Politics and Social Movements*. Philadephia: Temple University Press, 1995.

Davis, Eric, and Nicolas Gavrielides, eds. *Statecraft in the Middle East*. Miami: Florida International University Press, 1991.

Eickelman, Dale F. *Moroccon Islam*. Austin: Texas University Press, 1976.

Eickelman, Dale, and James Piscatori. *Muslim Politics*. Princeton: Princeton University Press, 1996.

Eisenstein, Elizabeth. *The Printing Press as an Agent of Change: Communications and Cultural Transformations in Early–Modern Europe*. 2 vols. New York: Cambridge University Press, 1979.

Eley, Geoff. "Nations, Publics, and Political Cultures: Placing Habermas in the Nineteenth Century." In *Habermas and the Public Sphere*, ed. Craig Calhoun. Cambridge: MIT Press, 1992.

Eyerman, Ron. "Modernity and Social Movements." In *Social Change and Modernity*, ed. Hans Haferkamp and Neil J. Smelser. Berkeley: University of California Press, 1992.

Eyerman, Ron, and Andrew Jamison. *Social Movements: A Cognitive Approach*. New York: Cambridge University Press, 1991.

Esposito, John L. *The Islamic Threat: Myth or Reality?* Oxford: Oxford University Press, 1992.

Geertz, Clifford. *The Interpretation of Cultures*. New York: Basic Books, 1973.

———. *Islam Observed: Religious Development in Morocco and Indonesia*. New Haven: Yale University Press, 1968.

Gellner, Ernest. *Encounters with Nationalisms*. Oxford: Blackwell, 1994.

———. *Muslim Society*. Cambridge, England: Cambridge University Press, 1983.

———. *Nation and Nationalism*. Oxford: Blackwell, 1983.

———. *Postmodernism, Reason and Religion*. London: Routledge, 1992.

Giddens, Anthony. *Central Problems in Social Theory*. London: Macmillan, 1979.

———. *New Rules of Sociological Method: A Positive Critique of Interpretive Sociologies*. New York: Basic Books, 1976.

Gillis, John R., ed. *Commemorations: The Politics of National Identity*. Princeton: Princeton University Press, 1994.

Gilsenan, Michael. *Saint and Sufi in Modern Egypt*. Oxford: Clarendon Press, 1973.
———. *Recognizing Islam*. London: Tauris, 1990.
Goldberg, Ellis, Reşat Kasaba, and Joel Migdal. *Rules and Rights in the Middle East: Democracy, Law, and Society*. Seattle: University of Washington Press, 1991.
Göle, Nilüfer. *The Forbidden Modern: Civilization and Veiling*. Ann Arbor: University of Michigan Press, 1996.
Goody, J., ed. *Literacy in Traditional Societies*. Cambridge: Cambridge University Press, 1968.
Gülen, Fethullah. *Essays, Perspectives, and Opinions*. Rutherfordf, NJ: Fountain, 2002.
Heper, Metin, and Ahmet Evin, eds. *Politics in the Third Republic*. Boulder, CO: Westview Press, 1994.
Honneth, Alex. *The Fragmented World of the Social: Essays in Social and Political Philosophy*. New York: State University of New York Press, 1990.
Hourani, Albert. *The Emergence of the Modern Middle East*. Berkeley: University of California Press, 1981.
İnalcık, Halil. *The Middle East and the Balkans under the Ottoman Empire*. Bloomington: Indiana University Press, 1993.
Kayalı, Hasan. *Arabs and Young Turks: Ottomanism, Arabism, and Islamism in the Ottoman Empire, 1908–1918*. Berkeley: University of California Press, 1997.
Kazamias, Andreas M. *Education and Quest for Modernity in Turkey*, 1966. Chicago: University of Chicago Press.
Kedourie, Elie. *Democracy and Arab Political Culture*. Washington, DC: Washington Institute for Near East Policy, 1992.
Khoury, Philip S., and Joseph Kostiner, eds. *Tribes and States Formation in the Middle East*. Berkeley: University of California Press, 1990.
Kramer, Heinz. *A Changing Turkey: The Challenge to Europe and the United States*. Washington, DC: Brookings Institute Press, 2000.
Lapidus, Ira M. *A History of Islamic Societies*. New York: Cambridge University Press, 1989.
Larana, Enrique, Hank Johnston, and Joseph R. Gusfield, eds. *New Social Movements: From Ideology to Identity*. Philadelphia: Temple University Press, 1994.
Lerner, Daniel P. *The Passing of Traditional Society: Modernizing the Middle East*. New York: Free Press, 1964.
Lewis, Bernard. *The Emergence of Modern Turkey*. 2nd ed. London: Oxford University Press, 1969.
———. *The Political Language of Islam*. Chicago: University of Chicago Press, 1988.
Luciani, Giacomo, and Hazem Beblawi. *The Rentier State*. New York: Croom Helm, 1987.
MacIntyre, A. *After Virtue*. Notre Dame, IN: Notre Dame University Press, 1981.
Mardin, Şerif. *Cultural Transitions in the Middle East*. Ed. Serif Mardin. Leiden: Brill, 1994.
———. "The Nakshibendi Order of Turkey." In *Fundamentalism and Society*, ed. Martin E. Marty. Chicago: Chicago University Press, 1993.
———. *Religion and Social Change in Modern Turkey: The Case of Bediüzzaman Said Nursi*. New York: State University of New York, 1989.
McCarthy, Justin. *Death and Exile: The Ethnic Cleansing of the Ottoman Muslims (1821–1922)*. Princeton: Darwin Press, 1995.
Meeker, Michael E. "Oral Culture, Media Culture, and the Islamic Resurgence in Turkey." In *Exploring the Written: Anthropology and the Multiplicity of Writing*, ed. Eduardo P. Archetti. Oslo: Scandinavian University Press, 1994.

Mehmet, Özay. 1990. *Islamic Identity and Development: Studies of the Islamic Periphery.* London: Routledge, 1990.

Melucci, Alberto. "Social Movements and the Democratization of Everyday Life." In *Civil Society and the State,* ed. John Keane. London: Verso, 1988.

Messick, Brinkley. *The Calligraphic State: Textual Domination and History in a Muslim Society.* Berkeley: University of California Press, 1993.

Özbudun, Ergun. *The Role of the Military in Recent Turkish Politics.* Cambridge, MA: Harvard University Center for International Affairs, 1966.

Özdalga, Elizabeth. *The Veiling Issue, Official Secularism and Popular Islam in Modern Turkey.* Richmond, Surrey, England: Curzon, 1998.

Özdalga, Elizabeth, Tord Olson, and Catharina Raudvere, eds. *Alevi Identity.* Istanbul: Swedish Research Institute in Istanbul, 1998.

Reed, Howard A. "Islam and Education in Turkey: Their Role in National Education." *Turkish Studies Association Bulletin* 9 (1988): 1–5.

———. "Revival of Islam in Secular Turkey." *Middle East Journal* 8, 3 (1954): 267–82.

———. "Turkey's New Imam Hatip Scools." *Welt des Islams* 4, 1–2 (1956): 150–63.

Richards, Alan, and John Waterbury. *A Political Economy of the Middle East: State, Class and Economic Development.* Boulder, CO: Westview Press, 1990.

Robinson, Francis, ed. *The Cambridge Illustrated History of the Islamic World.* New York: Cambridge University Press, 1996.

Shankland, David. *Islam and Society in Turkey.* Huntingdon, U.K.: Eothen Press, 1999.

Shaw, Stanford J., and Ezel Kural Shaw. *History of the Ottoman Empire and Modern Turkey.* New York: Cambridge University Press, 1977.

Sivan, Emmanuel. *Radical Islam: Medieval Theology and Modern Politics.* New Haven: Yale University Press, 1995.

Snow, David A., and Robert D. Benford. "Master Frames and Cycles of Protest." In *Frontiers of Social Movement Theory.* ed. Aldon D. Morris and Carol M. Mueller. New Haven: Yale University Press, 1992.

Sunar, İlkay. *State and Society in the Politics of Turkey's Development.* Ankara: Siyasal Bilgiler Fakültesi Yayınları, 1974.

Stokes, Martin. *The Arabesk Debate: Music and Musicians in Modern Turkey.* Oxford: Oxford University Press, 1992.

Tachau, Frank. *Turkey: The Politics of Authority, Democracy, and Development.* New York: Praeger, 1984.

Tapper, Richard. *Islam in Modern Turkey: Religion, Politics and Literature in a Secular State.* London: Tauris, 1994.

Taylor, Charles. *Multiculturalism and "The Politics of Recognition."* Princeton: Princeton University Press, 1993.

———. *Sources of the Self: The Making of the Modern Identity.* Cambridge: Harvard University Press, 1989.

Tibi, Bassam. *Islam and the Cultural Accommodation of Social Change.* Trans. Clare Krojzl. Boulder, CO Westview Press, 1989.

Toprak, Binnaz. *Islam and Political Development in Turkey* Leiden: Brill, 1981.

Touraine, Alain. "An Introduction to the Study of Social Movements." *Social Research* 52, 4 (1985): 749–87.

Van Bruinessen, Martin. *Agha, Shaikh and State: The Social and Political Structures of Kurdistan.* London: Zed Books, 1992.

———. *Mullas, Sufis and Heretics: The Role of Religion in Kurdish Society.* Istanbul: Isis, 2000.

Wagstaff, Malcolm, ed. *Aspects of Religion in Secular Turkey.* Durham, UK: Centre of Middle Eastern and Islamic Studies, 1990.

Weber, Max. *Economy and Society.* Ed. Guenther Roth and Claus Wittich. New York: Bedminster Press, 1968.

———. *From Max Weber: Essays in Sociology.* Ed. H. H. Gerth and C. Wright Mills. New York: Oxford University Press, 1958.

Weiker, Walter F. *The Turkish Revolution: 1960–1961.* Washington, DC: Brookings Institute, 1963.

Young, Crawford. *The Politics of Cultural Pluralism.* Madison: University of Wisconsin Press, 1976.

Zürcher, Erik J. *Turkey: A Modern History.* New York: Tauris, 1997.

WORKS IN TURKISH

Akarlı, Engin. *Osmanlılarda ve Avrupa'da Çağdaş Kültürün Oluşumu 16–18. Yüzyıl.* Istanbul: Metis Yayınları, 1986.

Akdeniz, Sabri. *Milli Eğitimimizde İmam Hatip Okullarının Yeri ve Köy Enstitüleri.* Istanbul: Tohum Yayınları, 1971.

Akel, Ali. *Erbakan ve Generaller.* 2nd ed. Istanbul: Şura, 1999.

Aktaş, Cihan. *Tesettür ve Toplum.* 2nd ed. Istanbul: Nehir, 1992.

Aktay, Yasin. *Türk Dininin Sosyolojik İmkanı.* Istanbul: İletişim, 1999.

Albayrak, Sadık. *Türk Siyasi Hayatında MSP Olayı.* Istanbul: Araştırma Yayınları, 1989.

Atay, Tayfun. *Batı'da Bir Nakşi Cemaati: Şeyh Nazım Kıbrısi Örneği.* Istanbul: İletişim, 1996.

Bahadıroğlu, Yavuz. *Bediüzzaman Said Nursi.* Istanbul: Yeni Asya, 1993.

———. *Mecburen Atatürkçü.* Istanbul: Yeni Asya, 1994.

Barbarosoğlu, Fatma K. *Moda ve Zihniyet.* Istanbul: İz, 1995.

Başar, Ahmed Hamdi. *Atatürkle Üç Ay ve 1930'dan Sonra Türkiye.* Istanbul: Tan Matbaası, 1945.

Başgöz, İlhan. *Türkiye'nin Eğitim Çıkmazı ve Atatürk.* Ankara: Kültür Bakanlığı, 1995.

Başlangıcından Günümüze Refah'ın Tarihsel Gelişimi. Istanbul: Pelikan Yayınları, 1996.

Baydar, Mustafa. *Hamdullah Suphi Tanrıöver ve Anıları.* Istanbul: Menteş Yayınevi, 1968.

Baydar, Mustafa C. *İslam ve Radyo Televizyon.* Ankara: Diyanet Vakfı Yayınları, 1994.

Behar, Büşra Erşanli. *İktidar ve Tarih: Türkiye'de Resmi Tarih Tezinin Oluşumu.* Istanbul: Afa, 1992.

Berk, Bekir. *Türkiye'de Nurculuk Davası.* Istanbul: Yeni Asya, 1975.

Bilgin, Beyza. *Eğitim Bilimi ve Din Eğitimi.* Ankara: A.Ü. İlahiyat Fakültesi Yayınları, 1988.

———. *Türkiye'de Din Eğitimi ve Liselerde Din Dersleri.* Ankara: Emel Matbaacılık, 1980.

Bölügiray, Nevzat. *Sokaktaki Askerin Dönüşü.* Istanbul: Tekin, 1991.

Bulaç, Ali. *İslam ve Ulus-Devlet.* Istanbul: İz, 1996.

Burçak, R. Salim. *Türkiye'de Demokrasiye Geçisi 1945–1950.* Ankara: Cam Matbaası, 1970.

———. *Yassıada ve Ötesi.* Ankara: Cam Matbaası, 1976.

Çakır, Ruşen. *Ayet ve Slogan.* Istanbul: Metis, 1990.

Çalışlar, Oral. *Fethullah Gülen'den Cemalettin Kaplan'a.* Istanbul: Pencere, 1997.

Can, Eyüp. *Fethullah Gülen Hocaefendi ile Ufuk Turu.* Istanbul: Ad, 1996.

Cerit, Sevil. "Türkiye'de İller Arası Göçler 1950–1980." *Turkish Journal of Population Studies* 8 (1986): 88–99.

Cizre, Ümit. *Muktedirlerin Siyaseti: Merkez Sağ-Ordu-İslamcılık.* Istanbul: İletişim, 1999.

Coşan, Esad. *Gayemiz.* 3rd ed. Istanbul: Seha, n.d.

———. *İslam Çağrısı.* Istanbul: Seha, 1993.

———. *Yeni Dönemde Yeni Görevler.* Istanbul: Seha, 1993.

———. *Yeni Ufuklar.* Istanbul: Seha, 1992.

———. *Zaferin Yolu ve Şartları.* Istanbul: Seha, 1994.

Coşkun, Zeki. *Aleviler, Sünniler ve Öteki Sivas.* Istanbul: İletişim, 1995.

Deveci, İbrahim Ethem. *Ben Dindar Bir Cumhuriyetçiyim.* Istanbul: Yeni Asya, 1994.

Dilaçar, A. *Atatürk ve Türkçe, Atatürk ve Türk Dili.* Ankara: Türk Dil Kurumu, 1963.

Dilipak, Abdurrahman. *Sorunlar, Sorular ve Cevaplar.* Istanbul: Beyan, 1993.

Dinçer, Nahit. *1913'ten Bugüne İmam Hatip Okulları Meselesi.* Istanbul: Yağmur, 1974.

Dönmez, Şerafettin. *Atatürk'ün Çağdaş Toplum ve Din Anlayışı.* Istanbul: Ayışığı, 1998.

Dursunoğlu, Cevat. *Milli Mücadelede Erzurum.* Ankara: Ziraat Bankası Matbaası, 1946.

Emre, Süleyman Arif. *Siyasette 35 Yıl.* 3 vols. Istanbul: Cuma, 1993.

Erbakan, Necmettin. *Milli Görüş.* Istanbul: Dergah, 1975.

———. *Milli Görüşün İktidardaki Hizmetleri (1974–1978).* Ankara: RP, 1995.

———. *Yeni Oluşum: Büyük Değişim.* Ankara: RP, 1993.

Erdoğan, Latif. *Fethullah Gülen Hocaefendi "Küçük Dünyam."* 38th ed. Istanbul: AD, 1995.

Erdoğan, Mustafa. *Rejim Sorunu.* Ankara: Vadi, 1997.

Ergin, Osman. *Türkiye'de Maarif Tarihi.* 5 vols. Istanbul: Eser Matbaası, 1977.

Ergün, Mustafa. *Atatürk Devri Türk Eğitimi.* Ankara: A.Ü.D.T.C.F. Yayınları, 1982.

Erkal, Mustafa, ed. *İslamiyet, Millet Gerçeği ve Laiklik.* Istanbul: Aydınlar Ocağı Yayını, 1994.

Erkaya, Güven, and Taner Baytok. *Bir Asker Bir Diplomat.* 4th ed. Istanbul: Doğan, 2001.

Güvenç, Bozkurt. *Dosya Türk-İslam Sentezi.* Istanbul: Sarmal Yayınları, 1991.

Gülen, Fethullah [M. Abdülfettah Şahin]. *Asrın Getirdiği Tereddütler.* 4 vols. İzmir: T.O.V., 1994.

———. *Çağ ve Nesil: Zamanın Altın Dilimi.* 4 vols. İzmir: TOV, 1992.

———. *İrşad Ekseni.* Istanbul: Zaman, 1998.

Güngör, N. *Arabesk: Sosyokültürel Açıdan Arabesk Müzik.* Ankara: Bilgi, 1990.

Gürdoğan, Ersin. *Görünmeyen Üniversite.* 2nd ed. Istanbul: İz, 1991.

Güreli, Nail. *Gerçek Tanık: Korkut Özal Anlatıyor.* Istanbul: Milliyet Yayınları, 1994.

Gürsel, İbrahim Ethem. *Kürtçülük Gerçeği.* Ankara: Komen, 1977.

Haydar, Ali. *Milli Terbiye.* Istanbul: Milli Matbaası, 1926.

İlyasoğlu, Aynur. *Örtülü Kimlik.* Istanbul: Metis, 1994.

İnalcık, Halil. *Osmanlı Toplumu.* Istanbul: Eren, 1993.

İnuğur, Nuri. *Türk Basın Tarihi.* Istanbul: Gazeteciler Cemiyeti, 1992.

Kafesoğlu, İbrahim. *Türk-İslam Sentezi.* Istanbul: Aydınlar Ocağı, 1985.

Kalafat, Yaşar. *Şark Meselesi Işığında Şeyh Sait Olayı. Karakteri, Dönemindeki İç ve Dış Olaylar.* Istanbul: Boğaziçi Yayınları, 1992.

Karataş, Turan. *Doğu'nun Yedinci Oğlu: Sezai Karakoç.* Istanbul: Kaknüs, 1998.

Kapacalı, Alpay. *Türk Kitap Tarihi.* Istanbul: Cem Yayınevi, 1989.
Kırboğa, Ali Rıza. *Din Eğitimi ve İmam Hatip Okulları Davası.* Istanbul: Milli Gazete, 1975.
Kırkıncı, Mehmet. *Bediüzzaman'ı Nasıl Tanıdım?* Istanbul: Zafer, 1994.
———. *Mektuplar Hatıralar.* Istanbul: Zafer, 1992.
Kara, İsmail. *Amel Defteri.* Istanbul: Kitabevi, 1998.
———. *Şeyhefendinin Rüyasındaki Türkiye.* Istanbul: Kitabevi, 1998.
———. *Türkiye'de İslamcılık Düşüncesi: Metinler ve Kişiler.* 3 vols. Istanbul: Risale, 1986.
Kınacı, Selahattin. *Şeyh Muhammed Raşid (K.A.S.)'in Hayatı.* Adıyaman: Menzil, 1996.
Koloğlu, Orhan. *Basımevi ve Basının Gecikme Sebebleri ve Sonuçları.* Istanbul: Gazeteciler Cemiyeti Yayınları, 1987.
Kotku, Mehmet Zahid, *Tasavvuf Ahlakı V.* Istanbul: Seha, n.d.
———. *Alim.* Istanbul: Seha, 1985.
———. *Cihad.* Istanbul: Seha, n.d.
———. *Hadislerle Nasihatler 1–II.* Istanbul: Seha, n.d.
———. *Muminlere Vaazlar 1–II.* Istanbul: Seha, n.d.
———. *Faiz.* Istanbul: Seha, 1985.
———. *Nefsin Terbiyesi.* Istanbul: Seha, n.d.
———. *Tevhid.* Istanbul: Seha, 1985.
Mert, Nuray. *Hep Muhalif Olmak.* Istanbul: İletişim, 2001.
———. *İslam ve Demokrasi.* Istanbul: İz, 1998.
Mürsel, Safa. *Bediüzzaman Said Nursi ve Devlet Felsefesi.* Istanbul: Yeni Asya, 1995.
Oçak, Ahmet Yaşar. *Alevi ve Bektaşi İnançlarının İslam Öncesi Temelleri.* 2nd ed. Istanbul: İletişim, 2000.
———. *Türkler, Türkiye ve İslam.* Istanbul: İletişim, 1999.
———. *Türk Süfiliğine Bakışlar.* Istanbul: İletişim, 1996.
Öcal, Mustafa. *İmam-Hatip Liseleri ve İlk Öğretim Okulları.* Istanbul: Ensar, 1994.
Okutan, Ömer. *Cumhuriyet Dönemi Milli Eğitimimiz.* Istanbul: M.E.B. Yayınları, 1983.
Onur, Necdet. *Erbakan Dosyası.* Istanbul: M. Yayınevi, n.d.
Ortaylı, İlber. *İmparatorluğun En Uzun Yüzyılı.* Istanbul: Hil Yayınları, 1983.
Özdenören, Rasim. *Müslümanca Düşünme Üzerine Denemeler.* Istanbul: İnsan, 1985.
———. *Ruhun Malzemeleri.* Istanbul: Risale, 1986.
———. *Yaşadığımız Günler.* Istanbul: İnsan, 1985.
———. *Yeniden İnanmak.* Istanbul: Nehir, 1988.
Özek, Çetin. *Din ve Devlet.* Istanbul: Ada, 1982.
———. *Türkiye'de Gerici Akımlar ve Nurculuğun İçyüzü.* Istanbul: Varlık, 1964.
Özel, İsmet. *Neyi Kaybettiğini Hatırla.* Istanbul: İklim, 1995.
———. *Üç Mesele: Teknik, Medeniyet, Yabancılaşma.* Istanbul: Dergah, 1978.
———. *Zor Zamanlarda Konuşmak.* Istanbul: Risale, 1986.
Özel, Mustafa. *Devlet ve Ekonomi.* Istanbul: İz, 1995.
Şahiner, Necmettin. *Bediüzzaman Said Nursi ve Nurculuk.* Istanbul: Yeni Asya, 1979.
———. *Bilinmeyen Taraflarıyla Bediüzzaman Said Nursi.* 13th ed. Istanbul: Nesil, 1998.
Sarıbay, Ali Yaşar. *Türkiye'de Modernleşme Din ve Parti Politikası: "MSP Örnek Olayı."* Istanbul: Alan Yayıncılık, 1985.
Sencan, Hüner. *İş Hayatında İslam İnsanı (Homo Islamicus).* Istanbul: MÜSİAD, 1994.

Sevilgen, M. Gündüz. *MSP'de Dört Yıl (1973–1977)*. Ankara: İstiklal Matbaası, 1979.

Şişman, Nazife. *Kamusal Alanda Başörtülüler*. 2nd ed. Istanbul: İz, 2001.

Soydan, Mehmet Ali. *Türkiye'de Refah Gerçeği*. Erzurum: Birey, 1994.

Tarhanlı, İstar B. *Müslüman Toplum, "laik" Devlet: Türkiye'de Diyanet İşleri Başkanlığı*. Istanbul: AFA, 1993.

Toker, Metin. *Şeyh Sait ve İsyanı*. Ankara: Bilgi, 1994.

Tunaya, Tarık Zafer. *İslamcılık Akımı*. Istanbul: Simavi Yayınları, 1991.

Tunçay, Mete. 1981. *Türkiye Cumhuriyetinde Tek Parti Yönetiminin Kurulması (1923–1930)*. 3rd ed. Istanbul: Tarih Vakfı, 1999.

Ülken, Hilmi Ziya. *Türkiye'de Çağdaş Düşünce Tarihi*. Istanbul: Ülken, 1979.

Ünal, İsmail. *Fethullah Gülen'le Amerika'da Bir Ay*. Istanbul: Işık, 2001.

Üstel, Füsun. *Türk Ocakları (1912–1931)*. Istanbul: İletişim, 1997.

Üstün, Kemal. *Menemen Olayı ve Kubilay*. Istanbul: Çağdaş Yayınları, 1990.

Üzüm, İlyas. *Günümüz Aleviliği*. Istanbul: Isam, 1997.

Yalçın, Soner. *Hangi Erbakan*. Istanbul: Başak, 1993.

Yıldırım, Ergün. *İktidar Mücadelesi ve Din*. Istanbul: Bilge, 1999.

Yıldız, Ahmet. *Meşrutiyet'ten Cumhuriyet'e İktidar Kavgaları ve Sanal İrtica*. Istanbul: Pınar, 2000.

UNPUBLISHED DISSERTATIONS AND THESES

Aktay, Yasin. "Body, Text, Identity: The Islamist Discourse of Authenticity in Modern Turkey." Ph.D. diss., Middle East Technical University, Ankara, 1997.

Cakı, Fahri. "New Social Classes and Movements in the Context of Politico-Economic Development in Turkey." Ph.D. diss., Temple University, Philadelphia, PA, 2001.

Çınar, Menderes. "The Republican Character of Islamism in Turkey from the Perspective of 'The Political.'" Ph.D. diss., Bilkent University, Ankara, 1998.

Eskicumalı, Ahmed. "Ideology and Education: Reconstructing the Turkish Curriculum ror Social and Cultural Change, 1923–1946." Ph.D. diss., University of Wisconsin–Madison, 1994.

Kömeçoğlu, Uğur. "A Sociological Interpretative Approach to the Fethullah Gülen Community." M.A. thesis, Boğaziçi University, Istanbul, 1997.

Kuru, Fazıl. N. "Menzil Nakşibendiliği Merkez Cemaati Üzerine Sosyolojik Bir Araştırma." M.A. thesis, Erciyes University, Kayseri, Turkey,1999.

Maccaferri, James Tilio. "Ottoman Foreign Policy and the British Occupation of Egypt: The Hasan Fehmi Pasha Mission of 1885." Ph.D. diss., University of California, 1983.

Mermer, Ali. "Aspects of Religious Identity: The Nurcu Movement in Turkey Today." Ph.D. diss., Durham University, U.K., 1985.

Tarhan, Mehmet. "Religious Education in Turkey: A Socio-Historical Study of the Imam-Hatip Schools." Ph.D. diss., Temple University, Philadelphia, PA, 1996.

I

Index